Mountaincraft and Leadership

Third Edition

A Handbook for Mountaineers and Hillwalking Leaders in the British Isles

ERIC LANGMUIR

Mountain Leader Training Board

THE SCOTTISH SPORTS COUNCIL

D0193379

Published jointly by:

The Scottish Sports Council
Caledonia House
South Gyle
Edinburgh EH12 9DQ

The Mountain Leader Training Board
177–179 Burton Road
West Didsbury
Manchester M20 2BB

First published as *Mountain Leadership* 1969
Second edition published as *Mountaincraft and Leadership* 1984
Eight reprints with amendments to 1994
Third edition 1995
Reprinted 1996, 1997, 1998

Printed in Glasgow by Rexam Cartons & Print Scotland Limited

Book design by Fred Pollock

British Library cataloguing in publication data
A catalogue record for this book is available from the British Library

ISBN 1 85060 295 6

Trade distribution by Cordee
3a De Montfort Street
Leicester LE1 7HD

This edition of Mountaincraft and Leadership *is dedicated to the memory of Duncan Ross, Chairman of the Scottish Mountain Leader Training Board from 1987 to 1990, who provided gentle inspiration to so many aspiring mountain leaders.*

Contents

Foreword

I first experienced the responsibility, as well as the satisfaction, of introducing beginners to the mountains during a training course which I organised in 1942 at the Climbers' Club Hut, Helyg, in North Wales, for members of an armoured brigade in which I was serving at the time. It was an experience born of necessity; but even in the exigences of training for war, for those who took part it was a revelation of something far more far-reaching and enduring. Quite apart from acquiring some elementary mountaineering skills, they learned a good deal about one another, and a great deal about themselves. What they did not learn was to appreciate the mountains themselves; the environment was simply a training area for battle. As for myself, that experience had some bearing on the opportunities which later came my way to bring young people to the mountains in more normal times.

Those of us who had a hand in establishing the National Mountaineering Centre at Capel Curig in the early 1950's had little notion of the dimensions to which mountain training would be developed in the years ahead, to the point it has reached today. Yet even then it was apparent that something exciting was astir; there was an urge for adventure in post-war Britain for which the mountains could provide an outlet. There was a feeling abroad of a dynamic new age, at the end of that conflict and the beginning of a new era.

But this soon gave rise to anxiety about safety. There were far too many groups of young people, too large in number, unsuitably equipped and led by too few adults with too little experience and skill. The need to establish a code of standards and to draw up schemes for the certification of adult leaders – though frowned upon by some mountaineers of the time – became essential in the interest of safety. This demand for qualifications as a safeguard for youthful parties in the mountains led, for a while, to unfortunate misapprehensions over the title of the Mountain Leadership Certificate. It seemed to imply a greater degree of experience than any limited training course could provide. Today, these courses are better understood while their value is widely accepted.

Looking back over this span of time, I marvel at what has been achieved in giving so much pleasure and satisfaction to so many people – especially young people – within reasonable parameters of safety. I say 'reasonable' purposely, for safety in the mountains is, and should be, a relative term. If you seek to eliminate it altogether, you remove the magnet of adventure, in which an element of risk is an essential ingredient; risk is the honey-pot which lures us to the mountains. Most of the satisfaction in every 'risk' sport lies, not in courting hazards unprepared, but in matching danger with your skills, and in extending your experience in order to step up, with impunity, the degree of risk which you seek.

Much has happened since this book was first published to give cause for that other concern: the need to protect the mountains from damage to which they are subjected by us humans. Save for the exceptional circumstances of military training, most people enjoy the mountains partly, at least, for the beauty and grandeur of the scenery, as well as for the challenges they offer. That aspect has become increasingly under threat as a result of the sheer numbers of people who visit our hills, and the commercial services which supply the demand. A conservation strategy cannot be purely negative; it is not an acceptable policy to ban access to the crags and uplands. But our personal responsibility not to damage or pollute them is greater now than it was before; the chapter on 'Access and Conservation' is especially important.

A word about 'Leadership'. Its concept has changed a good deal since those days during and shortly after the war. But leadership remains crucial to the enjoyment, success and safety of all who come as learners to the mountains. I hope that those who, with the help of this book, set out to qualify as mountain leaders will also learn the skills and the pleasures of teaching those whom they lead over the mountains and moorlands; giving them responsibilities under their guidance and not acting as mere conductors. I say this with feeling, for in my own boyhood I spent six seasons in the European Alps, both in winter and summer, climbing many big peaks with professional guides, yet learning very litttle and missing much of the fun and satisfaction of graduating as an all–round mountaineer.

I hope that all of you who study this book and apply its teaching to your own knowledge of the mountains will find as lasting a joy in them as I have over the last seventy years or so, since I first started as a ten year old, walking in the Alps.

John Hunt
Patron
The British Mountaineering Council

Acknowledgements

The most obvious changes in this new edition are the new chapters on 'First Aid' and 'Nutrition'. 'First Aid' has been written by Dr Duncan Gray, a specialist in accident medicine and an experienced outdoorsman. 'Nutrition' is a topic which has engaged public interest in recent years. Lynne Douglas has condensed a great deal of information into one small chapter. Other areas of the the book have received attention, some more than others. 'Security on Steep Ground' remains a controversial area and this has been addressed by John Cousins, Secretary of the Mountain Leader Training Board.

I am also grateful to Bill Wright of the British Mountaineering Council for updating Mark Hutchison's chapter on 'Access and Conservation' and to Doug Jones for bringing a fresh approach to 'Mountain Rescue'. Ken Ogilvie's chapter on 'Leadership' and Hamish Brown's on 'Campcraft' remain substantially unchanged.

The list of people who have contributed in one way or another to this book and its predecessors is legion. To all those unacknowledged here, my warm thanks. However I must single out Blyth Wright, Tom Redfern, Nigel Williams, Douglas Patterson, Bob Barton, Phil Kennet, Aido Liddle, Allen Fyffe and Nick Halls for their individual contributions to specific chapters.

As with previous editions the work of review has been overseen by an Editorial Board comprising Duncan Ross, Bob Pettigrew, John Cousins, Alastair Craik, Iain Davenport, Anita Hible, Alastair Morgan, Ian Peter, Fred Pollock and Ken Ogilvie. I should like to record my thanks to them for their encouragement and support. All the illustrations have been drawn or redrawn by Douglas Godlington.

Finally, it is fitting to remember that it was Lord Hunt, who has written the Foreword to this book, who chaired the first meeting of the Working Party which laid down the foundation of the Mountain Leader Training Schemes.

1

Navigation

Navigation is fun! It is an intensely interesting aspect of mountaincraft, the proper practice of which brings considerable personal satisfaction. It is one of the most important keys which unlocks a whole new world of adventure and discovery but it is a skill which you ignore at your peril. Far too many accidents are caused by original errors in route finding. It is not enough just to be able to follow a set course in fine weather at low level. Experience of blind navigation in the most severe weather conditions is essential if you wish to aspire to the freedom of the hills.

The ancient peoples of the world learned to navigate through the meticulous observation of natural phenomena; the sun, the moon and stars, the migration of birds, the wave patterns in the oceans, the behaviour and signs of other species and so on. Observation is still the keynote to successful navigation today although this is sometimes obscured by our tendency to rely on gadgets or the recorded experience of other experts, such as the map makers themselves.

There is perhaps one further lesson to learn from the navigators of old and that is to keep track of a journey as a whole rather than as a series of disconnected sections. It is quite possible to complete a route successfully without ever knowing where you are in relation to your starting point or even to the country immediately outside the narrow corridor of your route. From time to time you should stand back from the absorbing detail and think of where you are in a wider context. This self-orientation will not only help you to anticipate what lies ahead but will enable you to respond positively should some mishap occur requiring a change of plan.

One final word of advice. Do not leave it to someone else to do all the navigating. Even the best can make a mistake and you may be asked to pick up the threads at a moment's notice. Keep involved and in touch with all that is going on.

MAP SYMBOLS

Most maps contain hundreds of thousands of bits of information about the ground, not all of which are relevant to the mountaineer. Indeed, most maps in general use are a compromise between the sometimes conflicting demands of different groups and interests. The selection of information to portray is one problem for the map makers; another is the actual presentation of that information on the map. Because of the severe limitations of space a system of shorthand is used by which means a great deal of information is conveyed by 'conventional signs'. With a little practice these signs are easily recognised and if in doubt you can refer to the key which is given in the margin of the map. Of particular interest to the hillwalker is the convention which is used to represent relief and associated signs such as those depicting outcrops and cliffs. These are dealt with in more detail later. Footpaths and boundaries of various kinds can be easily confused and you should familiarise yourself with the appropriate map symbols.

While it is important to be able to extract the maximum amount of information from the map, it is just as important to know what the map does not tell you. In the first place maps are not produced just for the benefit of mountaineers, although this is an assumption too readily made by many of us. They do not, for example, tell us very much about the nature of the terrain and how easy or difficult it is to walk over. There is no map symbol for knee-high heather or for a dissected peat hag! The special maps produced for orienteering do go some way towards providing the kind of information which is particularly relevant to the hillwalker, but their use is generally confined to lowland and forest areas. If you have the opportunity, try navigating with the aid of an air photograph. Although the technique of 'reading' air photographs is a specialised art, you will be surprised how much additional information you can learn from one and it will serve to illustrate some of the limitations of conventional maps.

WHICH MAP ?

The first thing you have to decide is what scale of map is suited to your purpose. The scale of a map is always printed on the front cover and is expressed as the ratio between a unit of length on the map and the equivalent distance on the ground. A scale of 1:25,000 means that one unit of length on the map is equivalent to 25,000 units on the ground, or, to put it into actual units, one centimetre is equivalent to 25,000 centimetres or 250 metres. In the same way 1:50,000 means that 1cm on the map is equivalent to 50,000 cms or 500 metres on the ground.

(Table 1) *Some common map scales and their use:–*

SCALE	MEANING	USE
1:15,000	1cm=150m	Orienteering map
1:25,000	1cm=250m	Ideal for walking, but you may require more than one map to cover your area
1:40,000	1cm=400m	Harveys Walkers maps for a number of popular mountain areas
1:50,000	1cm=500m	The most popular map for walking
1:100,000	1cm=1,000m	Cycling, hostelling, holidaying, route selection
1:250,000	1cm=2,500m	Cycling, motoring, etc
1:1,000,000	1cm=10km	Map of UK

For the hillwalker the choice seems to be between the 1:50,000 and the 1:25,000 published by the Ordnance Survey, or the excellent maps produced by Harveys for a number of popular areas at a scale of 1:40,000.

Obviously, it is possible to show a great deal more detail on the larger scale map, but this advantage is offset by the fact that you have to carry twice as much map. Your final choice is inevitably a compromise between the two. Additional information about these scales is provided at the end of this chapter (page 59).

MEASURING DISTANCE

Once you know the scale of a map it is a relatively simple matter to measure the length between any two points in centimetres and convert this into distance along the ground. Nearly all compasses are provided with a centimetre scale. The grid lines on all Ordnance Survey maps are spaced 1km apart, irrespective of the scale, so it is possible to estimate distance quite quickly, simply by counting the number of grid squares separating the points. It is useful to know that the diagonal from corner to corner of a grid square is approximately 1.5km. (Fig.1) If you are doing a lot of route planning a map measurer is a useful gadget, otherwise a length of string or the edge of a piece of paper can be used quite satisfactorily to measure distances.

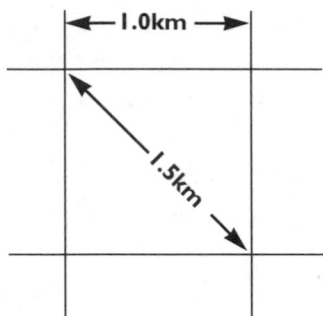

Fig. 1   **_The grid lines on Ordnance Survey maps are 1km apart. The diagonal is approximately 1.5km or 1 mile._**

Looking after your Map

Only a few maps, such as some of the 1:25,000 leisure maps and Harveys Walkers maps, are provided with any protection against the weather. The ideal arrangement is to cover the map completely and preferably on both sides, with a transparent adhesive film such as 'transpaseal'. The treated map should then be refolded in the manner which allows any part of it to be viewed by a single opening of the folds. The expense of protecting a map in this way is probably only justified if it is in fairly constant use. A clear plastic envelope or bag serves well enough and the map should be prefolded so that the route for the day is exposed. Some people favour map cases and boards, but it should be remembered that such items can become unmanageable in high winds.

THE NATIONAL GRID

If you look at any Ordnance Survey map you will see that it is overprinted with a grid of vertical and horizontal lines. These grid lines are 1km apart and form part of a larger National Grid which covers the whole of mainland Britain. The system was introduced as a sort of index system so that every point in the country could be given a unique reference number which would enable it to be identified. Indeed, it was once suggested that such a system could provide a postal code for every home in the land.

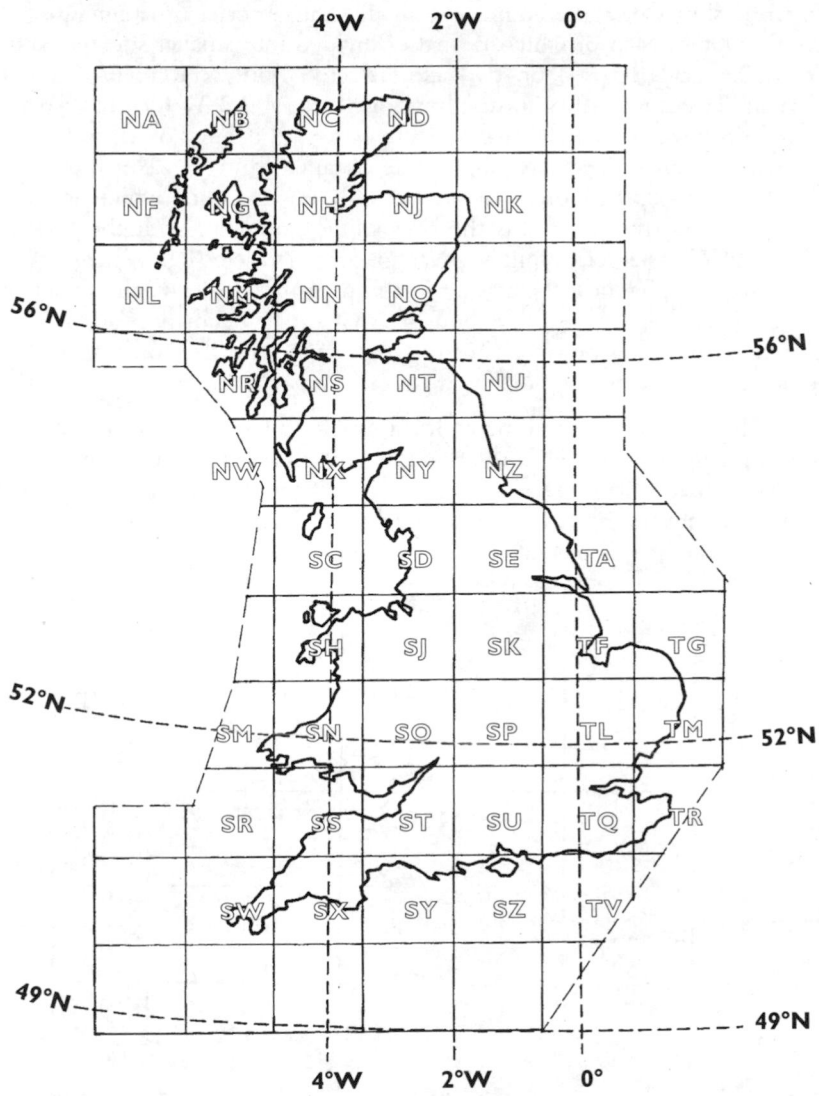

Fig. 2 *Each large square on the National Grid is 100km x 100km and is identified by a two letter code. There is not an exact correspondence between lines of latitude and longitude and the National Grid. In fact, true north differs from grid north by as much as 4° in the far northwest.*

Figure 2 shows how the country is divided into a series of larger squares, 100km x 100km, each of which is further divided into smaller squares, 1km x 1km. The grid is based on two axes selected from convenient lines of latitude and longitude, 49°N for the horizontal axis and 2°W for the vertical. Being a rectilinear pattern this grid differs from the lines of latitude and longitude, the difference increasing as the distance from the axes increases. You will appreciate, therefore, that there is only one grid line which actually points to true north and that is the one which coincides with the line of longitude 2°W. The remaining vertical grid lines differ slightly from true north, and this difference is recorded in the map margin for each corner of the sheet. It is never more than about 4°. As we shall shortly see it is grid north which we use as our reference for navigating with the compass so that the difference between true north and grid north is of academic interest only.

Since the grid lines are numbered it is possible to refer to a particular 1km square by giving the number of the two lines which bound it on the west and south. The vertical grid lines, known as eastings because they are numbered eastwards, are always given first, followed by the horizontal lines, known as

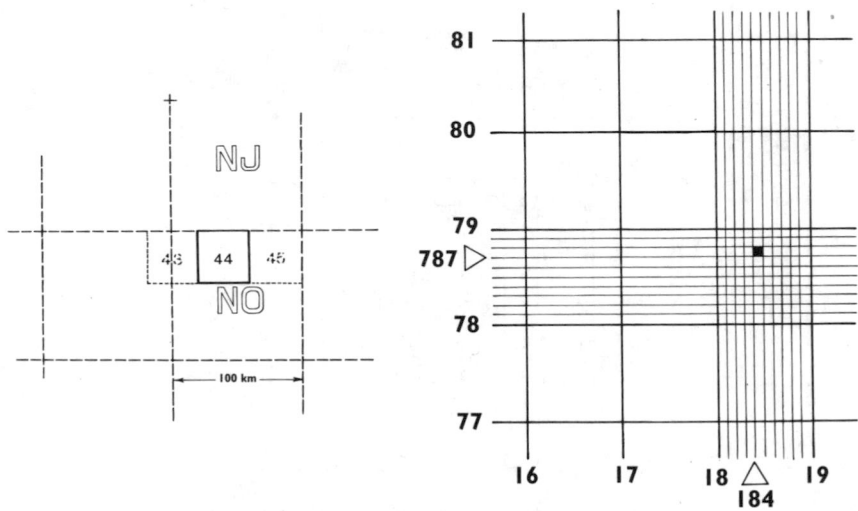

Fig. 3 *The grid reference for the 100m square is 184 (eastings) 787 (northings). To make the reference unique you must add the grid letters appropriate to your position, in this case, NO. The complete reference is therefore NO 184787.*
The inset shows the 100km squares of the National Grid and the coverage of three O.S. map sheets, nos. 43, 44 and 45.

northings because they are numbered northwards. By further subdivision, co-ordinates can be given for individual 100m squares. So it is important to realise that a six figure grid reference refers to an area 100m x 100m, not a point. You should also appreciate that any six figure grid reference is duplicated in each one of the larger 100km squares. To make it unique you need to add the two grid letters which identify the particular 100km square. The appropriate letters are to be found in the map margin.

Setting the Map in relation to the Ground

Since the map is a plan representation to scale of the actual ground it should be possible to turn the map in such a way that with your own position as the

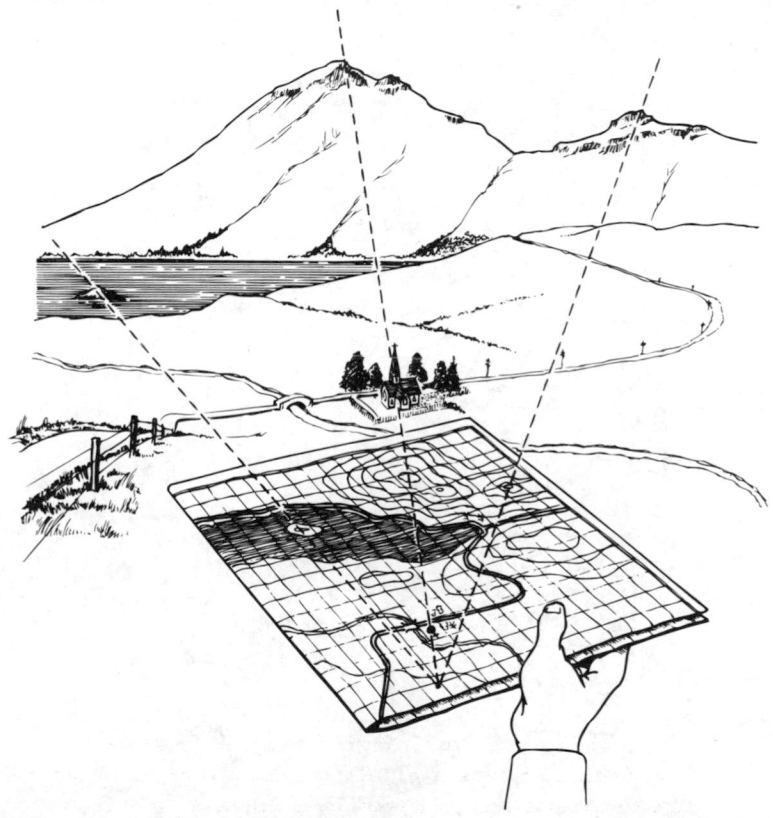

Fig. 4   *Setting the map by reference to identifiable features on the ground. The feature, its position on the map, your position and your eye must all be in the same vertical plane.*

central point all the features that you can see around you are in their correct relative positions. This is called setting or orienting the map and is one of the first and most important techniques of map reading. You may also use the compass to set the map if identifiable features are not visible. This technique is described later (page 24). Once the map is set, you can identify all the features which can be seen and most importantly select a route across country to reach an unseen objective.

If you are following a linear feature such as a path it is usually unnecessary to identify other features. Simply turn the map until the path lines up with the real path you are walking on. You can then anticipate changes in direction, junctions and the appearance of features which will confirm your actual position along the path.

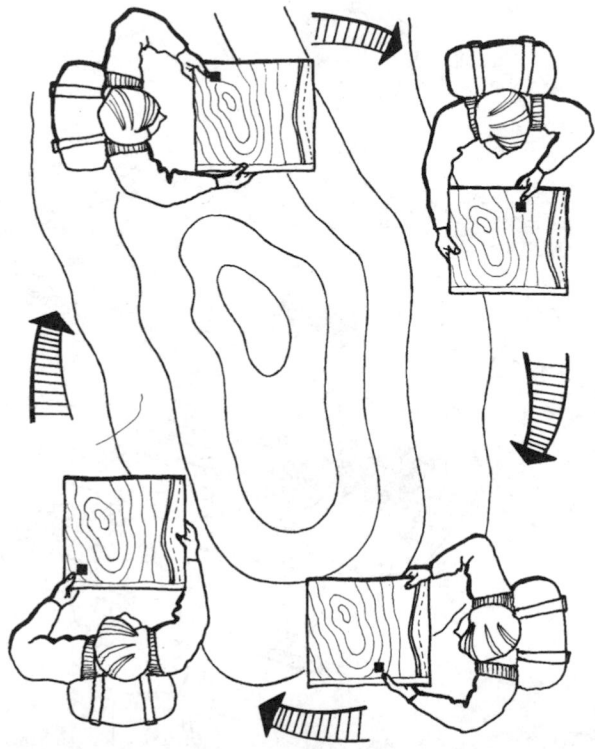

Fig. 5 *Get into the habit of walking with the map "set". If you need to refer to it fairly often it is a good idea to place your thumb just behind your last known position.*

Get into the habit of walking with the map set. If you do this (and it takes a bit of getting used to because the place names and so on may be upside down) the features that you see on the map match those that you see around you. This correct orientation is far more useful in relating the map to the ground than being able to read the place names. Try to think of the map as a three dimensional model, rather than a book which has always to be held the right way up. The right way up for a map is when it is set.

Relief

It is one thing to represent the ground surface on a horizontal plane; this basic technique of map making has been used from the earliest times. It is quite

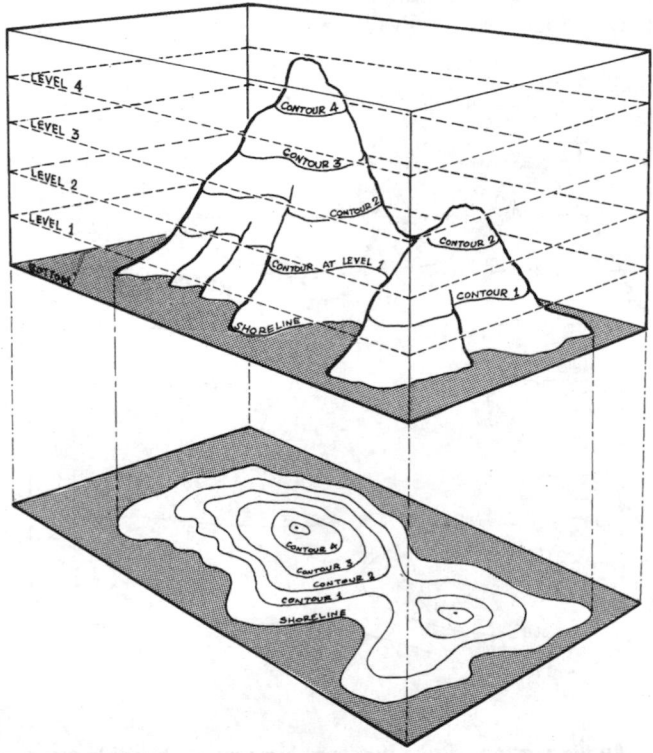

Fig. 6 — *Contour lines can be visualised as successive shore lines formed by raising the level of the sea in a series of equal vertical steps. The map, in effect, is a plan showing how these shore lines would appear on a horizontal plane when viewed from above.*

another to depict the ups and downs, the shape of the ground, on such a plane. It is a problem that map makers wrestled with until the contour line was invented. Curiously enough, the contour principle was first used in 1730 to show the shape of the sea bed, but it was not until much later that contour lines made their appearance on maps in general use to show relief.

It is important to appreciate that a contour line represents the intersection of a horizontal plane with the surface of the ground. The coast line is a good starting point since, in a way, it is the only "real" contour line and is the one from which all others are derived. Raise the level of the sea in increments of 10m and you have a succession of new shore lines or contour lines, each one 10 metres vertically above the other. When you are looking at a map the arrangement of the contour lines should allow you to build up a 3-D picture in your mind of what the ground actually looks like. The closer the contour lines are packed together, the steeper the slope.

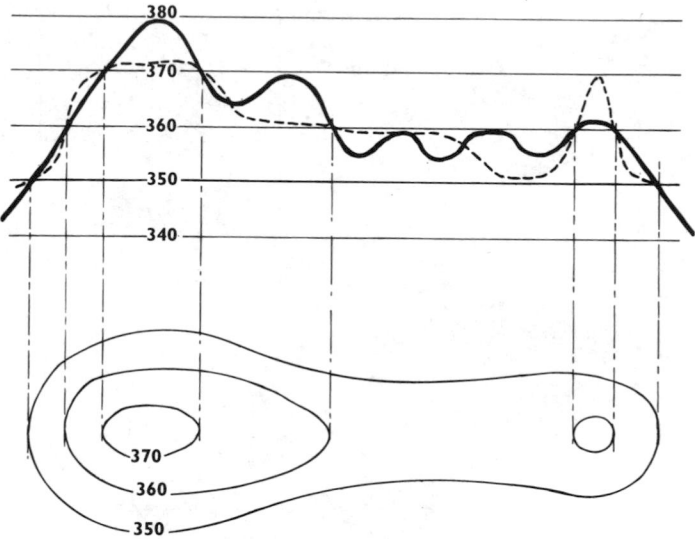

Fig. 7   *An illustration of two different but equally possible interpretations of the same map. Knobbly ridges are notoriously difficult to follow in thick mist. A 10m knoll is as big as a four storey building and there are three of them on one of the ridge profiles (solid line) which do not show up on the map below.*

There is a limit to the amount of information which can be conveyed by contour lines because they only give the shape of the ground at certain predetermined intervals. They do not tell you what is happening in between. It is quite possible, therefore, for small features to be completely missed because they fall within two contour lines.

With practice you will quickly learn to associate certain characteristic arrangements of the contour lines with particular mountain forms, such as ridges, valleys, cols, concave and convex slopes and so on.

HOW STEEP ?

It follows from what has been said that it is the closeness of contour lines in a particular area on the map which gives a measure of the steepness of the ground in that area. But how steep? This is not an easy question to answer and yet it is one of considerable importance to the mountaineer.

Steepness can be measured in two ways:

(i) By measuring the angle of the slope from the horizontal. It is surprising how few of us think in terms of angles and there is a general tendency to overestimate the steepness of slopes, even amongst climbers and skiers, two categories of outdoor sportsmen to whom such information is critical. The truth of the matter is that there is no easy way to measure slope angles in the field without the aid of a clinometer, itself a simple enough instrument, but not one which is normally carried.

(ii) By comparing the vertical and horizontal components of a slope and expressing this as a percentage gradient. This is the number of vertical units in one hundred horizontal ones.

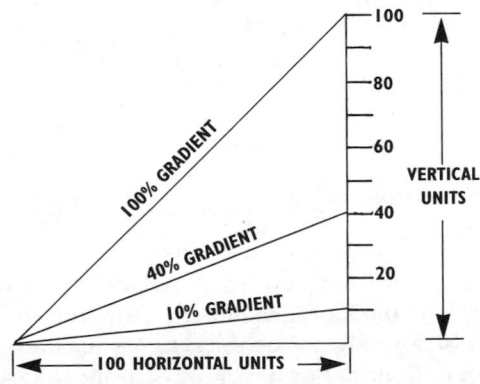

Fig. 8 *Gradient is expressed as the number of vertical units in 100 horizontal ones.*

Thus a 20% gradient is a slope which rises by 20 units for every one hundred horizontal ones. 100% gradient is a slope which rises by 100 units in the same horizontal distance, ie a 45° slope. Beyond 45°, gradients exceed 100% and indeed at very high angles the system becomes meaningless as gradients approach infinity. However, it is not difficult to work out an approximate percentage gradient from the map. All you have to do is to count the number of contour lines in 1cm of the slope under examination.

Take an example from a 1:50,000 map with a contour interval of 10m and let us say you count 8 contour lines in 1cm of map.

8 contour lines in 1cm (500m)

∴ 16 contour lines in 2cm (1,000m)

16 contour lines = 160m vertical (10m per contour)

So the gradient is 160m vertical in 1,000m horizontal which is the same as 16m vertical in 100m horizontal which is a gradient of 16%.

Table 2 will help you to compare gradients and angles and to relate these to slopes with particular characteristics.

Obviously it is extremely important to develop an awareness of the steepness of slopes as represented by the density of the contour lines. In practice, with the map scales in common use, it quickly becomes impossible to include all the contour lines, because there is just not enough room for them and some are simply left out. Take for example the 1:50,000 O.S. maps with a vertical interval of 10m and a thicker contour line every 50m. At a slope angle of approximately 27°, or 51%, the intermediate 10m lines start to be faded out. One of the effects of this is that slopes just less than 27° appear to be very steep because of the overcrowding of contour lines.

STEEPNESS OF SLOPE FROM CONTOUR LINES

On steeper slopes it is unrealistic to expect details of individual gullies and smaller cliff features to show up. Here we are at the mercy of the artistic licence accorded to the cartographer. For this reason and also because of fading out, it is best to rely on the thicker contour lines when estimating the steepness of slopes from the map. Get used to judging slope angles from the density of the thicker lines. When you change the scale of the map or the contour interval you change the spacing of the contour lines for any given

Table 2 *Slopes and Gradients.*

Slope angle	Gradient percent	Description of Slope
5°	9%	gentle slope – normal walking – equivalent to a fairly steep road
10°	18%	walk directly up – very steep road gradient – easy ski slope angle
15°	27%	good ski-ing terrain – limit of road gradient
20°	36%	route selection and care in placing feet – if hard snow/ice care is required, especially in descent
25°	47%	probably start zig-zag walking – steep ski slopes
30°	58%	zig-zag up, but go straight down – into avalanche country
35°	70%	start to pick way up and down – rock scrambling
40°	84%	care required in descent – near max angle of repose for scree
45°	100%	graded snow/ice climbing
50°	119%	angle of 'scarp' slope below cornice – near limit of friction on rock
55°	143%	steep snow/ice pitch
60°	173%	extremely steep climbing on rock or ice
70°	275%	hands touch rock/ice when held horizontally in front

Table 3 *Showing the relationship between slope angle and the spacing of thick contour lines.*

SLOPE ANGLE	1: 50,000		1: 25,000	
	EXACT SPACING OF THICK CONTOUR LINES WITHIN 1cm OF MAP	NO. OF THICK CONTOUR LINES IN 1cm OF MAP	EXACT SPACING OF THICK CONTOUR LINES WITHIN 1cm OF MAP	NO. OF THICK CONTOUR LINES IN 1cm OF MAP
10°		2		1
15°		2.6		1.3
20°		3.5		1.8
25°		4.3		2.2
30°		6		3
35°		7		3.5
40°		8		4
45°		10		5
50°		12		6
55°		14		7
60°		16		8

The spacing of contour lines tells you how steep a slope is. Since the fine contour lines begin to be faded out above slope angles of 27° it is best to rely on the thicker contour lines to estimate steepness. Table 3 tells you how many thick contour lines there are in 1cm on the map for a range of slope angles from 10°- 60°. The table has been reproduced to scale so that the spacing of the thick contour lines is exactly as they would appear on 1:50,000 and 1:25,000 scale maps.

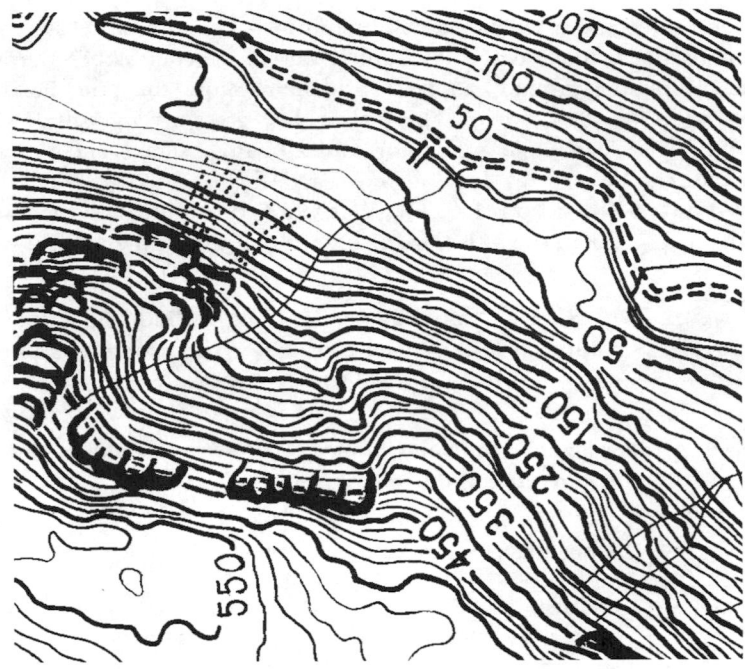

Fading out contour lines. Note how the intermediate contour lines are left out when the space becomes too constricted.

slope. Table 3 shows the exact spacing of the thick (50m) contour lines on 1:50,000 and 1:25,000 scale maps for a range of slope angles.

In attempting to interpret the hieroglyphics which are used to depict outcrops of rock and cliffs it is prudent to refer to the contour lines. The main change in the newer maps is that outcrops are now shown with a continuous line at the bottom of the rocks, in contrast to cliffs which are shown with a continuous line at the top. The distinction between the two features is not always clear and many a cliff is shown as an outcrop and vice-versa. (Fig. 9)

FORESHORTENING EFFECT

Remember that a map is really a projection of the landscape on a horizontal plane. Imagine looking down onto the ground from an aircraft; a cliff will appear as a single line or perhaps a narrow band whereas in fact it may be 300m high. Similarly, a steep slope will appear to be shorter than it actually is because of this foreshortening effect. Under normal circumstances it does not amount to much and can be discounted but on steeper slopes the actual distance along the ground can be considerably more than the horizontal distance indicated by the map. The table below gives a rough guide to the relationship between slope angle, horizontal (map) distance and the actual distance. It can be seen that on a slope of say 30° the extra distance travelled to that shown on the map is 15%. In other words if you measure the distance from the map as 200m the actual distance to be walked on the ground will be 230m.

However, beyond this slope angle, the extra 'hidden' distance is considerable. For instance, a horizontal distance of 200m becomes an actual distance of 280m on a 45° slope and 400m on a 60° slope.

Table 4   *Showing the additional distance travelled to that shown on the map as a result of the foreshortening effect.*

Slope Angle	Additional Distance Travelled
10°	1.5%
20°	6%
30°	15%
40°	31%
50°	56%
60°	100%

The effect of this is relatively slight on the sort of slopes normally frequented by hill walkers. It is taken into account in the various formulae used to estimate time and distance. Nevertheless, it is important to be aware of the problem. It not only seems longer when you are slogging up a steep hillside; it actually is longer. It's a comforting thought!

The Compass

It is said that the Chinese discovered the principle of the compass more than 5,000 years ago. It has retained its essential simplicity over the centuries and even today it is nothing more than a magnetised bar of metal suspended in the earth's magnetic field. It has been and remains the mainstay of the explorer and an essential tool of the mountaineer. It is when conditions are at their most severe that the compass becomes an indispensable aid to safe navigation.

It is true to say that there is a compass available for almost every specialist requirement from deep sea diving to rally driving. Whatever the use, it is a precision instrument on which the success or failure of an enterprise may depend. For the hillwalker the range of models is bewildering and it is perhaps worthwhile to look for a moment at the features which help to make a compass suitable for use on the hill.

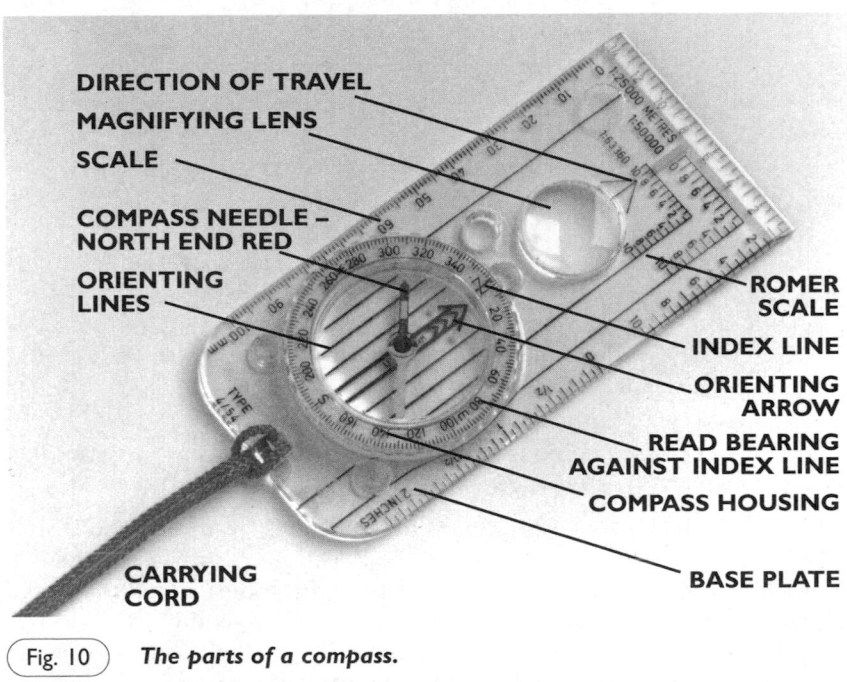

(Fig. 10)   *The parts of a compass.*

In the first place the compass should be compact, robust, light in weight and easy to handle and to operate in adverse conditions when you may have to use it with gloves on. The needle should settle down quickly when the compass is rotated and for this the capsule which holds the needle must be liquid filled. The compass should be able to be used as a protractor to measure angles on the map as well as giving a clear indication of the direction of travel when used to follow a bearing across country. Some models are specially adapted for sighting by incorporating a mirror or prism. To a certain extent this is a matter for individual preference but any more advanced gadgetry is inappropriate. It should have a romer scale engraved on the base plate for use with 1:50,000 and 1:25,000 maps. This can be used to measure distances up to 1km, or to give an accurate grid reference. At the very least it should have

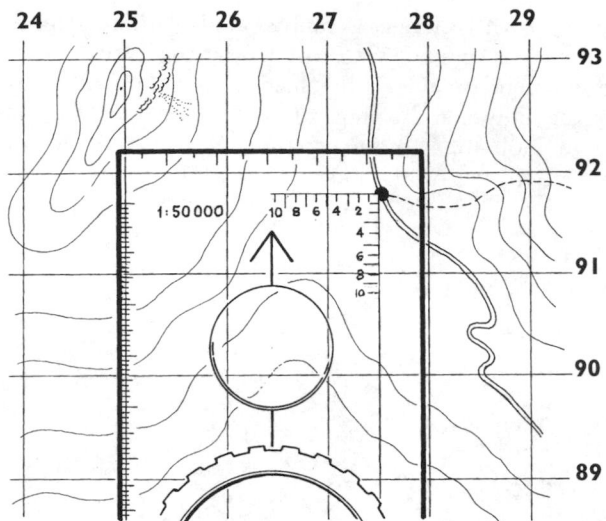

Fig. 11 *Using a romer to find a grid reference. In this example the grid reference is 275918.*

a metric scale marked out along one edge. Some models have a detachable plastic scale which can be changed when a different scale is required.

The rim of the housing is usually marked off in 360°, although models are available with other scales. The figures and subdivisions must be clearly visible and it is useful to have some means of keeping the compass oriented in the dark without having to use a torch. Few compasses are equipped to do this satisfactorily and rely on spots of luminous paint on the north end of the needle, the orienting arrow and the direction of travel arrow.

Like all precision instruments the compass requires careful handling. Try not to drop it and when you are not using it put it away in its case. If you do not have a proper case an old sock or a section of tubular bandage will serve equally well. Store apart from other compasses and electrical equipment such as TV sets, telephones, doorbells etc. After a period of time some compasses develop an air bubble inside the capsule. Provided it is not too large this does not interfere with the functioning of the compass.

DEVIATION

Since the compass needle is a magnet it will respond to magnetic fields other than the earth's. Any object containing ferrous metal, if large enough or close enough to the compass, will distort the earth's magnetic field in its vicinity. This distortion causes the compass needle to 'deviate' from its true orientation. Even quite small objects can have a disproportionate effect; a metal badge, a watch, a camera, a wire fence and so on. On a larger scale there are certain types of rock that cause compass deviation, notably the rough gabbro of the Cuillin of Skye, but fortunately this is the exception rather than the rule. Normally, if you keep your compass well clear of metal objects you should have no problems.

TRUE NORTH

True north and south are at the geographical poles, the points at which the earth's axes meet the surface. In the northern hemisphere the direction of the north pole is indicated by the Pole Star which can be found by following the pointers in the constellation of the Plough or Great Bear as it is more properly known. With a little more difficulty it can also be found from the orientation of the 'W' of Cassiopeia.

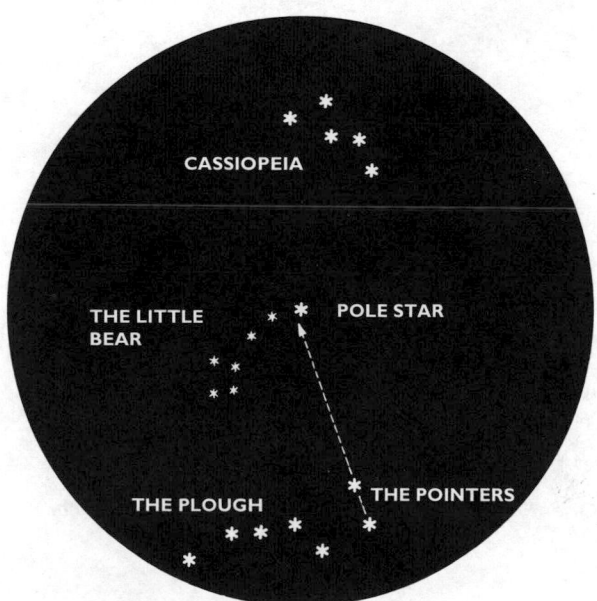

Fig. 12   *Finding True North by the stars. Follow the pointers to the Pole Star which always lies to the north of the observer. Alternatively, use the "W" of Cassiopeia.*

If you can see the sun it is also possible to orient yourself, provided you have a watch. Hold the watch horizontally and point the hour hand towards the sun. Now bisect the angle between the hour hand and 12 o'clock. This line will point due south. When using British Summer Time (April – October) bisect the angle between the hour hand and one o'clock. If you have a digital watch you can still find south by drawing a conventional clock in the margin of your map and using that instead of a watch.

SOUTH

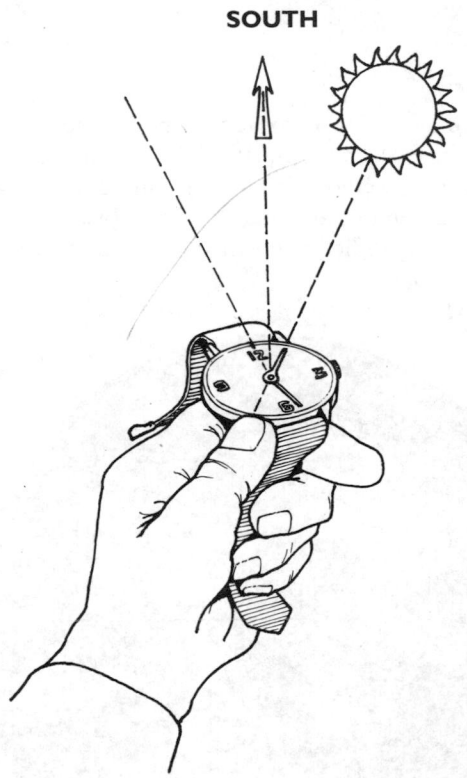

(Fig. 13)   *Orienting yourself by using the sun and your watch.*

GRID NORTH

As has been shown earlier in this chapter, O.S. maps are oriented to grid north which differs slightly from true north except along longitude 2°W. Since all our bearings are taken from Grid North this difference can be ignored.

MAGNETIC NORTH

The earth behaves just like a gigantic magnet creating its own magnetic field within which a suspended magnetised object, such as a compass needle, will align itself. Unfortunately for map users, the magnetic north pole does not coincide with the geographical north pole; in fact it is to be found in Canada, somewhere north of Hudson Bay. From the British Isles the magnetic north pole is currently some 5° west of the geographical pole. In other parts of the world this 'magnetic variation', as it is called, may be different. In the Alps for example, it is only one or two degrees west. In some areas of the world magnetic north is east of grid north. Since maps are oriented to the National Grid rather than to true north it is customary for the angle between grid north and magnetic north to be given in the map margin. Naturally, this magnetic variation has to be allowed for when converting a map bearing (angle from grid north) to a compass bearing (angle from magnetic north) or vice versa. Since magnetic north is to the west of grid north in this country, the compass or magnetic bearing is always the greater of the two.

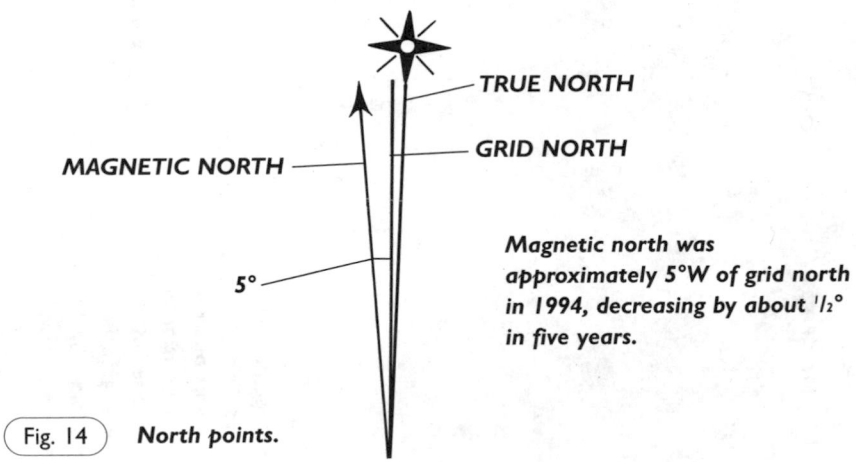

TRUE NORTH

GRID NORTH

MAGNETIC NORTH

5°

Magnetic north was approximately 5°W of grid north in 1994, decreasing by about $^1/_2$° in five years.

Fig. 14   **North points.**

There is a further complication due to the fact that magnetic north is not a fixed point. It changes its position over a period of years. Fortunately, the movement can be predicted and an appropriate adjustment made to the magnetic variation. At the present time magnetic north is moving in a direction which reduces the westerly variation from locations within the British Isles by approximately ½° in 5 years.

Some compasses are adapted to take account of magnetic variation so that once set you no longer have to worry about it. (page 36)

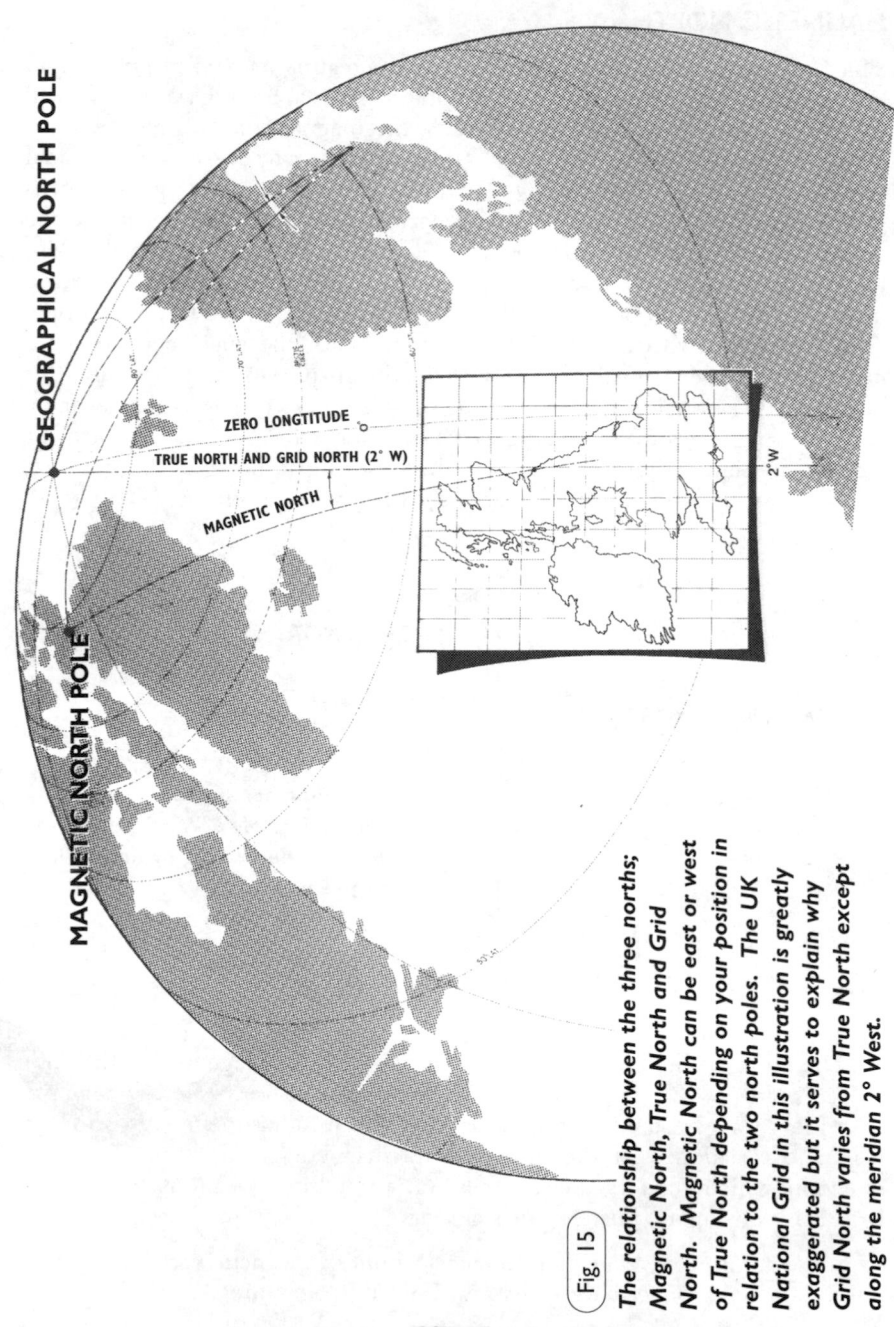

GEOGRAPHICAL NORTH POLE

MAGNETIC NORTH POLE

ZERO LONGTITUDE

TRUE NORTH AND GRID NORTH (2° W)

MAGNETIC NORTH

2°W

Fig. 15

The relationship between the three norths; Magnetic North, True North and Grid North. Magnetic North can be east or west of True North depending on your position in relation to the two north poles. The UK National Grid in this illustration is greatly exaggerated but it serves to explain why Grid North varies from True North except along the meridian 2° West.

Setting the Map with the Compass

Quick Method

In poor visibility it is useful to be able to set the map quickly using the compass. To do this simply place the compass on the map and turn both compass and map until the red end of the needle points to north on the map. You can allow for magnetic variation by turning map and compass that little bit more so that the needle points just to the west of true north.

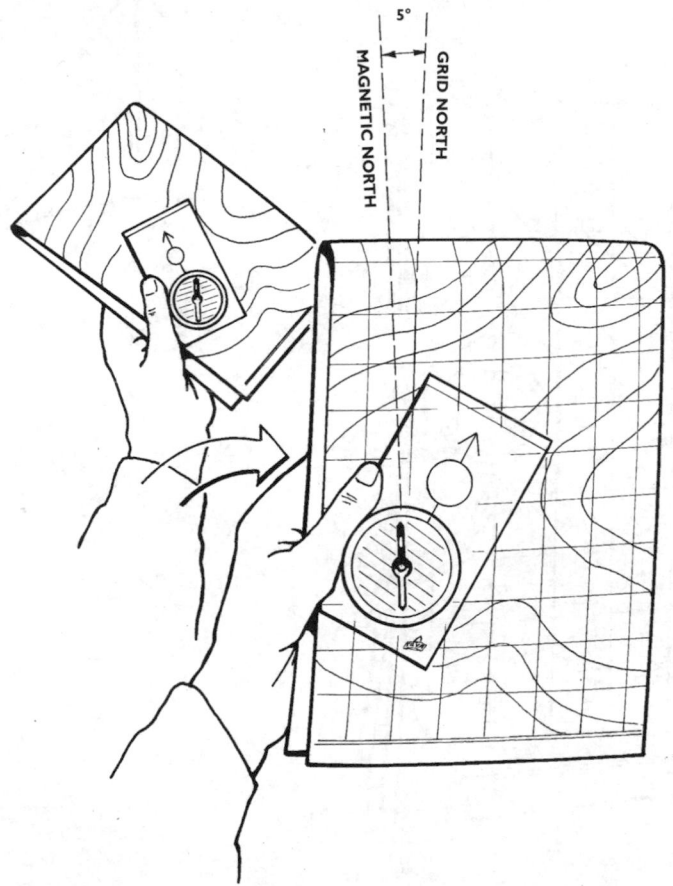

Fig. 16 *Setting the map with the compass - Quick method.*

23

Accurate Method

Set the actual variation on the dial, then match the edge of the compass with the N – S grid lines and turn both map and compass until the needle falls inside the orienting arrow. Your choice of method will depend on the circumstances and the need or otherwise for accuracy.

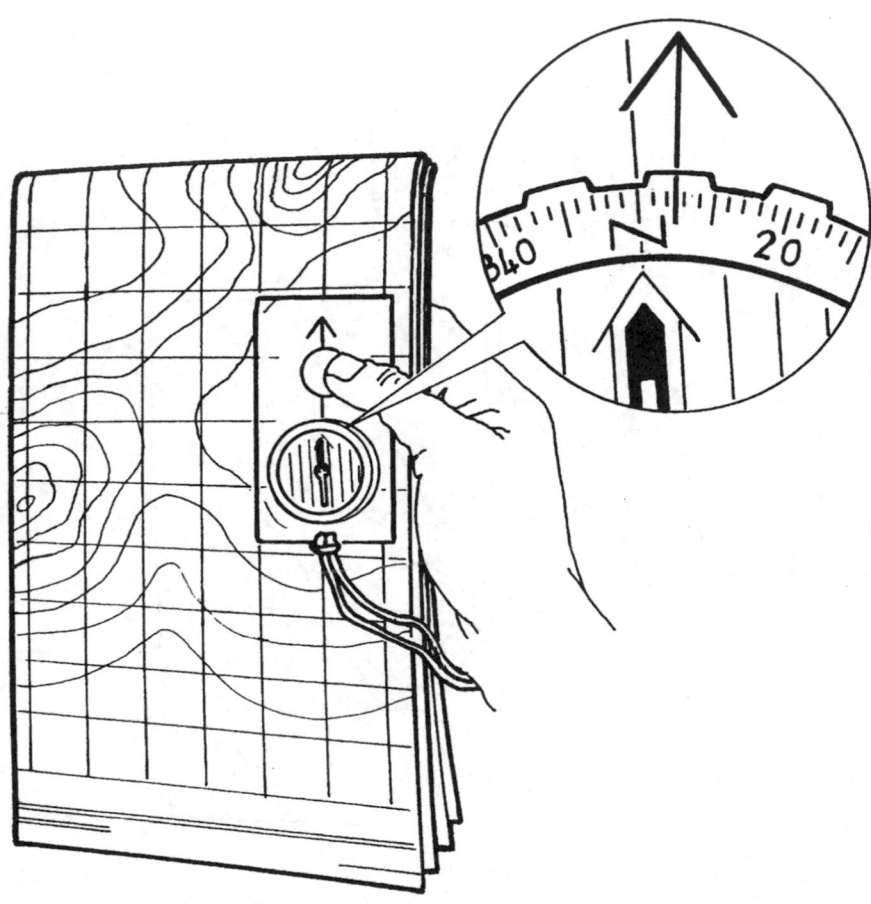

Fig. 17 **Setting the map with the compass - Accurate method.**

Some emphasis has been placed on keeping the map 'set' as you go along. (page 7). It is possible to use this technique combined with the compass to follow a course to your next objective. In Fig 18 you want to get from the stream junction at A to the next one at B. Place one edge of the compass along the desired line of travel on the map and holding both firmly together with your thumb and fingers turn them until the north end of the compass needle is aligned with magnetic north on the map. This will have to be estimated but since it is only 5° to the west of the N/S grid lines it should not present too much of a problem. Now, simply follow the direction indicated by the direction of travel arrow on the compass. This simple and practical technique can be used when a high degree of accuracy is not required.

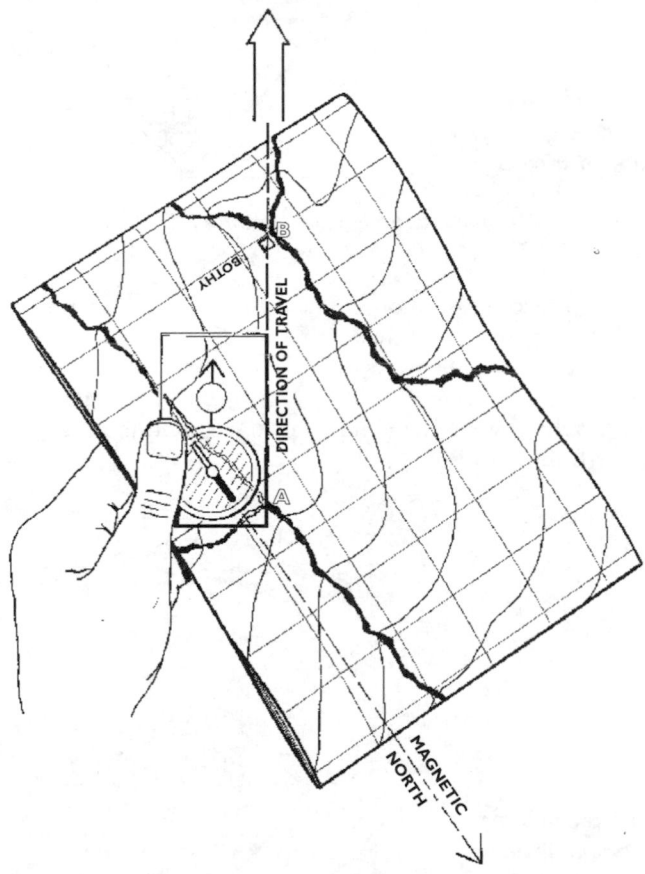

Fig. 18 *Following a course with the map set.*

To take a compass bearing from the map and follow it on the ground:

In good visibility it should rarely be necessary to take a compass bearing. In mist or at night it is the norm.

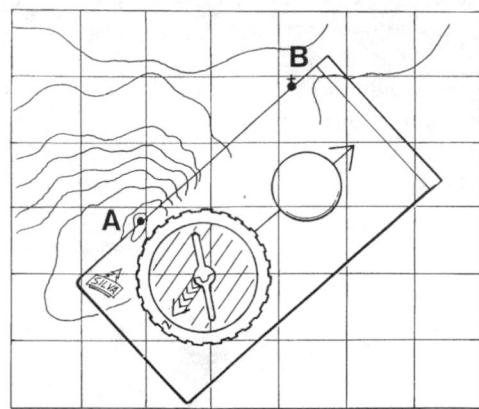

STEP 1: Place the long edge of the compass along the line of travel.

(Fig. 19) **Taking a compass bearing from the map. Steps 1, 2, 3, 4.**

The first step is to measure on the map the angle between grid north and your intended direction of travel. To do this you use the compass as a protractor. Place the compass with one of the long edges along the line joining your present position, A, with your objective, B, making sure that the direction of travel arrow on the compass plate is pointing in the direction you want to go, ie from A to B.

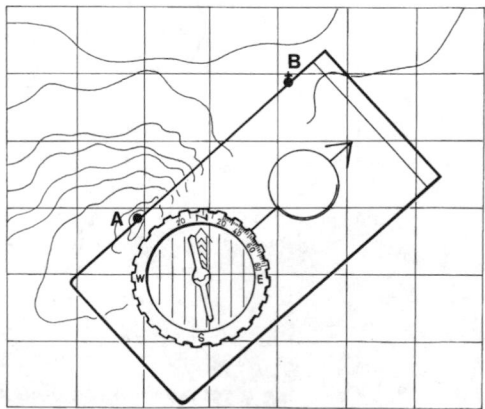

STEP 2: Turn the housing so that the orienting lines are parallel to the grid lines.

Now hold the compass plate firmly in this position on the map and rotate the compass housing so that the lines engraved on it are parallel to the north-south grid lines which can be seen through the housing. Make sure that the north arrow on the housing is pointing towards north on the map. The number of degrees between grid north and your intended direction of travel is shown on the rim of the compass housing against the direction of travel arrow. This is the bearing of your objective and at this stage it is worth making a visual check against the map that the figures are of the right order and not 180° out, as can all too easily happen.

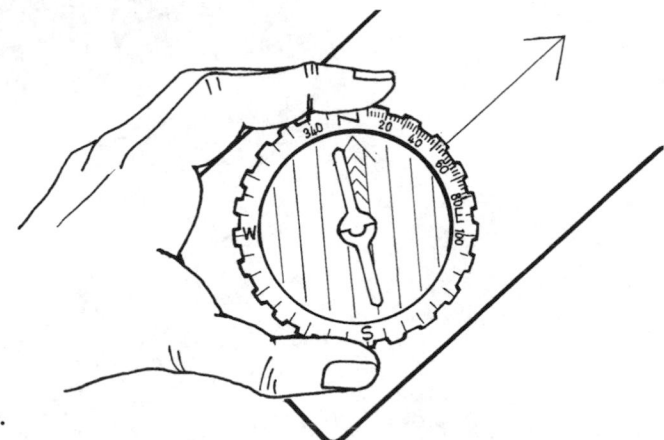

STEP 3: Add the magnetic variation.

To find out where this direction is on the ground you need to refer to the compass needle. But the compass needle does not in fact point to grid north, but towards the magnetic north pole. Therefore, you have to make an allowance for this. Since magnetic north is to left or west of grid north and since bearings are measured in a clockwise direction you will understand that for any given direction of travel the angle between that direction and magnetic north will always be greater than that between the direction of travel and grid north. And it will be greater by the number of degrees that magnetic north is to the west (left) of grid north, ie the magnetic variation.

There are all sorts of rhymes and tricks to help you remember whether to add or subtract the magnetic variation eg. "Add for mag get rid for grid" or "mag for magnitude". However, if you understand why the compass bearing is different from the map bearing you will always be able to work out whether to add or subtract. The next step therefore is to take the compass off the map and to add the magnetic variation. (Step 3)

STEP 4: Turn your body and the compass until the needle falls inside the orienting arrow. Walk in the direction indicated by the direction of travel arrow.

The final step is to use the compass to follow the magnetic bearing you have now set. Hold the compass in front of you with the direction of travel arrow pointing directly away from you. Turn your whole body, still holding the compass in front of you, until the compass needle falls within the arrow engraved on the bottom of the compass housing, with the red end of the needle at the arrowhead. Walk in the direction indicated by the direction of travel arrow.

HOW DO I KEEP ON COURSE ?

In reasonably good visibility pick out features along your line of travel and simply walk to them. The ideal is to have the actual line indicated by the alignment of two features. In this way you avoid drifting to one side of your course.

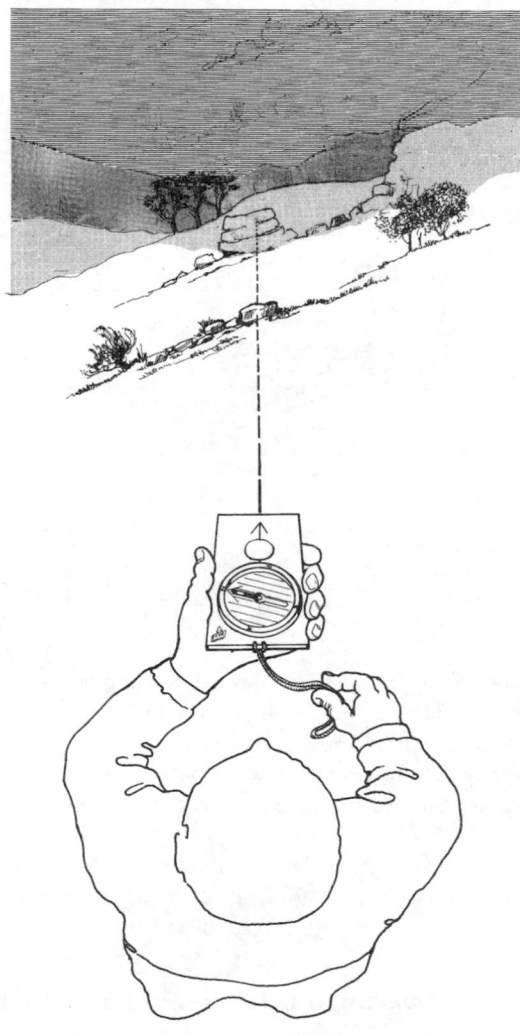

Fig. 20   *Keeping on course.*

In good visibility you may hardly have to refer to the compass, especially if you are following the advice given earlier and are taking note of features as you go along. The advantage of this approach is that you do not become the slave of the compass, but can make allowances for terrain by contouring round obstacles, following the line of least resistance and yet sticking to your overall course. One of the hallmarks of the good navigator is that the compass is only used when it is necessary.

In poor visibility it is, of course, much more difficult to hold a line. In some circumstances two navigators can sometimes be better than one, with the one behind checking up on the navigation of the leader and calling out corrections as required.

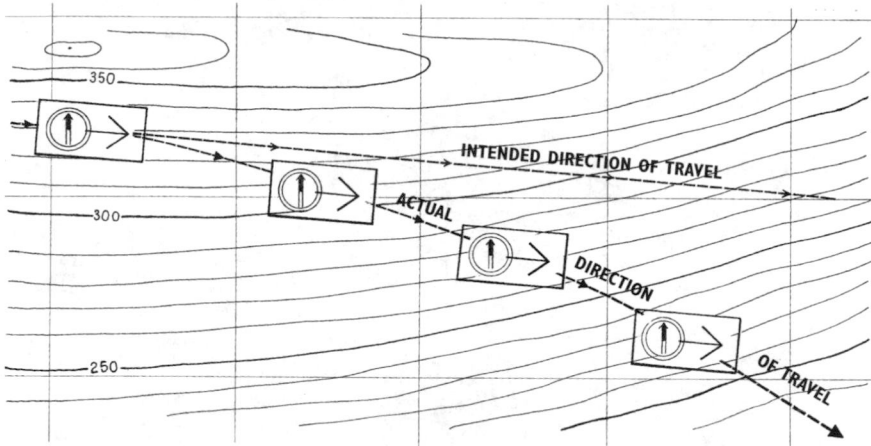

Fig. 21   *Drifting. Even following a compass bearing it is easy to drift downhill. This can happen if you try to follow a bearing on your compass without relating it to features on the ground. It is especially easy to drift downwards when traversing a hillside. A crosswind can also cause you to drift downwind.*

Remember that the compass can be affected by metal objects either on your person, such as camera, watch, pocket knife, ice axe, or in your immediate vicinity, such as fencing, power lines etc. (page 18)

To take a compass bearing on the ground and transfer it to the map

It is sometimes necessary to take a compass bearing and convert it to a map bearing. It may simply be to put a name to a peak or some other feature you can see or it may be to help you to pinpoint your own position by taking compass bearings to visible features which you can identify on the map. Whatever the reason the technique is the same.

1 Point the direction of travel arrow at the feature.

2 Holding the compass in this position, turn the housing until the orienting arrow lies directly underneath the north end of the compass needle.

3 The figure which is given at the base of the direction of travel arrow is the angle between magnetic north and the line to the feature, ie the magnetic bearing to the feature, in this case 295°.

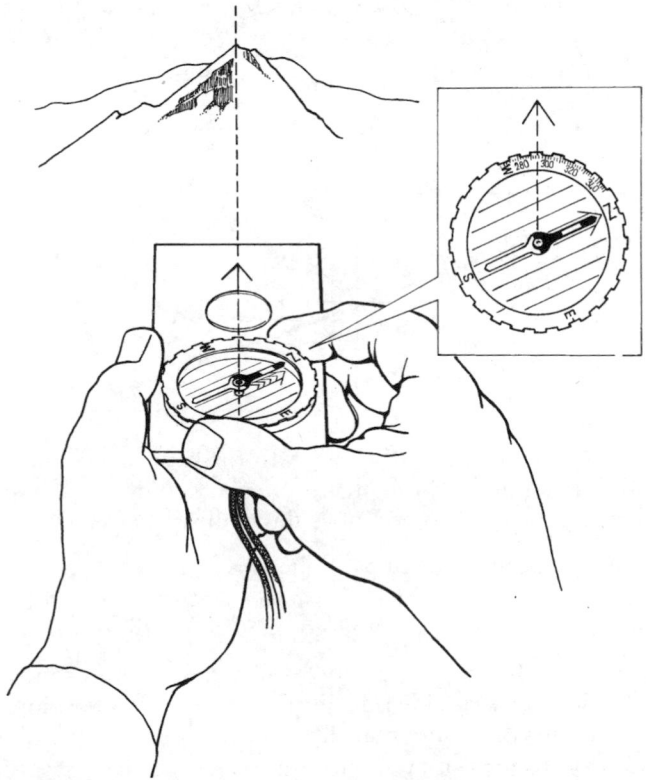

Fig. 22   **Compass to map.**
STEPS 1-3: Point the direction of travel arrow at the peak and turn the housing until the arrows coincide.

(Fig. 22) **Compass to map.**
STEPS 4-8: Subtract magnetic variation and by moving the whole compass align the orienting arrow with the north grid lines at the same time as matching up the edge of the compass with either the peak or your own position, whichever is known.

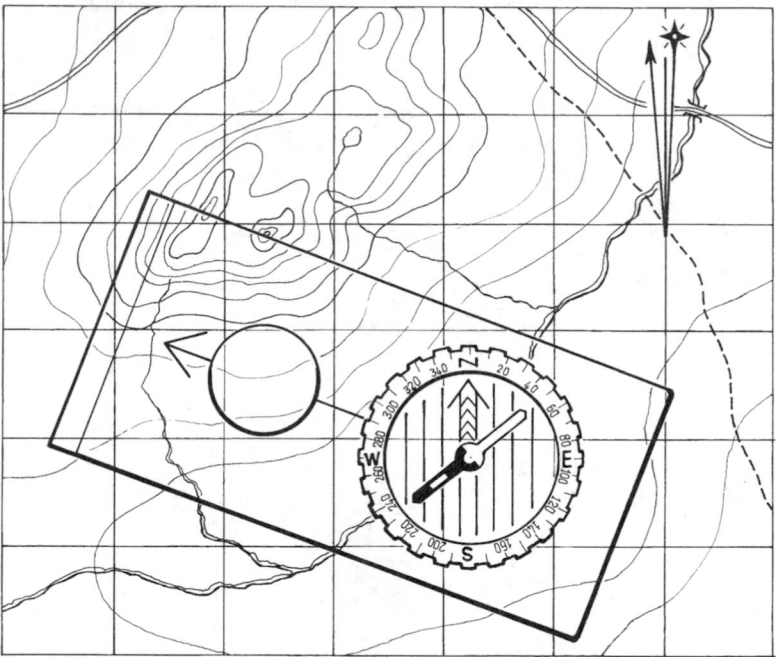

4 Now subtract the magnetic variation for your locality to arrive at the grid bearing and set this figure on your compass, 295°-5° = 290°. From this stage on do not move the compass housing.

5 Place the compass on top of the map in such a position that the orienting arrow and lines are parallel to the N–S grid lines, making sure that the arrow is pointing to the top (north) of the map.

6 Now move the compass on the map into a position so that one of its long sides intersects either the feature or your own position, whichever is known, making sure that the direction of travel arrow is pointing away from your own position.

7 If you are trying to identify the feature, you know that it is somewhere along the edge of the compass or an extension of it. What, of course, this exercise does not tell you is the distance to the feature.

8　In just the same way, if you are trying to find your own position from a known feature, you know that it will be somewhere along the line indicated by the edge of the compass, but in the opposite direction from that indicated by the direction of travel arrow, in other words on the back bearing.

Finding Your Position from Identifiable Features

USE OF TRANSITS

When two simultaneously visible features which can be identified on the map are on the same line of sight they are said to be 'in transit' with you. An extension of the line joining the two features on the map must therefore pass through your present position. If you are on some linear feature such as a path, a stream or a ridge then the transit will give a fix on your position. (Fig. 23) Sometimes a linear feature, such as a road or a stream or the edge of a forest, will provide the same information (Fig 24)

BACK BEARINGS

By using the compass you can eliminate the need for a transit. A glimpse of an identifiable feature should be sufficient to enable you to take a bearing

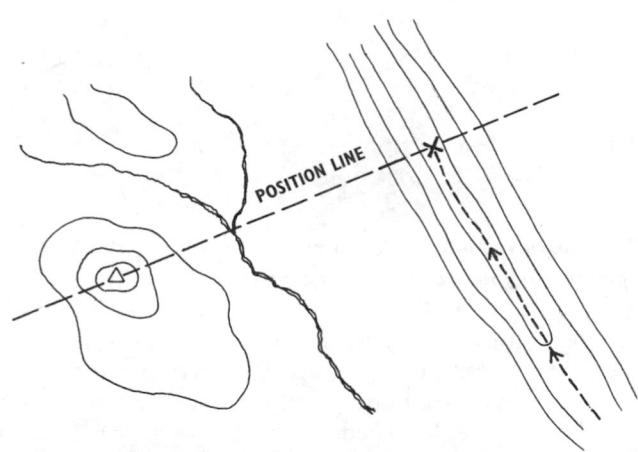

POSITION LINE

Fig. 23 *The use of a transit to pin point your position on a ridge. When the stream junction and the peak are in line (transit) you must be at point X on the ridge.*

towards it. Take, for example, a situation where you are following a path across a featureless plateau (Fig. 25). In the distance to one side you can see a peak which you can identify on the map. You take a bearing to the peak. Since it is a magnetic bearing it will be greater than the grid bearing. You therefore subtract the magnetic variation of say 5° to arrive at the grid bearing and set this on your compass. Place the compass on the map in such a way that the orienting lines on the housing are parallel to the N–S grid lines on the map with the orienting arrow pointing to the top of the map and the direction of travel arrow pointing towards the peak. Slide it into a position where one of the long sides of the compass plate crosses the peak. Your position on the path is where this side, or an extension of it, intersects the path. This technique assumes, of course, that you know which footpath you are on.

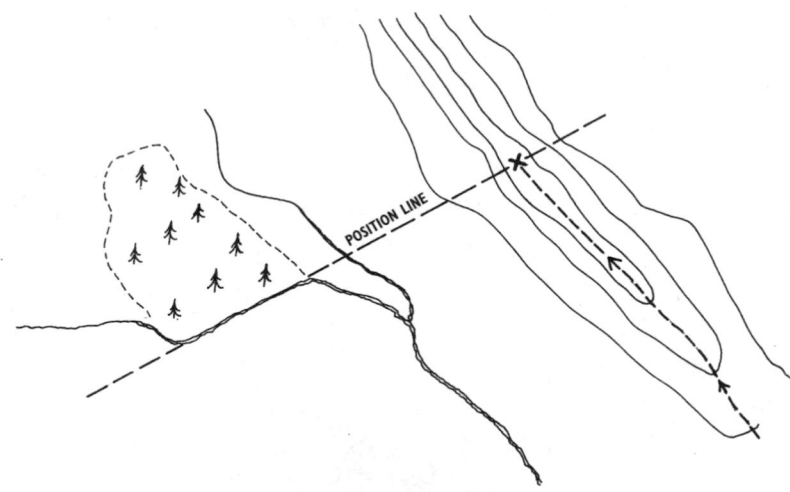

POSITION LINE

Fig. 24   *The straight section of the stream or the edge of the forest provides a pointer to your position on the ridge.*

Strictly speaking, a back bearing is a bearing towards you from an object. It is the reverse of the bearing from you to the object and is therefore 180° different from it. To find a back bearing you must add or subtract 180° from the bearing. In the example illustrated in Fig. 25 the back bearing of 60° is 60° + 180° = 240°. However, in practice it is unnecessary to do this mental arithmetic since what you want is a 'position line' and that is provided by the edge of the compass plate. The back bearing is simply in the opposite direction to that indicated by the direction of travel arrow.

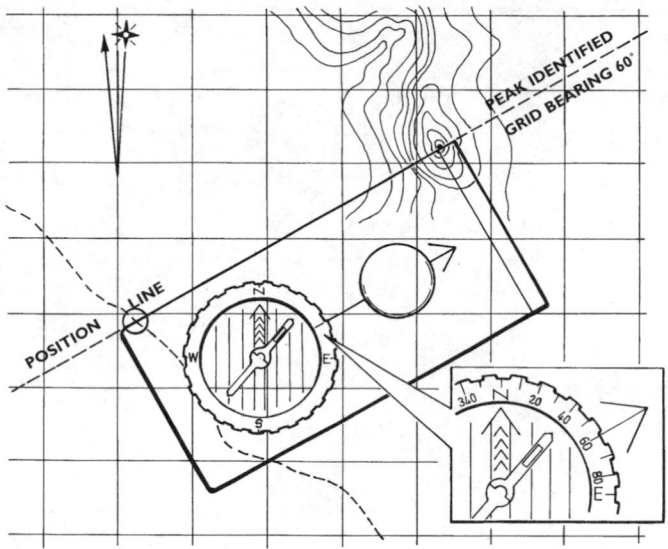

Fig. 25   *The use of a back bearing, having subtracted the magnetic variation, to pinpoint your position on the footpath.*

RESECTION

In some circumstances you may be in open country with only a very general idea of your position. In this event you require at least two and preferably three features which you can definitely identify and which should not all be within the same 180° arc. Take a compass bearing to each of the features and convert them to grid bearings. Plot these bearings on to the map (page 32, steps 5–8). Your position will be in the centre of the small triangle or 'cocked hat' formed by the intersection of these lines (Fig. 26). If the three features are all within the same 180° arc there is a possibility that your actual position will lie outside the cocked hat. The procedure is known as 'resection'.

Resection is a fairly time-consuming procedure, and in adverse conditions you are unlikely to be able to identify the three features required for an accurate 'fix'. You are much more likely to catch a brief glimpse of the way ahead or a sight of some landmark which you can identify on the map. Be alert for these opportunities to get a quick fix on your position. The art of navigation lies in piecing together these various clues with all the other information which is available.

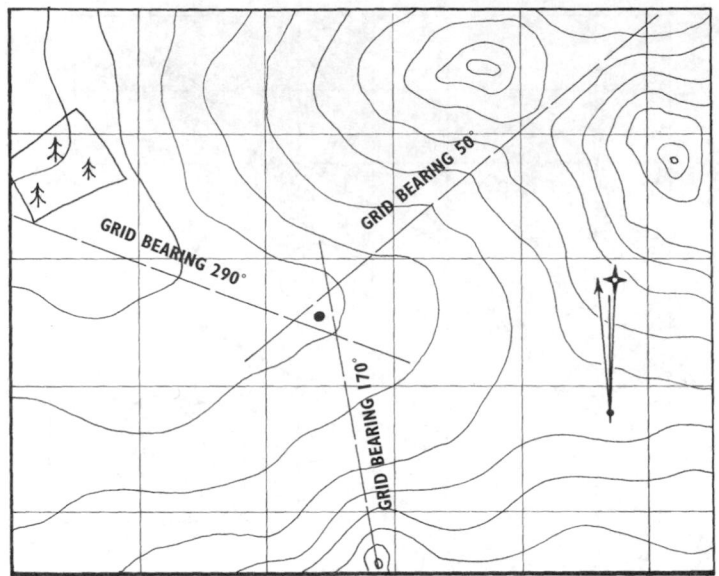

Fig. 26   *Finding your position by resection. Note the 'cocked hat' or triangle, within which your position must lie.*

SIGHTING COMPASS

One of the drawbacks of the conventional type of compass is that constant adjustments have to be made to take account of magnetic variation. On some sighting compasses, such as the Silva Ranger (Fig. 27), the orienting arrow can be adjusted by means of a small screw on the rim of the compass housing. This should be set so that it is inclined to the west of the engraved N/S lines by the angle of magnetic variation. Once this has been done there is no further need to take account of variation unless, of course, you go abroad where the variation is different. Then you will have to readjust the orienting arrow.

The advantage of this type of compass is that you do not have to worry about whether you add or subtract the variation, nor do you have to fiddle about making the adjustment when your hands are freezing. Once this bearing is set on the compass you simply match up the needle with the orienting arrow and go. The 'Ranger type' has other refinements. A hinged cover protects the compass housing and prevents accidental movement. Inside the cover is a mirror which can be used when a more accurate bearing is required. The compass is held at eye level with the cover open at 45° so that

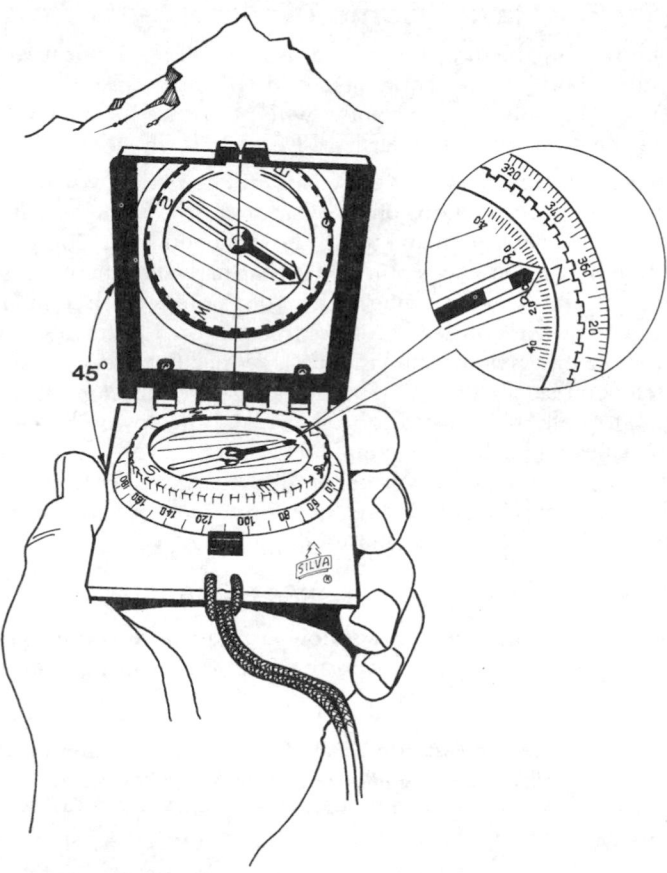

Fig. 27   *The Silva Ranger facilitates accurate bearings and does away with the need to make constant adjustments for magnetic variation which is preset on the orienting arrow (inset).*

the reflection of the housing can clearly be seen in the mirror. Having lined up the object in the sights the housing is turned until the compass needle falls inside the orienting arrow, red to red. The compass will then read the true bearing to the object (remember that magnetic variation has already been set). In transferring the bearing to the map exactly the same procedure is followed as with the regular compass (page 32, steps 5-8), matching up the engraved lines on the housing with the N/S grid lines on the map, making sure that the orienting arrow is pointing to north on the map.

"How Far Have I Come ?"

You know now the direction you want to proceed in, but it would be asking too much, both of your equipment and your expertise, to be able to hit the target spot on. So you must know when to stop. In other words, you must answer the question, "How far have I come?"

Well, if you know where you started and you know where you are and can identify these two positions on the map then it is a simple matter to measure the distance between them, using the scale on your compass to find out exactly how far you have come. But what happens when you set out from a known position and are trying to get to a point which is hidden from you, perhaps because it's buried in a forest, or out on a featureless moor or simply because the mist is down and visibility is reduced to a few yards? Your compass will tell you that you are going in the right direction, but unless you are lucky enough to walk straight into your objective, how do you know when to stop? If the shape and pitch of the ground does not provide sufficient clues then you must rely on your estimation of the distance travelled since your last check point. You can estimate the distance in one of two ways: timing and pacing. Timing is dealt with below, and pacing on page 47.

Estimation of Distance Travelled by Timing

If you know, or can at least guess, how fast you are walking you can work out how long it is going to take you to walk from your starting point to your objective (Table 5).

Table 5 — **Time and Distance Table. Time taken in minutes for a range of walking speeds and distances up to 1,000 metres.**

DISTANCE	SPEED KPH				
	2	3	4	5	6
1,000	30	20	15	12	10
900	27	18	13.5	10.8	9
800	24	16	12	9.6	8
700	21	14	10.5	8.4	7
600	18	12	9	7.2	6
500	15	10	7.5	6	5
400	12	8	6	4.8	4
300	9	6	4.5	3.6	3
200	6	4	3	2.4	2
100	3	2	1.5	1.2	1

Let us say you are at a stream junction and you want to get to a bothy which is 1.5km away as measured on the map. You reckon you will walk at a speed of 3km per hour. Well, if it takes 1 hour to travel 3km, it will only take half the time to travel half the distance, 1.5km. In other words it will take you half an hour. So after half an hour of walking, you stop, look around, and lo and behold there is the bothy.

It sounds easy, but there are a few possible snags which we will now consider. First of all it is not so easy to estimate how fast you are likely to walk over a given stretch of country. All sorts of factors affect your speed over the ground.

HEIGHT CLIMBED

Perhaps the most obvious of these is the amount of climbing you have to do. You are likely to go a lot faster downhill than slogging up a steep mountain side. So, you have to make some allowance for these variations in terrain. It is useful to have some basic formula for working out your speed over the ground and then adjust it as necessary. The traditional formula was that proposed by the Scottish Climber, Naismith, back in 1892. He advocated an allowance of 3 mph plus ½ hour for every 1,000ft of climbing. In metric terms this becomes 5 k.p.h. plus ½ hour per 300m. It is just as valid today as it ever was, provided one appreciates that it is an average time for a day's expedition undertaken by reasonably fit hill walkers.

NAISMITH'S RULE:-

5km per hour plus ½ hour for every 300 metres of ascent.

It is sometimes more convenient to express this formula in terms of the extra time required to climb a given number of contour lines. For example, it takes an additional minute to climb one 10 metre contour line or an additional 5 minutes for each thick contour line. So if you are working out the time for an individual leg of a route all you need to do is to count the thick contour lines you have to climb, multiply by 5 and add this number of minutes to your estimated time based on your speed on the flat.

To allow for height climbed, add 5 minutes for each thick (50m) contour line.

You will appreciate that if the contour interval is different then the time to allow for each contour will be different. For instance you may be using a Harveys map where the contour interval is 15m. In this case you would allow an additional 1.5 minutes for each contour or 7.5 minutes for each thick contour.

Going Down

Going downhill poses a bit of a problem. Most walkers naturally increase their speed going down fairly gentle slopes of between about 5° and 12°. There comes a point, however, at which the time taken is more than would be taken walking the same distance on the level because of the extra care that is required. Over a day's journey it is normal practice to discount descent, on the assumption that increased speeds on the gentle descents will be compensated by slower speeds on the steep ones. However, for individual sections it may be necessary to make some allowance as follows:

Corrections for short distances :

going gently downhill : - 10 mins/300m of descent

very steeply downhill : + 10 mins/300m of descent

Fitness

The question of fitness is important particularly where a group of youngsters is concerned and due allowance must be made for this. Remember, too, that a party can only progress at the speed of its slowest member. A speed of:

4 k.p.h. plus 1 hour for every 450m of climbing

is a more realistic estimate for such a party. (See Tranter's corrections to Naismith's Rule, Table 6, page 42).

Load

Another factor which affects your speed is the load carried. A heavy pack can reduce progress by 50% of the unladen speed, taking into account additional rest periods as well as speed over the ground. It is best to allow for this by simply estimating a slower speed, say 3 k.p.h. or even 2 k.p.h. in some circumstances.

Terrain

One thing over which you have no control and which can reduce your speed to a snail's pace is the nature of the ground. It is not always possible to tell from the map just how rough the ground will be. A boulder field, an unthinned plantation of conifers, breakable snow crust, boggy ground, and a host of other factors can reduce your performance dramatically. Here again, you must allow for slower progress across such terrain. In extreme conditions the estimated time can be exceeded by as much as 400%. It is worth noting that orienteering maps provide much more relevant information about the nature of the ground than do O.S. maps.

Notice the additional information provided by the orienteering map.

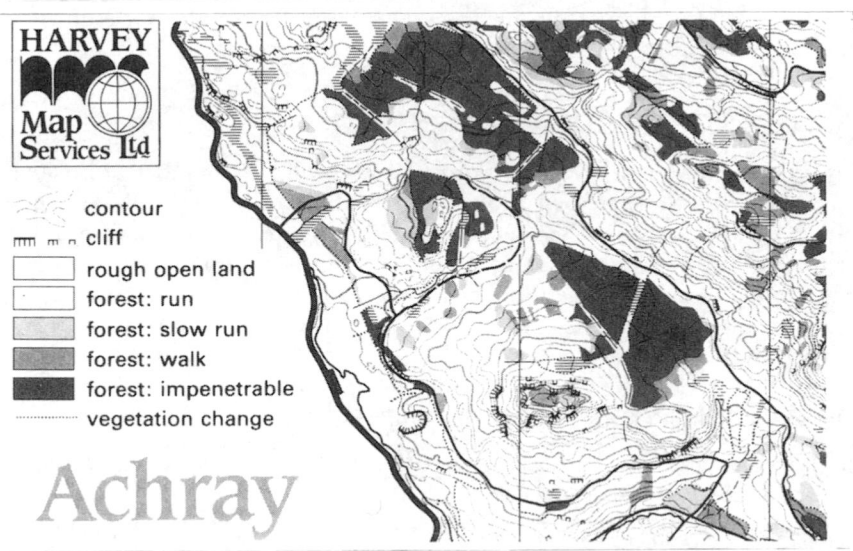

Fig. 28   *Extract from the orienteering map of Achray Forest, Stirlingshire. The scale is 1:15,000 with a 5m contour interval. The original is printed in five colours. Reproduced with the permission of Harvey Map Services, Doune. Notice the additional information provided by the orienteering map.*

Weather Conditions

Another factor outside your control is the weather and adverse conditions can play havoc with the most carefully worked out route plan. A strong headwind, with or without rain or snow, can reduce your speed on the flat to less than 2 k.p.h. Conversely, a following wind can greatly increase your speed, sometimes dangerously so! Modify your estimate of speed in the light of experience for each leg of your journey and always keep in mind the fact that it can be a hard fight if the homeward leg is against the wind in the gathering darkness.

With all these factors to take into account, you could be forgiven for thinking that it is a near hopeless task to arrive at a realistic estimate. Not so! It is largely a matter of common sense and you will get a lot better with practice. It should also be borne in mind that the technique of using time to estimate distances is inevitably somewhat inaccurate. If you manage to get within 10% of the actual distance you are doing very well. For this reason you must always be aware of the terrain as you go along, mentally checking off features as you pass them and comparing your actual time with your estimated time.

TRANTER'S CORRECTIONS

It is probable that on a given day's outing there will be a number of isolated bad patches and these are best allowed for on the spot once you know what you are up against. General corrections, such as Tranter's corrections to times calculated on the basis of Naismith's rule, are not applicable to separate legs of the route, but only to the route as a whole. In other words they are useful for estimating the total time of an expedition, not in working out the distance travelled over individual sections of it.

(Table 6) *Tranter's Corrections to Naismith's Rule.*

The Table gives the actual times adjusted according to fitness level for a range of times estimated according to Naismith's Rule.

Time taken to climb 300m in 800m

Individual fitness in minutes	Times Taken in Hours Estimated According to Naismith's Rule															
	2	3	4	5	6	7	8	9	10	12	14	16	18	20	22	24
15 *very fit*	1	1½	2	2¾	3½	4½	5½	6¾	7¾	10	12½	14½	17	19½	22	24
20		1¼	2¼	3¼	4½	5½	6½	7¾	8¾	10	12½	15	17½	20	23	
25			1½	3	4¼	5½	7	8½	10	11½	13¼	15	17½			
30				2	3½	5	6¾	8½	10½	12½	14½					
40					2¾	4¼	5¾	7½	9½	11½						
50 *unfit*						3¼	4¾	6½	8½							

Limit Line

Too much to be attempted

20 kg load carried- drop one fitness level.

Conditions underfoot - drop one or more levels according to conditions.

Conditions overhead - drop one level for journey at night or if wind is against you.

The fitness level is the time in minutes taken to climb 300 metres in 800 metres distance at your normal pace. It should be determined for each individual by timed trials. Allowance can be made for other factors by adopting a higher or lower fitness level as appropriate.

To use the Table start at the top with your estimated time based on Naismith eg 7 hours. Follow the vertical column down until you get to the horizontal line corresponding to your fitness level eg the 25 level. In this case it would take you $8\frac{1}{2}$ hours to do the same journey, i.e. $1\frac{1}{2}$ hours longer than by Naismiths. If your fitness is less than 40 then this particular trip is too much to be attempted.

Errors

The question of error is significant because it is perfectly evident that an error of 10% is unacceptable unless you do something about it. When you combine this with a possible error in direction of, say, plus or minus four degrees, you find that with increasing distance the area of uncertainty within which your objective must lie becomes very large indeed. As you can see from Fig. 29 the area of uncertainty is approximately 3 hectares at 1km, 11 hectares at 2km and a staggering 25 hectares at 3km (1 hectare = 100m x 100m). The area of a football pitch is 0.8 hectares. The moral is surely obvious. Keep individual sections of the route as short as possible and when conditions are tricky and it is vital that you locate your objective without too much casting about, use a more accurate method, such as pace counting, to estimate distance travelled.

HOMING IN ON THE TARGET

Let us say that you are following a compass bearing to an objective 1 km distant. You estimate your speed to be 3 k.p.h. and there are no further corrections. In 20 minutes. you know you are in the target area and at this point you must take stock of the situation. Refer to the map for clues, but failing these, you must set about a systematic search of the area to locate your objective. Wherever you happen to be in the area of uncertainty, provided your error is no greater than plus or minus four degrees in direction and plus or minus 10% of distance travelled, a search of a rectangle 200m x 140m is certain to lead to its discovery. Well, almost certain! You should resist the temptation to dash off in what you consider to be the most likely direction. If you happen to be wrong it greatly complicates the subsequent systematic search. The most effective method is to work outwards in a rectangular spiral from where you expected the objective to be (Fig. 30).

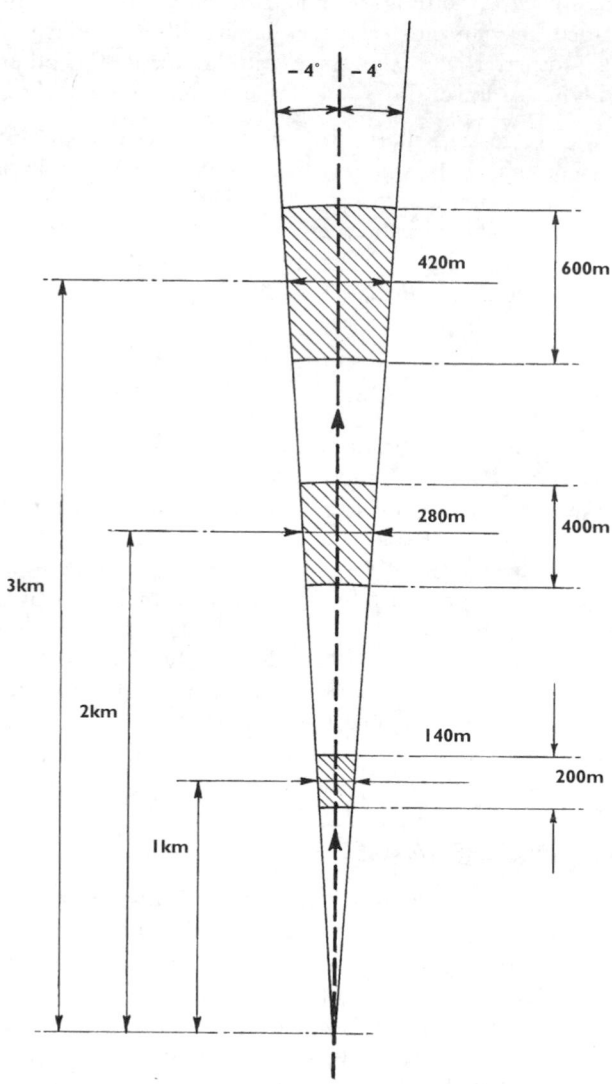

Fig. 29 *The effect of errors. The shaded areas represent the combined effect of a maximum error of plus or minus 10% in the estimation of distance travelled and a maximum angular error of plus or minus 4°, after walking distances of 1km, 2km and 3km.*

EXPANDING SPIRAL SEARCH

The steps are as follows:

(i) Search on a bearing for a distance equal to the visibility.

(ii) Turn 90° to the right and search for a distance equal to twice the visibility.

(iii) Turn 90° to the right and search for a distance equal to three times the visibility.

(iv) and so on, turning to the right by 90° at the end of each leg and increasing the length of the next leg by a distance equal to the visibility, until the objective is found.

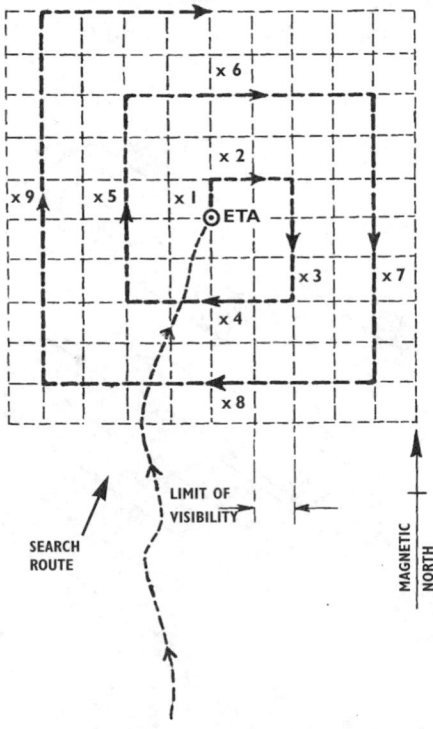

Fig. 30 *Searching for your objective at night or in poor visibility. The grid represents the limit of visibility and the heavy line the route which should be followed from your position at your expected time of arrival (E.T.A.). Note that every point within the grid is visible from somewhere along the search route.*

The route followed in this search pattern is such that no matter where the objective may lie it will be visible from some point on the expanding spiral. To simplify matters the initial bearing should be magnetic north, south, east or west. This also makes it easier to retrace ones steps to the original position should the objective not be found within a reasonable period. The method has the merit of simplicity and the advantage over other methods that the smaller the original error the quicker the objective will be found.

SWEEP SEARCH

One of the drawbacks of the spiral search is that it is difficult to take advantage of having a number of experienced mountaineers in the party. Using the sweep search method it is a relatively simple matter to space the party out so that they are still within visual contact and sweep back and forward across the area to be searched until the objective is found (Fig. 31).

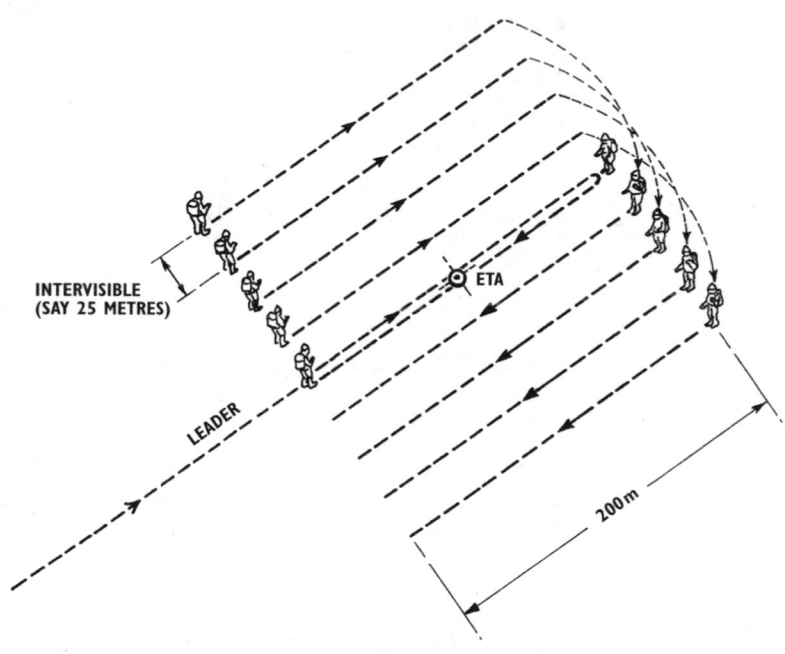

Fig. 31   *Sweep search.*

Estimation of Distance Travelled by Pace Counting

The trouble with calculating distance travelled on the basis of average speed and time taken is that it is at best a rough estimate. Such an estimate is permissible when conditions and visibility are reasonable, but in adverse conditions a mistake, or even a delay, caused by difficulties in the terrain could have serious consequences. At such times it is necessary to use a more accurate procedure; in fact to measure distance by counting the number of paces from your starting point. The technique is well-known to orienteers, the best of whom achieve an almost phenomenal degree of accuracy. Obviously, the length of a single pace varies not only between individuals, but also as a result of variations in terrain and slope angle. This is something that can only be arrived at for each individual by practice and experience. Count double paces (ie each time the same foot hits the ground) and as far as possible keep the distances which have to be measured in this way as short as possible. As a very rough guide an average double pace count for 100m of flat straightforward terrain would be 65. 'As a general rule therefore your double pace count will be two thirds of the distance in metres'. Work out for yourself what your pace count is across a variety of terrain and different slope angles.

One hopes that in the mountains you will not have to rely on pace counting too often. Intelligent use of the map, particularly in selecting a line which minimises the possibility of error, even though it may be a longer way round, pays dividends in the end.

SLOPE ASPECT

Lost? Slope aspect can often provide the vital clue. In Fig. 32 all you know is that you are somewhere in the square kilometre illustrated. Take a bearing straight down the slope. If it is 270° (West) you must be somewhere along the line W,W. If it is 135° (SE) you must be somewhere along the line SE,SE. If it is 360° you must be on the line N,N. If it is flat you must be on the col. Wherever you are the slope aspect will give you a position line. Additional information is required in order to pin point your position along the line. If the fall of the slope is the only information available to you, standing still is not going to improve matters. Depending on where you are trying to get to, walk on but keep a careful track of both direction and distance. Sooner or later you will identify some other features or a change of slope which will provide the clue you are looking for.

Awareness of slope aspect is an essential and often neglected navigational skill.

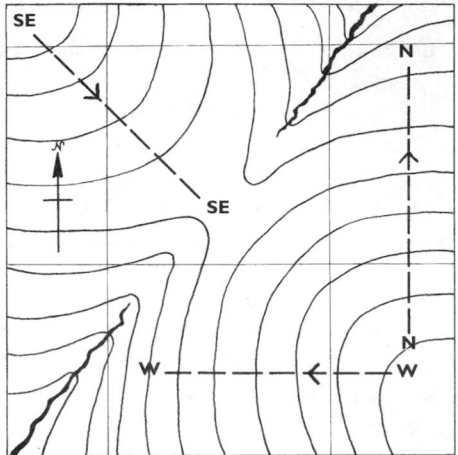

(Fig. 32) *Slope aspect can provide you with a position line.*

CONTOURING

Should we take a direct line even if this involves unnecessary climbing or should we contour round? This is a problem which all hillwalkers have to grapple with from time to time and it is not an easy one to answer. It is difficult to hold a constant height and even more difficult to keep track of your course when contouring. It is usually safe to contour when visibility is good or when you are heading for some collecting feature, such as a stream in the next valley which will prevent you from going too far. Provided that you can maintain a truly horizontal course (and that takes a lot of practice) an accurate estimate of distance travelled should establish your position without too great an error. If accuracy is at a premium, as it would be in the dark with no collecting feature, it may be necessary to contour in a series of straight lines using the well tried method of pace and compass.

Taking the Long Way Round

Deciding whether it is quicker to take a direct route which involves climbing or take the long way round is another matter. We have seen (page 39) that each thick contour line means an additional 5 minutes to your route time. In 5 minutes you could walk 417 metres on the flat (at 5 k.p.h.). So as a general rule, and as a guide to the length of detour you could afford to make to avoid any given ascent and descent, allow 400 metres for each thick contour line you would have to climb.

In the example illustrated by Fig 33 there are three thick contour lines to be ascended on the direct route from A to B so you can allow 3 x 400 = 1,200 metres over and above the 1,000 metres distance, ie a total of 2,200 metres for contouring. In other words you could afford to contour for more than twice the direct distance between A and B in the time it would take you to go over the top.

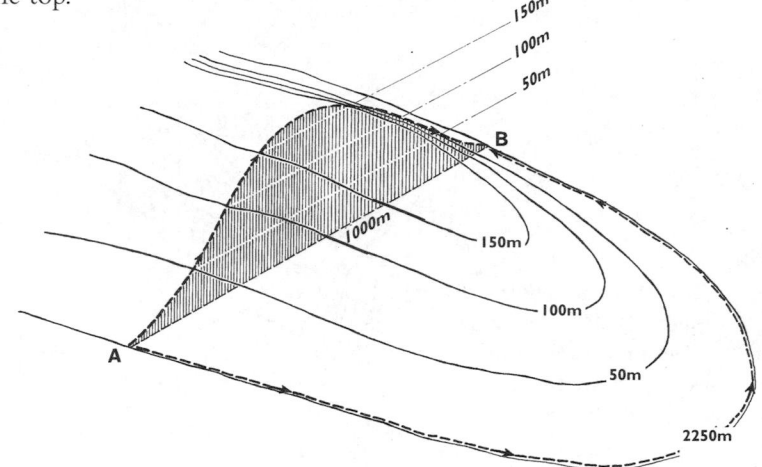

Fig. 33 — *The direct route from A to B 'over the top' will take an extra 15 minutes based on Naismith's Rule. In that time you could walk an additional 1250m on the flat at 5k.p.h. In other words the long way round from A to B is just as quick and certainly less tiring.*

FOLLOWING FEATURES

This is something that many will do instinctively, but it is well worth making a mental note of various features which you will come across en route and tick them off as you actually pass them on the ground. If a feature does not appear on schedule you will know immediately that something is wrong. Common sense dictates that it is sensible to follow any well marked feature if it is leading in the general direction that you wish to go such as fence lines, footpaths, streams, in fact anything that is fairly easy to identify and follow.

AIMING OFF AND ATTACK POINTS

Let us say you are heading for the bothy shown in Fig 35 from a known position, "X". The bothy is 600m away on a magnetic bearing of 350°. If you take a direct line to it in poor visibility you stand a very good chance of missing it altogether (Route C). Instead, head for the unmistakable feature,

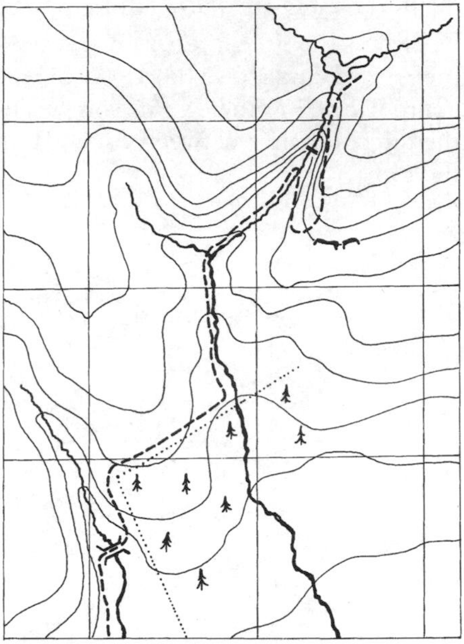

Fig. 34 *Navigating using features as guidelines: the bridge, the forest edge, the stream, the waterfall, the small crags, the lochan.*

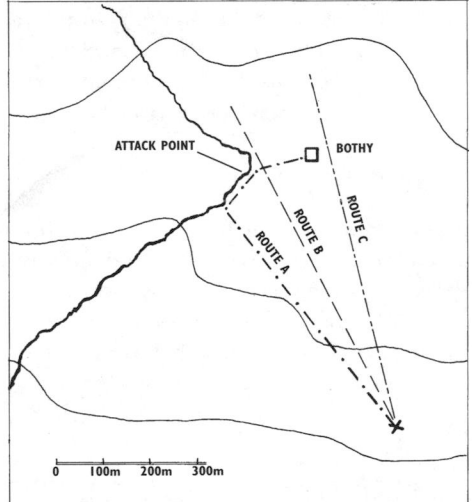

Fig. 35 *Aiming off and attack points.*

_ . _ .   *Aim off to be sure of getting to your attack point. Route A*

_ _ _   *Direct route to attack point is very risky. Route B*

_ . _   *Direct route to the bothy is even more risky. Route C*

the bend in the river, from which you can home in on the bothy by pace and compass (Route A). The river bend is known as an 'attack point'. Do not head directly for the bend (Route B) because a small deviation to the right could result in missing it. Aim off a few degrees to the west so that you are certain to hit the stream which you can then follow to the bend. These techniques have many applications on mountainous terrain but remember that an attack point to be of any use should be close to the objective and should be appreciably easier to find and identify than the objective itself.

PARALLEL ERRORS

One of the most common mistakes in navigating is to pick up the wrong feature, thinking it was the one you were heading for. Look-alike features, particularly contour features, are commonplace on the map and in poor visibility it is easy to mistake one for another. Parallel errors arise from situations, such as that illustrated in Fig 36, where two or more similar

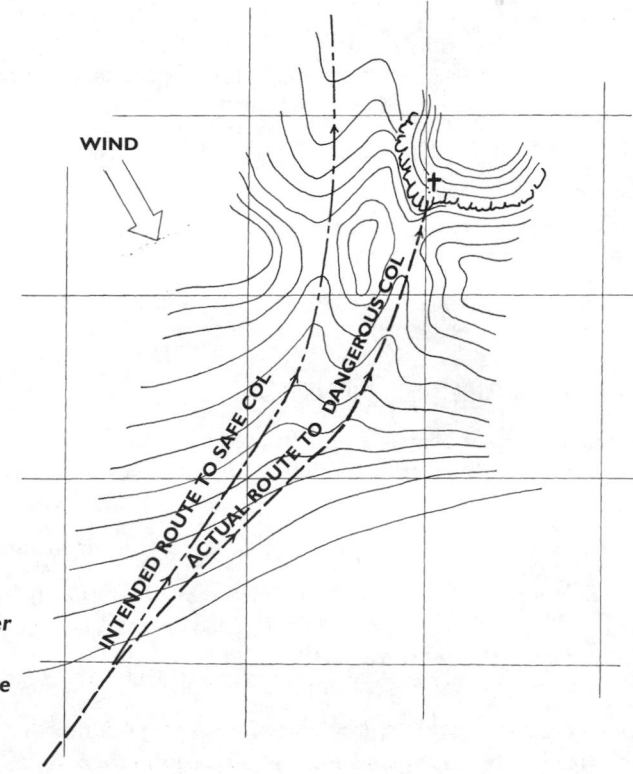

(Fig. 36)

Parallel Error. The intended route is to the west col. The NW wind and the slope of the terrain has caused the walker to drift to the right into a parallel feature which leads to the wrong col.

features, in this case two cols, lie adjacent and parallel to each other. Once at the col it is extremely difficult to tell which one you are on and the consequences of a mistake could be serious. Good contact with the map, accurate compass work and above all, awareness of the possibility of error should ensure that you hit the right target.

Navigating at Night or in Bad Weather

Navigating in reasonable conditions and good visibility should present no great problems to the mountaineer. In bad weather it is not new techniques which are required but a more skilful and determined application of those already learned. Nevertheless, it is worthwhile drawing attention to certain aspects of navigation which require special consideration in such conditions.

Be Prepared!

Your route card should not only take note of possible escape routes, but it should also record compass bearings, distances, and estimated times for any sections which might prove difficult in bad conditions. A little advance planning at this stage can forestall a lot of potential trouble later on.

Check through your equipment and make sure it is all in working order and readily accessible. Have you got a couple of spare batteries for your torch?

'Transpaseal' is an ideal protective cover for your map. Cover both sides and then fold the map so that the area of your route is exposed, or use a polythene bag.

Be prepared to modify your route should conditions justify a change of plan.

PARTY DISCIPLINE AND ORGANISATION

Keep the party together and impress on each person that it is his or her responsibility to keep in touch with the person immediately in front and behind.

Appoint a responsible member of the group to bring up the rear.

Appoint another to check your navigation and in particular to ensure that you follow the correct compass bearing without drifting to one side. Obviously you must be within sight and hearing of each other so that corrections can be made from time to time as necessary.

Morale can fall to a low ebb under severe conditions with confidence in the leader being sapped by anxiety, ignorance and unexplained delays.

Proceed at a steady pace and keep your party well informed and involved, with everyone feeling that they have a job to do.

TECHNIQUES

Have the map correctly oriented at all times and be fully aware of changes in the terrain, particularly changes in both the steepness of slopes and in their aspect.

As far as possible keep your compass legs short, moving from one easily identifiable point to the next even if this involves a detour. Play safe and use the techniques of aiming off, attack points, catching features to full advantage.

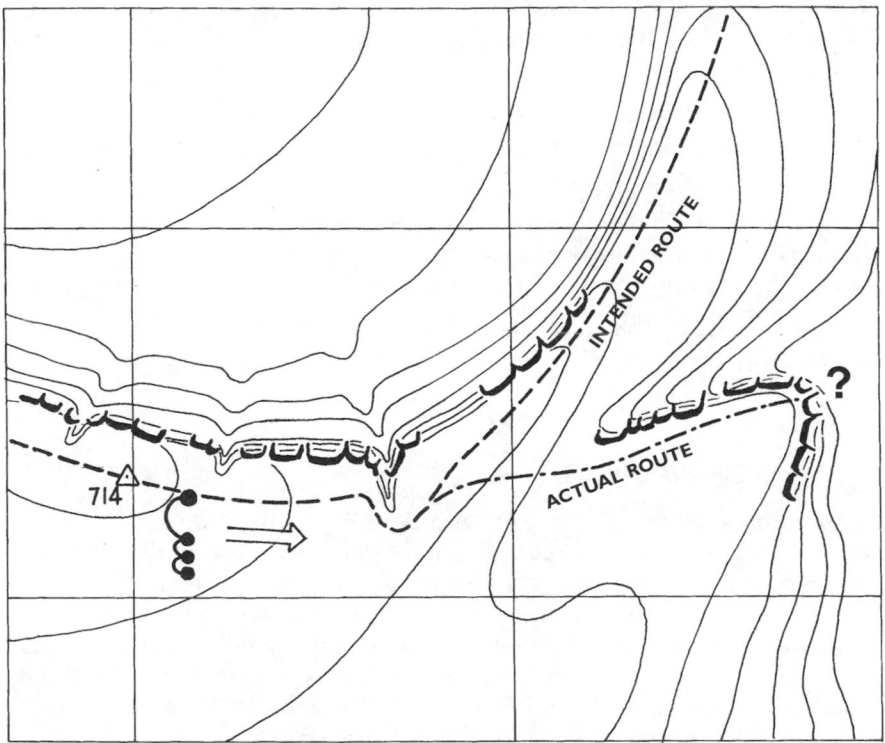

Fig. 37 *The party is lined up correctly in relation to the cliff edge, but note how a slight error can lead to a dangerous situation, disguised by the fact that they still have a cliff edge to their left.*

Continual reference to the map at night using a powerful torch can seriously impair your night vision. Use your torch sparingly. It takes almost 1 hour for your eyes to become fully acclimatised to the dark after exposure to bright light. To a certain extent you can protect the night vision in one eye by closing it when you use your torch. Another useful tip is to use a red filter in your torch or your goggles. Red light does not bleach out the pigment in the eyes on which night vision depends. Unfortunately, brown contour lines tend to disappear in red light. Glare from a head torch can also affect night vision. If you use one make sure that it is set at the correct angle and if necessary use insulating tape to adjust the beam.

In extreme conditions, which most commonly occur during the winter months, it may occasionally be necessary to rope the party together, particularly in the vicinity of cliffs or cornices. In some circumstances it may be sufficient just to hold the rope without actually tying on. Allow plenty of margin for error in taking your compass bearings and choose a route well back from potential danger.

If roped together in this situation, align the party at right angles to the cliff edge. The leader should adopt the position nearest the edge on a long length of rope from the second.

In white-out conditions it is impossible to judge scale, distance and the steepness of slopes. Throwing a snowball ahead can sometimes provide a focal point for the eye and reveal the snow surface.

Take advantage of any break in the weather or improved visibility to check on your position and to take a compass bearing along the route ahead.

A WORD OF WARNING

Lest it be thought that all problems of bad-weather navigation can be solved by use of map and compass techniques, it should be pointed out that there are certain bad-weather problems where map and compass are of limited use. One particularly awkward case is the traverse of a narrow and complex ridge in thick weather. Not even 1 : 25,000 maps indicate sufficient detail of such ridges to allow accurate 'blind' navigation. For sure and reasonably rapid movement over such ground it is necessary to know the structure of the ridge from clear weather experience. Otherwise, large amounts of time may be spent in pursuing side-buttresses and missing tiny cols between minor tops or pinnacles. Lacking clear weather knowledge, party leaders would be well advised to consider alternative courses of action. Though more circuitous, they may save time and lessen anxiety.

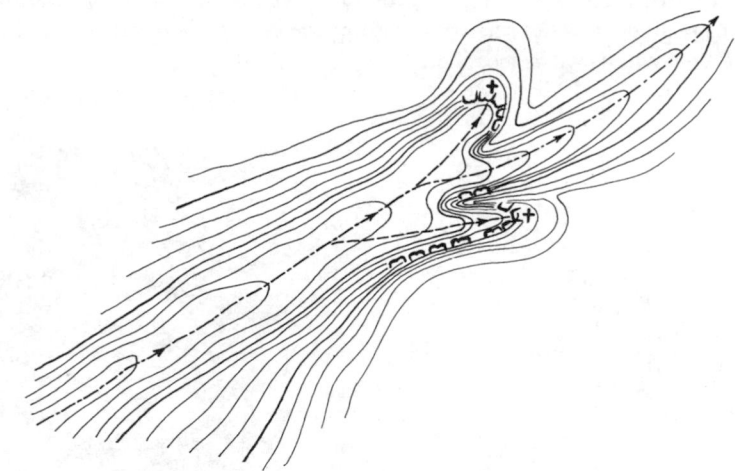

Mistakes are made much more frequently in descent. In severe weather without an altimeter or detailed local knowledge it is difficult to know exactly when to turn off the ridge to follow the safe route down. Careful pace counting and accurate compass work are absolutely essential.

The Altimeter

Atmospheric pressure reduces with altitude at a rate of approximately 10 millibars for every 100 metres of altitude above sea level. So if we measure the atmospheric pressure at any particular point it should also give us a reading for our altitude at that point. Altimeters measure air pressure and are calibrated to read in height above sea level. Until comparatively recently they were expensive instruments and their use was limited to a small number of people mountaineering in the higher ranges. Today they are readily available in a wrist watch format and cost little more than a good quality compass.

It is perfectly possible to navigate accurately without reference to an altimeter. Nevertheless, there are many situations when a knowledge of your height may help to pin point your position when identifiable features are lacking. Take a situation involving a complicated descent in thick mist down a ridge with intricate detail which is too small in scale to be shown on the 1:50,000 map (Fig 40). At some point you have to turn due east off the ridge on to a subsidiary one but the junction is not at all obvious. Straight forward navigation will keep you on the crest of the ridge but without any visual references it would be virtually impossible to know when you had reached the junction. An altimeter would provide that vital piece of additional information, since you can see from reading the contour lines that you should turn due east when you reach 725m.

A wrist watch altimeter.

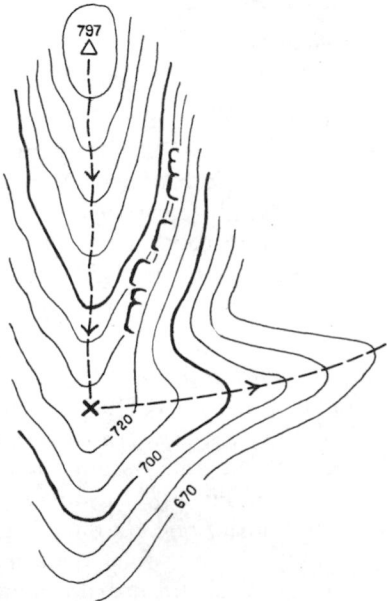

Fig. 40 **Using the altimeter to identify the point on the descent of the south ridge at which to turn east to hit the subsidiary ridge.**

Unfortunately, the altimeter has not been invented that can distinguish between pressure changes brought about by changes in altitude and those brought about by changes in weather. In a period of rapidly developing weather the atmospheric pressure may change by as much as 4mb in one hour. This is equivalent to a change in altitude of 40 metres. Clearly that is an unacceptable margin of error. It is important therefore to reset the altimeter throughout the day at places, such as spot heights, trig points etc, where the height is known. This keeps the altimeter up to date with pressure changes caused by the weather.

GLOBAL POSITIONING SYSTEM (GPS)

Satellite navigation technology has been available for some time and is extensively used in aircraft and ship navigation systems. The GPS is essentially a system of orbiting navigation satellites each of which transmits an accurately timed signal which is picked up by a receiver on the ground. Just as in the technique of resection (page ...) signals from several satellites are necessary to fix the receivers position; in this case a minimum of four. The greater the number of signals received the greater the accuracy of the fix. The equipment currently available is able to compute the distance and direction of travel to fixed points whose map co-ordinates are known and are keyed into the receiver's computer. Accuracy is within plus or minus 100m horizontally and plus or minus 150m for altitude. Clearly, estimates of altitude can not be relied upon. Greater levels of accuracy are available through a Precise Positioning Service (PPS) which, at the present time, is available for military use only. There is no doubt that in the not too distant future improved models will become more generally available and, as the price comes down, so GPS will become a more popular aid to land navigation. However, it is vitally important that it should be viewed in this light, as an aid and not as a substitute for conventional map reading skills.

Teaching Navigation

No person is entirely safe in the mountains without the ability to use map and compass, no matter how knowledgeable and experienced the leader. For reasons outside their control the members of a party can become separated and therefore it is important that individuals should be given sufficient basic instruction to enable them to find their way to safety. In the field of navigation the party leader must be able to give such basic instruction. Considerations of safety apart, it is surely important to encourage the less experienced to strive for a level of competence which will enable them to undertake expeditions without being led.

It is not easy to teach map reading as an extra to be slotted in at odd moments during a day's hill walking. Avail yourself of every opportunity of doing some preliminary ground work. Simple navigation courses can be great fun if intelligently laid out. They should if possible encircle the base so that a bad mistake can always be rectified by a quick return for further instructions. Courses should not be too long and should become progressively more difficult towards the finish. In safe country it is best to travel singly or in pairs. If the groups are larger than this, most of the navigation tends to be done by one person.

Problems of all kinds may be set on route, anything in fact which will encourage the novice to practice the skills previously studied indoors. In the early stages concentrate on the use of the map before introducing the compass.

Orienteering is not only a fine sport in its own right it is also a superb way of developing the skills of navigation. Courses can be set to cater for all levels of ability and it is one of the most attractive features of the sport that you will find the young and the not so young, the fit and the not so fit all competing together and enjoying themselves.

SOME IDEAS FOR MAKING MAP READING MORE FUN

1 Walk blindfold to estimate your tendency to drift to one side.

2 Blindfolded navigator talked through miniature course by accompanying guide.

3 Draw a map of your home town from memory to see if you are aware of the wider relationships.

4 'Mappo', an adaptation of the game Bingo, using map symbols.

5 Place code letters at a series of fixed points. These can be used in different combinations to provide courses of varying degrees of difficulty.

6 Map reading crossword games.

7 Find your fitness level. How long does it take you to climb 300 metres in 800 metres horizontal distance?

8 Draw a map of an area incorporating your own system of symbols and shading to give the maximum amount of helpful information to someone following a route across it.

9 Indoor orienteering. Follow a series of compass bearings round the building. A box can be placed over the head of such a size that it allows the navigator to see his feet and avoid obstacles, but no more.

10 Treasure hunt with clues involving pace counting, recognition of features, compass bearings etc.

11 Use maps of different scales; 1:10,000, 1:25,000, 1:50,000 etc.

12 Compare old maps with new to see how the countryside has changed over the years.

13 Measure your pace count over different terrain eg. path, heather, uphill, downhill etc.

14 Follow as closely as possible a route marked on the map with a continuous line. Unmarked controls may be placed at any point on the route.

15 Improve your map memory. Set a course with a map at each control showing the route to the next control point which has to be memorised.

16 Follow a route marked on an air photograph.

17 Draw a route on a map and then cover over or cut out appropriate sections. Try to follow the route.

18 Night navigation exercise. This must be carefully prepared and supervised.

There are many other games and courses which can be devised. They are fun in themselves, but remember that they are a preparation for finding your way across the high tops where conditions may be much more severe and the margin for error considerably smaller. As with most aspects of mountain training it is experience and practice which tells in the end.

Maps for hillwalking
Ordnance Survey Land Ranger Maps

A complete series of 204 maps at a scale of 1:50,000 which cover England, Wales and Scotland. Each map covers an area of 40 x 40km. The contour interval is 10 metres. This popular map is perfectly adequate for most purposes. It has the advantage of including on a single sheet of manageable proportions an area within which many walks may be accomplished without straying on to adjacent sheets.

Ordnance Survey Pathfinder Maps (green cover)

A complete series of 1,373 maps at a scale of 1:25,000. Most cover an area of 20km (E/W) x 10km (N/S). The contour interval is 10m (5m in lowland areas). There is no doubt that this is an excellent map for mountain walking and the 'Pathfinder' Series provides additional information which is of particular interest to hillwalkers. Inevitably, because of the large scale, it is often necessary to use two or more maps to cover a single expedition.

Ordnance Survey Outdoor Leisure Maps (yellow cover)

Some 32 maps at a scale of 1:25,000 cover popular areas including, the Peak District, the Cairngorms, the Lake District, the Cuillin and Torridon Hills, Snowdonia, North York Moors, Dartmoor, Ben Nevis and the Mamores.

Irish Maps

1:50,000 sheets are available for the whole of Northern Ireland. At the time of writing (1995) about one third of Eire is covered by 1:50,000 series which includes many of the holiday and mountain areas. The remainder is covered by the half inch to one mile series.

Harveys Walkers Maps

A dozen maps of popular mountain areas specially produced for walkers at a scale of 1:40,000 with contours at 15m intervals. These maps are on waterproof and tear resistant paper and include detail of particular relevance for the walker. The following maps are available: Cairngorm, Ben Lawers, Trossachs, Arrochar, Arran, Cheviots, Galloway, Lake District, Howgill Fells, Peak District, Snowdonia and Dartmoor.

2

Hillwalking

Preparation and Planning

Careful preparation can make all the difference to the success of an outing, whether it be a short afternoon stroll or a two-week camping expedition into the mountains. Clearly, the amount of time which should be devoted to advance planning must be related to the nature and duration of the trip, but the principle remains the same; the more thought and care you put into your planning, the more likely you are to enjoy a successful experience. Most local education authorities and many of the voluntary organisations have their own set of guidelines for teachers and leaders who intend to take groups of children into the hills. To some these rules may seem somewhat restrictive and there is no doubt that if too onerous they can inhibit the spontaneity and excitement of outdoor education. However, if pitched at the right level they provide a useful check list of tasks to be accomplished, they ensure an adequate level of communication between the party leader and those involved, including headteacher, pupils and parents and they provide a very necessary assurance to parents and those in authority that the enterprise, whatever it may be, will be conducted according to agreed procedures by someone with an appropriate level of experience.

What follows is a necessarily brief summary of what is required by way of advance preparation for an expedition of several days duration involving a group of young people under the auspices of some official organisation, such as a local education authority.

Consultation   Initially with controlling authority, eg. the headteacher and later on with pupils and parents. It is vital that all should be aware of exactly what is involved in the expedition.

Objectives   It is important to articulate the objectives right at the start so that the programme can be arranged in a way which will help them to be achieved.

Choice of area, route etc.	This should be selected to suit the experience and capability of the group. The temptation always to choose areas of national reputation should be resisted.
Sources of information	The more information you can find out about the area and the people who live there, the better. Visit your local library, obtain copies of appropriate reference books and guides and talk to people who know the area.
Maps	Obtain sufficient copies of the 1:50,000 O.S. map of the area and allow all the group to be involved in the selection of routes.
Familiarity with area	With a party of inexperienced youngsters the leader should get to know the area beforehand. It may be possible to arrange a visit in advance of the expedition.
Fitness	The enjoyment of the whole group will be greatly enhanced if there is a general level of fitness which all can attain. For the longer expeditions some pre-trip training can be very useful in this respect and also serves to sort out possible problems with boots and other equipment.
Medical	Medical clearance is usually a requirement of the sponsoring authority for longer expeditions away from home. It is important to know of any medical condition which may affect a young person's performance in taking part in strenuous physical activity eg asthma, epilepsy, heart weakness, recent illness, etc.
Skills	It may be possible to teach certain skills in advance so that the maximum enjoyment and interest can be obtained from the trip. e.g. navigation, lighting a primus stove, pitching a tent, the geology of the area and so on.
Safety and emergency procedures	It is important that every one should be aware of the possible hazards and of the need for a disciplined approach where matters of safety are concerned.
Budget	An accurate estimate of costs should be made as soon as possible and submitted to parents. It is better to overestimate if in doubt. Under certain circumstances a deposit may be appropriate. Firm advice should be given on pocket money since it is invidious if there are large differences between members of the group.

Insurance

It is prudent to be aware of the situation regarding liability and insurance. In most circumstances the leader of a party is deemed to be "in loco parentis" and is required, "to take such reasonable care of the party as careful parents would take of their children, having regard to all the circumstances". Check the insurance cover provided by the sponsoring organisation. Does it extend to mountain activities? Do you require to take out additional cover for baggage, travel etc?

Clothing and equipment

A list of what is required should be given to parents in plenty of time. Insist on critical items, such as boots and anorak, but be as flexible as you can on non-essential items. Make a thorough personal inspection of the main items a week before you are due to leave to allow time for last minute changes and adjustments.

Food

Menus should be prepared in advance and the appropriate quantities of food purchased or ordered. You will have to decide how you are going to organise the catering, cooking as a single unit or in small groups. Also the type of fuel and stoves to be used, bearing in mind considerations of safety and the experience, or more likely lack of it, of the party. Pre-trip practice can be a great help in this respect. Resist the temptation to live entirely out of cans which, although they can provide a quick meal, are heavy to carry and tend to be left behind after the contents are eaten. Remember that the quality of catering can make or mar an expedition.

Helpers

If your party is a large one you may need to have additional help. The role of assistants should be clearly defined at the outset and if they are to be involved in leading groups on the hill they must have appropriate experience.

Programme

Careful planning pays dividends. This does not mean that you have to prepare a rigid plan and stick to it come what may, but rather that you assess thoroughly the potential of the area and identify specific objectives, features, places of interest, summits and so on which can be included in the programme at the appropriate time. Give a lot of thought to what you can do in bad weather. Discuss the programme with the members of your party and as far as possible get them involved and contributing to the detailed planning.

Access Find out well in advance whether there are likely to be any problems of access to the countryside and hills at the time of your visit and if necessary obtain clearance from the landowner. The appearance of a large party can be very disturbing to activities such as deer stalking and grouse shooting. It is only reasonable that you should discuss your plans with those concerned with the management of the land, preferably in advance, but if not, on the spot.

Travelling arrangements All too often the first and last experience of an expedition is the trauma of travelling; discomfort, travel sickness, hunger, boredom, all take their toll. With some forethought a great deal of this can be eliminated. Safety should be a prime consideration and this applies to travelling by public transport as well as by private minibus. If the latter, make sure that you are familiar with the Minibus Act 1977 and other legal requirements.

Consent It goes without saying that for all officially sponsored expeditions into the hills involving minors, written parental consent is required. A document should be prepared for signature which gives a clear statement of the nature of the expedition and the activities to be undertaken. It may be convenient to include a certificate of fitness to be signed by the family doctor. It is important that parents be given an address or telephone number to contact in case of emergency.

NUMBER IN PARTY

Without a doubt this is one of the most important and yet at the same time one of the most neglected of all the factors concerned with mountain safety. Perhaps this is because it can never be formulated as an inflexible rule. There are too many other factors which have a bearing on the number of people who can safely be taken on a mountain walk: the length of the route, the type of ground and special difficulties of the terrain such as rock ridges and so on, the conditions to be expected overhead and underfoot, for example, wind, rain and snow and the fitness, age and sex of the members of the party. Not only are large parties of 15, 20 and sometimes even 30 highly dangerous on the hill, but they stifle interest and make good instruction impossible.

One person cannot possibly look after such large groups even in the easiest of terrain and when things go wrong troubles tend to multiply in proportion to the number of people in the party. As a general rule hillwalking groups should number between three and ten, the ideal being about six; the sort of number the leader can be aware of without actually counting heads. If the route is a long one or perhaps one which involves some scrambling or ridge walking, six should be taken as the maximum. Three is taken to be the minimum safe number since in the event of an accident one member of the party can stay with the injured person while the other goes to summon help. This minimum becomes the maximum if long sections of difficult ground are to be encountered. An experienced assistant in the party can be an invaluable asset, particularly in the event of an accident to the leader.

The leader should never allow any member of the party to go off alone in potentially dangerous country. This should not be taken to mean that a group must always be accompanied by a 'qualified' person. Programmes should be planned to encourage initiative and independence, but within a carefully chosen framework, which is judged by the leader to be well within the capabilities and experience of the group. For example, at an appropriate stage in their training, it may be more profitable for a party of young mountaineers to plan and execute a journey on their own through easy hill country, than to follow a more difficult route in the wake of an experienced leader. There is a time and a place for both in the scheme of things, but the opportunities which exist in the more gentle hills, usually closer to home, should not be ignored.

Going solo in the hills is almost universally condemned by those who are not themselves hillwalkers, usually on the grounds that if something goes wrong there is no one to raise the alarm and as a consequence a great deal of unnecessary time and effort may have to be put in by the search and rescue services. This is a narrow view. The desire to be alone from time to time is a powerful and basic human need and where better to fulfil this than in the mountains? There are few, if any, experienced mountaineers who have not, at some time in their lives, deliberately sought the solitude of the hills. Solo hillwalking can be a profound and rewarding experience, but it demands judgement and experience of a high order. In particular it brings a responsibility to make doubly sure that nothing does go wrong and that as a result of foolhardiness or thoughtlessness others are not put to unnecessary inconvenience and risk.

Clothing

If you go walking in Antarctica you can be reasonably confident that your double-thickness Ventile anorak with fur-lined hood will protect you from the worst of the weather. No such certainty exists in the British hills where within the span of a single day you can experience conditions which range from the subtropical to the subarctic. It is the variety of our weather as much as its ferocity which makes it difficult to find the ideal clothing assemblage.

The most vital component in this assemblage is the anorak which has four primary functions: to be wind proof, to keep water out, to keep heat in, and to allow water vapour to escape.

It is useful to know why these functions are so important and how they are achieved in the garments. If water is allowed to penetrate the outer garment it is quickly absorbed by the inner clothing which, as a direct consequence of this, loses most of its insulating qualities. Body heat is conducted outwards through the layers of wet clothing to the surface where evaporation leads to still further heat loss. Cotton clothing is particularly prone to give rise to this refrigeration effect. It is vital, therefore, to have a fully waterproof outer shell and this is usually achieved by 'proofing' a basic nylon fabric with a coating of neoprene or other proofing agent. Unfortunately, having an airtight shell creates other problems since it prevents water vapour produced as a result of exertion from escaping into the atmosphere. Instead, this water vapour condenses on the inside surface of the anorak which can quickly lead to a situation where the inner clothing is as wet as if there was no anorak at all. But there is a difference. Clothing wet from within remains warm; in fact it acts as a primitive kind of wet suit. This is an infinitely preferable situation than being wet-through to the surface where evaporation can lead to serious loss of body heat. Materials, such as Goretex, provide an answer to this problem by allowing the passage of water vapour but not liquid water. Condensation is thereby reduced to a tolerable level. It goes without saying that a garment which is waterproof will also be windproof although clearly the converse is not necessarily true. The prevention of loss of body heat is more a function of the inner clothing but the anorak does contribute to this especially by reducing radiative heat loss and by containing the circulation of warm air within the garment.

The function of inner clothing, fleece sweaters, shirts, vests, long-johns and so on, is to provide insulation, and it does this by trapping a relatively large volume of air within the fibres which go to make up the clothing. By and large the degree of insulation is proportional to the thickness of the inner clothing. If the air temperature is at freezing point a walker requires about a 2-cm thickness of inner clothing to provide effective insulation against heat loss. Clearly the rate of heat loss is determined by the work-load as well as by the environmental temperature. The greater the work-load the less insulation is required to keep the body warm. Since this is a factor which varies even more sharply than the air temperature it is sensible to be able to adjust the insulative properties of the inner clothing. This is best achieved by wearing multi-layers of clothing which can be taken off or put on as circumstances require. Wool is the best of the natural materials since it retains much of its insulation qualities when wet. Nylon pile and modern spun synthetics have the advantage of retaining their structure when wet and drying out more quickly. Polypropelene underwear acts like a wick and transfers moisture from the skin surface into the outer layers leaving a dry layer next to the skin. This nullifies the refrigeration effect previously referred to. Cotton is not satisfactory for winter use. In general then, many layers of inner clothing are better than one or two and you must be prepared to ring the changes as dictated by the prevailing conditions and the amount of energy you are expending at the time. To give a practical example, it makes no sense at all to work flat out and fully clothed to construct a bivouac shelter only to settle down in it to be frozen by the evaporation of all the sweat you have produced.

The same general principles apply to clothing below the waist although it is rather more difficult to achieve the right balance between water proofing and adequate ventilation. In cold wet conditions many walkers rely on medium to heavy-weight stretch fabric trousers or salopettes, which dry out quickly, overlapped by a long anorak or cagoule. Overtrousers should be carried. The most effective have zips which enable them to be put on and taken off quickly without removing your boots.

It is not widely appreciated that up to 1/3rd of the body's heat loss can take place from the head. A balaclava or ski hat that pulls down over your ears can make a substantial contribution to heat conservation. In hot weather the converse is equally true and it is sometimes necessary to wear a white sun hat or improvise one by tying a knot in each corner of a white handkerchief. In cold weather mitts or gloves complete the protective shell, the former providing a greater degree of warmth. It is very difficult to keep gloves dry, especially if you are constantly taking them off and on. It is important, therefore, that they should remain functional when wet and that brings us back to wool or synthetic pile or fibre. Proofed nylon or waxed cotton overmitts are useful. Leather gloves must be treated with candle wax or other proofing but in spite of this it is next to impossible to keep them dry. Leather does however furnish a firm grip on the shaft of an ice axe. In winter for general warmth and practicability it is hard to beat pre-shrunk woollen Dachstein mitts.

Footwear

The first thing to realise is that there is no such thing as the ideal boot. Ideal for what and for whom? The average hill walker can only afford to invest in one pair of boots and will use them in winter and in summer, for squelching through bogs and for tip-toeing delicately across slabs. In other words what is wanted is a boot that will perform well in a whole range of conditions and circumstances. Unfortunately, such a boot does not exist. The characteristics which are required to perform well in one situation are the very ones which make it less suitable in another. So, one is obliged to compromise and select, from a bewildering array of models, a boot that will be comfortable to walk in and yet sufficiently robust to offer the support and protection that is required, together with a measure of rigidity for walking on hard snow or steep grass. The alternative, of course, is to buy a light-weight boot for summer use and a more robust stiffer soled boot for winter.

On the whole, you get what you pay for as far as the quality and durability of the leather is concerned. The boot should be high enough to provide support for the ankle, with firm toe and heel counters to provide additional protection in these areas. A bellows tongue is essential in this country to keep out surface water. The attachment of the upper to the sole is critical in boot construction, and may be welded, screwed, sewn, glued or any combination of these. Ask the retailer to explain the method of construction. A narrow welt is to be preferred, and the sole should have good adhesive qualities, and be of sufficient thickness to protect the feet from sharp rocks. A rubber-cleated lug sole is best. PVC is not a suitable material since it is extremely slippery on wet rock. The degree of stiffness of the sole is an important consideration, and the final choice will depend partly on personal taste, and partly on technical requirements. A boot for the high mountains, for the Alps or for winter mountaineering in this country requires a stiffish sole to give the boot an edge, to take crampons, and to stand up to the pounding of kicking steps on hard snow. The stiffness is usually provided by a steel shank set into the sole. A boot for general hillwalking can afford to be more flexible in the sole, and altogether lighter in weight. Nevertheless, some torsional rigidity is required to eliminate the sudden twist which would inevitably result from a bendy sole. A simple test of this is to take hold of the boot by toe and heel and twist. It is a common failing in the cheaper range of boots with moulded soles. It is not easy to give advice on fitting boots because it is such a personal thing. Ideally, one should wear the boots around the house for a day or two before clinching the deal, but this requires a very understanding retailer. When you try them on in the shop make sure that you wear the type of socks or stockings which you would normally be using. You should be able to wiggle your toes and they must not be touching the toe of the boot. A useful test is to see if you can get a finger down inside the boot just at the back of your heel with your toe just touching the front of the boot.

A lot of foot problems can be traced to a lack of care and maintenance of the boots. The cardinal sin is to dry out the boot too quickly in front of a fire or on top of a radiator. The result of such maltreatment is a hardening and buckling of the leather which in extreme cases may even crack right open. Boots must be dried gently, preferably stuffed with newspaper and placed in a moderately warm room. Boot leather normally contains natural vegetable oils as a result of the tanning process which must be topped up from time to time, particularly after drying out. Several suitable preparations are available for this purpose.

Plastic boots have few of these problems. They are robust, light in weight and absolutely waterproof, an attribute not to be lightly ignored in a land which contains so much bog. Some find them sweaty and complain of a lack of feel on stoney ground but there are many models to choose from. Some have an inner boot which can be removed and dried separately.

BLISTERS

Although a relatively minor injury, the blister can cause discomfort and disability out of all proportion to its medical significance. It is by far the commonest of all mountain ailments, and as such deserves serious consideration by party leaders. The cause is invariably due to rubbing of the foot against some part of the boot. This can be caused by ill-fitting boots, inadequate socks/stockings, loose lacing, or simply by the fact that the feet are unaccustomed to boots. The first question to ask is, 'are boots really necessary for the activity planned?' For many low level summer outings training shoes or similar footwear is more appropriate, but make sure that the tread on the sole is deep enough to give a good grip on wet grass or rock. If boots are necessary, they should have been well broken-in before being used on more demanding terrain. Unfortunately, hired boots rarely provide the degree of personal fit and comfort that is required, and special care is needed to both guard against and treat the blisters which will almost certainly result from their use.

The first rule is to keep your feet in good order and insist that those in your charge do the same: wash regularly, use clean, snugly-fitting socks or stockings (a single pair of loop stitched stockings is probably best), cut toe-nails straight and short and periodically apply surgical spirit to harden the feet.

At the first sign or sensation of discomfort stop and treat the problem. Cover the area with a broad plaster, cutting it as necessary to avoid making any creases. Self-adhesive chiropody felt makes light work of plastering a blister. The toes can be taped with micro-pore. If a blister is already present improvise a ring plaster which serves to keep the pressure off the blister. Given time the fluid will be reabsorbed into the blood stream.

In a severe case it may be necessary to prick the blister with a sterilised needle having first washed the feet thoroughly. The fluid is then expressed taking care not to touch the pricked holes. Cover with a sterile dressing and change daily.

I Sterilising the needle:

2 Pricking the blister:

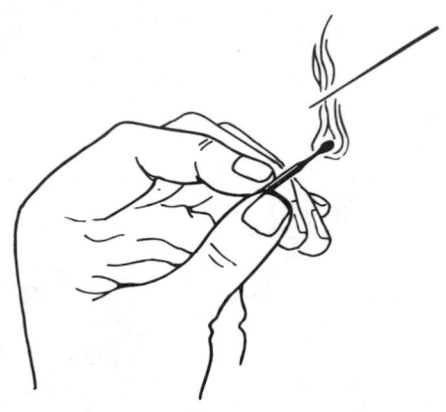
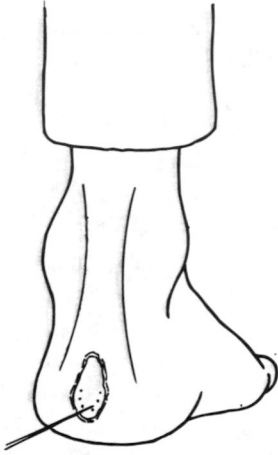

3 Plastering:

4 A ring plaster

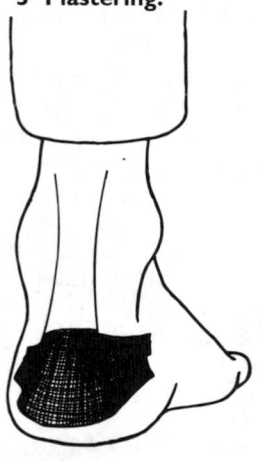
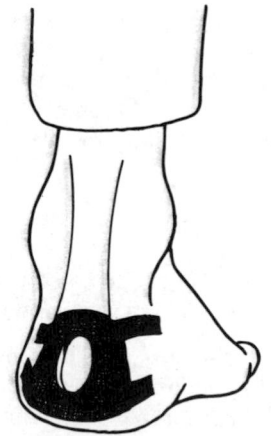

Fig. 41   *Treating a Severe Blister.*

Walking

On roads or flat ground, journeys are usually measured in kilometres or miles, but on the hills it is more expedient to measure in hours. A rough guide when estimating the time of a walk for an average lightly equipped party is to allow five kilometres per hour plus half an hour for every three hundred metres of climbing (see page 37-42 for further discussion on this subject).

One of the golden rules of party leadership is that you must leave details of your intended route with someone who can raise the alarm should you not return before the deadline given. While this is the main purpose of filling in a route card, there are other more positive benefits in so doing. It is a discipline which forces you to consider in some detail the demands which a particular route is going to make on your party. It involves the estimation of time and distance and compass bearings in the comfort of basecamp which, on the day, might be difficult and time-consuming to take because of bad weather or darkness. Finally, it reminds you to consider ways of cutting short your chosen route should circumstances necessitate a retreat. The route card illustrated in Table 6 is a suggested format for an organisation which requires a standard procedure. For the smaller independent party it is usually sufficient to leave a brief description of your intended route and expected time of return, and take with you a note of any compass bearings which you think may be of use.

A route card is an aide-memoir. It should not be thought of as something written on a tablet of stone to be slavishly adhered to come what may. Circumstances arise which could not possibly have been foreseen and which necessitate a deviation from the planned route. The fact that you have left a route card behind should not deter you form taking appropriate action.

Speed is of less importance than economy of effort. To hurry, except in extenuating circumstances, is foolish. Tail enders must be encouraged and not left to struggle on their own to become exhausted and depressed. When you notice that someone is having difficulty, bring them up alongside where you can keep an eye on them and provide a bit of encouragement. Keep together and on no account send any member of the party back on his own. Except in dire emergency the party should act as a single unit.

There is no best position for the leader of a party. It may be at the front, at the back, or in the middle. The position adopted will depend on the circumstances prevailing at the time. Normally, of course, the leader will be in front, having appointed the next most experienced member of the party to bring up the rear.

Rhythm is essential to good hill walking: jerky movements, springing and flexing the knees by taking too high a step tire the muscles and should be avoided. The leg should be allowed to swing forward like a pendulum; the natural swing of the body assists this movement. There should be no conscious use of the leg muscles. To assist rhythm and balance the hands should be kept free, particularly in descent. Spare clothes etc., should be carried in the rucksack or tied round the waist.

To maintain rhythm, the same speed of pace should be used on all types of ground, the length of the pace being shortened for steep or difficult ground and lengthened for easy ground.

The feet should be placed down flat with a deliberate step, resting the heels on any available projections such as stones or tufts of grass. Where the slope is very steep, zig-zagging will assist the walker. Good rhythm and setting the feet is the sign of the experienced hill walker.

When descending, overstriding and putting the foot down heavily should be avoided as these jar the body and therefore fatigue the walker. Running downhill, though good fun, can be tiring. An experienced walker uses downhill periods to rest his muscles.

Scree running is also fun, but it is bad for boots and unless closely supervised can be dangerous. If you have to negotiate a scree make absolutely sure that your party is deployed in such a way that loose stones do not fall onto those below. (See page 150-1). Remember too, that screes are a habitat for hardy rock plants. Indiscriminate scree running will destroy the plants and eventually transfer the habitat to the bottom of the slope.

Constant stopping and starting breaks up walking rhythm and should be avoided. Short rests should be taken at regular intervals, say 5 minutes every hour, depending on the party and the terrain.

OTHER FACTORS

Large meals should be avoided – 'little and often' being the better approach during a day on the hills. It is a good plan to retain a portion of the day's food and so maintain a reserve of food in case of emergency. Alternatively, an emergency ration should be carried. (Chapter 4).

Most mountain streams in the British Isles are fit to drink from. The body needs to replace fluid lost in sweat, in breathing, etc., and contrary to popular belief drinking is to be encouraged, 'little and often' once again being the safest maxim to follow.

Constant vigilance should be exercised, as weather conditions can deteriorate with extreme rapidity in hill country. Check the weather forecast before leaving. The vital thing is to anticipate changes and to adjust your route plan to take account of them.

Act before the weather dictates its own terms (Chapter 8).

Exposure is an ever present danger with young people in the mountains and all leaders must be familiar with its recognition and treatment. If your party is fit, dry, well fed and watered and in good spirit you have little to fear. If they are not, then you must modify your route to suit their condition and capabilities (Chapter 9).

No attempt must be made to cross mountain streams in spate where there is possible danger to life unless each member of the party can be adequately safeguarded. Youngsters should not be given routes to follow independently which might involve the crossing of such streams (Chapter 7).

Severe electrical storms are unusual in British mountains. In the event of one, do not seek shelter under overhangs or in cracks in the cliff face or against large prominent boulders. Avoid being the prominent object in the neighbourhood. Get off peaks and ridges and sit it out on open coarse-blocked scree. There is no need to throw away your axe, camera or other ironmongery - you may need them later and they do not attract lightning any more than you do yourself (Chapter 8, page 226).

Rope the party together when visibility is very poor and when there is the likelihood that a slip might develop into a dangerous slide. Remember that a small error in navigation can lead you to the edge of a cliff or on to a cornice.

In addition to its chilling effect, the wind can exert sufficient force to sweep a party off its feet. In round terms a wind of 80 Km.p.h. (50 m.p.h.) exerts a force of 23 kg. (50lbs) on a standing adult. The lesson is obvious: do not stand. Crouch down or crawl. Get out of the wind into the lee of a ridge. Keep your party close together and if necessary rope up. Be particularly careful round the tops of corries or on exposed ridges where a fall could be disastrous.

Good technique and safety measures can be learned. Good leadership and instruction is an art which embraces more than mere technical skill. Your job as a leader of a party is to stimulate interest and safe enjoyment in everything which the mountains have to offer.

Table 7 *A Simple Route Card.*

Tuesday 16 May 1000 hours.
E Langmuir and A N Other
Capel Curig to Nant Peris via the Glyders and Twll Du.
Return by bus or hitch.
Etr: 1630 Capel.

Table 8 *Sample Route Card for Party.*

Route Card							
Main Objective:				Date:			
From	To	Magnetic bearing	Distance	Height		Description of ground	Time
				Gained	Lost		
Total							
Add ten minutes per hour							
Time Out:				Time Back:			
				Is it dark at:			
ESCAPE ROUTES							
1	2		3				

Table 8 *Sample Route Card for Party, reverse side.*

NAMES OF PARTY	EQUIPMENT IN PARTY		
LEADER	IN SUMMER		
ASSISTANT	Anorak	Map	Whistle
	Boots	Compass	Rations
	Safety rope	Watch	First Aid
	Survival bag/tent	Flares	
	EXTRA IN WINTER CONDITIONS		
	Ice axe	Crampons	Torch
	Balaclava	Over-trousers	Sleeping bag Duvet
	Gloves/Mitts	Goggles	Gaiters
	WEATHER FORECAST		
	WIND		
	Speed/Force		Becoming
	Estimated at altitude		Becoming
	Direction		Becoming
	TEMPERATURE		
	Sea level		Becoming
	Estimated at altitude		Becoming
	Cloud base		Becoming
	Freezing level		Becoming
	Outlook:		

3

Campcraft and Expeditions

The use of a tent to provide shelter from the elements may not be as old the hills but it certainly has its origins far back in prehistory when man first learned to fashion the skins of animals to improve his own living conditions. It is surely one of the greatest attractions of lightweight camping that in essence it remains a primitive technique which depends for its success on the skill and fortitude of the practitioner. To many people the perfecting of that technique and the satisfaction and enjoyment which that brings is a sufficient goal. To others, camping is seen as a means towards the achievement of some other goal; a peak perhaps or a scientific study in a remote corner of the globe. Of course the two goals are not mutually exclusive and in reality it is very much a question of emphasis. The plain truth is that the more demanding the primary objective is, the more efficient the campcraft has to be to increase the chances of achieving it.

There are several different types of camping each designed for the attainment of specific objectives, and requiring quite different equipment and organisation. We are concerned in this chapter with mobile camping, which may be defined as living under canvas and moving through remote country carrying all that is required on your back. It is generally regarded as the most advanced form of campcraft requiring considerable stamina, skill and experience. Perhaps because of this, it can be one of the most rewarding of mountain experiences, but it is not one to be entered into without due thought and preparation, indeed it is hard to think of any aspect of mountaincraft which demands more comprehensive planning and application to detail. Without a doubt it is the most educational of outdoor activities, and its potential in this area has been eagerly exploited by almost every youth organisation from the Scouts to the local education authorities. Done properly, it is a good way to introduce young people to outdoor life, and for many it may prove a key which will unlock the door to a marvellous world of untamed places. Many aspects of camping and expedition activity can be rehearsed beforehand and this is essential both for personal assurance and for the safety of young people who cannot be watched all the time. Much of this training can take place in and around the city, perhaps culminating in a trial overnight camp not too far from home. Pitching and striking tents, packing a rucksack, filling and lighting stoves, cooking a meal, working out a menu and shopping list, drawing up a budget, all these things and a lot more should be familiar to the youngsters before they set out on a mobile camping expedition.

One of the problems about camping is that it is potentially very damaging to the environment. Inconsiderate and incompetent campers can do irreparable harm to sensitive sites. The higher you go, the thinner the soil and vegetation cover and the more fragile it is to structural damage. Rubbish pits, drainage channels, turfs removed, fires, all leave scars which may take tens of years to be erased, if at all. Pollution from a badly managed camp site may destroy 80% of the aquatic life in a mountain lochan. Those who go camping on the hills have an obligation to ensure that they and their charges do nothing which would result in change or harm to the environment. This is the first law of the mountain camper.

THE PARTY

The party should be reasonably fit before starting. Care should be taken not to over-burden. Check for anyone with disabilities or special medical requirements.

THE TIMETABLE

The timetable should be flexible and there should be some progression from easy to more difficult undertakings. If the weather is severe, stay put if possible; do not move merely to stick to an armchair plan. Mountain weather is unpredictable. Allow for this when planning. Do not attempt too long marches. Very hot weather can also be exhausting: if necessary be up at five and finish the day's walk by noon. Use local knowledge as well as maps, guides, etc.

DAILY ROUTINE

An early start always pays off. Work out a system that can be used by the party each day. Everyone should be employed. From waking to departure should not take longer than two hours for an efficient team. Try to be settled in a new site before evening. Tents should, as far as possible, operate as independent units, though, if the weather is set fair, it may be quicker for each tent to deal with one part of a meal. Two tents, pitched door to door, can also operate as a unit. Do not hesitate to stop for a brew-up or a swim during the day. These are valuable mentally and physically. Check at the end of a trip to see what was carried and never used – question whether to take it again.

FOOD AND COOKING

Adequate and appetising food is a vital part of any well-run expedition. See to it that your party takes a hot breakfast and evening meal each day. A communal brew of hot, sweet tea immediately on arrival at the camp site is an excellent morale booster and paves the way to a good meal. Lightweight expeditions can make use of the wide range of dehydrated foods now available on the market. Be careful to select those which have a reasonably short cooking time and which can be cooked in a single pot. Dehydrated foods are of course expensive, but allow a great saving in weight and therefore of energy.

Before preparing a meal, make sure that everything you are likely to need is within reach. Work out a cooking plan so that food which takes longer to cook is put on first. Ring the changes on the stove – some things cook away quite happily in hot water and just need the occasional boost on the stove. Rice, for instance, can be brought to the boil for three minutes and then put aside for fifteen. Use pans with well fitting lids. This builds up a level of steam which will help to keep food hot and cooking when taken off the stove Resist the temptation to lift the lid to see how it is getting on. This lets the steam escape and reduces the pressure. A towel or sweater makes a convenient cosy to conserve heat. By judicious rotation of the pots on the stove the various components of the meal can be timed to arrive on the table cooked to perfection.

For a more detailed discussion of energy requirements and mountain diet refer to Chapter 4, 'Food and Nutrition', page 93.

PERSONAL CLOTHING AND EQUIPMENT

Essential items of personal clothing, anorak, boots etc., have been dealt with in the previous chapter on Hillwalking (see pages 65-69). Additional equipment required for lightweight camping is covered in this chapter and includes a discussion of tents, sleeping bags, stoves etc. A comprehensive list of recommended clothing and equipment is given in Appendix 3.

As far as clothing is concerned it is important to note at this stage that a dry set of clothes should always be kept for night wear or emergency. Wet clothes can often be dried out over night and in any case it is normally better to put on damp clothes in the morning than risk wetting your dry ones.

Never assume that the members of your party are properly kitted out. Before leaving inspect all equipment and personal clothing.

LOAD PACKING AND CARRYING

One of the most difficult of camping skills to acquire is that of being able to separate essential from non-essential items of equipment. Nothing is more calculated to kill enjoyment than to be labouring under an enormous pack, bursting with extras taken along, just in case. All this does is to increase the likelihood of the anticipated emergency actually taking place. Your total load should never exceed one third of your body weight and for a party of young people 15kg (33 lbs) should be regarded as the absolute maximum. Beware the effect of rain on the weight of gear which was previously within the limits.

Rucksacks are made in every conceivable size and shape, but whether you prefer a framed or frameless sack there are certain basic requirements. First of

THIS **NOT THIS**

Fig. 42 *Carrying a Rucksack.*

all the sack should be made from waterproof fabric, and this means its closures as well as the material it is made from. However, no sack is completely waterproof, so use a polythene liner. It should have a capacity appropriate to its intended use. Some sacks are adjustable in this respect using extensions and/or compression straps. It should sit comfortably, carrying the load high and close to the back. Sacks come in various sizes, or are adjustable within limits to fit different sizes of people. Make sure yours fits. The critical measurement is from the nape of your neck to the small of your back. The straps themselves should be firmly attached to the sack (a common weak point), well-padded and easily adjustable for length. A hip belt, again quick to tighten or release, is an essential feature, and in the framed sack it can be used to distribute more of the load onto the hips. The addition of pockets and separate compartments is mostly a matter of personal taste, the main advantages being that they enable you to have access to certain items without opening the main sack and that you can separate the stove and fuel from clothing, food etc. A reinforced bottom (or corners) is useful and assorted straps may be used to carry such items as ice axe, crampons etc. Those items excepted, you want to avoid having too many things dangling or projecting from your pack. Apart from the discomfort and uneven weight distribution they can be dangerous to your companions as well as yourself.

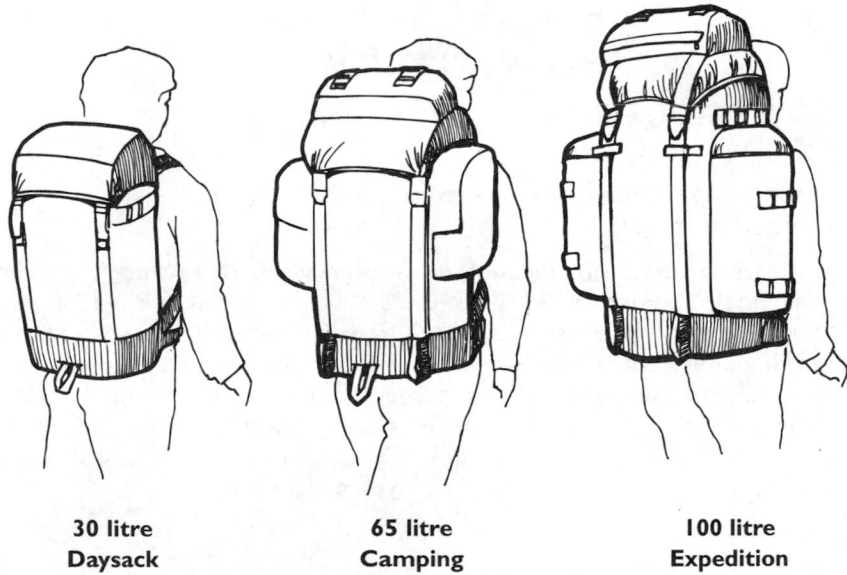

| 30 litre | 65 litre | 100 litre |
| Daysack | Camping | Expedition |

Fig. 43   *Different Sacks for Different Purposes.*

The pack frame really comes into its own where heavy or awkward shaped loads have to be carried. Its main advantages are, that it enables the load to be carried higher, (though at the cost of some stability). It distributes the load evenly across shoulders, back and hips and it allows air to ventilate the space between the pack and your back. The adjustment of the hip belt and shoulder straps is critical for comfort and stability. Its only real disadvantage is that it is an awkward shape, difficult to tuck away inside a tent and liable to snag on branches and rocky projections while on the move.

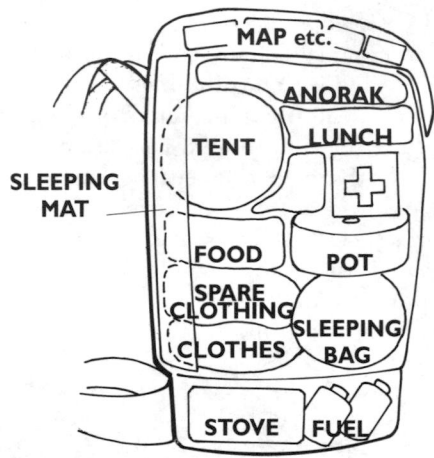

Fig. 44   *Packing a Rucksack.*

How a rucksack is packed can make a surprising difference to the ease and comfort of carrying it.

Articles needed during the journey or immediately on reaching the camp site should be on top or in side pockets, i.e. food for the day, first aid kit, tent and so on. Do not have articles dangling from the outside of the sack. Heavy items should be kept as high as possible. Balance the weight and avoid sharp edges and corners against the back. Stove and fuel should be kept in a well sealed polythene bag and stored in a separate pocket or well away from food. All clothing and sleeping bag should be kept in polythene bags and the sack itself might benefit from a 500 gauge polythene bag liner.

Tents

In many respects a mountain tent is required to perform a similar function to the outer layer of clothing. It is expected to protect the occupant from the wind, it is expected to be hard-wearing yet reasonably light in weight and it is expected to keep out the rain, but at the same time discourage excessive condensation on the internal surfaces. As with clothing, all these attributes are obtainable, but at a price, and as with clothing there is a premium on keeping out the rain. The traditional solution to the waterproofing – condensation problem is to provide two layers, an outer waterproof fly sheet and a lightweight inner tent which 'breathes' and provides a dry inner haven. For the wet and windy conditions so common in the British Isles it is advisable to have a sewn-in ground sheet and a down- to-earth all-round fly sheet.

The actual design of tent varies enormously and within the constraints previously mentioned it is very much a matter of personal taste and what you can afford.

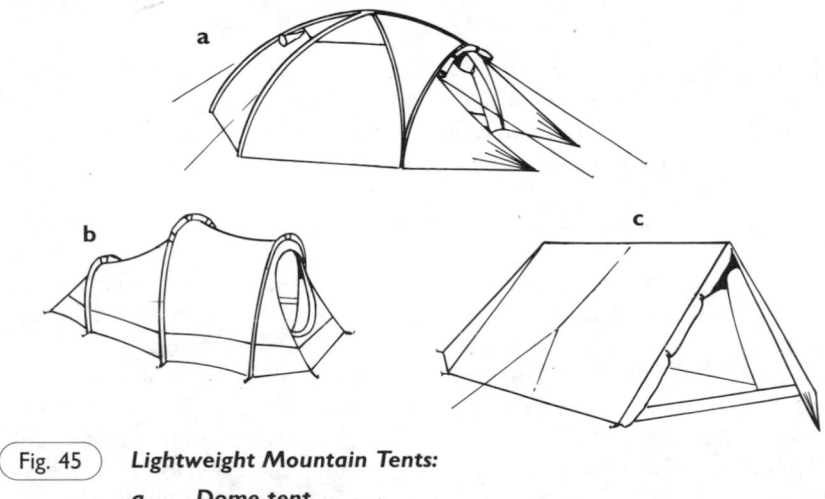

Fig. 45   *Lightweight Mountain Tents:*

a   **Dome tent**
b   **Hoop tent**
c   **Ridge tent with fly sheet and double bell-end**

Hoop and dome designs are supported from a framework of flexible fibreglass or aluminium wands. They have the advantage of providing the maximum amount of space for a given floor area and they use the minimum number of pegs and guys. In fact a dome tent can be moved short distances by the simple expedient of picking it up like an unfolded umbrella. Both designs can be recommended for experienced campers, but do require careful handling. The more traditional 'ridge' design still has much to recommend it. Ridge tents are generally tough and durable and are still available in cotton fabric.

Other secondary, but none the less important considerations are:

Ventilation	—	especially important in completely sealed waterproof tents.
Storage space	—	for rucksacks, wet boots, anorak etc. This is one of the advantages of the double bell-end.
Cooking area	—	A well ventilated porch or bell-end is useful for cooking when weather conditions make it impossible outside.
Entrance	—	Rain and snow can get into the tent if the entrance is poorly designed.
Colour	—	There may be some justification for brightly coloured tents in the Himalaya but certainly not in the mountains of the British Isles.

With a group it is good practice for each tent to act as a self-contained unit making its own arrangements for cooking, sleeping etc. Quite apart from the benefits of experience, mountain tents are not intended to hold more than 2 or 3 people. Any more than this and accidents are likely to happen.

CHOOSING A CAMP SITE

A good site should provide shelter from the prevailing wind. The ground should be as flat as possible and relatively free from lumps, tussocks and boulders. It should be well drained and safe from potential flooding. A handy water supply is almost essential though do not pitch too near a noisy mountain stream if you want an undisturbed night's rest. Trees may provide some protection from the wind but do not pitch directly underneath them; although they offer some immediate shelter from the rain, eventually large drops form and these are much more effective in penetrating the fly sheet.

If frost is expected avoid hollows into which the cold air sinks at night. Try and find out if the site is accessible to domestic animals which can wreak havoc with tents, guy lines and food supplies. One of your first tasks will be to investigate the immediate surroundings for possible safety hazards such as old mine workings, near-by crags, fast flowing streams etc. Your party may have to be warned about them and if youngsters are involved they may have to be placed out-of-bounds.

PITCHING TENTS

Even if the weather seems set fair, allow for the worst when pitching your tent. Put the back end into the wind and peg out the groundsheet first, to ensure tent shaping. Erect the windward end first and peg out all main guys, making sure that the ridge is taught. Other guys are pegged out in line with the tent seams. Rubber guys should be stretched before pegging. The pegs may be weighted with stones, but do not place stones on top of guy lines. In a wind the sawing action frays them through in no time. There should be no wrinkles in the canvas and any unnatural strains should be corrected by adjusting guys. Door tabs should be tied in bows not knots. Do not dig a drainage trench round your tent – a sure sign of a badly sited tent. Such a practice eventually leads to a scarred site on which no one can camp. If your tent gets flooded; move it.

STRIKING CAMP

As far as the tents are concerned this is largely a matter of reversing the procedure for pitching. In bad weather it is usually possible to fold up the inner tent first under the protection of the fly sheet. All pegs should be cleaned and all the parts stowed away in their bags. Check the site before leaving to see that nothing is forgotten and no litter is left. After a few days it should be hard to tell that the site has been used. On returning to base, tents should be hung to dry out thoroughly and examined carefully for any damage before storing: tents stored wet for any length of time will become mildewed and eventually rot.

SLEEPING BAGS

The first thing to realise is that a sleeping bag can never provide complete insulation against loss of body heat by conduction to the ground. A separate mattress, air bed or mat, depending on taste, is necessary to do this, and at the same time to give that little bit of extra comfort. The trouble is that sleeping bag fillings, whether they be down or synthetic fibre, rely on their ability to trap air for their insulative qualities. Under compression the air is expelled, and one is left with a fairly compact layer of the material itself, which is a much less effective insulator. In some respects compressibility is a very useful characteristic, since it means that the sleeping bag can be packed into a small space for carrying. What matters is its ability to regain its loft, and its natural thickness, when it is unpacked. Good quality down, which is outrageously expensive, has this quality par excellence. It is also extremely effective in trapping air, and this provides an almost ideal filling for a sleeping bag. Alas, it behaves very badly when wet and is well nigh impossible to dry out in the field. This criticism does not apply to polyester sleeping bags which, with the advances made in the manufacture of synthetic fibre, can provide almost comparable insulation. Polyester bags are moisture resistant and retain most of their loft when wet. For these reasons they are becoming increasingly popular as a less expensive alternative to down. The actual design of the bag is not a critical matter although for a really warm bag the 'mummy' design is probably the most effective.

In the case of loose fillings, such as feathers or down, the bag must be constructed in a way which eliminates the formation of cold spots along seams and zips and also prevents the filling from migrating from one part of the bag to another. This can be achieved, first of all, by compartmentalising the filling and, secondly, by ensuring that at no place does the stitching pass through both surfaces of the bag. The technique used is generally known as 'box quilting' although in practice the filling is contained within a series of overlapping tubes.

OFFSET LAYERING

SEWN THROUGH

BOX QUILTED

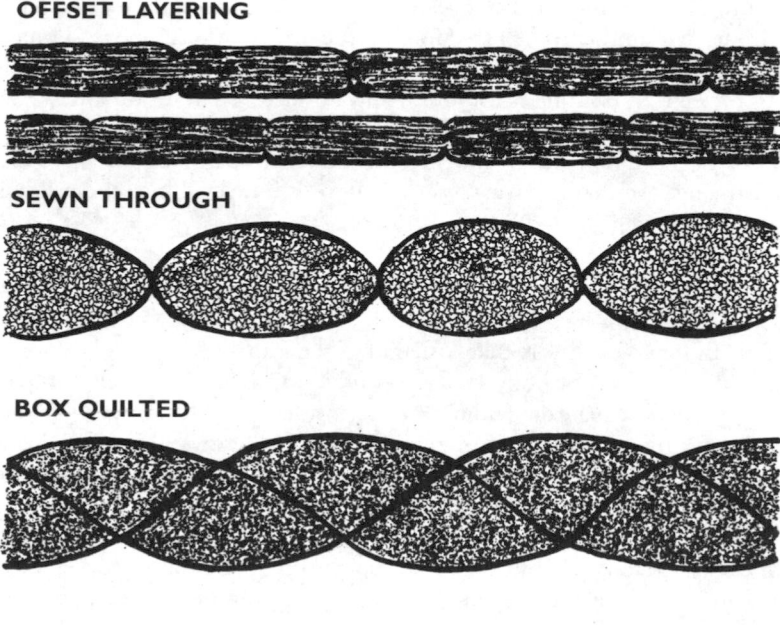

Fig. 46   *Construction of Sleeping Bags.*

In the case of polyester sleeping bags, the migration of the filling is not a problem, but the layers or batts of material do have to be stitched together, so that the same criticism applies to the 'sewn through' method of construction.

A great deal of body heat can be lost from the exposed head, so, if the bag does not cover it, wear a hat. Zips do make getting in and out a lot easier but they also give rise to cold spots unless the zip has a draft baffle behind it. Another advantage is that to a certain extent they allow you to adjust your heat loss according to the environmental temperature.

SOME FURTHER TIPS FOR WARMTH AND COMFORT

In winter insulation from ground cold is essential. It is sometimes possible to pack the underside of the groundsheet with bracken, heather or grass to improve comfort and insulation. If you do not have a sleeping mat then improvise one by making a mattress from your rucksack, spare clothing, rope etc. If you do use a second sleeping bag try to ensure that it provides a fairly loose fit with the first. Always do something about cold. Don't just lie there shivering.!

It is more comfortable to sleep head uphill if on a slope, and on your stomach if the ground is rough and stony.

Polythene bags are useful for storing unwanted or wet clothes, personal belongings, sugar, salt, potato powder or anything else in breakable packets. They can also be used as emergency bags for travel sickness.

Boots should not be worn inside tents. Wet clothes should be taken off before entry if possible. If soaked to the skin, remove all clothing, put on dry underclothes, get into your sleeping bag and prepare hot, sweet drinks.

Store tins, wet clothes, ropes and anything animals will not eat, under the flysheet. Pans, stoves and water carriers should be easily within reach.

Resist the temptation to wrap the sleeping bag tightly around you. This expels the warm insulating air which is trapped within the filling.

It is not a good idea to attempt to dry-off wet clothing either by wearing it or by taking it inside your sleeping bag. You will only end up with a wet bag as well as wet clothing. When the weather improves improvise a clothes line or, if on the move, tie some of the wet garments to the outside of your pack. In really cold conditions it may be necessary to bring your boots and gloves into your sleeping bag at night to prevent them freezing up. If you do this make sure you wrap them up well in a polythene bag.

Newspapers can be used for a variety of purposes: for insulation under bedding, for cleaning material, to keep under supplies, cutlery or pans to prevent dirt or grease spreading, under a pullover for body insulation, drying boots and starting fires.

The following are some useful additional items: torch (reverse battery to avoid accidental switch-on in travel); alloy 'Sigg' bottle or equivalent for fuel; tin opener (small ones, 'jiffy-type', can fold into a wallet); matches in waterproof container; toilet/kitchen paper; sponge (for mopping up leaks and spills, and for using as a wet-cold cover for perishable foodstuffs in hot weather); 5m of boot-lace nylon; multi-bladed knife; one or two cooking pans with lids, non-stick (if you can afford them, and if you can persuade your friends not to stir the food with metal spoons or clean them out with brillo pads); nylon pot scrubber; cutlery; deep plate and mug (not china); training shoes (wear on bare feet if wet, avoiding wet socks); a small-size fish slice is valuable; as is an egg whisk for mixing milk powder; dubbin for boots; writing materials; transistor (for weather forecasts); anti-midge cream and/or spray (May to October); alarm watch or clock; first-aid kit including burn dressing and treatment for stomach upsets; repair-spares kit for tent and stove; water purifying tablets. For some types of expedition a pressure cooker may be worth the extra bulk and weight.

RUBBISH DISPOSAL

The burning and burying of rubbish can no longer be recommended. The accumulation of buried waste in some mountain camp sites has reached such proportions as to seriously affect their continued use. Unearthed rubbish pits are unsightly, unhealthy and a danger to both domestic and wild animals. In future the guiding principle must be:

RESPECT THE MOUNTAINS
TAKE YOUR RUBBISH HOME

A certain amount of rubbish can be burnt and liquid waste may be disposed of in a pit dug well away from the camp site and its water supply. Tins should be opened at both ends, burned, then flattened between stones, tied in a polythene bag and taken home.

Glass is unnecessary. Use plastic bags or containers or light tins and transfer the contents into these. On no account must glass be smashed. Take your empties home! Polythene bags are particularly lethal to animals.

HYGIENE

A safe and adequate water supply is the first prerequisite of any campsite. An adequate supply is not usually difficult to find in the mountains but whether it is safe or not it is a matter for conjecture. Unless you are completely satisfied that the supply is unpolluted, precautions will have to be taken to render it safe for consumption either by using sterilising tablets or by boiling (ten minutes is sufficient). Water should be collected above the site and personal ablutions carried out below.

Personal cleanliness is essential and with young people this must be insisted upon and checked. Hands must be washed thoroughly with soap after using lavatories, filling stoves etc. and at all times before handling food. Cooking utensils, plates, cutlery etc. should be washed thoroughly in hot water immediately after meals.

Toilet facilities depend on length of stay. Where at all permanent, a latrine trench is advisable. Excrement must be buried 15 - 20 cm (6 - 8 inches) below the surface and at least 60m from any open water. When filled in there should be absolutely no trace left.

With a mixed party separate arrangements may have to be made for male and female toilet and washing facilities, although how elaborate they are will depend very much on the situation and the length of stay.

Stoves, Cooking and Safety

Gas: This is clean, requires no priming, but is expensive and, for half an hour before a cartridge runs out, burns at an infuriatingly low pressure. They are less suitable for winter use because of the reduction of gas pressure at low temperatures (below O°C).

Pressure Stoves: These require priming with solid 'Meta' fuel or meths, but give a wide variety of pressure. They are very cheap to run. Petrol stoves are not recommended for inexperienced young people.

Meths Burners: The most popular system is the Trangia which consists of a lightweight aluminium body housing a methylated spirit burner. The fuel is allowed to burn naturally, and not under pressure and this heats the various utensils which are included in the kit. It is light in weight, compact and very simple to operate, but do remember that meths burns silently and with a flame which is almost invisible in direct sunlight. Meths stoves are cheaper to buy but more expensive to run than paraffin pressure stoves and they are less efficient under normal operating conditions. On the other hand, unlike the pressure stoves, there is very little that can go wrong with them and they burn well in windy conditions.

SAFETY FACTORS

Changing gas cartridges or filling stoves must be done in the open and away from candles or any naked flame. Used cylinders may contain some residual gas and there is often a leak of gas under pressure as the new cylinder is tightened up.

Experience in using stoves is essential before going off on expeditions when they may have to be lit and used within tents or shelter.

As with all stoves, there is considerable danger of setting the tent alight when cooking is done inside the tent. If cooking outside is not possible because of weather conditions, adequate ventilation must be ensured. In addition to burning oxygen, incomplete combustion produces carbon monoxide gas which may be highly dangerous in a sealed atmosphere.

Gas is heavier than air. During sleep, gas from leaking appliances could accumulate in a layer on the groundsheet (particularly if sewn in). Quite apart from the obvious danger of explosion, this layer could rise to nose level, with fatal results. Store gas stoves and cylinders outside.

Paraffin pressure stoves in fact burn paraffin vapour and pumping too soon will result in flooding. This causes dangerous flaring and soot is deposited which will ultimately choke the nipple. Pricking (only when needed) to clear stoves, as well as priming, should be done outside, if possible.

Make sure you have the correct fuel. Parties of young people are advised to avoid using petrol stoves.

Do not overfill a stove. When doing anything to a stove, always remove pans. When stirring pans, always hold on to the handle. Scalding accidents are common. Make sure handles are up or extended properly so that they do not hang down near the flame to become dangerously hot.

When cooking outside a great deal of heat can be lost in combating the wind. In the first place the stove must be kept going at full blast or it will go out and in the second place heat is constantly removed from the sides of the pan. Under these circumstances an effective wind shield made from stones or turfs will greatly increase the efficiency of the stove.

Patience is the most important point in stove control.

FIRE IN TENTS

The main causes are: mis-use of stoves/cigarettes/candles or other lighting.

Precautions

See above, but also, do not fall asleep smoking or with a candle or stove left burning. (Elementary - but it happens constantly!). Long candles should be snapped in half to make them less unstable. Even placing them on top of a tin usually ensures that if they topple they land end on and so extinguish the flame. Some safety holder is easily created. With other forms of lighting – wick or pressure lamps, etc., care must be taken to ensure adequate ventilation.

A small internal fire can quickly be smothered with a sleeping bag, with little damage to the bag but, if the roof or walls go up, it is vital to get out fast. Poles and, if necessary, main guys, should be collapsed to smother the fire. Any other method is too slow and ineffective. A stove giving real trouble should be thrown outside at once. Work stoves near the entrance – if you must have them inside at all.

Fires out of doors are particularly damaging and nearly always leave long term scars on the ground. Only light fires in areas designated for this purpose and ensure that they are properly extinguished before departure.

Camping makes a great impact on young people. It is after all concerned with survival in a potentially hostile environment using only the material which can be carried on your back. To be able to be comfortable under such circumstances is no mean achievement, but it is one which requires determination, meticulous organisation and a willingness to co-operate with others to achieve a common goal. Camping has many lessons to teach about living as well as merely surviving, but perhaps the most important of all is that it should foster a sense of harmony with the mountain world.

4

Food and Nutrition

Most mountaineers would agree that food is of paramount importance in the success of any expedition. Not only is it a physiological necessity but it has important psychological benefits. Sufficient quality and quantity of food, will help to maintain the motivation to complete an expedition and to enjoy it.

Food provides the cells in the body with energy. Extra energy has to be taken from food to allow the body to exercise. In addition to energy the body also requires, protein, vitamins, minerals, fibre and water. This chapter is concerned with the amount and type of food which is required for journeys into the mountains of relatively short duration, that is day trips up to expeditions of two weeks.

The longer the sojourn into the hills, the more thorough the planning has to be to ensure that the correct quantity and quality of food is taken to avoid food shortage, boredom and carrying unnecessary weight Despite the popularity of mountaineering there are very few guide-lines available on what types and amounts of food should be taken on an expedition. There are several factors which have to be considered when planning the food provision for a trip. These include, the age, sex and number of members in the party, weather conditions, shopping availability, type of accommodation and duration.

We will look not only at how to calculate the amount of food required, but also the physiological effects of food and how to make meals on the mountain palatable and interesting. The needs of vegetarians will be considered and how to adapt the menu appropriately without adding unnecessary weight to a calculated food pack.

Why we need food

Food is essential to all cells in the body as it provides us with energy. There are three energy giving nutrients found in food; fat, carbohydrate and protein.

The energy found in food is expressed on food packets in both kilojoules(kJ) and kilocalories (kcal).

Kilocalorie: One kilocalorie is the amount of heat or energy necessary to raise the temperature of 1,000gm of water 1°C. The symbol is 'kcal'.

Joule: The Joule is a 'Systeme Internationale' derived unit of work, energy and quantity of heat. The symbol is 'J', 1000 J = 1kJ. To convert kcal to kJ, multiply kcal by 4.184. To convert kcal to megajoule (MJ) multiply kcal by 0.0041

Throughout this chapter we will give the value in kilojoules first followed by the value in kilocalories in brackets. Where the figure is very large megajoules (MJ) will be used as the unit of energy. Other nutrients such as vitamins and minerals are essential in small quantities to perform specific functions in the body. For example, iron is a mineral which is essential for the formation of red blood cells which carry oxygen to the exercising muscles. Fibre and water are both essential for health and need to be consumed daily.

The amount of energy needed by the body to go hillwalking will depend on the body weight, age and sex of the hillwalker, plus the length of the walk and the total height to be climbed, in other words the amount of work to be carried out. Energy requirements, therefore, are determined by both individual and external factors.

The greater the demands on the body the more energy is required to fuel it. If the body does not receive an adequate quota of energy from food, it resorts to consuming body fat and eventually muscle to function. However, food intake would have to be reduced for a considerable period of time before weight loss occured. More immediately in hillwalking the working muscles use carbohydrate as their source of energy and also fatty acids from fat. Once the carbohydrate has been used the muscles are not able to continue working at the same rate and you have to slow down.

How does the body use food

Food provides the body with the nutrients it needs at rest and during exercise. In this section we will look at these nutrients individually and the role they play in exercise.

CARBOHYDRATE

Carbohydrates are found in nature in varying forms, monosaccharides (eg, glucose) which have the smallest molecules to polysaccharides (eg. starch), which have the largest, providing the body with 15.7kJ (3.75 kcal) per gram.

These different types of carbohydrates are referred to as simple and complex carbohydrates respectively. Together they should provide us with 60-65% of our total energy intake.

Simple sugars such as table sugar, honey and fruit sugars are digested easily by the body and pass into the blood stream a short time after eating. Starches on the other hand such as bread, rice and pasta have to be digested by the body and broken down into simple sugars before they can be absorbed into the bloodstream. Starches are beneficial in exercise and help to sustain activity if they are eaten in the correct quantity.

Excess glucose, the product of carbohydrate digestion, is stored in the muscles and liver as GLYCOGEN. Once the body's glycogen stores are full excess glucose is converted into fat and is stored in the body. The amount of energy which can be stored by the body in the form of carbohydrate is small:-

Glucose within blood: 210kJ (50 kcal)
Liver Glycogen store: 1050-1250kJ (250-300kcal)
Muscle glycogen store: 1700-2100kJ (400-500kcal)

If this was the only fuel source available to the body for the days energy requirements, there would not be enough as we expend 6300-16,800kJ (1500-4000kcal) per day.

During exercise carbohydrate is a major source of fuel to skeletal muscle, enabling the muscles to contract and you to perform the exercise. Different activities require different amounts of energy and will consequently use up glycogen at different rates. Hillwalking, although strenuous, is a long duration low intensity activity and glycogen along with fat will be used by the muscles for energy.

The intensity of exercise will vary depending on the nature and steepness of the terrain. For example, walking along a flat path at a steady pace all day would ensure that glycogen stores lasted for 5-6 hours, whereas if you were to increase the intensity of activity and walk up a steep hill for several hours, glycogen would run out rapidly. As there is a limited amount of carbohydrate in the body, energy for hillwalking is also provided from the body's fat stores.

FAT

Fat is a very concentrated source of energy providing us with 37.6kJ(9kcal) per gramme. A diet high in fat that is greater than 35% of total energy intake is harmful to health in the long term, and is associated with heart disease, obesity and cancer. It is essential in the diet and provides us with fat soluble vitamins A,D,K and E which perform specific functions in the body.

Fatty meals take longer to be digested and create a feeling of fullness. Consequently at the end of a days hillwalking a hot meal containing some fat will be satisfying and prevent feelings of hunger for a while.

Fatty acids which are obtained from the digestion of fat are used as an energy source by skeletal muscle in hillwalking. Even without fatty acids from food digestion the body has an abundance of stored fatty acids. The average 70kg male body consists of 20% fat representing an energy store equivalent to 527,184kJ(126,000kcal).

In exercise such as hillwalking, skeletal muscle will use carbohydrate and fat as fuel. Initially carbohydrate will be used and after a short time a mixture of carbohydrate and fat.. The more trained the muscle, the more capable it is at utilising fatty acids for fuel and hence sparing glycogen and allowing you to exercise for longer. If glycogen becomes depleted, fatty acids alone cannot provide sufficient fuel and fatigue will become apparent.

After several days hillwalking if the diet has not been high enough in carbohydrate to refuel the muscles glycogen stores will be low and it will be difficult to sustain a long walk. Symptoms such as general tiredness and heavy legs may be experienced.

The emphasis, therefore, in the hillwalkers diet should be on foods containing carbohydrate and only a small amount of fat.

PROTEIN

Protein is important to the body as it is involved in growth and repair and is needed amongst other things, for the manufacturing of important body proteins such as haemoglobin which carries oxygen to cells in blood and immune proteins needed to fight infection.

Protein provides the body with 16.7kJ (4kcal) per gm, and is sometimes used to provide energy although this is not it's primary function. It is found in many foods of both plant and animal origin. To ensure that the body can use the protein it is essential to mix the types of protein at meal times particularly if you are vegetarian. Animal proteins can be used by the body on their own but plant proteins have to be mixed, for instance by combining grains with pulses, eg beans on toast.

It is estimated that 10% of energy used during exercise comes from protein. Under extreme conditions, eg starvation or very high energy expenditure, much more protein would be used for fuel. Excess protein from the diet which is not used by the body is converted into fat. 1.0–1.2 grammes of protein per kilogram of body weight per day is the required amount of protein needed for health. Children and teenagers may need more as they are actively growing. In Western civilisation we eat too much protein and most people will eat more than the recommended amounts. Generally 10–15% of the total energy intake should come from protein.

VITAMINS AND MINERALS

Vitamins and minerals are required by the body in minute quantities to perform specific functions and they are known to be essential for life.

Vitamins may be classified as water soluble or fat soluble. The government published a report in 1991 with new recommendations on the amount of each vitamin which is required on average by an individual to remain healthy. The amount required is referred to as a 'dietary reference value' (DRV). Table 9 documents the source, function and DRV of these vitamins.

In excess vitamins can be toxic, particularly fat soluble ones. As we have a large store of fat soluble vitamins in our bodies, supplementation is very rarely required. If the quality of food eaten is poor, that is highly processed food, vitamin deficiencies may occur.

A deficiency in any vitamin would be a limiting factor during exercise as many of the water soluble vitamins (Table 9) are involved in energy release. It is therefore recommended that a diet which contains a good variety of fresh produce is eaten to ensure adequate vitamin status.

In expeditions of less than two weeks, it is unlikely that a vitamin deficiency would develop and only in longer expeditions where the availability of fresh food may be limited would a multi vitamin supplement possibly be recommended.

Minerals such as iron and zinc are important in exercise as iron is needed for the production of haemoglobin which carries oxygen to the working muscle. Without oxygen the muscles are unable to contract after a short time. A lack of iron in the diet can lead to iron deficiency anaemia. Anaemia would reduce the body's work capacity as oxygen demands would not be met and the individual would be very tired. Iron is found in red meat, eggs and also some vegetables. The iron from animal products is more readily absorbed than the iron from plant sources.

Zinc is a trace element which is involved in energy releasing reactions and is an essential component of some enzymes. The richest source of zinc is oysters, not that you will find many of these in the British mountains! It is also found in animal products, such as red meat and also in seeds.

Table 9 *Source, Function and Dietary Reference Value (DRV) of Vitamins.*

Vitamin	Source	Function	DRV
Fat Soluble			
A	carrots, green vegetables, dairy produce, fish oils	Growth, eye function	600–700ug/d
D	dairy products sunlight, fortified foods, margarine	calcium metabolism	★
E	vegetable oils dairy products wholegrains	antioxidant	>3mg/d★★
K	green leafy veg cereals, meats	blood clotting	1ug/kg/d
Water soluble			
Thiamin	dairy products	carbohydrate metabolism	0.8–1.0mg/d
Riboflavin	dairy products cereals	oxidative processes	1.1–1.3mg/d
Niacin	cereals, dairy produce	energy metabolism	13–17mg/d
B6	vegetables, pears	protein metabolism	1.2–1.4mg/d
C	citrus fruits	antioxidant	40mg/d

★ No DRV, elderly and those indoors, 10mg/d,   ★★ Safe intake no DRV

Reference: Department of Health 1991.

FIBRE

Dietary fibre or non starch polysaccharides are important to every day health as they facilitate normal gut function and prevent the bowel from becoming sluggish resulting in constipation and diverticular disease. There are two types of fibre; soluble and insoluble fibre both of which need to be eaten in the diet. Insoluble fibre comes from cereals and grains and soluble fibre is found in fruit, vegetables and pulses. During a hillwalking expedition it may be necessary to reduce the amount of fibre eaten as it is bulky and leaves you feeling full. This may limit the amount of food eaten. Normally 30gm of fibre is recommended but it would not be harmful to health if this was reduced for a short period of time during an expedition.

How much food do we need and when ?

Now that we know what food is made up of it is appropriate to look at what we need and when.

As we have seen it is important that we eat the correct balance of nutrients to make up our daily energy requirements. To summarise, the proportion of our daily energy intake which should come from carbohydrate, fat and protein is 60-65%, 25-30% and 10-15% repectively.

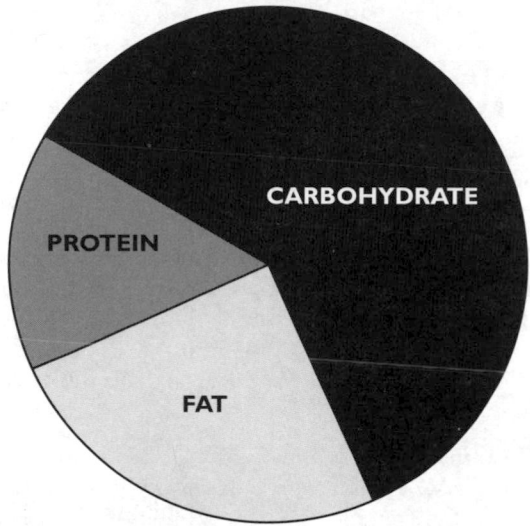

Fig. 47 *Pie Chart showing percentage energy intake from various food sources.*

To translate this into practical guide-lines imagine the above pie chart as a dinner plate, more than half the plate should contain pasta, potatoes or rice (the carbohydrate foods), a quarter should contain vegetables, eg. carrots, peas (carbohydrate + protein) and the remainder should contain lean meat, fish or chicken (protein + fat foods).

This type of diet is recommended to everyone all the year round to remain fit and healthy. Throughout an expedition the total amount of food eaten should increase to meet the increased energy requirements.

As we have seen carbohydrate is an important source of fuel for skeletal muscle in hillwalking, and the diet should remain high in carbohydrate throughout the expedition. Carbohydrate can be taken while on the move to help top up carbohydrate stores and snacks such as dried fruit, cereal bars and chocolate are ideal for this throughout the day. After hillwalking the muscles refuel glycogen most effectively in the two hours after exercise stops. Foods such as sandwiches, with a low fat filling eg, banana, honey, dried fruit, tea with sugar, biscuits and bananas are good foods to help the refuelling process. It is very important that muscles are refuelled following exercise particularly if the party is to walk on consecutive days.

In addition to energy the body also needs fluid to stay alive. The adult body is comprised of approximately 60% water. We will now look at ways to prevent dehydration when hillwalking.

Preventing dehydration when hillwalking

To remain healthy the average 70kg man requires 30mls water per/kg body weight per day, ie 2.1 litres of water per day. During exercise and or in hot weather the water requirements will increase as much as 3 fold.

Water is required by the body to maintain body temperature. When we exercise the body produces sweat on to the skin and it is the evaporation of this sweat which cools the body down. All the fluid lost in sweat has to be replaced by drinking fluid. If the body is dehydrated the heat will not be as effectively dissipated and heat exhaustion may occur due to a rise in body temperature.

When water is ingested it is absorbed from the small intestine into the circulation. There are several factors which are known to delay the absorption of water, for example, if a concentrate such as orange juice is added to water the rate of absorption will be slower due to the increased concentration. As water absorption in the body is an energy consuming process the addition of glucose in small amounts along with sodium and chloride will aid water absorption. Isotonic sports drinks work on this formula and are effective in providing water to the body if made up in the correct concentration. Isotonic means that the solution is in balance with the body's own fluids and will not draw water from the tissues in the same way that highly concentrated sugary drinks (hypertonic) do.

You should never wait until you are thirsty while out walking before you drink. Thirst is a poor indicator of the need to drink and at this point 1-2% body weight may already have been lost as fluid. It is advisable to drink small amounts frequently when hillwalking, particularly in warmer weather. A minimum intake of 2 litres of fluid is required each day and some of this may be appreciated as a hot drink if the weather is cold. Water is extremely heavy and it is quite unneccesary to carry large quantities over hill and dale. Streams are in plentiful supply in the mountainous parts of the British Isles and fortunately, most are safe to drink from. If a water bottle is carried it should be topped up as the opportunity arises.

Suitable drinks to take include water, isotonic sports drinks, weak squashes and hot drinks which could be taken at camp in the evening or first thing in the morning such as hot chocolate (instant), tea, coffee, soup (instant) and hot squash. Instant drinks, like hot chocolate, provide a satisfying hot drink and are a good source of calories.

Food selection and menu planning

It is generally recommended that 1kg of food per person per day should be allowed for on an expedition. Consequently, careful planning is required to ensure that the quality and quantity of food taken will meet the demands of the group. Accommodation, cooking facilities, shopping facilities are some of the factors which will have to be investigated to ensure that appropriate types of food are taken. To assess the quantity of food required, the duration of the trip, the number of people taking part, the type of expedition and the energy requirements have to be determined.

CALCULATING ENERGY REQUIREMENTS

Energy is the key to all activity and even at rest the body requires energy to fuel the functioning of vital organs and maintain body temperature. It is crucial that adequate energy is consumed from food as lack of energy could have severe and limiting consequences on any expedition into the mountains. Research has been conducted to classify activity of different groups of people according to their energy needs. In general children and adolescents require more energy than adults because they are growing and elderly people require less since they have reduced muscle mass and consequently a reduced resting energy expenditure.

The energy the body requires at rest is known as the 'Basal Metabolic Rate' (BMR) and factors such as age, sex, muscle mass will influence this. 'Daily Energy Requirement' (DER) is the sum of the BMR plus the energy cost of work performed. The DER will be greater on the days you spend climbing mountains than on the days sitting at a desk.

Hillwalking is classified as 'moderate' work in relation to energy expenditure. This is obviously a subjective judgement and depends on factors such as age, sex, the severity of the walk and the weight of the pack. It is estimated that hillwalking requires 2520kJ (600 kcal) per hour. In a cold environment extra energy will be required to keep the body warm and to fuel the shivering response which is an energy consuming process. If the body does not have the ability to keep itself warm due to lack of energy hypothermia will result.

Table 10 gives an estimated guide to the energy requirements for various groups you may find yourself leading on a hill walking expedition. Do remember however that within these groups there are often substantial differences between individuals. The figures given represent average values and may well have to be adjusted either up or down to meet individual requirements.

Table 10   **_Estimated Daily Energy Requirements (DER)._**
[MJ/(kcal)]

Sex	Male		Female	
Age (years)	15–18	19–50	15–18	19–50
DER MJ (kcals)	11.5(2755)	10.6(2550)	8.8(2110)	8.1(1940)

Note: 1 megajoule (MJ) = 1000 kilojoules (kJ)

The DER above should be taken as the baseline figure for the energy requirements of individual members of an expedition. They indicate the energy needed by an average person in a particular age range to perform day to day tasks. Consequently the DER has to be increased by a factor to cover energy needs for various tasks.

Adjustments to be made to the DER to take account of external factors. Add 10% for each of the following:

> for every 500m ascent,
> in winter or adverse conditions, either overhead or underfoot,
> if a full rucksack is carried.

For example, calculate the DER for a 70kg man aged 23 undertaking a days walk in winter conditions with a total ascent of 1000m.

	MJ	(kcal)
baseline DER	10.60	(2550)
add 10% for winter conditions	1.06	(254)
add 20% for 1000m ascent	2.12	(508)
ESTIMATED REQUIREMENTS	13.78	(3312)

These energy requirements are only guide-lines and some individuals will need more and some will require less energy to perform the same task. It is important therefore that individuals carry sufficient food with them during the day to prevent exhaustion due to lack of energy. It is also important to make sure that the expedition is within the capabilities of the group otherwise exhaustion may occur regardless of the preparations made for food provision.

CALCULATING WHAT FOOD IS REQUIRED

Now we know what food contains, the contribution it makes to the body while hillwalking and how much we need, we can translate this into the actual food required for an expedition.

We shall distinguish between two types of mountain outing; there is the short trip lasting one to two days and the longer semi-expedition lasting a week or more. The type of food which could be taken on these trips varies. For instance, more fresh produce could be included in a short trip where the weight to be carried is not so critical as it is on a longer expedition. From the previous section it can be seen that the energy requirements of individuals hillwalking can differ by as much as 30%. Because of this and to simplify the calculations involved, it is suggested that an AVERAGE DER is selected for the group as a whole, taking account of the number of individuals in each category (table 10) and making due allowance for conditions and the strenuousness of the hillwalks to be undertaken.

It is not a practical proposition to vary individual portions for each meal. However the necessary adjustments can easily be made in the amount of food which is consumed during the day; those who require more energy eating more and those who require less than the average DER eating less.

Fig. 47 suggests how much of each nutrient should make up the total daily energy intake. In practice on the hill the contribution each nutrient makes to the energy intake may have to be altered. Foods which are light to carry and energy dense have to be used so that energy demands are met. Wherever possible foods high in carbohydrate should be used .

When calculating the food required for a trip, it is important to know what percentage of the energy intake should be taken and at what time. Fig. 48 shows how the energy intake may be distributed throughout the day. In practice, most hillwalkers prefer a more substantial evening meal providing up to 50% of their requirements, with a correspondingly lesser amount consumed during the day. There is some room for individual preferences here but in general it is not good practice to follow a routine of stuff and bust at the end of each day, the energy intake should as far as possible be spread out throughout the day.

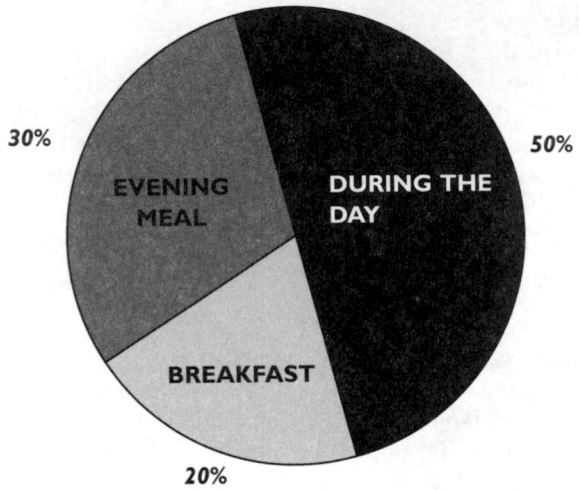

30%   50%

EVENING MEAL   DURING THE DAY

BREAKFAST

20%

Fig. 48   *Distribution of energy intake in one days hillwalking.*

With this information we can now consider planning a menu for a hillwalking expedition. Planning a menu for a trip can be as complicated or as straight forward as you like. For those who wish to calculate energy requirements for a hillwalking group, detailed information and examples are available in Tables 11 and 12 at the end of this chapter. To assist you in planning a menu a list of suitable foods and energy values are documented in Table 11.

When to eat food

If it can be arranged breakfast should eaten at least 1 hour before setting out. This allows the body time to begin processing the food and should prevent any feelings of nausea at the onset of exercise. On day trips it may be possible to eat breakfast several hours in advance as a lengthy drive is sometimes necessary to reach the mountains. In other situations it is worth making the effort and getting up earlier.

It has been said of hillwalking that, "when breakfast ends lunch begins". There is some truth in this as energy requirements are high and small amounts of food have to be eaten frequently to enable these requirements to be met.

Fifty percent of the days energy should be consumed between breakfast and the evening meal (Fig. 48). When planning a menu this should be kept in mind, with this food being high in carbohydrate such as dried fruit mixes, cereal bars, fruit cake. Hot drinks and cooked meals are best kept to breakfast and the evening meal.

The body refuels the muscles most effectively within the first two hours following the cessation of exercise. Foods high in carbohydrate such as sandwiches, cereal bars, chocolate or bananas should be eaten. Alternatively, a hot sweet drink would suffice to begin the refuelling process, eg hot chocolate, tea with sugar.

Proprietary foods such as 'Build-up' 1442kJ/100g(345kcal/100g) and 'Complan' 1870kJ/100g(444kcal/100g) which are complete meal replacements in powder form are useful to have in an emergency store as they contain a balanced source of fat, carbohydrate, protein, vitamins and minerals. They are available in sweet and savoury flavours and can be made up using powdered milk. Complan and Build-up soups can be made up with water.

ADAPTING THE MENU

Before planning the food for an expedition it is essential to find out if any members of the group have special needs. Occasionally you may get someone who is diabetic, coeliac or has some other special requirement. In this case it would be important to sort out in advance with this individual the food to be taken on the trip. The dietary needs of these individuals will not be discussed here but further advice on the menu adaptations which would be necessary if you did have someone with special needs could be obtained by contacting a local hospital dietitian or an organisation such as the British Diabetic Association or in case of coeliacs, the Coeliac Society.

As vegetarians do not have special dietary needs in quite the same way as diabetics or coeliacs and as vegetarianism is increasingly popular we will consider how to plan a vegetarian menu to ensure that suitable foods are provided. The only difference between vegetarians and non vegetarians is that the former do not eat meat, fish, chicken or products made from these foods. Lacto-ovo vegetarians eat milk cheese and eggs.

Alternative protein sources include, nuts, seeds, cheese, pulses, beans, textured vegetable protein and soya curd. Combined with vegetables, (fresh or dried), pasta and a savoury sauce an easy, palatable and nutritious dish can be made. There are endless combinations of any of the above foods which can be accompanied with rice, pasta, potatoes, noodles or bread. Many of the commercially available dehydrated foods are made from textured vegetable protein which some vegetarians may find unpalatable. You should discuss with the vegetarians in the group the types of foods they would prefer to eat.

Palatability

Many people, especially children, will starve rather than eat food they dislike. Therefore some market research prior to drawing up your menu is a good idea. The planned meals should be imaginative with a variety of simple and tasty meals included. The meals also have to meet the following criteria: have a high energy to weight ratio, be nutritious, be not too bulky to carry and easy to cook (preferably in a single pot).

PACKAGING OF FOOD

Due to restrictions imposed on weight it is important that food is packaged in light containers and not in heavy metal ones. Lightweight plastic containers may be used for liquids and for foods which are easily squashed or damaged such as bread, crackers, bananas, eggs etc but self sealing plastic bags, foil and cling film serve admirably for most foods which have to be packaged. Reducing the weight to be carried will ultimately help you in conserving energy. Tins should be kept to a minimum. Since the contents are usually precooked and dehydrated the additional weight has to be balanced against possible benefits in terms of ease of preparation and savings in fuel and cooking time. Most foods recommended in this chapter are dry and can be stored in plastic bags or containers. The portioning of food depends on the size of the group and the duration of the trip. Foods should, as far as possible, be packed in quantities which will be used in one day.

Remember that by failing to prepare you are preparing to fail. There are many benefits to be derived from devoting some thought and effort into the provision of sustaining and palatable food for the planned expedition. In this way both the physiological and psychological benefits of food will be obtained.

(Table 11)

Menu planner

FOOD	ENERGY/ 100gm MJ (kcal)	PORTION (gm)	HANDY MEASURE	ENERGY/ PORTION MJ (kcal)
BREAKFAST				
Porridge	1.66 (400)	30	1/2 cup	0.50(120)
B'fast cereal	1.5(368)	30	1 cup	0.45(110)
Muesli	1.5(368)	70	4.5 tablespoons	1.05(258)
Crackers	1.8(440)	28	4 crackers	0.5(123)
Bacon	0.95(228)	50	2 rashers	0.47(114)
Biscuit	1.9(471)	30	2 biscuits	0.60(143)
Peanut butter	2.5(623)	20	1 tablespoon	0.52(124)
Butter/Marg	3.0(740)	7	1 pat	0.21(52)
Jam	1.1(264)	15	1 teaspoon	0.15(36)
Dried fruit	1.0(246)	25	1 tablespoon	0.25(61)
Orange drink	0.45(107)	40	average concentrate	0.18(43)
Dried milk	2.0(490)	14	1 glass	0.28(67)

FOOD TO EAT THROUGHOUT THE DAY

Sandwiches eg				
2 slices bread	0.91(216)	60	2 slices	0.55(130)
butter	3.0(740)	7	1 pat	0.21(52)
Filling eg				
Peanut butter	1.6(406)	45	medium chunk	0.72(183)
Pepperoni sausage	2.2(556)	25	1 stick	0.5(139)
Cheese	1.6(406)	45	med chunk	0.72(183)
Oatcake	1.8(441)	26	2 round	0.47(114)
Biscuit savoury	1.8(441)	20	2 crackers	0.36(88)
Chocolate biscuit	2.0(493)	30	2 round biscuits	0.6(148)
Banana	0.3(79)	100	1 medium	0.3(148)
Dried banana	0.77(182)	25	2 tablespoons	0.17(140)
Apple	0.19(46)	112	1 medium	0.2(51.5)
Dried apple	0.45(107)	25		0.11(27)
Peanuts	2.4(570)	100	1bag	2.4(570)
Cereal bar	2.06(495)	33	1 bar	0.62(150)
Honey	1.2(288)	17	1 heaped teaspoon	0.2(49)
Raisins	1.0(246)	25	1 tablespoon	0.25(62)
Chocolate	2.2(529)	50	1 bar	1.1(314)

FOOD	ENERGY/ 100gm MJ (kcal)	PORTION (gm)	HANDY MEASURE	ENERGY/ PORTION MJ (kcal)
Fruit cake	1.5(490)	70	1 average slice	1.05(343)
Flapjack		60	1 average square	
Mars bar	1.8(441)	68	1 regular bar	1.2(299)
Mixed nuts				
& raisins	3.4(860)	30	1 small bag	1.02(258)

EVENING MEAL

FOOD	ENERGY	PORTION	HANDY MEASURE	ENERGY/PORTION
Instant soup	1.64(377)	26	1 sachet	0.63(145)
Oxo cubes	0.96(229)	6	1 cube	0.05(14)
Rice	1.5(361)	50	½ cup	0.75(181)
Savoury rice	1.7(407)	50	½ cup	0.85(203)
Pasta	1.6(378)	75	¾ cup	1.2(284)
Mashed potato	1.4(318)	120	2 scoops	1.6(381)
Sausage	1.1(274)	120	2 sausages	1.32(328)
Corned beef	0.9(217)	50	1 thick slice	0.45(157)
Tuna fish	1.2(289)	60		0.56(133)
Salmon	0.64(155)	60		0.38(93)
Cheese-hard	1.6(406)	120	2 large chunks	1.92(487)
-soft	1.2(300)	40	1/6th portion	0.48(120)
Mixed beans	0.64(152)	50	2 tablespoons	0.32(76)
Baked beans	0.27(64)	225	1 small tin	0.60(141)
Sauce mixes	0.82(198)	30	small portion	0.24(59)
Black pepper	NEG			
Cayenne pepper	0.97(233)			
Curry powder	0.97(233)			
Salt	0	0		
Tomato puree	0.28(67)	15	1 tablespoon	0.04(10)
Instant custard	1.5(354)			
Instant pudding	0.58(139)	120	1/2 packet	0.69(166)
Swiss roll	1.4(337)	30	1 slice	0.42(101)
Instant hot				
chocolate	1.1(277)	28	1 sachet	0.42(99)
Malted drink	1.6(396)	23	1 sachet	0.36(91)
Fruit drink	0.45(107)	40		0.18(43)

MISCELLANEOUS

Sugar	1.6(394)	5	1 teaspoon	0.08(2
Gatorade/				
Isostar	1.48(356)	15	2 scoops	0.2(53)
Butterscotch	1.3(327)	133	1 packet	1.69(425)
Mints	1.6(392)	50	1 packet	0.8(196)

Planning a Menu - an example

Plan a menu for a group of seven people, 5 males and 2 females, aged 20-35 years old, who will be walking without packs for two days in summer with an average ascent of 1000m per day. There are a number of factors to be considered:-

1. Energy requirements of group (Refer to Table 10, page 102).
   This will depend on:
   a. Age and sex of individuals in group
   b. Height climbed (average per day)
   c. Severity of conditions and load carried.
      Calculate the average DER (following adjustments)
2. Energy distribution throughout the day (Refer to Fig. 48 page...)
3. Planning the menu (Table 11)

From the information given the group will require;-

Average DER=11.8MJ (2808kcal), per day;
*Males require 10% more, females 10% less energy per day;
Energy should be allowed for as follows:

Breakfast;	2.4MJ	(571kcal)
Throughout day*	5.9MJ	(1404kcal)
Evening	3.5 MJ	(833kcal)
Total	11.8MJ	(2808kcal)

One days intake has been chosen from the 'menu planner' Table 11 and is set out in Table 12.

Table 12 *Meal satisfying the above requirements.*

FOOD	Average portion weight grams	Energy from one portion in MJ(kcal)	Weight in grams required for number in party, ie X 7	Weight in grams required for number of days ie X 2
BREAKFAST; AVERAGE ENERGY REQUIREMENT IS 2.4MJ (571 kcal)				
Porridge	30	0.50(120)	210	420
Dried fruit	25	0.26(61)	175	350
Biscuit sweet(2)	30	0.60(143)	210	420
Peanut butter	20	0.52(124)	140	280
Jam	15	0.15(36)	105	210
0.25 pint dried milk	14	0.29(69)	98	196
Tea/Coffee	7	neg	49	98
Sub total	*141*	*2.32(553)*		
THROUGHOUT THE DAY; AVERAGE ENERGY REQUIREMENT IS 5.9MJ (1404kcal)				
2 Sandwiches	330	2.11(502)	14 s'wiches	28 s'wiches
2 Choc biscuits	34	0.59(140)	238(14 bisc)	476
Peanuts	100	2.36(570)	700(7 packets)	1400
Apricots(dried)	42	0.33(76)	294	588
Cereal Bar	30	0.53(126)	210(7 bars)	420
Sub total	*536*	*5.92 (1414)*		
EVENING MEAL; AVERAGE ENERGY REQUIREMENT IS 3.5MJ (833kcal)				
Instant soup	26	0.63(145)	182	364
Pasta	75	1.2(283)	525	1050
Tuna fish	60	0.56(133)	420	840
Mixed beans	50	0.32(76)	350	700
Shortbread	15	0.31(75)	105	210
Dried apple	25	0.11(27)	175	350
Tea/Coffee	7	neg	49	98
Bedtime				
Hot chocolate	28	0.42(99)	196	39
Sub total	*286*	*3.55(838)*		
TOTAL	**963g**	**11.79(2805)**		

Notes

(i) Foods have been chosen with palatability, ease of cooking and weight in mind. Items such as salt, pepper, herbs and spices are not included and would be to the individuals taste. Milk is dried as it is less heavy to carry and the energy given is for full fat dried milk. Butter or margarine could be used and the energy content for this can be found in Table 11.

(ii) Adjustments should be made in the food consumed during the day to allow for different DER for males and females. If the females have one sandwich and one biscuit instead of two and the males share the spoils, this should give both groups approximately the correct DER.

(iii) The right hand column lists the weight of each item which should be taken for the whole group for the two days assuming that this menu was repeated on the second day. It is unlikely that these exact quantities would be available in retail packs. Repack where necessary into polythene bags and handy containers.

5

Access and Conservation

The Multi-use Mountain Environment

It has been estimated that there are well over three quarters of a million people who enjoy walking in the hills, and up to one hundred thousand mountaineers - all actively seeking their recreation on the hills, moors, mountains and crags of the British Isles.

This level of activity represents a rapid and sustained increase in participation since the end of the Second World War. In 1944, when the British Mountaineering Council was first established, it had 25 member clubs. By 1992 this figure had grown to 282. Similarly the Mountaineering Council of Scotland grew from about 20 member clubs in 1970 to 105 in 1992. Population growth; vastly improved mobility through increased car ownership and a much developed road network; an increase in leisure time; a higher standard of living, and a growth of outdoor activities within education have all been contributory factors.

Every walker or climber venturing into the hills is seeking an experience that may be based upon peace, solitude, natural beauty, the natural environment, excitement, adventure and risk. However, the mountain and hill land of Britain is much more than just a recreational playground; it is productive land on which some depend for a livelihood, and on which the entire population depends for some of the most basic amenities of twentieth century living. It is also the location of some of the few remaining large areas of semi-natural vegetation in the British Isles, most of the rest of the land having been developed or farmed in some way. For this reason it has special significance for conservation and supports a number of rare species of fauna and flora. Agriculture, forestry, water gathering, power generation, mineral exploitation, landscape and nature conservation, military training, sporting activities, tourism, recreation and education all take place, yet clearly not all are compatible. In some areas, by careful management an area of hill land supports several land uses but in others there are direct conflicts.

Into this complex scene the mountaineer fits with some difficulty. There are few areas managed with outdoor recreation as the priority use. Most landowners wish to secure a return from their holdings and there is no direct profit, apart from the provision of facilities such as camp sites or bunkhouses, to be made from hillwalkers or rock climbers.

Despite a campaign for free access to uncultivated land dating back over a century, there are still today few legal rights of access to hill and mountain land. Forty years ago the few hillwalkers seldom caused problems; the hordes of today are ill-concealed and frequently present a potential if not real conflict with other land uses. Instances of damage and disturbance can occur; access difficulties can result, and even the careful management by bodies such as the National Park authorities or National Trust applies only to limited areas.

The freedoms of mountaineering - of access and of practice - and the quality of the environments in which it takes place are traditionally highly prized, yet there remains room for improvement in standards of behaviour and attitudes towards the playgrounds of mountaineering.

A degraded environment lessens the enjoyment for those who follow. Damage or misuse give those who own, control or manage land reason to restrict, or even prevent access. If the tolerant attitudes of landowners on which access depends are to be maintained or the new legal rights so long sought in Parliament and elsewhere are to be won then there is a need for a responsible attitude, a new philosophy of minimum impact, and a depth or understanding of the multi-use environment of upland Britain. A new philosophy will not come overnight. It can come about in the long term by fostering an appreciation and responsibility in those people who take up mountaineering activities. In this respect leaders, teachers and instructors have a key role to play.

Management, Designation and Ownership of Land for Conservation and Recreation

A sophisticated designation system for land of scenic, scientific and recreational value has evolved in Britain since the Second World War. Areas of high quality are designated by the relevant government agencies, resulting in stringent planning policies, special consultative procedures for development control, special management arrangements, the injection of central government finance and in some cases special administrative arrangements for the designated areas. These arrangements vary depending on whether the areas fall within England, Northern Ireland, Scotland or Wales but do have some common provisions. In each country different government agencies or departments are responsible for promoting the enjoyment and protection of the countryside. The following notes provide brief descriptions of those agencies whose responsibilities are most closely concerned with those issues which affect hillwalkers and mountaineers and also the relevant systems of designation, management and ownership.

Statutory Organisations

THE COUNTRYSIDE COMMISSION

Formed in 1968 under the Countryside Act to succeed the National Parks Commission but with wider responsibilities it is the statutory agency which cares for the countryside of England and access to it. The Commission is the governments advisory body on countryside matters in England and has special responsibility for the designation of National Parks, Areas of Outstanding Natural Beauty, and Heritage Coasts and establishing National Trails. It provides grants and advice for projects which conserve the countrysides natural beauty and make it available for appropriate public enjoyment.

ENGLISH NATURE

English Nature was established in 1991 under the Environment Protection Act and is responsible for advising Government on nature conservation in England. It promotes the conservation of wildlife and natural features; selects, establishes and manages National Nature Reserves and identifies and notifies Sites of Special Scientific Interest (SSSI). It provides advice and information about nature conservation and supports and conducts relevant research.

THE COUNTRYSIDE COUNCIL FOR WALES

The Countryside Council for Wales was also established in 1991 under the Environment Protection Act but CCW combines the responsibilities for protection and enjoyment of the landscape and nature conservation in Wales that the Countryside Commission and English Nature have separately for England.

SCOTTISH NATURAL HERITAGE

Established in 1992 under the Natural Heritage (Scotland) Act 1991, SNH has similar powers and responsibilities for landscape protection and enjoyment and nature conservation that CCW has for Wales and the Countryside Commission and English Nature have separately for England. The most significant difference between Scotland on the one hand and England and Wales on the other is that there are no National Parks in Scotland and SNH has no powers to designate them. However, powers do exist under the Natural Heritage (Scotland) Act to establish Natural Heritage Areas (NHAs).

DEPARTMENT OF THE ENVIRONMENT (NORTHERN IRELAND) - COUNTRYSIDE AND WILDLIFE BRANCH

The Department of the Environment (N.I.) is responsible for the designation of Areas of Outstanding Natural Beauty, National Parks (presently none), National Nature Reserves and Areas of Special Scientific Interest; active management of some designated areas; research, surveys, financial support and education on conservation matters; and implementation of EC directives related to wildlife and countryside conservation.

Statutory Designations

NATIONAL PARKS

National Parks in England and Wales (see Fig 49) have been designated for the purposes of: conserving and enhancing natural beauty and amenity; providing appropriate opportunities for outdoor recreation; and for promoting the social and economic well-being of the local communities. Each park is administered by a National Park Authority, funded jointly by central government and local government.

The concept of national parks originated in the United States as a means of protecting large areas of completely natural habitat from development and exploitation, and making them available in a controlled manner for public enjoyment. This was achieved in the USA through land purchase by government. The idea rapidly spread and pressure grew from conservation and recreation organisations in Britain for the establishment of specially protected areas of landscape. The national park concept, adapted to British circumstances of inhabited, man-made landscapes and private ownership, became part of British government thinking in the 1940s. A series of reports was commissioned during the late 1940s and culminated in the National Parks and Access to the Countryside Act 1949 which laid down the procedures for the establishment of national parks. The National Parks Commission (which became the Countryside Commission in 1968) was given the responsibility for recommending areas for designation, and the first park, the Peak District, was formally established in 1951. Nine further designations were made during the 1950s; six in England: Northumberland, Lake District, Yorkshire Dales, North York Moors, Dartmoor, Exmoor; and three in Wales: Snowdonia,

Brecon Beacons and the Pembrokeshire Coast. The ten national parks cover 13,600 sq km, one-tenth of the land area of England and Wales. With the exception of Pembrokeshire, they are all major areas of upland or mountainous country. A further area of lowland, The Broads, which was designated in 1989 is administered as a National Park in all but name.

Each National Park is administered by a committee or board which is made up of two-thirds county and district councillors and one-third ministerially-nominated members who are intended to represent the national interests in the park. Each authority has a National Park Officer and supporting staff.

National park designation does not change land ownership; the authorities implement the aims through the essentially negative process of planning control and the more positive approach of management by formal agreement, co-operation and financial support. A national park plan has been produced for each park, carefully defining policies for all aspects of land use and management, and it is against these that the authorities consider all planning applications for development within the parks. The authorities' more positive roles include: providing facilities for the public such as car parks, toilets, picnic areas and local transport services; providing information and interpretation services, including a warden service to undertake practical works and reconcile local difficulties on the ground; seeking access agreements to open country.

As opportunities arise some national park authorities seek to fulfil their functions through purchasing important areas of land, for example, the Roaches Estate and the Eastern Moors and Edges in the Peak District.

AREAS OF OUTSTANDING NATURAL BEAUTY (AONB)

Areas of Outstanding Natural Beauty are designated in England, Wales and Northern Ireland for the purpose of conserving and enhancing natural beauty - the first only of the national park purposes. There is no statutory aim of provision for recreation.

By 1991 39 AONB had been identified in England and Wales by the Countryside Commission, and their designation confirmed - accounting for a total land area of over 20,000 sq km. A further 3 areas were under consideration with consultations in various stages of progress.

There are no major mountain areas designated as AONB (these are mostly national parks) but the 39 areas do include a wide variety of landscape types - Hills (eg the North Pennines, Malverns, Mendips and (proposed) the Berwyns), Downs, Vales, Coasts and Peninsulas. All planning and management responsibilities are carried out by County and District Councils, although a few have established joint Advisory Committees. Designation ensures a more stringent approach to planning policy and development control than elsewhere in order to conserve the high landscape quality. Although there is no statutory responsibility for recreation provision, increasing pressure has led to some provision and management, where this is consistent with conservation.

In Northern Ireland eight AONB including the Mourne Mountains were designated under the 1965 Amenity Lands Act. Subsequently, when passing the 1985 Nature Conservation and Amenity Lands order, it was felt to be necessary to re-designate those areas and review their boundaries. Three of these re-designations had been completed by 1990.

NATIONAL SCENIC AREAS (NSA)

National Scenic Areas (see Fig 50) are areas of the Scottish countryside that have been identified for their outstanding scenic qualities and for which special consultative procedures have been established to consider proposals for developments which could have a significant effect on those qualities.

Forty National Scenic Areas were identified by the Countryside Commission for Scotland (CCS) – the government agency formerly responsible for conservation of natural beauty and recreation for the general public in the Scottish countryside, whose powers were transferred to SNH in 1992.

NSAs cover a total of 10,000 sq km – about one-eighth of the land and inland water area of Scotland – and include many of the main mountain areas: The Cuillin Hills, Wester Ross, Knoydart, Kintail, Ben Nevis and Glencoe, the Cairngorms and Lochnagar.

The planning authorities consult SNH whenever planning applications are received for certain classes of development within the Scenic Areas, eg vehicle tracks above 300m altitude. If the planning authority and SNH are not in agreement on whether permission should be granted, the matter is referred to the Secretary of State for Scotland for a decision.

SITES OF SPECIAL SCIENTIFIC INTEREST (SSSI)

Sites of Special Scientific Interest are areas of land identified as being of particular importance for nature conservation because of the flora, fauna, physiographic or geological features they contain.

The sites are surveyed and identified by English Nature, Countryside Council for Wales and Scottish Natural Heritage and are selected to represent the best examples of the total range of ecological variety in Britain, the aim being to protect sufficient areas to support sustainable populations of all the natural wildlife and representative examples of geological and physiographic features.

In 1991 there were 5,671 sites covering 17,785 sq km of land; some of which are of international, importance. Many of the sites are in the upland and mountain areas and include a range of habitats such as blanket bogs; rare plants on cliffs and screes; heaths and grasslands, birch, oak and native pine woodlands. Some rivers and lakes are also SSSIs. Local planning authorities are notified of the existence of each site and the views of the relevant government body, ie EN/CCW/SNH, are sought on any planning application for development with potential to affect the site. In this way the nature conservation value of the site is taken into consideration in deciding whether development should be permitted.

Most SSSI are in private ownership and management and in 1981 the Wildlife and Countryside Act introduced measures whereby the owner and occupier of each SSSI is also notified by the relevant country body of operations or activities, such as agricultural improvement or afforestation, which could be harmful to the scientific value of the site. The owner is required to consult the relevant body before any such operation can proceed. If EN/CW/SNH consider that the operation would damage the interest of the site a management agreement can be drawn up whereby a modified management system is implemented and the owner is compensated if he/she is disadvantaged by the agreement. Landowners in Scotland have the power to appeal against SSSI designation.

NATIONAL NATURE RESERVES

National Nature Reserves are nationally important SSSI which are managed primarily by EN/CCW/SNH for nature conservation. They may be owned or leased by statutory or voluntary conservation organisations such as the RSPB, or managed jointly with a private landowner under a nature reserve agreement.

In 1991 there were 242 NNRs in Great Britain, and 45 in Northern Ireland many in the mountain areas. Examples are: Cwm Idwal, the Rhinogs, Snowdon, Cader Idris, the Cairngorms, Ben Eighe, Rhum and Ben Lawers.

There are usually no restrictions on access to NNRs in mountain areas. Exceptions occur where certain research or management operations are being carried out and prior permission to visit the NNR should be sought (eg the Isle of Rhum).

Further information about NNRs can be obtained from the Regional Office of the relevant bodies or from local staff.

THE NATIONAL TRUSTS FOR PLACES OF HISTORIC INTEREST OR NATURAL BEAUTY

The National Trust (England, Wales and Northern Ireland) and the National Trust for Scotland are both charities established to promote the preservation of buildings and land of great historic, landscape or amenity value for the nation's benefit. The Trusts are independent of governments and rely for income on rents, admission income, membership subscriptions, donations, bequests and grants (this last sources includes some government money via the Countryside Agencies). Both Trusts are of importance to the mountaineer in that they own many large and important tracts of mountain land, and through ownership manage these properties to conserve their high landscape qualities and to provide public access, subject to the needs of agriculture and nature conservation.

The Trusts have been given unique powers by Parliament. Firstly the National Trust is able to declare its property 'inalienable' ie it cannot be sold, mortgaged or given away voluntarily. This security has encouraged many donations of buildings and land to the Trust. The National Trust for Scotland does have the power to grant feus of land, although the consent of the Lord Advocate is required if the area exceeds eight hectares in extent. Secondly, even though government and most public authorities have the power of compulsory acquisition of property, both Trusts nearly always have the right to appeal to a joint committee of both Houses of Parliament if a compulsory purchase of Trust property is proposed.

THE NATIONAL TRUST

The National Trust was established in 1895 and in 1992 had over two million members.

The Trust owns very extensive areas of mountains and moorlands in many of the prime walking and climbing areas of England and Wales, as an examination of the relevant O.S. maps will reveal. Nearly one-quarter of the Lake District National Park, including much mountain land, has been brought into Trust ownership over the years by steady acquisition. In Snowdonia, the Carneddau, Tryfan and the northern side of the Glyders; in the Brecon Beacons the central massif including Pen y Fan, and in the Dark Peak the Howden Moors, Bleaklow and Kinder Scout are all owned by the Trust.

The Trust has also bought or been given restrictive covenants over many areas of land, particularly in areas where it is already a major landowner, eg the Lake District. The land remains with the owner but the covenants help to preserve the land from damaging change. The existence of covenants does not imply any right of public access.

While the Trust's policy is to give access on foot to all its open spaces, it is nevertheless very concerned about the intense pressure some of these are under from high levels of visitor use.

It is concerned to protect the fabric of the landscape - to halt footpath erosion, for example, and to protect areas of high nature conservation value but also to preserve the quality of experience that the open spaces provide - their remoteness and tranquillity.

The Trust has always adhered to the principle that conservation is the first task which must take precedence over public access and that it is essential to preserve for the future the qualities that so attract people that they are at times in danger of destroying them. Thus in order to reduce impacts, the Trust attempts to manage public pressure by careful provision of the facilities that promote public access to sensitive areas. This has meant matching the size and positioning of car parks and campsites, for example, to the capacity of the land they serve.

THE NATIONAL TRUST FOR SCOTLAND

The National Trust for Scotland was formed, well after the National Trust, in 1931, and in 1991 had 234,000 members.

The Trust now owns over 100 properties - castles, houses and gardens - and 400 sq km of land of high scenic quality.

The Trust's aim is to promote the permanent conservation for the benefit of the nation of its mountain and other properties, so far as is practicable. The Trust believes that in the case of mountain properties this includes the protection of their natural aspect and features, and animal and plant life; mountains and wild life are worthy of conservation for their own sakes, and not just for the enjoyment of man.

Some of Scotland's finest mountain land is owned by the Trust. The history of the acquisition of this property is a very interesting and relevant one for mountaineers. In 1935, only 4 years after its formation, a large Glencoe

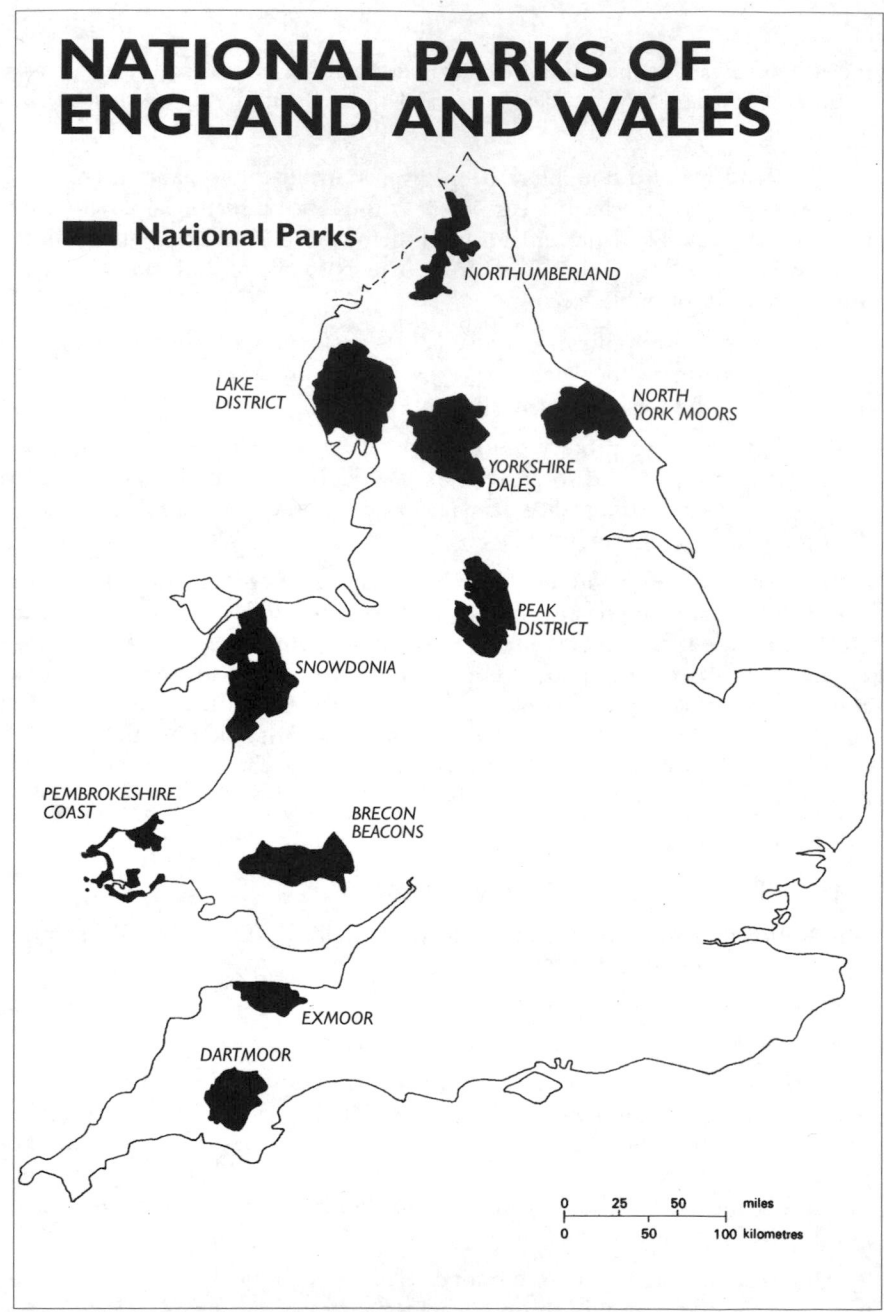

NATIONAL PARKS OF ENGLAND AND WALES

■ National Parks

NORTHUMBERLAND

LAKE DISTRICT

NORTH YORK MOORS

YORKSHIRE DALES

PEAK DISTRICT

SNOWDONIA

PEMBROKESHIRE COAST

BRECON BEACONS

EXMOOR

DARTMOOR

| 0 | 25 | 50 | miles |
| 0 | 50 | 100 | kilometres |

Fig. 49   *National Parks of England and Wales.*

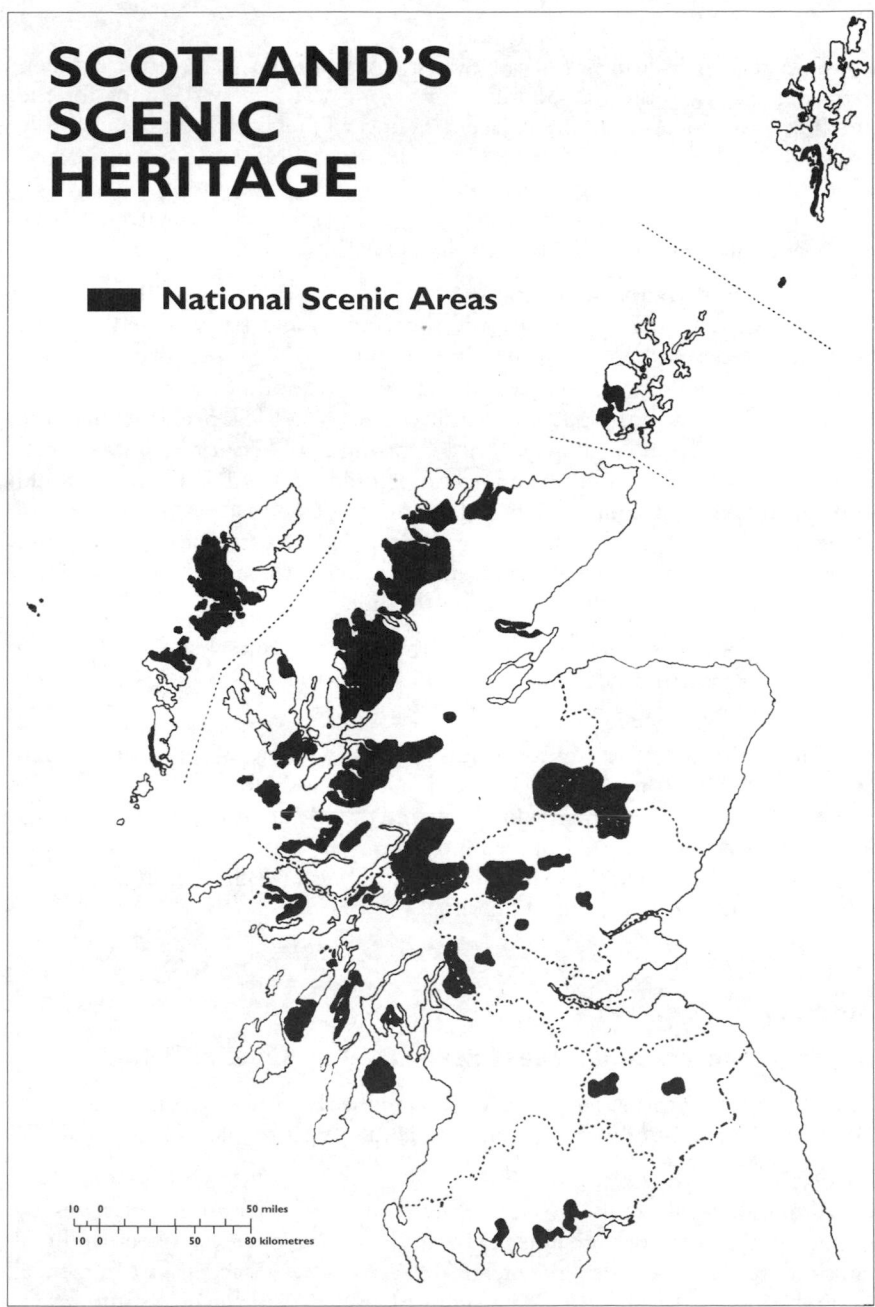

SCOTLAND'S SCENIC HERITAGE

■ **National Scenic Areas**

Fig. 50 *National Scenic Areas in Scotland.*

Estate including Bidean nam Bian, was put up for sale. A Scottish climber, Percy Unna, was largely responsible for raising the necessary funds for the purchase. Two years later the adjacent Dalness Forest, including Buachaille Etive Mor, became available and Unna, by then President of the Scottish Mountaineering Club, organised a national appeal amongst climbers which resulted in the money being raised and the land purchased. Unna made a large personal anonymous contribution to the appeal.

Following the purchase, Unna wrote to the Trust expressing the views of the subscribers to the appeal on how the land should be managed. These views have become known as the 'Unna Guidelines'. Summarised, they are that the land should be maintained in its primitive condition for all time with unrestricted access to the public. Primitive meant not less primitive than the existing state. Sheep farming and cattle grazing could continue but stalking, with the associated restrictions on access, should cease. Regulations should be kept to a very minimum. The hills should not be made easier or safer to climb and there should be no facilities for mechanised transport on the hills. There should be no new, improved or extended paths; no signs, waymarks, posts or cairns, nor any shelter built on the hills.

These guidelines were visionary for their time, for it would have been a farsighted person indeed who understood then the pressure this mountain land would be under in 50 years time.

Unna was instrumental in the acquisition by the Trust of further mountain properties. In 1944 he purchased Kintail anonymously for the Trust. In 1950 he handed over an investment which became the Mountainous Country fund. This fund then financed the purchase of Ben Lawers in 1951. The Trust also owns Goat Fell on Arran, the Torridon Estate, Wester Alligin, immediately to the west of Torridon and Ben Lomond.

Access

Rights of Access and Access Permitted by Official Policy

In comparison with the large area of land regularly visited by hillwalkers and climbers, the extent of mountain and hill land subject to a legal right of access is very limited.

Although legal rights are very slowly increasing through purchases by public bodies or formal agreements, mountaineering has always been and will continue to be largely dependent on 'de facto' access – access as of practice, unhindered by the landowner. The rights of access are nevertheless important. They exist through a complex array of legislation, some representing the historical rights of local inhabitants, and some more modern in response to the needs of the urban-based, recreation-seeking population of the post-war years. The differences between access rights in England/Wales and in Scotland are considerable and the two will be dealt with separately.

Depending on the type of access right, information may be readily available or it may be difficult to establish if a public right exists or not. In many situations, although a right of access exists, there will be restrictions, often by byelaws, on other activities which are considered unsuited to the area or its agricultural productivity.

PUBLIC RIGHTS OF WAY

England and Wales

Public footpaths, bridleways and byways open to all traffic are all public rights of way (also called public highways) - linear routes along which members of the public have a right to pass and re-pass. All public rights of way from footpaths to main roads are subject to the same protection in law. On footpaths there is a right of way on foot only; on bridleways there is also a right of way on horseback and on pedal cycle. In legal theory most paths become rights of way because the owner 'dedicates' them to public use. In practice very few paths have been formally dedicated, but the law presumes that if the public uses a path without interruption or hindrance for upwards of 20 years then the owner intends dedication. Local authorities can also establish rights of way by agreement with landowners or by 'creation orders'.

Public rights of way are shown on the Ordnance Survey Pathfinder and Outdoor Leisure maps (1:25,000), Landranger maps (1:50,000) and Tourist maps (1:63360). There may have been recent changes not indicated on the maps. For conclusive evidence that a particular path is a right of way one would need to turn to the definitive rights of way maps (each accompanied by a 'statement' of additional information) prepared for each county in England and Wales by the County Councils.

Appearance of a path on a definitive map is conclusive legal proof of its being a public right of way at the date of publication. However, a path may have been subsequently altered by a statutory diversion or extinguishment. A footpath not shown on a definitive map may still be a public right of way. The definitive maps are available for public inspection at county and district council offices, also often at public libraries.

County councils are the authorities to which all duties for public rights of way are assigned. They are designated as highway authorities - responsible for maintaining and repairing public rights of way and keeping them free from obstruction. In some cases the actual work of carrying out rights of way duties has been delegated to the District Councils. Obstructions and other path problems should be reported to the highway authority or, where appropriate, the District Council. The authority or council has the duty and the powers to act but some are hesitant or short or cash to do so. If there is no progress towards solving the problem, it should be referred to a relevant councillor or the Ramblers' Association, or the BMC.

It is not unusual for rights of way to be blocked by new fences, ploughing or newly planted crops or other obstruction. Such obstructions can be moved sufficiently to allow passage but should normally be reported to the local authority, which has a duty to deal with them. Intimidation or harassment by, for example, the landowner or a fierce dog should also be reported to the highway authority.

A public right of way cannot be closed or diverted by the landowner, only by a local authority, central government, or a Magistrates' Court. Of course, the local authority may be persuaded to act by the landowner and a landowner may make an application for closure or diversion to a Magistrates Court. A local authority may make an order to close a path if it considers that it is no longer needed for public use, or to allow certain new developments to take place. A notice of the order must appear in at least one, easily available, local newspaper and a notice must be displayed in a prominent position at either end of the path affected by the order. Members of the public may make objections to orders. Objections will usually lead to a public hearing and a decision by the Secretary of State.

Many rights of way have their origins deep in the past as cross country routes used by local inhabitants; footpaths being the routes between different dwellings or from dwellings to a church or graveyard; bridleways more usually being routes used for movement of livestock to market or elsewhere. However, because the responsibility for recording rights of way information on definitive maps was created in 1949, by which time routes in the countryside were well established for recreational use, the recreational routes too have been recorded as rights of way. Hence there are many rights of way in the mountain and upland areas which owe their existence to use by hillwalkers. There are, for example, public footpaths leading to the summits of many of the Lakeland fells.

For those particularly interested or concerned with rights of way issues, there is an extremely useful guide available to Rights of Way in England and Wales (see bibliography).

Scotland

Footpaths, bridleways and highways exist in Scotland as public rights of way. However, a lack of any legal responsibility for any authorities to record comprehensively all public rights of way information means that the vast majority of public rights of way that exist in Scotland are not recorded on any register; there are usually no maps showing public rights of way; and it is, therefore, often difficult to determine whether a public right of way exists or not. Tracks and footpaths as shown on OS maps of Scotland give no indication of the existence or not of public right of way.

For a public right of way to exist in common law the route has to have been in use by the public for a continuous period in excess of 20 years; have been used as a matter or right, not simply tolerated by the landowner; connect two public places or places to which the public habitually and legitimately resorts and follow a route more or less defined.

It is not clear from these requirements whether public rights of way may exist to mountain summits through established use by hillwalkers, but there is no legal precedent on the matter.

Local authorities do have a duty to protect public rights of way by keeping them open and free from obstruction, and they have powers to create, improve and maintain rights of way. Some local authorities are undertaking the work of preparing maps and lists of rights of way. The only indication to a member of the public that a right of way exists in Scotland is where some of the major cross country routes have been signposted by planning authorities or by the Scottish Rights of Way Society.

The public also enjoys a legal right to follow the Long Distance Routes that have been established in Scotland, sections of which are common law rights of way. The remainder of the routes have been created by footpath agreements or access agreements. These routes are signposted throughout their length.

The Scottish Rights of Way Society produces a useful guide to rights of way law in Scotland (see bibliography).

Northern Ireland

Under the Access to the Countryside (NI) Order 1983 responsibility for the inventory and protection or rights of way was placed with local authorities.

PERMISSIVE PATHS

Permissive paths are linear routes that do not have the legal standing of public rights of way and do not appear on definitive maps. The landowner has simply agreed to permit the public to use the path, but usually with the intention that it does not become a public right of way.

Permissive paths are most common on land owned by statutory or public bodies – the National Trusts, Forestry Enterprise, National Park Authorities, or Water Companies – where the body will normally decide the alignment of permissive paths as part of a management plan for a particular area of land. Permissive paths may also occur where a local authority or National Park Authority has negotiated a route with a private landowner under a management agreement. The latter may occur if an access problem exists.

In mountain areas permissive paths will often be established in order to allow walkers to cross the lower enclosed land and so provide a convenient route to the open hill country which will cause the minimum of problems or disturbance.

Permissive footpaths may appear on Ordnance Survey maps, particularly Outdoor Leisure maps (1:25,000), and there will usually be information provided on the ground.

OPEN COUNTRY ACCESS LAND

England and Wales

Legal access exists to areas of land classified as 'open country' where an access agreement has been made under the National Parks and Access to the Countryside Act 1949 and/or the Countryside Act 1968. According to the 1949 Act, the definition of open country was land consisting wholly or predominantly of mountain, moorland, heath, down, cliff or foreshore. This definition was extended by the 1968 Act to include woodland and land alongside rivers, canals and other stretches of water.

A county authority may seek an access agreement with a landowner for an area of open country, or failing an agreement may declare an access order. In effect there are very few situations where access orders have actually been employed. In return for access, the landowner may receive compensation. Necessary practical works such as stile building will be undertaken by the authority, which may also provide a warden service.

Byelaws will probably exist governing certain activities, particularly control of dogs, damage to property, lighting fires, etc, and possibly also camping. The right of access may be temporarily suspended, for example, during periods of high fire risk, or to allow game shooting. There are often signs permitting entry and giving information where roads or paths go near to, or cross, the access area boundary. A relatively small number of access agreements exist to areas of open country. The main areas are in the Peak District National Park, the Yorkshire Dales National Park, and the Forest of Bowland. Details of the areas covered by the agreements are available from county councils or the national park authorities. Access land is also shown on Ordnance Survey Outdoor Leisure maps (1:25,000).

Scotland

Access may be formally secured to 'open country' land by planning authorities in Scotland under the Countryside (Scotland) Act 1967. The powers of the local authority and the arrangements for access closely parallel those in England and Wales. Probably because of the widespread de facto access and rarity of access problems, the powers have been little used except to small areas of land under heavy recreational pressure and at the time of writing, there are few access agreements to land of interest to mountaineers. However, linear access agreements have been used to create sections of the West Highland Way.

COMMON LAND

England and Wales

Commons are a remnant from the manorial system which formed the basis of the country's social and economic system in the Middle Ages. Common land was poor quality, unenclosed, 'waste' land to which the local inhabitants - the commoners - had rights for grazing animals, gathering fuel, etc.

Much of this common land was lost during the very extensive enclosures of the 18th and 19th centuries. However, over 6,000 sq km of common land still remains, and in many parts of the country common rights, especially of grazing, are of great agricultural importance; in others the traditional rights have fallen into disuse.

In the same way as any other land, common land is owned by some person or body, who holds it subject to the rights of commoners and to special Acts relating to common land. There is no general public right of access to common land, but some of these special Acts convey rights of access to specific kinds of common.

The Law of Property Act 1925 gives a public right of access on foot, for air and exercise, to all commons situated within pre-1974 local government reorganisation boroughs and urban districts. These areas are particularly important; many of the Lake District fells are common that were within the old Lakes and Windermere Urban Districts.

The Owner of any common may execute a Deed to bring a common under this same arrangement. Again this is of particular significance. The Crown Estate Commissioners, as owners of extensive commons in North Wales including many of the Snowdonia mountains, have made such a Deed.

In either case, there are three basic prohibitions: it is an offence to drive a vehicle, to camp, or to light a fire. There may also be byelaws controlling public behaviour where access is a right.

The Dartmoor Commons Act 1985 gives a public right of access to all common land within Dartmoor National Park. There are provisions to restrict this access to limited areas for a series of reasons such as protecting archaeological sites or repairing erosion damage. Entering a restricted area is an offence under the byelaws.

There are other categories of common land to which a public right of access exists, but these are of lesser significance to mountaineering and it may also be far from easy to discover where such rights exist.

In theory, the owner of common land to which no public right of access exists may take an action for trespass. In practice, the prohibition of fencing common land prevents the owner from effectively taking any action to exclude trespassers.

Full details are found within a useful publication on commons (see bibliography).

Scotland

Common land in Scotland is now virtually unknown. Local rights of pasturage do exist but these do not include any public access rights.

LAND OWNED BY THE NATIONAL TRUSTS

England, Wales and Northern Ireland

Although, strictly speaking, not a legal right, the National Trust's policy is to allow free access on foot at all times to its open spaces, subject only to the observance of the Trust's byelaws for commonsense behaviour which prohibit activities such as shooting, lighting fires or not keeping dogs under proper control.

There is not, however, unrestricted access to enclosed farmland, where walkers should keep to public or permissive paths in order to reach the open land; to young plantations and woods; or to certain nature reserve areas, particularly in the breeding season when the Trust is keen to protect rare flora and fauna. In certain areas the Trust also needs to restrict access either to make good damage such as erosion caused by access or to prevent it occurring.

National Trust property is indicated on Ordnance Survey maps, with usually, differentiation shown between those areas of country where there is unrestricted access and those properties such as gardens or houses where access is restricted.

Scotland

The National Trust for Scotland permits unrestricted access to all its mountainous properties at all times of the year. These are Torridon, Glencoe and Dalness, Kintail and Morvich, Falls of Glomach, Grey Mare's Tail, Loch Skeen and White Combe, Ben Lawers, Goat Fell, and Ben Lomond.

Whilst the Trust has the right to make byelaws under its constitution, none have so far been adopted for any of its mountain properties because there has been no need to do so. As part of its management techniques, however, local directions may be given to encourage walkers to avoid areas where there is erosion, or where protection is desired for plant or wildlife habitats.

LAND OWNED BY FOREST ENTERPRISE

Forest Enterprise is responsible for 12,000 sq km of land in Great Britain, most of which is low grade agricultural land, much of it located in the upland areas. A surprising proportion of this land is not in commercial timber production. Areas are left unplanted for landscape reasons or if a boundary extends above the tree line. Forest Enterprise welcomes the public on foot to all its holdings provided that access does not conflict with the management or production of the land or forest. Access on foot is free of charge. They also provide visitor centres, car parks, picnic places and camping sites and facilities and opportunities for specialist activities.

Trespass

When in the hills or mountains, unless one is on land which is included in one of the categories described, or one has received the permission of the landowner, one is, legally speaking, trespassing. Trespass is commonly misunderstood, no thanks to the oft-seen signs in the countryside announcing that trespassers will be prosecuted.

It can be simply regarded as being where one has no right to be; a civil wrong against the personal right of property but not a criminal offence.

However, trespass on land in the ownership of certain organisations, eg the Ministry of Defence or British Rail, is a criminal offence. Despite a commonly held belief, there is little difference in the law of trespass between England and Wales, and Scotland.

A landowner who objects to a person's presence on his property can only seek civil remedies against that person. The landowner or representative can tell the trespasser to leave the land and indicate the direction for leaving. The trespasser must be allowed to leave as quickly as possible but should be allowed to do so freely.

In the case of a persistent trespasser, the landowner can apply to the courts for an Injunction (England and Wales) or an Interdict (Scotland) to prevent a particular person from continuing to trespass or from re-entering the property. That person would then be in contempt of court - a serious offence - if trespassing again. The courts would require to be convinced of serious expectation of continuing or re-occurring trespass for an Injunction or Interdict to be granted.

A landowner can proceed against a trespasser by bringing a civil action in the courts for damage. In England and Wales, in theory, the landowner can succeed in such an action and recover nominal damages for the 'loss' suffered due to the trespass itself. In practice, however, it would normally only be worthwhile bringing a civil action for damages if the trespasser had damaged or destroyed property. In Scotland there is no penalty for trespass itself, and so a civil action can only be brought in the case of damage to property.

The only exception to this situation exists in Scotland under the Trespass (Scotland) Act 1865. This Act makes it an offence to camp on private property or lodge in any premises without the permission of the landowner; or to camp or light a fire on or near any private road, enclosed land, or plantation without the landowner's consent, or on or near any public highway. This Act was brought in to deal with tinkers and gypsies, but is still in force and could be effective against recreational campers.

AGGRAVATED TRESPASS

There has been some apprehension about the effect of Section 62 of the Criminal Justice and Public Order Act, 1994, which has created a new offence of 'Aggravated Trespass'. This section is directed specifically at those who deliberately set out to disrupt the legitimate activities of others on private land, and assurances have been given that it will in no way affect the position of walkers and mountaineers. Nevertheless, there is justifiable concern that the balance between the private and public use of land has shifted in favour of the landowner, the less sympathetic of whom may be tempted to use the provisions of the Act, or more simply the threat of prosecution in terms of the Act, to discourage access. Anyone experiencing difficulties of this nature should report the circumstances to the British Mountaineering Council, the Mountaineering Council of Scotland or the Mountain Council of Ireland.

De Facto Access and Access Problems

Despite the theoretical legal situation, there exists to most of the mountain and hill land in the UK a situation commonly described as de facto access: that is habitual access by the public, unhindered by the landowners. Where de facto access exists it is not common practice to seek the permission of a landowner prior to going on to land, but it may assist in establishing or maintaining good relations to do so, and is perhaps a good idea where access passes close to, or the most suitable parking place is prominent and close by the owner's house.

If challenged or asked to leave at anytime whilst on private land the best course of action, especially in the long term, is to resist any temptation to argue or defy the request, to leave, and to seek another route to the chosen objective. Putting a reasoned case, if discussion is possible, will help to establish the responsible intentions of those seeking access, and any information gleaned will assist others in solving the difficulties that exist.

Any such incidents or problems over access should be reported to the British Mountaineering Council (BMC), Mountaineering Council of Scotland (MC of S) or Mountaineering Council of Ireland (MCI). These organisations represent the interests of all hillwalkers and mountaineers in seeking to ensure that freedom of access without an unnecessary restrictions exists to all mountain and hill land. They are able to pursue difficulties through direct approaches to landowners, via the landowning or farming representative bodies, or via the local authorities or government agencies with responsibility for public access and the powers, if appropriate to secure legal access rights.

It is unusual for difficulties to persist for long periods. Any that are more than local and short term will usually be reported in the specialist climbing and rambling magazines.

If in doubt about a particular access situation, and information is required in the planning of activities, the BMC, MC of S or MCI will endeavour to provide advice, as will the National Park Authorities for areas within the national parks.

Temporary or Periodic Restrictions on Access

In many situations of legal access or de facto access, temporary restrictions may exist. These may be for example, seasonal restrictions applying annually to allow shooting to take place; periodic closures for exercises on land used for military purposes; or emergency suspension of access agreements in the case of a high fire risk or for nature conservation reasons.

Additionally, there may be particularly sensitive seasons related to agricultural use of mountain land or a particular nature conservation interest, when access is not restricted but great care is needed to avoid causing any damage or disturbance.

GAME SHOOTING

Moorland country managed as grouse moor totals 4,000 sq km in England and Wales, and 12,000 sq km in Scotland. The birds breed during May and June and the shooting season extends from 12 August (the glorious 12th) until 10 December.

Research work has shown that public access to grouse moors has no harmful effect on either the grouse population or grouse bags, and public access exists as a right by access agreements to some grouse moors. De facto access exists to many areas but owners' concern of possible disturbance is one of the most common reasons for access being restricted. Shooting and walking are not simultaneously compatible and, where formal access agreements exist, the right of access to the moors is withdrawn under the terms of the agreements for a number of days each year during the grouse shooting season for the shoots to take place. Anyone entering the access land whilst the agreements are suspended is no longer exercising a legal right but committing a trespass.

The moorland access land in the Peak District is divided into more than a dozen separate areas. Access is withdrawn to each area for not more than 12 days per year, some for as few as one or two days. In the Yorkshire Dales the access may be withdrawn for a maximum of 30 days. These restrictions occur primarily during August, September and into October, but never on Sundays. If days are lost due to high fire hazard early in the season, shoots may extend into October and November.

During shoots in the national parks, wardens may be present, particularly at access points, to warn people of the danger and to offer advice on other areas where access is not restricted.

Public rights of way across access land are not affected by these restrictions.

DEER STALKING

Many of the estates in the Scottish Highlands are managed as deer forests, Sportsmen, some visiting specially from abroad, are willing to pay large sums to stalk Red Deer, and consequently the estates derive a substantial income during the stalking season, and thus provide important employment.

The seasons for killing deer are laid down by law and are 1 July - 20 October for stags and 21 October - 15 February for hinds. It is the stags that provide the commercial stalking which usually commences in mid-August when the stags are in prime condition and antler growth is complete. Hinds are shot to control numbers, although these are nevertheless widely regarded as exceeding the capacity of the land to support them, and for venison production which provides the bulk of estate revenue. Public access to the estate land and stalking are not simultaneously compatible. There is an obvious danger to walkers whilst shooting is taking place, and there is the problem that the deer are disturbed by not only the sight, but also the scent, of humans.

During the stalking season hillwalkers are well advised to find out when and where stalking is taking place and so avoid unnecessary confrontation. Details about individual estates, including contact telephone numbers, are given in the joint publication of the Mountaineering Council of Scotland and the Scottish Landowners Federation, 'Heading for the Scottish Hills'. Day to day information is sometimes posted at the main access points and sympathetic owners will often recommend particular routes which will allow both activities to take place in harmony.

No stalking for sport takes place on the estates owned by the National Trust for Scotland. The Trust's own staff do kill both stags and hinds to control populations. However, this is done without the need to restrict access to these estates at any time of year.

WOODLAND DEER

The control of populations of woodland deer is essential to ensure that forest damage is minimised. Stalking or culling is carried out by professional stalkers or rangers, day permit holders accompanied by rangers, or by others authorised by the owner or manager of the forest.

Most control is carried out at dawn and dusk throughout the summer months and in daylight throughout the winter. Enclosed woodland deer are exempt from close seasons.

To avoid accidents to the public, it may be wise for those wishing to camp or walk through forests to use recognised campsites if they are available and to check with the local forest office or forest manager if they intend to use other than normal access routes.

MILITARY TRAINING AREAS

There are several Ministry of Defence military training areas in the moorland and upland areas, including some important and popular hillwalking country. The Dartmoor Ranges include much of northern Dartmoor and Warcop Range encompasses Mickle Fell, close to the Pennine Way above Upper Teesdale.

Most of the training areas are used as firing ranges, some are live ranges, others are dry (live ammunition is not used). There is access to many ranges, both dry and live, but mostly dry, on days when training is not taking place, but on some live ranges there is little or no access allowed. In most cases when access does exist, the ranges will be open more often than they are closed; usually at weekends, public holidays and during the high holiday season. Range areas are marked on OS maps 1:25,000 and 1:50,000, as 'Danger Area'. Special maps showing the exact boundaries and other details of those ranges where public access is most sought after are produced by the Ministry of Defence.

There are standard warning notices and procedures for providing on-the-ground information to prevent access when firing is taking place; red flags during the day, red lights at night. Other public information may be available in the form of advance notice of the dates and times when particular ranges are open. The emphasis on this depends upon the popularity of the area; hence for the Dartmoor Ranges the information is particularly comprehensive - firing times are advertised in the local press and displayed in local police stations, post offices and public houses; a map is available showing the different firing areas and there is a telephone information answering service. For other ranges the information available may not be so comprehensive; if not in the locality, it may simply be best to contact the relevant Range Liaison Officer.

There are byelaws for most of the firing ranges, which make it an offence to enter the range area during periods of closure.

FIRE RISK

Two vegetation types that are particularly susceptible to serious, long-term damage by uncontrolled fire are moorland and woodland.

There is a very obvious need for great care not to cause any risk of fire when walking in moorland areas. However, where rights of access exist to moorland through access agreements there are formal procedures for suspension of the agreements when the risk of fire reaches a critical level.

The suspensions result from consultations between farming, landowning and local authority interests and operate for one week periods. Notices usually appear in the press and signs are placed on all access points to the access land.

Public rights of way across access land are not affected by the access suspensions.

ANIMAL DISEASE

There is one, rarely occurring animal disease, 'Foot and Mouth Disease', which can result in restrictions on public access to the countryside. In order to prevent the spread of infection the Ministry of Agriculture has power under the Animal Health Act 1981 to close and restrict access to any area of land regardless of whether or not legal rights of access normally exist. Entry to a restricted area becomes an offence.

Since an epidemic in 1967-68 that resulted in widespread access restrictions, precautionary standards have improved significantly and only one outbreak has occurred, in 1981.

A Minimum Impact Approach

The mountains are a sensitive environment, under pressure from a whole host of activities and interests. Hillwalking and mountaineering contribute to that pressure and can themselves be damaging to the physical environment, can cause disruption to the interests of those who own and manage the land, and can mar the enjoyment of those who follow, expecting an unspoiled environment. The implications of continuing increases in the levels of participation in recreation are serious. There is a very real danger that the more popular areas in particular will become so degraded that either the potential for enjoyment will be severely reduced, or owners or authorities will seek to impose controls to reduce the impacts. If such situations are to be avoided and freedoms maintained, there is a need for a philosophy of responsibility and respect for the environment - a 'minimum impact' philosophy.

The following notes offer some advice on ways to minimise impacts associated with mountaineering without requiring any major limitation or curtailment of activity.

TRAVELLING TO THE HILLS

Mountaineers frequently approach the hills by private transport and there is a temptation to drive as close as possible to the chosen objective. However, car parking space and especially mini-bus parking space is not always conveniently available. Farmyards, lanes and gateways may not appear to be but are often in use, and bulky farm machinery needs considerable space for manoeuvring. For a farmer an inconsiderately parked vehicle can cause great inconvenience and annoyance.

- Vehicles should not be driven away from public roads on to bridleways, private roads or open country. (It is an offence to drive more than 15 yards from a highway without the landowner's permission.)
- Park with forethought and consideration. Allow sufficient room for farm vehicles to use gates and pass along narrow lanes. Enquire locally if in doubt.

ON THE HILLS

Paths and Erosion

The most popular paths are suffering serious erosion. Heavy soled boots easily trample and break up the surface vegetation which dies to reveal a generally unstable soil. Heavy rainfall on steep slopes washes the material away and gullying results. The eroded section becomes unpleasant for walking and small detours result in path widening. Eroded sections on some popular hill paths have measured as much as 50 metres in width.

A lot of money is being spent in the more popular areas on repairing eroded paths. This can be expensive and in some areas may not be practical if insufficient funding is available to deal with the problem sympathetically. Erosion on peat is particularly difficult to repair in keeping with the natural character of the area.

- Tread carefully, if possible walking on boulders or stony ground.
- Resist the temptation to cut corners on zig-zag descents.
- Avoid running screes.
- Co-operate with diversions etc where repair work is being carried out.
- If sections of paths have been rebuilt or repaired use them rather than the ground to the side.

Walls and Fences; Gates and Stiles

Dry stone walls and fences are extremely important boundaries for containing stock, and walls particularly are an important characteristic feature of the upland landscape. They can be easily damaged by climbing over and are extremely time-consuming and expensive to repair.

- Use gates or stiles even if it entails a short diversion. Close and fasten all gates unless it is obvious they have been left open by the farmer.

- If it is absolutely necessary to climb a wall, do so carefully, and replace any dislodged stones or in the case of fences cross at larger fence posts where the strain on fencing wire should be at a minimum.

- Keep to footpaths across enclosed land, looking for gates, stiles or waymarking.

Litter

The problem of litter is not unique to the hills, but there are many examples of severe litter problems that can only be attributed to hillwalkers or climbers. Vast quantities have been removed in 'clean-ups' of the worst spots. Litter looks unpleasant and it can be harmful to stock. It also attracts scavenging animals and birds such as, sea gulls and crows which prey on and displace the natural species of the area.

- Plan to minimise rubbish, particularly on overnight trips. Repackage food to keep 'shop' packaging to the minimum. - Don't carry breakable containers.

- Carry all litter down the hill to a proper waste bin; it is useful to carry a plastic bag for this.

- Don't bury it or throw it behind rocks - animals will dig it up.

- Don't bury it in snow - it will reappear in spring.

FIRES

Accidentally started fires can cause extensive, expensive and long-term damage to areas of moorland or woodland. Concern over fire is a significant reason for some landowners to deny public access to areas of open country. It can take between 10 and 20 years for a burned heather moorland area to recover and more than 30 years for the full establishment of the original level of growth. Common causes of fires are (a) discarded cigarette ends and matches; (b) camp fires and stoves; (c) bottles and broken glass.

- Take special care not to risk staring a fire, particularly during dry periods.

- At these times keep a special look out for anything that could start a fire.

CAIRNS

The proliferation of cairns on many paths is an unsightly urbanisation of the hills; as a form of signposting they diminish the wilderness quality. Those venturing into the hills should aspire to self-reliance, navigating when necessary by map and compass. The existence of cairns can give a false sense of security. Do not build or enlarge them.

PLANTS AND ANIMALS

Wild animals and birds can be disturbed by human presence. During the nesting season birds may desert a nest if disturbed, or may be frightened away for so long that the eggs or chicks may be predated or chill and die. Dogs can also cause severe disturbance by scenting out ground nesting or sitting birds. Our uplands hold populations of rare and uncommon bird species which depend upon open, undisturbed heather moors and blanket bogs. All birds are protected by law, but it is an offence even to disturb these rare species at or near their nest sites. So if you see any bird behaving in an agitated fashion close to you, or if you accidentally come upon a nest, then move away quickly and quietly until the bird returns, or you are out of sight.

The British mountains are also the last refuge for many plant species which cannot grow in other parts of the country for a variety of reasons and so special care should be taken not to damage or uproot any wild plant in the hills. Again, all wild plants are protected by law and it is illegal for anyone to uproot them or even to pick a part of these species without the permission of the landowner.

Details of these animal and plant species and the protection given to them can be found in the Wildlife and Countryside Act 1981 (amended 1985), or from the conservation organisations listed in this book.

- Avoid hanging round close to birds nests; move to another location if you are causing a disturbance.
- Do not pick or uproot plants. If a record is required take a photograph. Even mosses and lichens can be uncommon and important.

Even though they are not wild animals, stock, particularly sheep, can be worried by dogs not kept under control. Sheep are especially at risk during the lambing season and nothing should be done to disturb or frighten ewes in lamb.

STAYING OVERNIGHT IN THE HILLS

Camping, bivouacking or staying in a primitive shelter can be one of the most rewarding experiences to be had from going into the hills. However the use of additional equipment for shelter and cooking can result, unless great care is taken, in far greater impacts than single day activities.

Camping

Without attention to detail an idyllic campsite in the hills can easily degenerate into an unsightly and unhygenic mess.

- To avoid vegetation damage, tents should not remain pitched on the same spot for more than 2 or 3 days. At pre-exisiting sites try to avoid pitch marks to allow vegetation recovery.
- Don't dig drainage ditches around tents. If the site is too wet, look for somewhere else.
- Avoid using boulders to hold down pegs or flysheets as moving them destroys the microhabitat underneath.

Bivouacs

- If it is absolutely necessary to build a shelter wall, take it down in the morning and return rocks to their original positions.

Bothies

These rudimentary shelters provide excellent accommodation in remote areas Most are not regularly maintained and it is the responsibility of visitors to leave a bothy as they would wish to find it.

- Leave the bothy clean, and secure doors to keep out sheep and deer.
- Avoid going to bothies with a party large enough to fill it; others may want to use it also.

Fires

Fires can be very enjoyable, but they can also cause damage to the fire site and the ecology of the area. There is a very real danger of fire spreading to heath, scrub and woodland so the best rule is not to light fires except in areas designated for the purpose.

Pollution

A certain amount of personal and equipment washing is necessary, so care should be taken to minimise water pollution.

- All washing should be done well away from any source of drinking water and in a position where foul water can be drained into an absorbent soil. It should not be returned straight into the water source.

- Toilet waste should, if possible be buried in a hole at least 15cm (6 in) deep within the top soil layer, well away from any water source, and the soil and turf replaced and trodden down. If burying is not possible it is important to be discreet well away from paths and other popular gathering areas. Make sure that toilet paper is not left to blow about. Bury or burn it.

Obtaining Information and Advice

There exists, at times, a confusingly large number of bodies and organisations both governmental and voluntary, responsible for or concerned with the management of mountain land, the conservation of its natural beauty or scientific value, and its use for recreation. Some have very useful information services and are able to provide both information and advice on issues directly related to mountaineering activities. For example, the National Park Authorities are a good source of access information and will give guidance on environmentally sensitive areas or seasons, and ways to avoid causing damage or disturbance. In contrast, looking to the voluntary sector, mountaineering organisations will always be the best source for the users' view of access to a particular area.

For those wishing to look at access and conservation issues in greater depth, there is a series of voluntary organisations with a primary concern for the environmental and recreational issues of the upland areas. These vary from those with a national view point to those with a regional interest and some are quite definitely campaigning pressure groups. Most of the voluntary organisations produce magazines, newsletters or other material examining the issues of the moment, and almost without exception, they welcome interest in the relevant issues. Indeed, for those organisations with the specific aims of exerting influence on access and conservation issues in the mountain areas, the support of mountaineers is a crucial factor in the success of their work.

Although some of the organisations have more than one main concern, making categorisation difficult, for the sake of simplicity they can be grouped as follows.

THE MOUNTAINEERING ORGANISATIONS

The interests of hillwalkers, rock climbers and mountaineers are represented in the British Isles by three main organisations, with responsibilities divided on a geographical basis. The British Mountaineering Council (BMC) covers England and Wales; the Mountaineering Council of Scotland covers Scotland; and the Mountaineering Council of Ireland covers both Northern Ireland and Eire). All three bodies have closely parallel objectives the most important of which are securing and maintaining unrestricted access to mountain land, and promoting the conservation of the unspoiled qualities of the mountains and hills. They are often closely involved in access negotiations and are therefore well placed to provide advice from the mountaineers' viewpoint on the practical access situation in any given area. To function efficiently the bodies need briefing on any developments relating to access and are particularly keen to be told of any problems encountered.

The Ramblers' Association has a much broader brief in geographical terms, being concerned about access and conservation issues affecting all the British countryside. The Association is particularly interested in rights of way issues, and has a wealth of information and experience. The RA has campaigned actively in recent years for the establishment of a legal right of access to all unenclosed hill country.

NATIONAL PARK AUTHORITIES

The primary source of information and advice for areas within National Park boundaries in England and Wales is the National Park Authorities. The authorities, in general, run a three-tiered service for the public. This operates, firstly, in response to written or telephone inquiries; secondly, at information centres within the Park; and thirdly, via the National Park wardens who may be encountered out and about in the Park. Most of the authorities have a Youth and Schools liaison officer whose task is to try and ensure that visits of all types by school and youth groups are enjoyable and beneficial for those taking part and are not in conflict with other National Park purposes. The Officer can provide information on access, land ownership, footpaths, transport, accommodation and local services; environmentally sensitive areas; and links with conservation projects taking place within the Park that are often in need of support from volunteer workforces.

Published material ranges from a full information pack in some Parks to a basic advice sheet in others, where the officers prefer to deal with specific individual inquiries. Teaching packs or slide packs may be on sale or loan and some authorities have a reference or study room available.

LOCAL AUTHORITIES

Outside the national parks in England, Wales and Northern Ireland the County and District Councils, and in Scotland, the Regional and District Councils, have statutory responsibilities for access and conservation in the countryside. Few provide specific information services, but nevertheless inquiries may be made or advice sought. Most countryside matters are dealt with by the planning department which will usually have a Countryside Officer concerned with countryside management and informal recreation, and a Recreation Officer concerned with formal recreation and sporting activities. Rights of Way matters are the responsibility of the Highways Department, which may have a Footpaths Officer.

NATIONAL CONSERVATION ORGANISATIONS

There are several organisations concerned with land use, planning and conservation issues on a national basis. The Council for the Protection of Rural England (CPRE), the Council for the Protection of Rural Wales (CPRW), the Association for the Protection of Rural Scotland (APRS) and the Ulster Association for the Preservation of the Countryside express views on issues such as agriculture, forestry, motorway developments, new reservoirs or power stations, attempting to influence views at a national level but also through an involvement with significant local proposals.

The Council for National Parks (CNP) fulfils a similar role but is concerned soley with issues within the boundaries of the 10 national parks of England and Wales. It fulfils an essential watchdog role, ensuring that the purposes for which national parks were designated, conservation and recreation, are upheld against the almost constant threats of commercial exploitation and inappropriate development. The Scottish Council for National Parks has recently been reformed to promote the establishment of National Parks in Scotland. The Scottish Wild Land Group is concerned with the protection of wild land and wilderness areas in Scotland. Various LINK organisations act as umbrella bodies for the shared concerns of conservation and recreation organisations in each separate country.

LOCAL CONSERVATION ORGANISATIONS IN MOUNTAIN AREAS

There are local conservation organisations in many areas of the country and most of the upland areas are the concern of one group or another. Three bodies are particularly worthy of mention here, since their aims are quite specific to the conservation of premier mountain areas.

The Friends of the Lake District (FLD) represents the CPRE in Cumbria and concentrates effort on ensuring that the purposes of the national park designation are upheld in the Lake District. As a watchdog organisation the FLD monitors developments and proposals and has played a leading role in numerous public enquiries. The Snowdonia National Park Society fulfils a similar role in Snowdonia.

The Save the Cairngorms Campaign is a coalition of 15 voluntary conservation and outdoor recreation groups, including the Mountaineering Council of Scotland, North East Mountain Trust and BMC, which was founded in 1988 to present the case for better management of the whole Cairngorms area, from low ground to high tops.

6

Security on Steep Ground

There are very few mountains in the British Isles which can not be walked up, so that almost every peak is accessible to any reasonably competent hillwalker. Indeed, it is commonplace today to meet a dozen or more people in a day on some of the most remote summits. This accessibility creates a problem in that there is no obvious demarcation between what might be called walking terrain and the domain of the mountaineer such as exists in the Alps for example. It is quite common for walkers to find themselves in situations which call for the exercise of a full range of mountaineering skills. The vagaries of our weather complicate matters further by transforming what might be classed as a straight forward hillwalk into a serious mountaineering route. Those who aspire to lead others into these mountains need be aware of this uncertain threshold so that with experience they can judge what is an appropriate undertaking and what is not. Fortunately, the variety of terrain is such that no matter how severe the conditions it is always possible to find a route somewhere, perhaps at a lower level or in the forest, which can be accomplished in safety.

This variety of terrain does however mean that one cannot set off in any direction from a summit and be sure of a straightforward descent. The majority of British hills have steep slopes made up of screes, rocky buttresses, vegetated slopes, gullies, ridges and unbroken cliffs. Skill and experience are needed to lead a group in safety through such terrain and the judgement to decide what can safely be tackled and what can not.

The most difficult of these skills to acquire is good judgement. An over enthusiastic party, a longed for summit, a fellow walker in distress can all colour one's judgement and in turn lead the group into a more serious situation. Mountain leaders must accept that on different days, with different groups, the same piece of ground can provide an enjoyable challenge or an impenetrable barrier. If such a barrier is encountered in descent then difficult decisions will have to be made about alternative routes which may be both lengthy and exhausting, and may be made more difficult by darkness. Without good route finding skills, personal technique, confidence, the ability to manage the group and a thorough knowledge of the applications and limitations of the rope, mistakes can be made.

Some of these skills have to be acquired on the mountains themselves, for example, route finding or group management. Other aspects such as rope handling and tying knots may appear more daunting but can actually be practised on the staircase at home.

A length of rope in a leader's rucksack is as essential as a first aid kit. It may never see the light of day but it is there to be used in an emergency situation. And just as the first aid kit is not the exclusive preserve of the medical expert so the rope is not exclusive to the rock climber. There are many ways to connect leaders, people and mountain sides with a rope and in this chapter only the simplest and most easily remembered methods are shown. These have been chosen because they build a large margin for error into the security system. Aspiring leaders need to understand the underlying principles in order to judge for themselves whether or not a particular rope management system is adequate. Rock climbers may have many advantages over walkers in gaining these skills but they are inclined at times to dismiss techniques which require the minimum of specialised equipment. There will be mountain leaders who climb and mountain leaders who do not and each must use the skills and equipment they have available to achieve the same objective – high levels of security and the minimising of risk.

Personal Skills

Before taking responsibility for other people, potential leaders must first be able to look after themselves; they need to be at ease on steep ground and capable of selecting a suitable line on which they can stop at any time to reassure or direct the rest of the party. The specific skills required are those of balance, pace, use of boots and where necessary hands and familiarity with all types of terrain including steep grass, scree, boulders, shattered and solid rock.

Balance

There are major benefits to be derived from maintaining an upright posture on steep ground and avoiding excessive reliance on the hands and arms. Anyone capable of keeping their balance on rough ground will make sure that their centre of gravity is over their feet. This is particularly important on steep descents when an excess of caution can cause the walker to lean into the hill, thereby greatly increasing the likelihood of a slip.

Pace

Most walkers find there is a limit to the angle of slope which they can comfortably walk up or down. Beyond this the obvious solution is to zig zag taking an apparently meandering line on the hillside. Not only does this allow a moderate angle of ascent or descent to be maintained it also makes it easier to edge with the side of the boot. When walking on more moderate slopes, the key to minimising effort is to maintain an even pace that the party can sustain; too many halts break the rhythm and allow the muscles to cool and stiffen up. It is best to adopt a slow but steady pace which is suited to the weakest member of the party. Encourage correct and regular breathing.

Boots

To maintain footing on a hillside we use friction and grip. Friction relies on the composition of the boot sole, and the roughness of the surface underneath the sole. Good grip is achieved when the boot and the ground lock together either because of the shape of the sole pattern or, on steeper ground through the edge of the boot and the angle at which it is applied by the walker.

In selecting a suitable pair of boots there are a number of criteria that have to be considered. Beside comfort, cost and weatherproofness the boot needs to be sufficiently flexible to enable the sole of the boot to mould to the ground and yet stiff enough to use just the edges. Training shoe type boots would be excellent when trying to gain maximum friction from the sole but not so good when trying to edge and get a good grip. Conversely, rigid boots will edge on small holds but will fail to mould to the shape of the ground for improved friction. The usual compromise is a boot with good ankle support stiffened across the sole which should have square cut edges and be made of a material which provides good friction with the rock.

When selecting suitable footwear the effect on the fragile mountain environment should also be borne in mind. The BMC's booklet on conservation 'Tread Lightly' suggests that mountain walkers should "wear the lightest boots suitable for the terrain and tread carefully, especially in descent". A word of caution here. Boots with bevelled or inclined heels have become fashionable. While they may be comfortable and perfectly suitable for gentle terrain the heels do not provide the degree of bite which is required when descending steep or wet grassy slopes.

Vegetated Slopes

Steep vegetated slopes can cause problems especially in descent and particularly when they are wet. Great care should be exercised in crossing patchy vegetated rock when it may not be clear whether the turf has a firm attachment or whether it is simply resting on slabby rock below. With reasonably firm soled boots good progress can be made up or down steep grass slopes using the side edges of the boots and zig-zagging going up and digging the heels in coming straight down. A slip on grass may not be immediately painful but there can be serious consequences if the slope leads down to the top of a cliff or gorge.

Scree

Scree slopes can be a blessing or a curse depending on whether they are to be ascended or descended. In descent they can, on occasion, provide an escalator smooth ride where every step is gently cushioned and another metre descended. Unfortunately, the stones which comprise a scree slope are not always sufficiently uniform in size and many a twisted ankle and worse has resulted from an over enthusiastic descent.

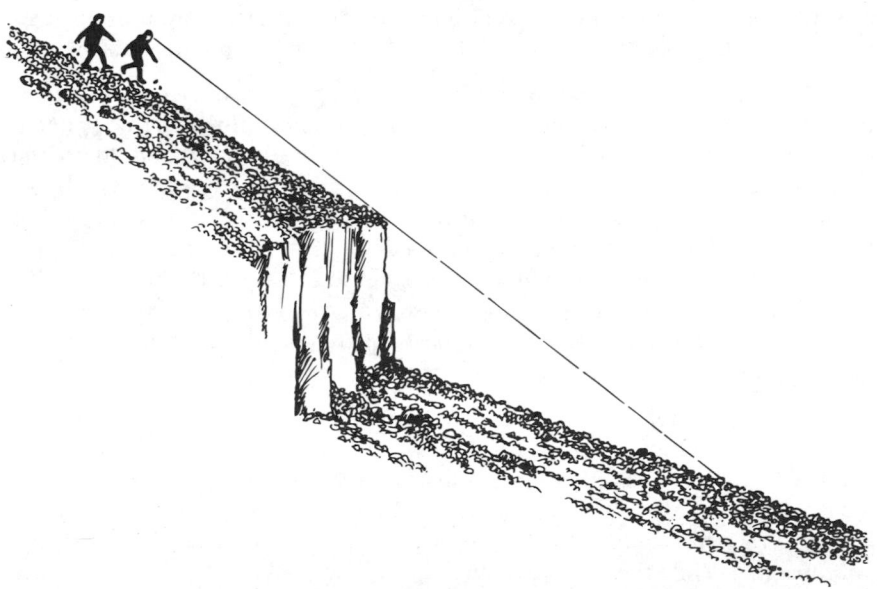

Fig. 51   *Beware! The cliff separating the scree slopes is not visible from above.*

The depth of screes vary and sometimes only a thin skin of loose rock covers the bedrock. If you hit one of these hard patches at speed it can cause a nasty fall. Be very cautious descending a scree slope in poor visibility or when you cannot see its entire length. A cliff in the middle of the slope may be quite indistinguishable from above until the very last moment, by which time it may well be too late to do anything about it. (Fig. 51)

On confined slopes the best approach is either to stay very close together so that the head of the person in front is above the feet of the person behind, or to descend one at a time and regroup somewhere safe. On wide slopes it may be possible to descend side by side or in a series of large zig zags but care must be taken to ensure that no one in the party finds themselves directly below anyone else and therefore in the line of fire. If you dislodge a stone that is likely to hit someone shout, "below!", at the top of your voice to warn them to get out of the way.

In ascent all the attractions of scree fade and it is easy to see where the phrase, "one step forward, two steps back" originated from. If it must be ascended then look for sections which are vegetated as this generally means they are more stable. In a confined gully the side walls will slow the movement of the scree to some extent just as the banks or a river will slow the current. When walking up scree bear in mind that the feet should be placed horizontally and each step made off the whole foot. Springing from the toe is likely to cause the scree to collapse and this can be very exhausting.

Boulder Fields

Some maps record boulder fields but most do not. Boulders may vary enormously in size and shape and may provide an easy staircase or a series of loose insurmountable obstacles depending on the nature of the rocks and how well lodged they are. Boulder fields are best avoided in descent and particularly at the end of a long day when concentration and agility are on the wane and especially if the party are carrying heavy rucksacks or in strong gusting winds.

Rock

When walking across rock consideration needs to be given to a number of factors such as its stability, the type and structure of the rock and the degree of friction it provides and the amount of vegetation, particularly lichen, algae and moss. On easy angled slopes a walker may encounter rock which has shattered through weathering. On steeper ground much of this loose material would fall to the screes below whereas on easier slopes the rock debris is more likely to accumulate. When scrambling across such ground care needs to be taken not to dislodge loose rock onto those below.

Scrambling is an excellent way of getting to know the strengths and weaknesses of individual members of a party. It is an activity that will quickly reveal who is sure footed and who is not, who is bold and who is apprehensive on rocky ground and demonstrate that one person's scramble may be another person's Everest.

Loose Rock

Handling loose rock requires a combination of care, balance and alertness. Injuries resulting from rock fall are common and the larger the party, the greater the risk. Although the leader can arrange things so as to minimise the danger to the party, it can not be eliminated entirely. A rock does not have to be very big, or fall very far, to do a great deal of damage. Each member of the party must be responsible for exercising the greatest care in handling loose rock. Hand and footholds should be tested gently. A suspect hold must be used in a way that tends to bed it more firmly into place with downward pressure. Never pull outwards on a loose hold. Climb placing the feet precisely and if stones are dislodged give a warning shout of "below!", so that those in the line of fire can take avoiding action or get their rucksacks over their heads. If the rope is being used, be particularly careful that it does not dislodge stones lying on ledges. One of the worst places for this is often on the top of a rock outcrop topped by scree.

Wet Rock

Provided the rock is clean, the fact that it is wet should not make very much difference. Rock made greasy by lichen or other vegetation is a different matter and care must be exercised, particularly on slabs, or when using sloping holds. Certain types of rocks, such as mica-schist, can become extremely treacherous when wet and special care is required.

Wind

A strong wind can upset balance and confidence on steep ground. The force exerted by the wind on a person walking is roughly proportional to the square of its velocity, so that a regular increase in wind speed results in a relatively much greater increase in the force which it exerts on your body. An

80km/hour (50 mph) gale will exert a force of approximately 25kg (55lbs), certainly enough to knock you off your feet if it comes in a gust; and remember that winds in excess of 200km/hour (180 mph) have been recorded! A steady or gusting wind that has an average speed of 30-40 miles per hour constitutes a danger in that it saps energy and heat and makes the movement of groups slow and clumsy.

Clearly, in such conditions it is essential to get off the tops and other exposed areas. It may even be necessary to rope the party together to prevent people literally being blown away. In the case of an extreme gust everyone should stop and crouch down. At all costs one should plan a safe route of descent downwind. To fight into the wind, or have to descend exposed steep ground with a strong gusting wind crossing the line of travel invites an accident. It is in contexts such as this that planning in the knowledge provided by a weather forecast is most important.

Route Finding

Route finding on steep group should not be confused with navigation. It is a continuous process which involves a whole range of skills and observations of which navigation is but one. It starts before you set foot on the hill and it only finishes when you are safely back at base. A careful study of the map before you set out will enable you to spot those places where you are likely to meet steep ground. Just how steep will be indicated by the closeness of the contour lines (page 14), while the more substantial cliffs and outcrops should be marked with the appropriate symbol. Quite often an understanding of the local geology can provide useful clues as to what to expect in a particular area. For example, in Torridon in Wester Ross, if you were to rely on the evidence of the map alone you would be justified in believing that a 30 degree slope could safely be descended. However, the knowledge that Torridonian Sandstone occurs in massive horizontal sheets and outcrops in a succession of vertical walls would make you cautious in taking a direct line of descent.

Other clues may be gleaned from guide books but there is no substitute for first hand experience and leaders are well advised to make a familiarisation visit to any mountain area prior to visiting it with a group.

Clearly, visualising the ground from studying the map has its limitations. There is much information of relevance to the hill walker which the map may or may not show: boulder fields, peat bogs, tussock grass and many other impediments to progress. The crude plan hatched in the comfort of home must be adjusted when confronted by the real thing. On the approach you should constantly be looking ahead from whatever viewpoints are available, working out your overall route plan as well as how to negotiate the obstacle immediately in front. Every viewpoint has its limitations: from the other side of the valley many hillsides look impossibly steep – on the other hand you do see everything in its correct relative position; from below ledges and terraces may be invisible while foreshortening distorts the scale of the upper slopes; from above convex slopes obscure what is below and terraces become disproportionately obvious; from the side the true angle of the slope is revealed but not the detailed line to follow. Nevertheless, each of these viewpoints is a piece of a jigsaw puzzle which when fitted together gives an impression of the terrain and a better indication of the most appropriate way up or down.

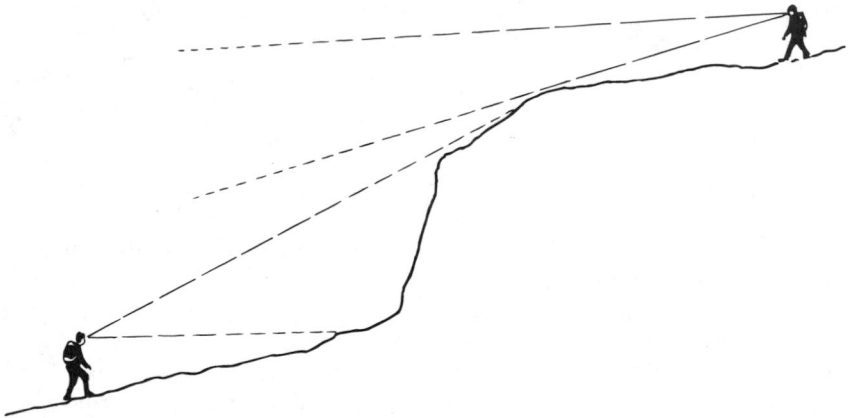

Fig. 52 *Visibility for route finding. Notice how the steep section is visible on the way up, but not on the way down.*

There may be specific marker features which can be identified, such as a peculiarly shaped or coloured rock, a tree, a band of quartz etc which will help to confirm progress. From time to time you should look back down the way you have come. Things can look very different from this perspective and after all, this is what you will see on the return journey.

DESCENT

The ability to find a good safe route of descent down a rocky hillside is a valuable skill that only comes with experience. It can be a wearisome business, retracing your steps to find the right line, so gain a lot of experience in different sorts of terrain. Gullies should normally be avoided, unless they are known to be safe. They tend to consist of a series of vertical steps, often with huge boulders wedged between steep side walls forming overhanging pitches. They also funnel stone fall. Furthermore, on a rock face, they frequently follow lines of weakness where the rock is perhaps softer or more broken and this given rise to an accumulation of debris which can be particularly hazardous to a large party.

Loose rock is probably the greatest hazard on any descent on steep rocky ground and the larger the party, the greater the risk. Do not let the party get strung out and brief everyone on the dangers of standing about in the line of stonefall from those higher up. An orderly descent with everybody adequately conscious of the possible hazards is the best strategy for reducing the risk.

As far as technique is concerned it is best to face outwards as long as possible, using downward pressure holds with the heel of the palms. Keep the upper body bent forward, partly to see where you are going to put your feet and partly to ensure that your weight is applied vertically downwards on to

Fig. 53 *Climbing down. As a general rule face outwards on easy terrain, sideways on intermediate and inwards on steep or difficult rock.*

them. On steeper ground it will first be necessary to turn sideways, using the inside hand, leaning out occasionally to get a better view of the next moves. On the steepest rock it is necessary to face the rock and go down as you would come up. Confident foot placement and balance is the key to mastering this skill. When you are climbing up it is easy to see the holds ahead of you. Climbing down, the holds are often out of sight below the feet. This makes it particularly difficult to make the linked series of moves which one does almost without thinking on the way up.

Why Carry a Rope?

It is worth remembering that there are many situations, apart from graded rock climbs, when the rope is at least desirable and sometimes essential, eg to safeguard the party up or down some unforeseen difficulty or to provide a safety rope in an exposed situation. Leaders should be aware of the technical difficulties as they appear to the novice and be sympathetic towards their mental condition. Psychological or physical succour brought about by the timely and effective use of the rope can mean the difference between an enjoyable day or one filled with avoidable anxiety.

The decision to put the rope on and belay each individual member of a party on a section of rock is not always an easy one, especially if there are other pressing factors to consider, such as approaching darkness. It requires judgement and experience. There are no hard and fast rules about when to rope-up. This is a decision which is influenced by a number of interrelated factors. These are:- Exposure - would a slip result in injury?; Difficulty - is the terrain difficult to a degree that makes a slip a possibility?; Ability - how do individual members of the party react to exposure and how do they perform on steep ground?; Security - can the situation be properly safeguarded by the use of the rope?; The time factor - speed is often a safety factor in itself. Is the saving of time more important under the circumstances than the additional security which can be provided by roping up?. If, having weighed these factors, you decide to rope-up, you must see to it that the rope is used as effectively and efficiently as possible. Roping up in itself is no guarantee of safety.

Sound belaying is the only key to safe practice. This depends on the selection of a safe and suitable anchor for the rope and on a thorough appreciation both in theory and practice of the technique of belaying.

Among rock climbers and mountaineers it is almost universally accepted practice to wear a helmet. It is not expected that all mountain walkers will wear them but there are likely to be occasions during training when it would be sensible to do so.

THE ROPE

The purpose of the rope is to provide a measure of security to those who use it, whether they be climbers or hill walkers. In the case of climbers the rope is deployed continuously, its primary function being to hold a fall, should one occur, although it may also be used to provide direct support, as in abseiling, or when a tight rope is called for. More often than not the mountain walker's rope never sees the light of day. It remains in the leader's pack only to be produced on those rare occasions when the situation demands additional security, or in an emergency which may be circumvented by the timely introduction of the rope.

Carrying the Rope

The most convenient way of transporting the rope is in a small bag. The bottom of the rope is attached to the bag and the rope then "poured" in and the other end tied off at the top. Alternatively, an adjustable waist loop can be tied in the end, ready to be brought into use at a moments notice. The stuff-sac is a nondescript bag in the rucksack yet, if necessary it can be deployed very quickly.

The traditional method is to coil the rope as illustrated in Fig 54 and to carry it over the shoulder. However, it does tend to kink the rope.

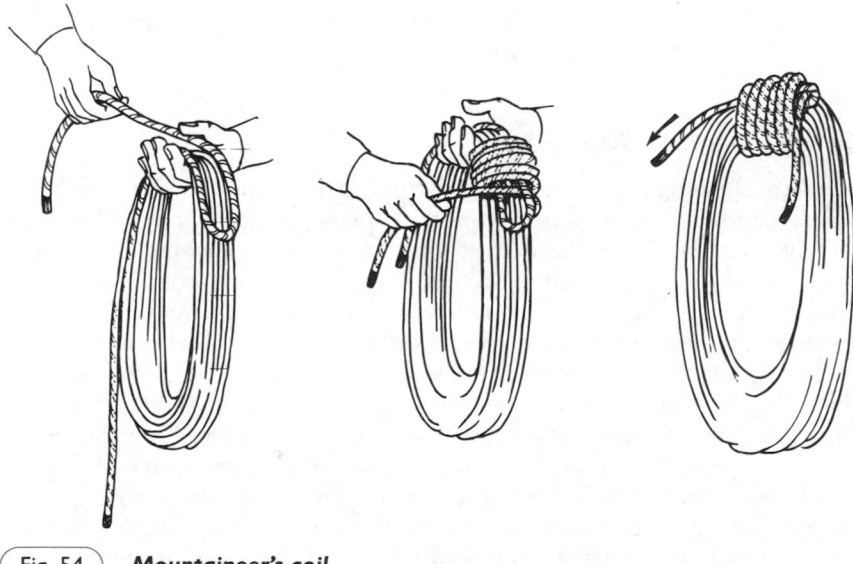

Fig. 54   *Mountaineer's coil.*

An alternative method is to flake the rope as show in Fig 55. The rope is "flaked" on either side of the holding hand until about 4m of rope remains. This is wrapped several times round the whole bundle of rope and a loop pushed through the space below the holding hand. This loop is then folded back over the top of the coils and the end pulled tight. This method avoids kinking the rope. It also enables the rope to be brought immediately into use without handing. If the rope is coiled doubled the two free ends can be used to secure the rope to the back, provided a rucksack is not being worn.

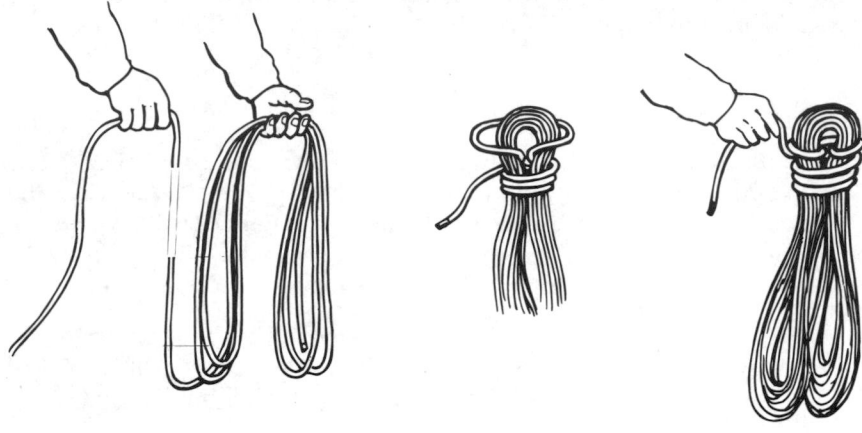

Fig. 55 *Butterfly coil - handy for carrying a large volume of rope which is usually coiled doubled.*

Construction and Dimensions

Modern climbing ropes are of kernmantel construction. This consists of several bundles of nylon fibres enclosed in a woven outer mantle. The design and manufacture of ropes has come a long way since the days of Manilla hemp but the modern rope is still a compromise between sometimes conflicting requirements and so it is important to understand its limitations. One of the most important characteristics is that it should be sufficiently elastic to absorb the energy of the impact of a fall without imposing an unacceptable strain on the falling body or, for that matter, on the person belaying. Clearly the rope must also be sufficiently strong to withstand the very considerable forces which are generated in a leader fall. This means that the rope must be of a minimum weight or thickness, all of which adds to the burden to be carried by the climber. The hillwalker, on the other hand, is extremely unlikely to be in the position of having to hold a falling climber, even in the most dire emergency, so it seems reasonable that some of this extra strength should be sacrificed in the interests of lightening the load. But one must not take this too far. The thinner the rope, the more difficult it is to handle and ropes of 7mm diameter and·under are difficult to hold. It is unlikely, too, that the hillwalker will be contemplating even the remote possibility of long abseils, so that 30m of 9mm diameter rope should be sufficient for most purposes. Choosing between different brands is largely a matter of personal taste but do make sure that the rope has been properly tested and meets the requirements laid down by the Union International des Associations d'Alpinisme (UIAA).

One serious disadvantage of nylon as a material for a climbing rope is its very low melting point. Considerable heat can be generated as a result of friction, if, for example, a moving rope is pulled through a static loop. Under such circumstances enough heat may be generated to cause the static loop to burn through. Another disadvantage is that it is relatively easy to cut, especially when the rope is under tension. Sharp rock edges and excessively abrasive surfaces can do a lot of damage to the mantle. It is important to look after the rope. On no account stand on it or let anyone else stand on it. It should not be used for any other purpose such as a washing line or, the ultimate sin, as a tow-rope. If it gets dirty give it a thorough wash to get rid of all the small particles of grit which can damage the fibres. A cool detergent-free wash in a washing machine, in a bag, is as good a way as any of doing this. Make sure that the rope ends are fused before you do this.

Inspect the rope thoroughly every so often and discard it if any serious damage is discovered, such as a cut mantle. Keep the rope away from hot objects and store it in a cool place out of direct sunlight. It is difficult to give firm advice on when to retire a climbing rope. Much depends on the level of use - and abuse. Obviously, a rope used very occasionally by a hillwalker will last a lot longer than the same rope used constantly by a rock climber. If in doubt, discard.

THE KNOTS

Tying knots is an essential skill but it is only a small part of the range of skills required to safeguard a party on steep ground. The following is a list of the most useful· knots needed by mountain leaders. It is by no means comprehensive and there are many alternatives to these knots which would be just as effective. They have been chosen because they are simple, have several applications and allow for a margin for error when being tied eg a figure-of-eight if incorrectly tied ends up as an overhand knot or a figure-of-nine, both of which are perfectly satisfactory knots.

Fig. 56   ***Overhand loop.***
An overhand knot tied in a doubled rope provides a loop for belaying or
for a waist loop.

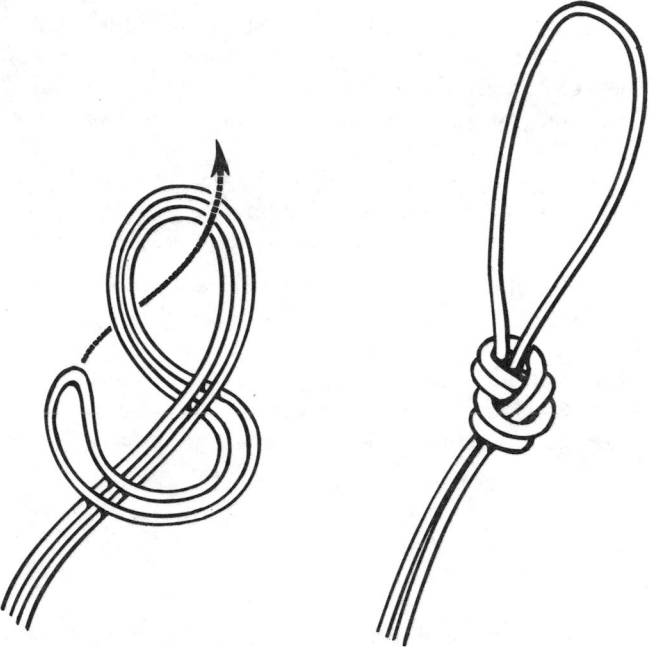

Fig. 57   ***Figure-of-8 loop.***
A more effective knot than the overhand for forming a waist loop. It can
easily be untied after loading. It is good practice to tie an overhand or
stopper knot in the free end. Although this does not add to the strength
of the knot itself, it does ensure that a sufficient length of tail is left after
tying the figure-of-eight.

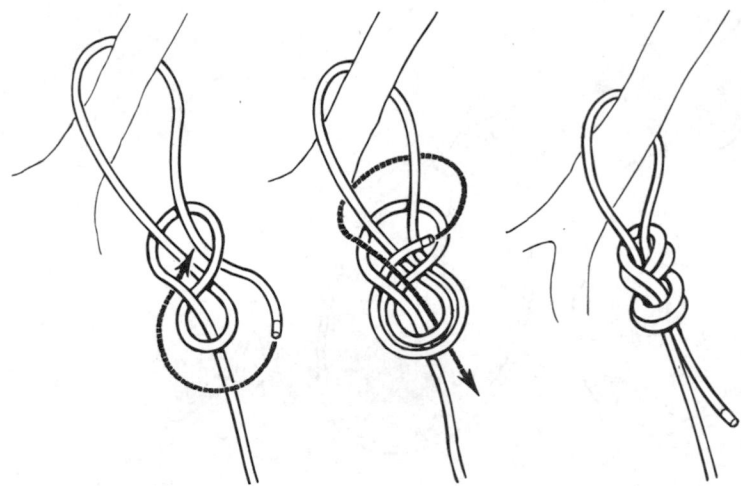

Fig. 58 **Figure-of-8 rewoven.**
A figure-of-eight knot is tied in the single rope. The end is passed through or round the anchor point. Then, in reverse order, the exact line of the rope in the original figure of eight is followed. This is a useful knot for attaching the rope to the waist, round a tree or for making a thread belay, etc where it is not possible to slip a loop over the top.

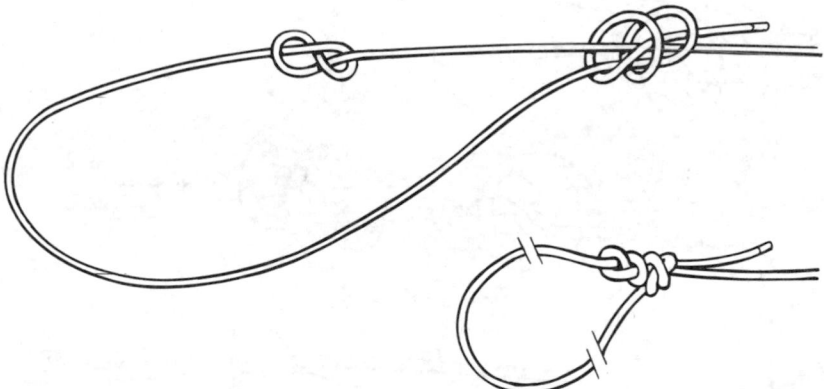

Fig. 59 **Figure-of-8, with fisherman's or Stoppered slip knot.**
This is useful when you need one knot that will fit several people without having to re-tie each time. The figure-of-eight acts as a stop knot. The size of the waist loop can be adjusted by changing the position of the figure-of-eight. Note that this knot should not be used for lowering or short roping.

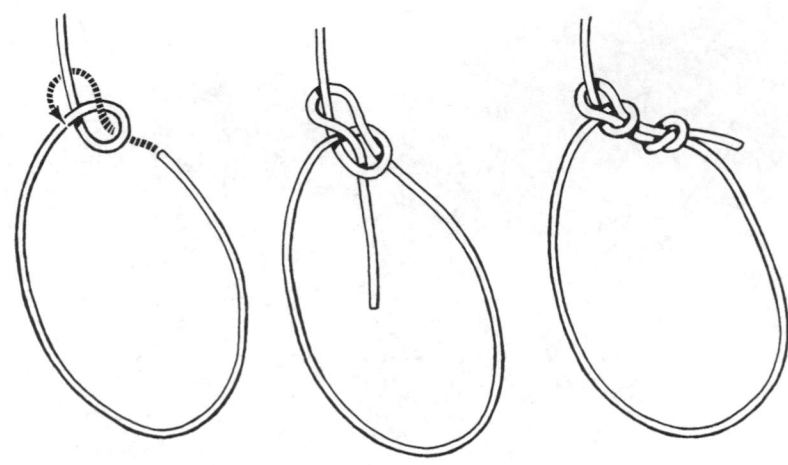

(Fig. 60)   ***Bowline.***
Still the most popular knot for tying on to the end of the rope. Do not
have the knot too tight round the waist; it should ride up round the
lower rib cage. Allow 12-18 inches of tail and secure it with an overhand
knot tied round the waist loop. It is also an ideal knot for tying on to the
anchor point, especially a thread.

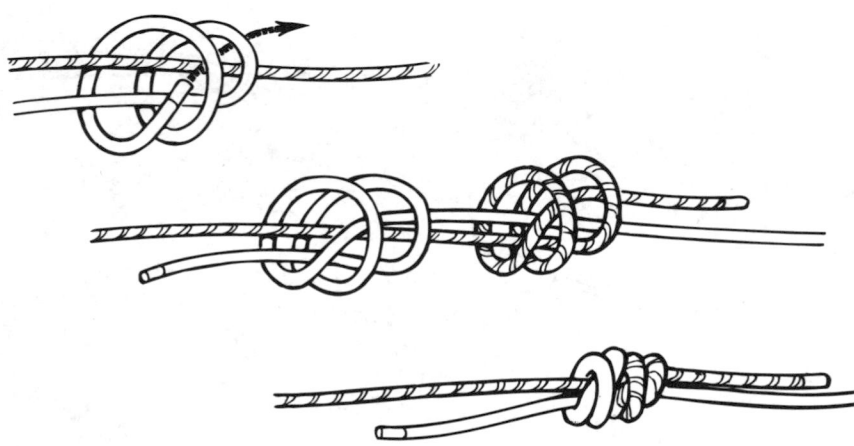

(Fig. 61)   ***Double Fisherman's.***
This is the most secure knot for tying two ropes together or for tying the
two ends of a length of rope to make a sling. Each end is passed twice
round both ropes and back through the loops so formed. Leave about
6-9 inches of tail.

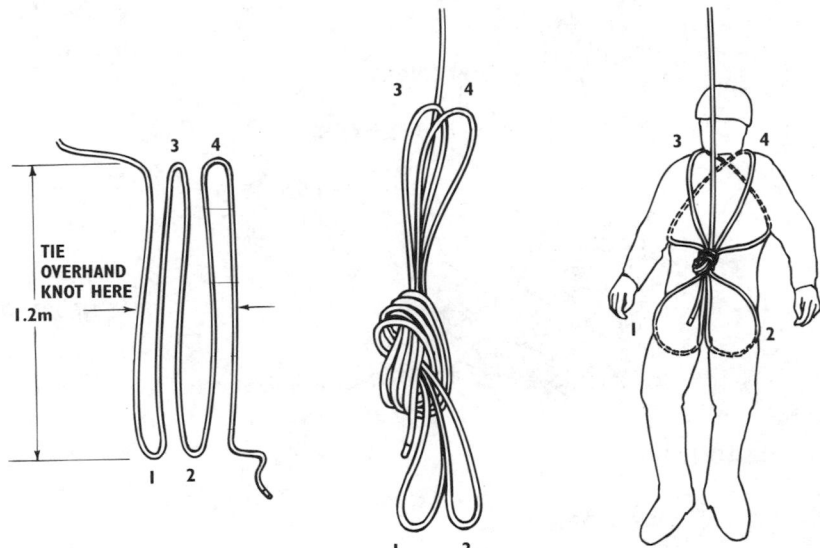

Fig. 62 *Thompson knot.*
This provides a reliable and easy-to-tie body harness which can be used for lowering. Make two dangling loops at the end of the rope from about shoulder height to the ground, making five strands of rope in all. Take the five strands and tie an overhand knot in the middle to form four loops. Step into the two loops (1 and 2) and pass the other two (3 and 4) over the head and under each arm. The position of the overhand knot determines the length of the loops and should be positioned so that the knot is above the navel to give a high centre of gravity. The loops should fit tightly with the body hunched up. To prevent the shoulder loops slipping off a rucksack can be worn. To facilitate quick fitting for different members of a group the loops should be made longer and the final adjustment is made by tying overhand knots in the excess rope (rabbit's ears) at the shoulders and adjusting the central knot to be at the sternum. Note that this knot must only be used for lowering - the leg loops catch behind the knees if climbing up or down.

In the figure labels: TIE OVERHAND KNOT HERE, 1.2m

Belaying

The purpose of belaying is to provide mutual protection for the members of a party by the use of the rope. The principle is that only one person is actually moving at any one time and that this person is secured by the rope which is held by the belayer who is himself secured by a loop of rope to the rock face.

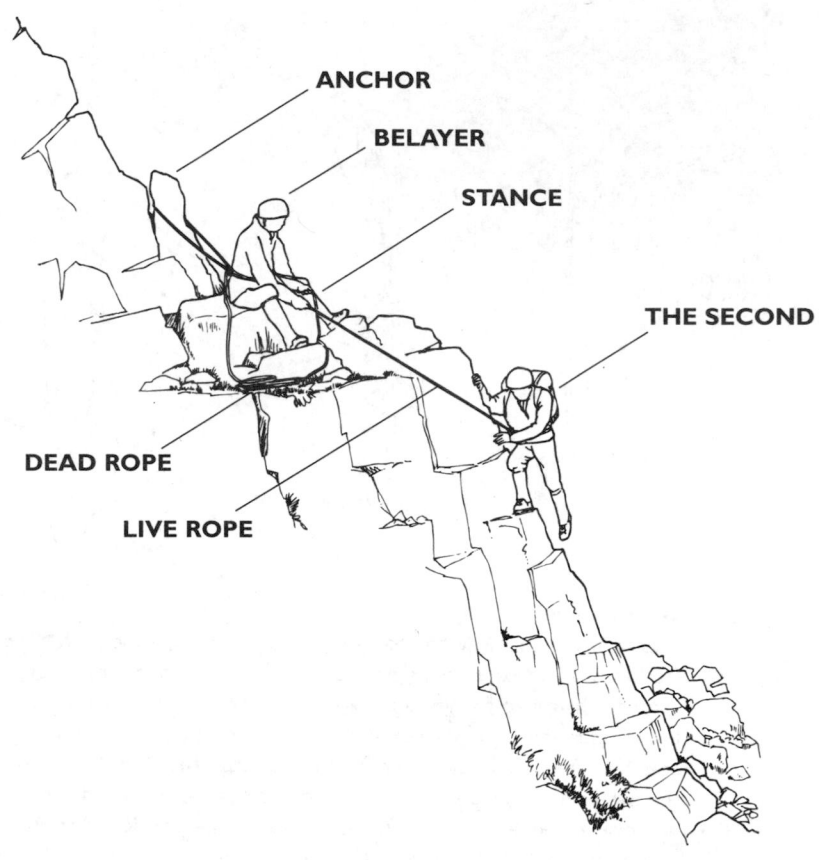

ANCHOR

BELAYER

STANCE

THE SECOND

DEAD ROPE

LIVE ROPE

Fig. 63   *The components of the belay system.*

In the mountain walking situation it is highly unlikely that the leader of a group would ever be required to hold a fall from above. Nevertheless, it is as well to be prepared for the worst and you should have some experience of the very considerable forces which can be generated by a 'leader fall'. A more likely scenario is that the rope would be used to safeguard the party down a short rock step. In these circumstances it is possible to provide a tight rope even to the extent of taking the whole weight of an individual on the rope and lowering them to the bottom.

It will be appreciated that a belay system has several interdependent components and like all such systems it can only be as good as its weakest link.

A faulty knot, a moment's inattention, a weak anchor point, and the strongest rope is made worthless.

Anchors

There are three types of anchor available when tying on with a rope;

1   a spike or flake of rock or free standing boulder over which a loop of rope can be passed;

2   a gap in the rock through which a rope can be threaded and then tied off; and

3   a tree which, like the thread, can be tied off.

The stability of an anchor is generally related to its mass and whether it is firmly attached to the surrounding rock. Its shape, too, is critical since there must be no tendency for the rope to slide off the anchor when any load is placed upon it. It is important, therefore, in choosing an anchor to take account of where you are going to sit or stand (the stance) and the likely direction of the strain along the rope connecting the belayer to the anchor.

An ideal anchor would be in the shape of a mushroom and be attached to bedrock. This would give it great strength with very little possibility of the rope jumping off and yet provide an even amount of resistance when pulled from one side. Finding out whether the spike is part of the mountain is easier said than done. If there is a lot of vegetation around this may well be difficult to determine. When in doubt treat it as a free standing piece of rock. The rope should always pull downwards as low down the spike as possible, rather than outwards higher up.

Trees, if available and of sufficient size and strength, can provide excellent anchor points with no possibility of the rope jumping off. When tying in to a tree remember the principle of leverage and that the higher up the tree the rope is the greater the leverage and therefore the potential load on the tree.

Threading a rope through a gap in the rock and re-tying it can often provide the most reliable form of anchor because of its ability to take a pull in most directions. "Threads", as they are called, are occasionally formed naturally in rock but more often occur when either two pieces of rock meet or when a smaller stone becomes jammed in a crack (known as a chockstone). Chockstones may be found naturally or can be wedged in place by the leader. The disadvantages of the thread are the greater need for judgement when assessing the worth of the anchor and the way v-shaped notches around its sides can cause the rope to jam making it difficult to adjust for length and which may even cut it if it is subjected to a sudden load.

DIRECT BELAY

A direct belay involves connecting the person climbing to the chosen anchor point so that in the event of a fall all the load is taken by the anchor, assisted by the friction of rope around it. In the case of a very small anchor point with limited friction it is advisable for the belayer to take the rope around the body as in the indirect belay. The attraction of this system is the speed with which it can be set up as well as the fact that it is the anchor that takes the strain. A disadvantage is the lack of security provided to the leader, although there is no reason why a belay should not be taken, even using the same anchor, provided the live rope is not running over the anchor loop. However the greatest problem is that it relies absolutely on the quality of the anchor and as such requires first class judgement from the leader as to when and how to apply it.

Fig. 64   *A direct belay. If necessary the belayer could tie on to a separate anchor.*

The best anchors for direct belaying are normally spikes or trees. In the case of a spike care must be taken to ensure that the rope does not roll up and over the spike as it passes around it. Avoid using anchors with sharp edges which could damage or even cut the rope, unless the edge can be padded with a gaiter or similar item.

The belayer faces the anchor point from below and passes the rope going to the climber round the anchor, grasping the ends of the rope with the hands and looking over their shoulder at the person being protected. When paying out rope each hand stays on the respective rope but when taking in two hands may be needed on the dead rope. It is imperative there is always at least one hand on the dead rope ie the rope on the side of the anchor away from the person being safeguarded. This is the rope which is gripped tightly in the event of a fall, friction around the anchor providing the major part of the braking force. Since some of the strain is likely to come on the hands it is useful to wear gloves.

INDIRECT BELAY

The indirect belay involves the imposition of the belayers body between the person climbing and the anchor. In this system the first impact of a fall is taken by the belayer who in turn is supported by the anchor. Although it is the most reliable arrangement it is unfortunately the most elaborate to set up.

As with the direct belay the anchor needs to be more or less directly above the line to be descended or ascended. The leader must take up a stance somewhere along that line, as appropriate (Fig. 65). In selecting a stance a decision will have to be taken whether to sit or stand always bearing in mind this principle of keeping straight line between the three points: anchor, stance and the person climbing or, more accurately, the point from which the expected strain would come. When standing it is usually possible to have a better view down the line of ascent or descent and also to pull the rope with more force if required. The overwhelming attractions of sitting down are stability and security. By sitting in a depression with legs bent and feet behind a lip in the ground the leader is in a very stable position and able to contribute a great deal to the strength of the belay (Fig. 67).

There is a range of options in the way that the belayer is secured to the anchor all of which to be effective must be safe, adjustable and economical of rope. Safe rope systems are simple ones which do not come apart. The need for an adjustable system is not just for convenience but also for safety. If the process of adjusting the tension on the rope between anchor and belayer is too involved then safety may be compromised by leaving the rope between the anchor and belayer too slack. Wherever possible the rope must be used economically since many anchor points can be a long way from the stance and if four strands are used then the entire rope can be employed to anchor the leader with nothing left to protect the group.

Fig. 65   *The relationship between anchor, stance and climber.*
The best situation is when all three are in the same vertical plane.
The dotted figures show what may happen if they are not in line.

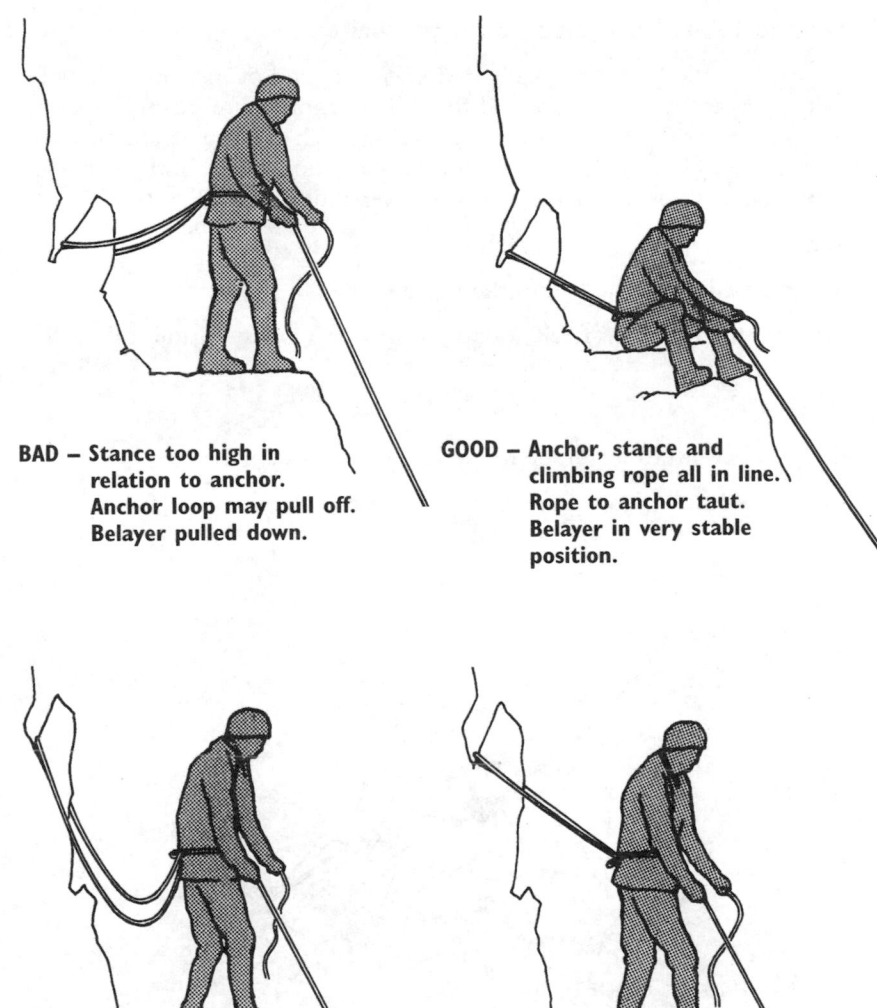

BAD – Stance too high in relation to anchor. Anchor loop may pull off. Belayer pulled down.

GOOD – Anchor, stance and climbing rope all in line. Rope to anchor taut. Belayer in very stable position.

BAD – Slack rope between belayer and anchor. Belayer likely to be pulled off stance.

GOOD – Anchor, stance and climbing rope all in line. Rope to anchor taut. Belayer in stable position.

Fig. 66   *Examples of Good and Bad stance and belay.*

Belaying to a spike anchor tied off at the waist

In this method the leader is already tied on to the end of the rope. A bight of rope is placed over the spike and the belayer moves into position on the stance. A loop of the trailing rope is passed through the waist loop and tied off in a figure-of-eight, ensuring that the knot is tied round both strands of rope and that there is no slack between belayer and anchor. (Fig. 67)

Advantages:

*   leader is tied on to the end of the rope.

*   provided the rope runs freely round the anchor it is easy to adjust from the stance.

Disadvantages:

*   can be awkward to feed rope round certain types of anchor eg boulders.

*   uses two strands of rope between belayer and anchor.

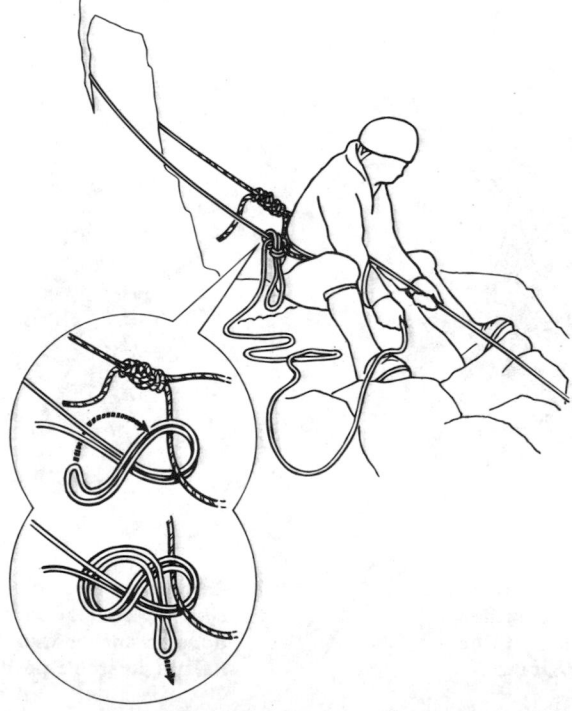

Fig. 67   *Belaying to a spike anchor, tied off at the waist.*

Belaying to a spike anchor tied off at the anchor. Method 1.

Initially the leader is not tied on. A loop is made in the end of the rope using a figure-of-eight on the bight and placed over the spike. The belayer then makes a waist loop just uphill of the chosen stance in such a position that the rope to the anchor will come tight when the belayer moves into position on the stance. Fine adjustments are made by feeding the rope through the figure-of-eight at the waist (Fig. 68).

Advantages:

- most economical of rope, using one strand only.

- easy to move into position on stance.

- avoids friction at anchor point.

Disadvantages:

- leader untied until belay is set up.

- awkward making adjustments through figure-of-eight.

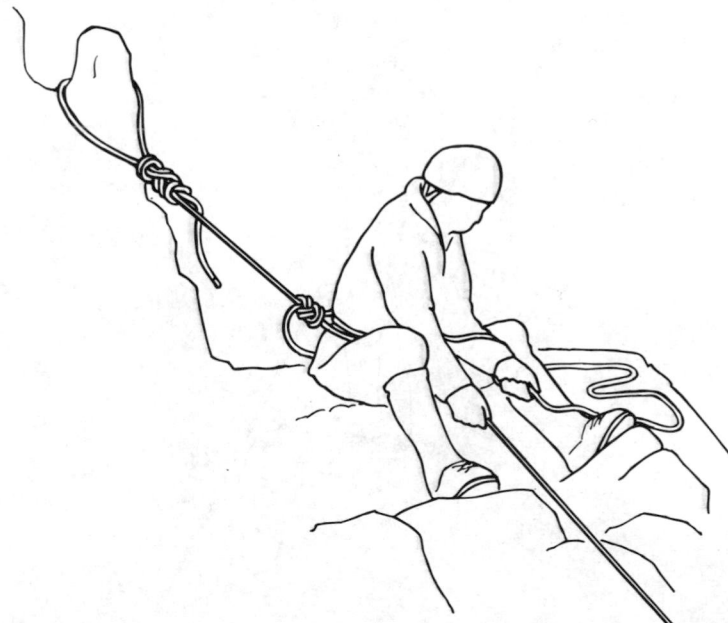

Fig. 68 *Belaying to a spike anchor tied off at the anchor.*
Method 1. The anchor loop is placed before the waist loop is tied.

171

Belaying to a spike anchor tied off at the anchor. Method 2.

The leader is already tied on to the end of the rope. Having selected the anchor and stance a loop is tied in the rope in such a position that when placed over the spike the rope to the belayer will come taut when the stance is taken up (Fig. 69).

Advantages:

*   leader is tied on to the end of the rope.

*   leader can untie from the system by lowering the load on to the anchor.

Disadvantages:

*   can not be adjusted from the stance if the anchor loop is out of reach.

Fig. 69   *Belaying to a spike anchor tied off at the anchor.*
Method 2. The belayer is tied on before the anchor loop is placed.

172

Belaying to a thread anchor tied off at the anchor

In this method the leader is not tied on until the belay is set up. The end of the rope is passed through the thread. It is then tied off at the thread either with a bowline or with a figure-of-eight rewoven. The latter requires a figure-of-eight to be tied at an appropriate distance from the end of the rope before it is threaded. The leader moves to the stance where a figure-of-eight on the bight furnishes the waist loop. Fine adjustments are made by feeding rope through this knot. (Fig. 70)

Advantages:

- most economical of rope.

- ropes does not have to move round thread and therefore will not jam.

- easy to move into position at stance.

Disadvantages:

- leader is untied until belay is set up.

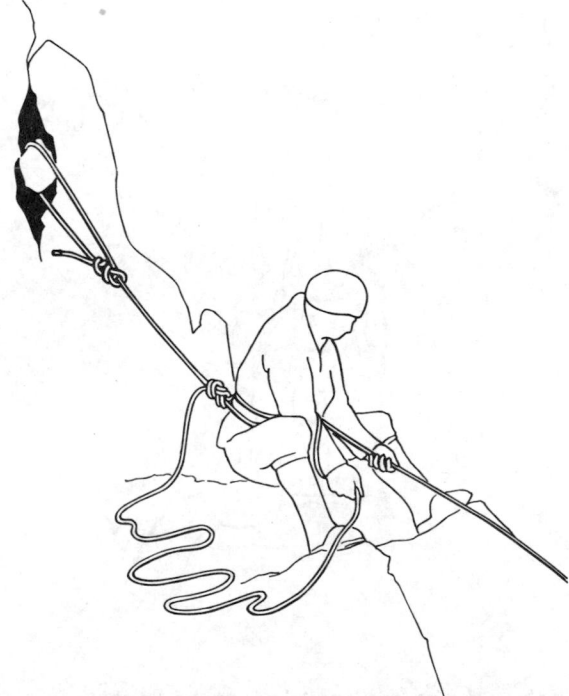

(Fig. 70) *Belaying to a thread anchor, tied off at the anchor.*

173

Belaying to a thread anchor tied off at the waist. Method 1.

Initially the leader is not tied on. The end of the rope is passed through the thread and back to the belayer at the stance where it is tied on at the waist with a figure-of-eight on the bight. A loop of the trailing rope from the thread is passed through the waist loop and tied off in a figure-of-eight (Fig. 71).

Advantages:

- easy to adjust from the stance provided the rope runs freely at the thread.
- dead rope is tied off securely at the waist.

Disadvantages:

- leader is untied until belay is set up.
- can be awkward to feed rope through the thread, particularly if there is a lot of friction and the stance is some distance from the anchor.

Fig. 71 **Belaying to a thread anchor tied off at the waist.**
Method 1. The rope is threaded before being tied to the waist.

Belaying to a thread anchor tied off at the waist. Method 2.

This is an adaptation of the method described for using a spike anchor tied off at the waist. The leader is already tied on to the end of the rope. A bight of the rope is passed through the thread and back to the belayer's waist where it is tied off in a figure-of-eight once the stance has been taken up. For the reasons explained below this method is best used when the stance is adjacent to the thread (Fig. 72).

Advantages:

- leader is tied on to the end of the rope.

Disadvantages:

- the most uneconomical of rope, four strands being used.
- awkward to feed rope through thread, especially if stance is some distance from the thread and there is friction at the thread.
- dead rope goes directly to the thread although it can be tied off separately at the waist.

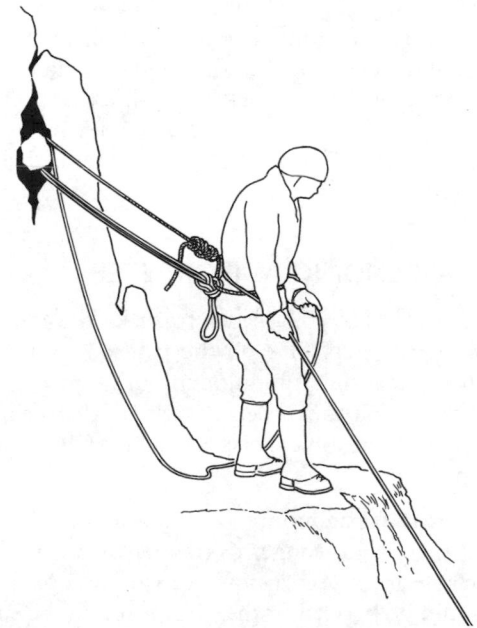

Fig. 72   *Belaying to a thread anchor tied off at the waist.*
Method 2. The belayer is tied on to the end of the rope before a
loop is threaded.

Whatever method is used the rope between belayer and anchor must be tight so that in the event of a load coming onto the rope the belayer is not pulled suddenly forward and the anchor loaded with the weight of two people. It can not be emphasised too strongly that no single method is completely satisfactory under all circumstances. Each has its limitations and the leader must choose the method appropriate to any given situation. For example if economy of rope is important because the stance is a long way from the anchor then it may be necessary to use a method where the rope is tied off at the anchor.

THE BELAYER

The final link in the chain of security is the belayer whose responsibility it is to ensure that the rope is taken in or paid out as required and to provide a firm rope to give support to the person ascending or descending. Because of the energy absorbing quality of the modern climbing rope it is no longer necessary to provide a dynamic brake in the event of a fall. The belayer's job is to hold on to the rope as tightly as possible and let the rope do the rest. The hip belay is undoubtedly the most reliable method available which does not involve the use of special equipment. It is simple and depends for its satisfactory operation in the event of a fall on achieving the maximum amount of friction between the rope and the back of the hips. It is important to use this part of the anatomy which has a bony framework rather than the waist which is soft and vulnerable. The hands, too, are vulnerable and should be protected by leather gloves.

A SCENARIO ON ASCENDING A SHORT STEP

Sound judgement should enable the leader to make the decision to use the rope prior to ascending the step. Tie on the first person to ascend the step after the leader, ensuring that the group understands how the adjustable belay loop works and is aware of the order in which they will climb – (the psychology of the most vulnerable person ought to be considered at this point).

The safety of the party is paramount. If the leader decides to tie on they must be satisfied that there is no danger to the person at the other end of the rope. It is unreasonable to expect a novice to belay a leader effectively so either the novice should be belayed or the terrain should be such as to render belaying unnecessary.

If the leader decides to move to the top of the step without tying on then all they have to do is to convey the end of the rope to the top of the step by whatever means seems most convenient at the time. On arrival the leader is free to construct the most appropriate belay for the particular situation.

The leader may wish to place their rucksack in a safe place as a point to which the rest of the group will go when they have arrived at the top of the step. The rope is then taken in quickly hand-over-hand until it tightens on the second. It is then passed over the head and down to the hips. The dead rope is twisted once round the forearm before being firmly held in the braking hand. The second person can now be brought up using the technique shown in Fig 73.

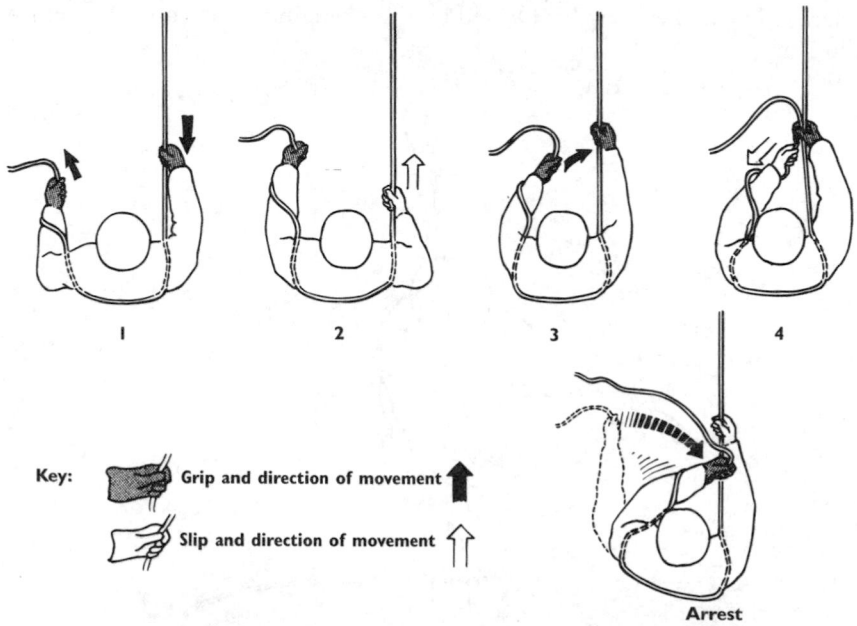

Fig. 73 *Sequence of actions for taking in the rope. In this case the right hand is on the 'live' rope and the left hand is on the 'dead' rope.*

1   Take in with both hands gripping the rope until the left arm is fully extended and the right arm retracted.

2   Grip the rope with the left hand and slide the right hand out to its fullest extent.

3   Bring both hands together.

4   Grip both ropes with the right hand and slide the left hand towards the body.

The live rope should be kept under just the right degree of tension so that the rope provides positive support to the person climbing. In the event of a slip the rope is held tightly in the braking hand which is moved across the front of the body so as to provide the maximum contact and friction between the rope and the hips. (Fig. 74) Even a short fall can impose a tremendous load on the belayer that can severely test both strength and skill. It is a technique which is well worth practising so that you are better prepared for the real thing. If the fallen climber is unable to resume climbing they should be lowered to the bottom of the pitch. It is very important for the belayer to keep alert at all times and be aware of the various components of the belay chain and how they may be affected by the changing position of the person climbing.

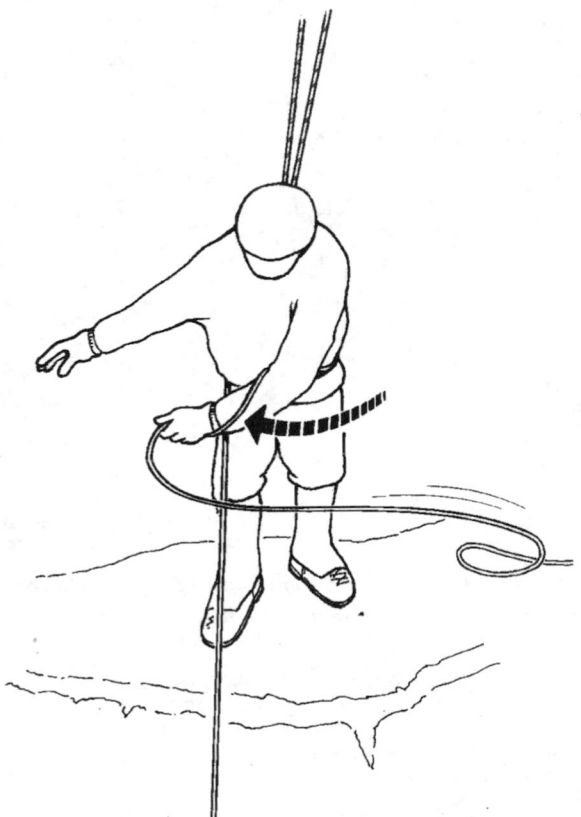

Fig. 74 *The body belay. The dead hand and arm are brought across the front of the body to provide maximum friction round the hips. The live leg should be forward to resist rotation.*

SECURITY ON DESCENT

It is not appropriate for inexperienced hill walkers to belay each other down steep rock. In the context of mountain walking one is talking about a relatively short section of rock where, because of the combination of exposure and difficulty, the leader deems it necessary to put on the rope. Under these circumstances the leader must come down last after each member of the party is safely down. How this is achieved depends on the circumstances, but whatever method is used, it should be used safely and swiftly - in that order. The simplest method is for the leader to take a belay at the top of the difficulty. An adjustable waist loop is tied on the end of the rope and each member of the party in turn slips on the loop and is secured on a tight rope to the bottom. When they get down they slip off the loop and stand well out of the way while the rope is retrieved to be attached to the next in line. When all are safely down the leader must decide whether to descend roped or unroped. If roped, their first responsibility is to ensure that there is no possible danger to those below, remembering again that it is unrealistic to expect a novice to give a satisfactory belay.

This is a time-consuming method, even when it is conducted by an experienced leader. If the steep section is short and not too difficult a direct belay round a suitable projection can save a lot of time and effort.

Abseiling

There is a tendency in some quarters to treat abseiling as if it is a risk free sport in its own right. It is not. It is potentially very dangerous. It is worth remembering that even experienced climbers have been killed abseiling and often as a result of some careless elementary mistake. As a technique for descending difficult rock, it is used in the Alps but in the British Isles it is normally possible to find an easy way to circumvent a difficult section. Nevertheless, there are occasions when it may be necessary for the leader of a non-climbing party to abseil. It must be stressed therefore, that in the context of hillwalking, abseiling is an emergency technique to be used by the leader of the party and not by the individual group members. In real situations, a safety rope will not be available and some practice should be experienced without having the security of an extra rope from above.

THE CLASSIC ABSEIL

This is the basic method involving the use of the rope alone and all mountaineers should be familiar with it. (Fig. 75) It has the considerable merit of simplicity. Take great care in selecting a suitable anchor point for the doubled rope. It should, if possible, be above chest level and it must allow the rope to move freely when one end is pulled to enable the rope to be retrieved from below when the abseil is completed. If the rope does not move freely then it may be worth sacrificing a short section to use as a sling around the anchor. The rope itself is threaded through the sling. Test the anchor before you start applying your full weight to the rope. Wear gloves. Getting started

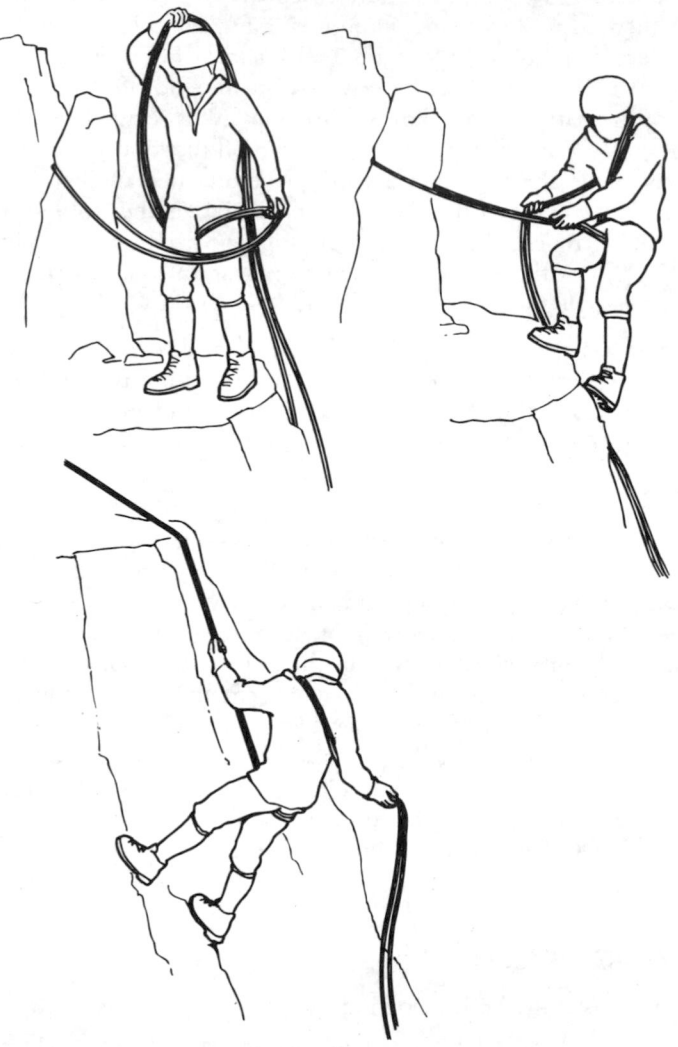

Fig. 75   *Abseiling. The 'classic' method using the rope alone.*

is usually the most difficult manoeuvre and may involve climbing down a step or two until you are in a good launching position. Take it steady. The friction, will usually limit your speed of descent. Do not try to support your weight by clutching onto the rope with the upper hand. The lower hand is the one which controls your rate of descent; indeed it may be necessary for you to feed the rope round your body to overcome the friction. Resist the temptation to try to climb down. This upsets your body position, which should be well out from the rock face and almost perpendicular to it, with your feet pushing against the face and about 18 inches apart. Turning the upper body sideways towards the lower controlling hand can relieve some of the discomfort associated with this method. Be constantly on the look out for loose rock and make sure that no one is standing at the bottom in the line of descent. When you get down, the rope is retrieved by pulling steadily on one end. Before doing so, separate out the two strands of the doubled rope so that there are no twists and remove any knots or kinks.

There is no doubt that using a sit–sling and karabiner makes abseiling a lot more comfortable although not necessarily safer. It is extremely unlikely that the non–climbing leaders would ever have to use this technique except in the most dire emergency. It is better, therefore, to rely on a system which requires no other equipment than the safety rope.

Confidence Roping

This chapter began by explaining that security could be provided on steep ground in different ways without recourse to the rope. Many people associate ropes with rock climbing and assume that it is only in this context that they can be used. However, there are a number of relatively common situations in which a rope can provide assistance on easier terrain. Either because of weariness or inability, one member of a party may be struggling to keep up, even on relatively straightforward ground and it is here that a leader can provide support with the rope.

The technique is not dissimilar to keeping a dog on a tight lead and indeed is sometimes referred to as 'dog leading'. It is normally used descending steep vegetated or mixed ground and is a way of providing actual physical support as well as confidence to someone who is experiencing difficulties. The rope is attached to this person with a figure-of-eight knot or similar; you may want to grab the waist loop itself so a slip knot will not do. The majority of the rope is best stored in the leader's rucksack, uncoiled or in a bag in case more is needed. The leader should be as close to his charge as practicable so as to ease communication and minimise complications and stretch in the rope. A small hand loop is tied between the two to provide a firm grasp on the rope which is held in the lower (outer) hand and kept under tension to ensure that there are no sudden shocks. To reduce further the possibility of unbalancing the leader the arm should be kept bent and the body in a flexed position, both of which will enable any sudden movements to be absorbed. Irrespective of the direction that the two people are walking, up down or across a slope the leader must always be uphill of the second so ensuring that they can not pendulum downhill. It goes without saying that this technique should only be used on ground on which the leader is completely happy and able to guarantee both the safety of the second and that of the rest of the group.

Fig. 76   *Short rope technique used to safeguard descent.*

A useful adaptation of this system involves the use of a sling about 2 metres long. This is placed over the second's head and down to the waist where it is held in place by wearing a rucksack on top of the sling. The leader takes a firm hold of the other end and provides direct support for the second as he or she descends.

Additional Equipment

It has already been established at some length that this book is not a rock climbing manual and that when moving in the hills with a group, the rope is in the second or third line of a leader's defences. Any additional equipment must be considered very carefully before being included in the day to day load.

7

River Crossing

One glance at the rainfall map of the British Isles should be enough to convince anyone that mountains and rain go together and that in these islands we sometimes appear to get more than our fair share of the latter. One of the effects of this, of course, is that our mountain areas abound with streams which, in times of heavy rainfall, literally gush from the mountain sides. The evidence of the power of such streams is there for all to see, the deeply cut gorges, the waste of transported boulders and debris and yet how often do we take this into account when drawing up our expedition plans? There can be few mountain days when it is not necessary to cross a stream, however small, and even the smallest stream can become impassable when fed by torrential rain or melting snow. Almost every year someone is drowned while crossing a river which should never have been attempted. So, while the techniques of making a crossing safely are important, it is much more important to be able to make a proper assessment of the situation, including the alternatives to crossing.

Planning Ahead

There is, unfortunately, no simple relationship between the amount of rain that falls and the volume of water in the streams and the rate at which it increases. However, in the mountains, as a consequence of the relatively thin soil and vegetation cover, run-off is usually very rapid and streams can quickly become impassable. The converse is, of course, equally true, that when the rain stops the volume of water in the streams diminishes just as rapidly and this is a fact worth bearing in mind when considering alternatives. It is sensible, then, to anticipate these fluctuations in water volume and plan your route taking into account the size of the catchment area, the weather forecast, the time of year and the possibility of a spate caused by melting snow and even such events as the release of water from hydroelectric schemes. In general, the completion of your route should not require the fording of a stream which could be hazardous in conditions of high water. When descending it is usually best to keep as high as possible on the ridges following the watershed between river systems. By doing this you avoid being halted in your tracks by uncrossable side streams feeding into the main river.

TO CROSS OR NOT

Nevertheless, even the most meticulous planning cannot provide for all unforeseen circumstances and eventualities. It is in the nature of mountaineering that the unexpected happens, the sudden emergency or forced change of plan which may lead you into a situation where you are faced with a difficult choice; to attempt a crossing or not? If the crossing is straightforward and there is no element of risk involved, select the most convenient place and get on with it. If, however, there is any doubt at all in your mind about the outcome, then you must carefully consider all the alternatives before committing yourself to the crossing.

As with most other aspects of mountaincraft sound judgements are based on experience and a good measure of common sense. Factors to take into account in making your assessment would include the width of the river, the depth of water, the colour or opacity of the water, the current and turbulence of the stream and the nature of the stream bed. Quite apart from these technical considerations you should reassess the physical condition of your party and ask yourself the question, "how safe is this crossing for the most vulnerable member?" Let us assume that you have some doubts about the wisdom of attempting to ford the stream. What are the alternatives?

Alternatives

(a) First of all, a great deal will depend on the remoteness of the location. In the British Isles it is highly unlikely that the situation will make a fording imperative, and if it is then you are unlikely to have the resources necessary to make a safe crossing. You should be wary of the psychological pressures to which you will be subjected, usually in favour of crossing. After all, it is only human nature to want to get it over with, when you can see the bothy and the prospect of a hot meal just a stone's throw away. Do not be misled.

(b) Examine the map very carefully both upstream and down. Where is the nearest bridge and what would be the implications of making a detour to it?

(c) Bearing in mind the weather forecast, you could decide to wait until the water level dropped to a safe height. A long wait might mean a night out in the open. What would be the effect of a forced bivouac on your party? If you do decide to sit it out remember to mark the water level so that you have some idea of the rate of fall and how much it has dropped during the night.

(d) If your party is fit and you have time in hand you might elect to follow the river upstream and ford the tributaries where the volume of water will be less. But how far will you have to walk and over what sort of terrain? How certain can you be of finding safe crossing points and have you the stamina to see it through? These are questions which you will have to attempt to answer.

It cannot be stressed too strongly that fording a river by whatever method, where there is some degree of risk, is an emergency procedure, only to be adopted when the alternatives to crossing are more hazardous than the crossing itself.

Inspection

If you decide that the river can be forded safely you will want to inspect as much of it as practicable to find the best crossing point. It is a great help to be able to interpret the surface movement of the river since this is largely determined by the nature of the bottom. The main flow of water is usually indicated by a large 'V' of smooth water pointing downstream. Large stationary 'standing waves' are the tell-tale signs of boulders on the river bed which deflect the water upwards towards the surface. They are not dangerous in themselves but they reflect an irregular bed which could make for a difficult crossing. Closer to the surface such boulders create eddies immediately downstream where the current runs counter to the main flow. Where the obstruction is large and the fall steep a vertical eddy can sometimes be formed causing a very strong back-flow towards the obstruction on the downstream side. These vertical eddies, or 'stoppers' as they are called, can be extremely dangerous since once caught in one, it can be almost impossible to escape.

Submerged or partly submerged obstructions, such as tree branches, are particularly dangerous. Provided you are moving down with the current the force of the water is not apparent. As soon as you lodge against some obstacle the full force and power of the river is brought to bear and can easily trap you.

The 'Vee' of smooth water indicates the line of the main flow. Note the eddies behind obstructions such as boulders or trees where the flow is counter to the main flow of the river.

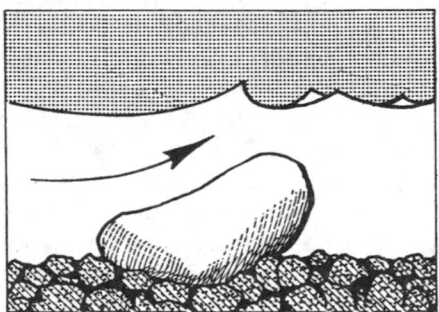

Standing waves produced by an uneven bottom.

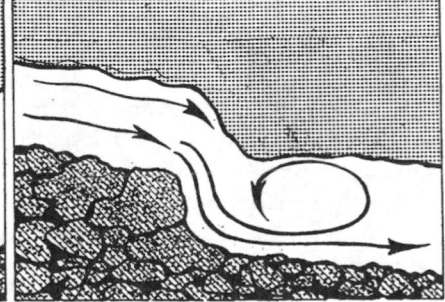

A stopper, commonly formed where there is a sharp fall in the river level, such as at a weir, waterfall, etc.

Fig. 77   *Reading moving water.*

SELECTION OF CROSSING POINT

In selecting the best crossing point, these and many other factors must be carefully considered:

Look at the map again to see if it provides any helpful clues. Remember that streams wider than 8m are shown with a double line on the O.S. Second series, 1:50,000 maps. The 1:25,000 map may well show places where the stream is braided into a number of smaller streams which may be crossed more easily than the main stream.

It is sometimes possible to ford a river near its mouth. Mountain streams running into lakes normally flatten out and consequently slow down in the last half mile or so. Generally, the water is quite deep but slow flowing. However, great care must be taken in crossing, particularly with the non-swimmer.

The area selected should be free of obstructions, submerged or otherwise, such as large boulders or fallen trees, which could snag ropes or trap a swimmer. Avoid high banks and make sure that the exit point is reasonable, with good access along both banks. Inspect the outflow. As far as possible it should also meet the above conditions.

Man-made obstructions such as collapsed bridges or broken down weirs provide additional and often unforeseen hazards.

The current is usually strongest on the outside of bends. Here you are likely to find undercut banks and deep, fast-flowing water which is not conducive to a safe crossing.

The river bed should be as even as possible, of uniform depth and free of boulders, rock outcrops or clinging mud. Shingle makes an ideal surface.

Do not rely on always being able to cross a river at a particular point. A rise in water level can change a safe ford into a dangerous one.

To some extent the selection of the best crossing point will be influenced by the limitations of the equipment carried by the party. If the crossing cannot be safeguarded by the use of a rope then it should be abandoned. The length of the rope itself limits the width of the river which can be crossed to one-quarter of the total length of the rope. Crossings wider than this can only be safeguarded by the use of some type of flotation or personal buoyancy or by joining two or more ropes together.

Finally, you should run through in your mind what would happen if someone should fall in and be swept away. How can they be safeguarded, if at all?

Preparations

Once you have selected the crossing point you must choose the method best suited to the situation and the physical condition of the party. Do not rush. A little extra time spent on preparation at this stage is time well spent. Brief the party carefully on procedure: how to tie on to the rope if one is to be used, how to adjust clothing, how to stand against the water, which bank to go for in the event of a swim and so on. Agree on the order of crossing and make sure that everyone knows exactly what their responsibilities are. It may be necessary to number the party or to arrange them in groups according to size and strength. Go through a dry run on the bank to make sure that the whole operation will go smoothly. A good simple system of visual communication is essential. Rivers can be noisy places, particularly if there is any white water around. If a rope is being used, clear signs are needed for taking in and letting out.

River Crossing Techniques

Many streams can be crossed without any more thought than that required to find the narrowest place to jump across. Just remember that even a 1.5 metre leap may present a daunting prospect to some of your party, especially if they

Fig. 78   *Crossing with the aid of a stick.*

are carrying heavy packs. In the same way, hopping from boulder to boulder may be a fine way of demonstrating your agility, but for the less able it may be the quickest way to a ducking or to a sprained ankle, or worse.

Choose a method of crossing which is well within the capability of every member of the party and be particularly careful crossing on wet or greasy boulders and on cold winter days when the rocks may be glazed with ice. Better to take to the water and suffer wet feet than risk an accident trying to cross dry-shod.

If you decide to take to the water there is a basic technique for crossing which can be adapted to suit all the methods described whether roped or unroped. The first rule is to keep your boots on. They protect the feet from bruising and provide a much firmer placement than bare feet. By all means take off your stockings and keep them dry in your pack, but put your boots back on. If you have gaiters, keep them on too. They add to the protection and help to insulate the legs against the numbing cold, as well as stopping small stones from accumulating in your boots. Since remaining dry is no longer an issue, remove any over trousers or roll them up above water level and tuck your anorak into your trousers. Baggy clothing is to flowing water what a sail is to the wind. As far as possible you want to reduce the surface area you present to the current. Keep your rucksack on, but do not secure the waist belt so that you can shed your sack in the event of a mishap. Your sack will almost certainly float. Indeed, you can ensure that it does by packing clothing, etc., in sealed polythene bags and by pulling out the bivouac extension and tying it off tightly so that it acts as an air bag. Now, if the worst should happen, you have a ready-made life raft.

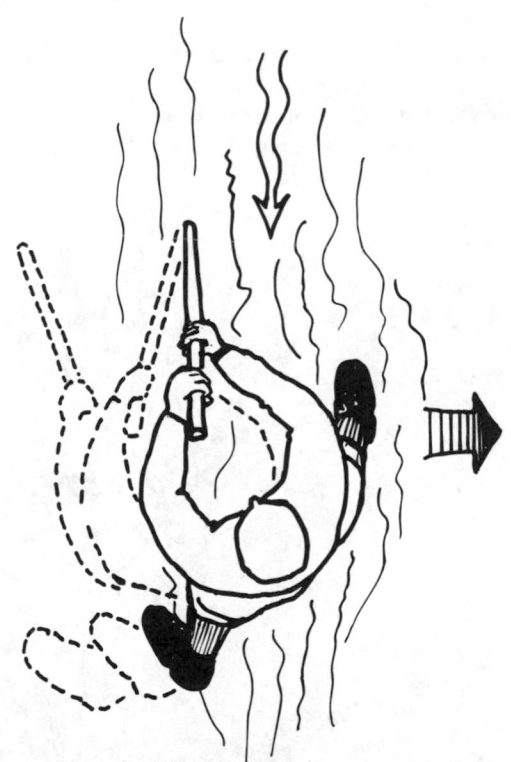

(Fig. 79)   *'Ferry glide'.*

In the water always face upstream with the feet half a metre apart. If you face the other way the force of the current acting on the back of the legs can cause the knees to give way. Avoid crossing your legs but rather proceed by a series of sideways shuffles making sure that one foot is firmly placed before moving the other.

Try to maintain foot contact with the bed of the stream. It can sometimes help progress to stand at an angle to the current so that it pushes you in the direction you wish to go. Your back should be half turned towards the bank you are heading for to achieve this 'ferry-glide' effect. (Fig.79)

A stout stick, if available, placed upstream acts as a third leg and greatly improves stability. It can also be used to probe for depth.

Crossing without a Rope

No attempt should be made to cross a river without the security of a rope unless it is obvious that the crossing can be accomplished in complete safety. In other words the methods which are now described are appropriate for low water crossings when the consequences of a slip are likely to be no more than a wetting. The three methods all depend on the principle of mutual support and the additional stability afforded by a group configuration as compared with a single individual.

Fig. 80   *'The Huddle'.*

Three people, preferably of similar height, get into a huddle with their arms linked (as shown in Fig.80). The strongest one of the three should face upstream. Holding firmly on to each other the group proceeds across the stream supporting each other when required. If the bottom is very uneven it may be necessary to move one at a time. Otherwise the group should move at the command of the leader. Take particular care when entering or leaving the stream because it is at these points that one of the team must release their grip to gain or leave the bank.

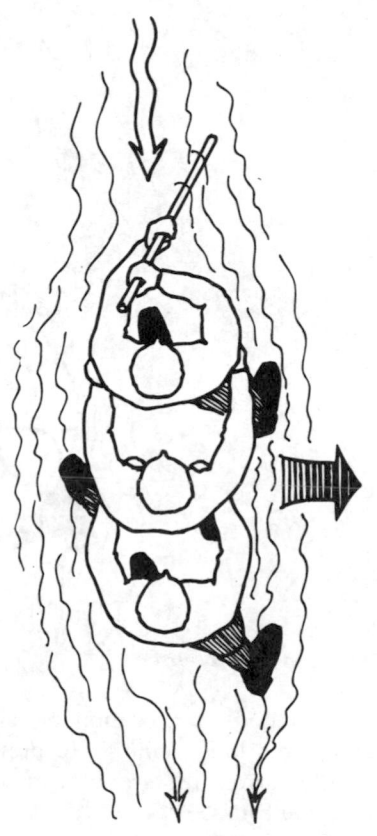

(Fig. 81)   *In line astern.*

A group of three or more takes up position as shown in Fig.81, each member facing upstream and holding on to the waist of the person in front. The leader should if possible, use a stick for support. The whole line should move sideways simultaneously, each shuffling step being co-ordinated by the leader.

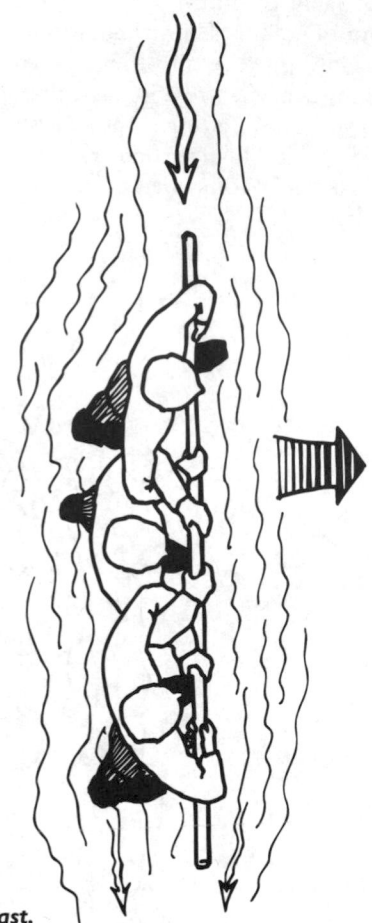

In line abreast.

In this method, three or more people cross in line abreast linking arms and holding on to a long branch. To present as small an area as possible to the force of the current the group faces across the stream with the branch held parallel to the banks.

Falling In

If the worst happens and you lose your footing and are swept away, remember that you are likely to remain buoyant for some time before your clothing becomes saturated. Don't panic. If you are on a rope you will either pendulum in to the bank or you will be pulled ashore on the downstream side. If you are not on a rope, take off your rucksack which should already be unbuckled, but keep a firm hold of it and float feet first downstream so that you can fend yourself off from rocks or obstructions. Your rucksack will act as a life raft, particularly if it contains one or two sealed containers or polythene bags. In any event it will take some time before it becomes waterlogged. Do not try to fight the current, but rather strike out across it to one bank or the other using any eddies or slack water to make progress. Choose a landing spot which is clear of submerged branches.

Once Across

A dry river crossing is a rare luxury. It is nearly always a cold and sometimes a frightening experience. Once you and your party are safely across get your dry socks on and put on any spare clothing you may have. A hot brew at this point can be a great morale booster.

Crossing with the Aid of a Rope

THE PENDULUM METHOD

In the Pendulum Method, one end of the rope is held from a point upstream on the opposite side of the river from the person crossing. This provides support and in the event of a fall ensures that the swimmer is swung into the bank they are heading towards.

The first person to cross, who must be one of the larger and stronger members of the party, ties into a slack loop at the mid point of the rope. One of the free ends is tied back into this waist loop to form a continuous loop which must be sufficiently long to span the width of the stream with some to spare for handling on each bank. The other free end is held by the belayer who takes the rope round any convenient anchor as far upstream as the rope length will permit. If no anchors are available a body belay is acceptable and in fact may be preferred because it allows better feedback from the person crossing. Other members may have to assist in holding the rope. (See Notes 1 and 2, page 198).

A then crosses the stream facing upstream and leaning back for support on the rope held by B. B will have to ease out the rope gradually as A is crossing. In the event of a slip A will pendulum back to the near bank assisted by C hauling in the doubled rope. Should this happen to A, who is one of the strongest in the group, the leader should reassess the decision to cross, taking account of the fact that once the control of the pendulum has passed to the far bank it will be very much easier for those who follow.

(Fig. 83)   *River crossing using a rope. The Pendulum Method.*

First person crossing.

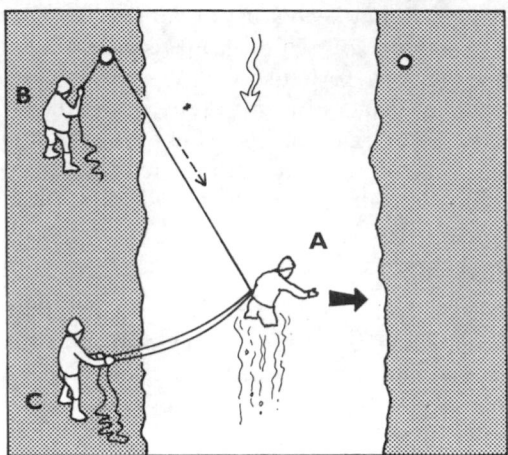

Once A is safely across there are two ways of getting the second person over.

- (i) A slips out of the waist loop and all the ropes are returned to the near bank. The second person then crosses in exactly the same way as the first.

(ii) A slips out of the waist loop but retains hold of the doubled rope so that as the second person crosses A can provide assistance, particularly at the exit point which is often awkward.

Second person crossing.

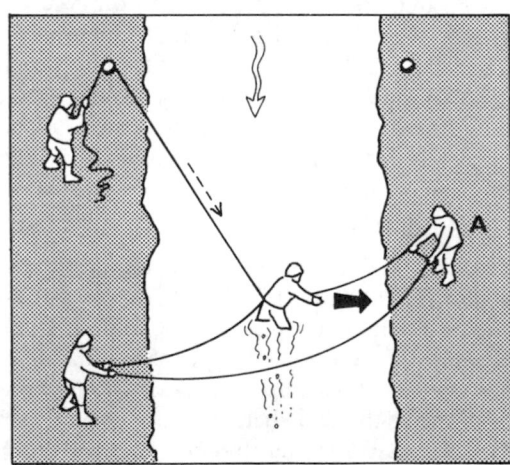

When two people have reached the far bank the pendulum can be put into operation. The pendulum rope is transferred to the far bank, if it is not already there, and is passed round a suitable anchor and held firmly by one of the two who have crossed. The other takes up a fielding position as shown. The remaining members of the party then cross in turn and after each crossing the waist loop is passed back across the stream for the next. The pendulum rope now offers not only support but positive impetus in the direction of travel. If someone should fall in they will automatically swing in to the far bank where they can be fielded by the person holding the recovery loop.

Remainder of party crossing.

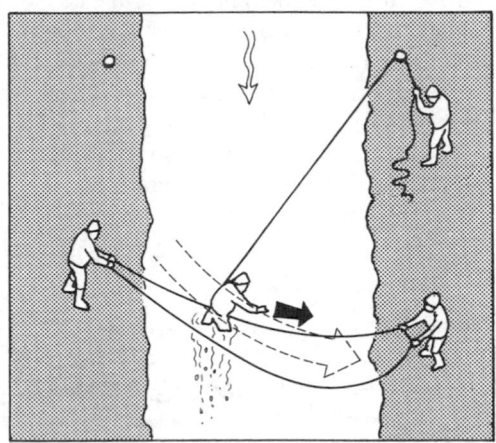

The last person crosses in the same way as the first except that the pendulum is now secured on the opposite bank of the stream.

Last person crossing.

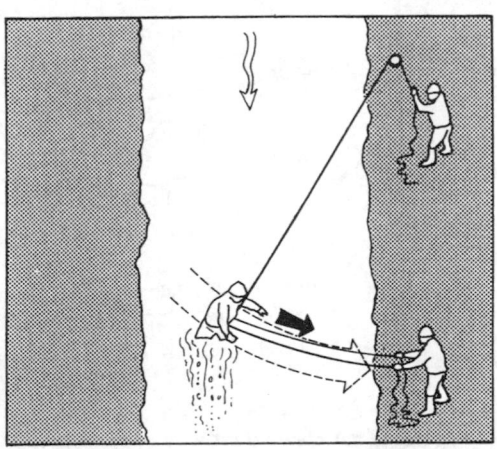

Notes

1. The loop used to secure those crossing should be two or three times the size of a waist loop. It is held closed by marrying the excess in the hands. This allows the person crossing to escape from the system should that be necessary. If a rucksack is carried a larger loop can be worn, draped over one shoulder and passing under the other arm. This enables the loop to be released without first having to take off the rucksack.

2. An alternative and convenient way of setting up the system is to lay out the rope in four equal lengths. One side will have two bights, the other one bight and the two ends. Marry together the single bight and one of the ends and tie an overhand knot with them, forming a loop of about 2m circumference. This loop is at the mid-point of the rope and will be the waist loop of the person crossing. The remaining rope is in two equal lengths, one with a free end – this will be the pendulum and the other in a loop – this will be the recovery rope. (Fig 84)

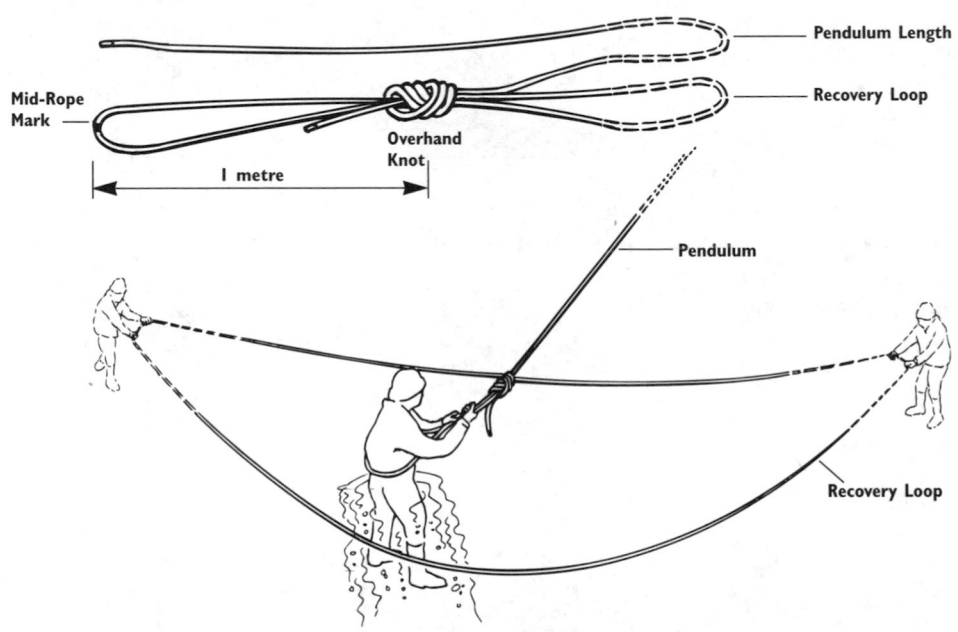

Fig. 84 — *A convenient way of setting up the pendulum and recovery loop.*

3. The method as described can be used to cross streams whose width is one quarter or less than the length of the rope. Thus, if a rope of 45m is carried, streams up to 10m wide can be crossed.

4. The longer the pendulum rope the better the support - it is more directly upstream of the person crossing.

5. The method requires three strong and perhaps well built people to cross first, second and last.

6. The anchor for the pendulum rope should be as high as possible on the bank. This avoids drag and the possibility of snagging on rocks or other obstacles in the stream.

If the stream is wider than one quarter of the length of the rope available it may be too wide to cross safely. However, if it is judged to be crossable two ropes may be used, one to act as the pendulum and the other as the recovery loop.

Conclusions

It must be appreciated that there are many variations of roped crossings. The Pendulum Method gives effective support to those crossing and ensures that they are delivered to the far bank if they fall in. Whatever method is used it is imperative that you make a thorough assessment of all the relevant factors both at the crossing point itself and downstream.

Streams and rivers are part of the mountain environment and learning to cross them safely is an essential element in the making of a mountaineer. Water on the move is a powerful and occasionally awe-inspiring force. Recognise this in your planning and avoid leading your party into a situation where you may be forced to consider a risky crossing as the least risky of several options. Sound judgement based on experience and a thorough knowledge of the various techniques and their limitations is the key to a safe passage. Better by far to make a lengthy detour than to risk a life in attempting a difficult river crossing.

8

Mountain Weather

Weather is a constant theme in the conversation of those who walk and climb in the mountains The reason is not hard to find. We are fortunate enough to live in a country which lies at a meeting place of great air masses of contrasting character which are constantly vying for supremacy in the atmosphere. The result is a continually changing pattern of weather, softened by the more benign influence of the surrounding and relatively warm sea. The effect of mountains is to accentuate these changes and in some cases to introduce an entirely new local dimension into the general pattern. Mountaineers are immersed in weather; it is the medium within which they move and is as much a part of their total environment as the more solid rock under their feet. At all times comfort, and on occasion safety, depend on it and on an ability to anticipate changes and to find an appropriate response. To equip yourself to do this you require:

(a) to be able to recognise the main pressure systems and the cloud and weather patterns associated with them;

(b) to be aware of the sources of information, including forecasts, and to be able to use and interpret them;

(c) to appreciate the effect of local conditions and altitude in modifying forecast conditions.

Finally, and most importantly, you must learn to blend your theoretical knowledge with the real-life situation on the mountain. If the wind is forecast to freshen in the afternoon, how will this affect you and your party and, as a consequence of this, do you need to modify your route? No doubt you will be asking yourself some questions such as: will it be a head-wind or a tail-wind, how strong will the wind be at 500m, how tired is the party likely to be at this point in the day, is there likely to be any loose snow on the tops which could mean spin-drift or even white-out conditions, what will the wind chill be at 500m? To answer these questions you need more than theory or a weather forecast. The most accurate forecast possible would not save you from benightment, unless you made that vital link between theory and practice Fortunately, practice is not too difficult to obtain. Weather is there all the time. It can woo you with warmth and sunshine or it can be a killer. It is an ever present dimension of the outdoor scene without which our mountains would be a good deal less interesting.

Fig. 85   *A satellite photograph dated March 1980 showing the general atmospheric circulation.*
Clouds are white, oceans dark and land surfaces grey. The Central and South American coastline is clearly visible. Notice the Great Lakes in the top centre of the photograph with the frozen surface of Hudson Bay to the north. Thick cloud associated with the depressions of the temperate latitude low pressure belt can clearly be seen.

The Global Circulation

The earth's atmosphere is constantly on the move. Photographs taken by weather satellites orbiting the earth are displayed daily on our television screens and show the swirling masses of clouds moving across the continents and seas of the world (Fig 85). At first sight there seems to be little order in the general turbulence, but closer examination reveals a pattern which can be explained in terms of the global circulation.

The energy to drive the world's atmosphere is derived from the sun which heats the earth's surface unevenly with the result that warm air rises at the equator and flows towards the poles at high levels, while cold air sinks at the poles and returns towards the equator at the surface. This basic vertical circulation is modified in a number of ways, and one should consider the situation in the northern hemisphere, remembering that a similar situation exists in the southern hemisphere. As the warm equatorial air moves northwards it becomes crowded because there is less room towards the pole and some of it descends where it gives rise to the subtropical high pressure belt which encircles the globe.

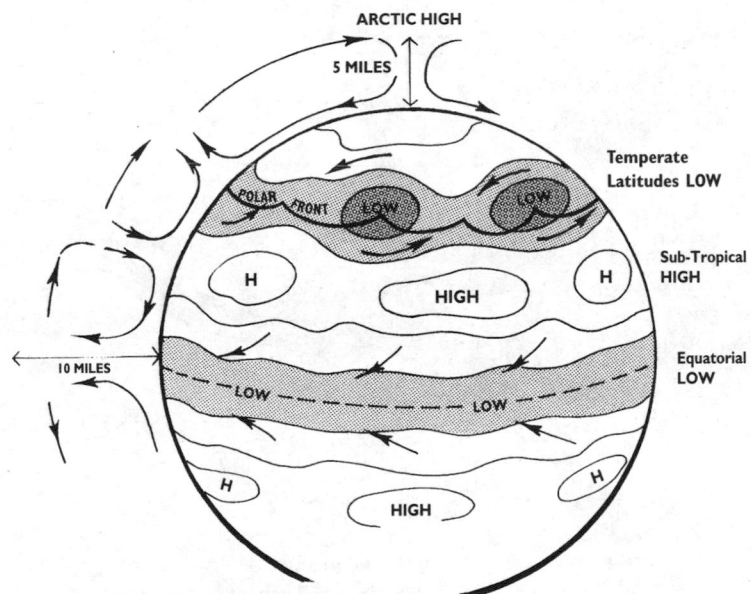

Fig. 86 *A diagrammatic interpretation of the general circulation showing the four main pressure belts in the northern hemisphere. Compare this diagram with the satellite photograph.*

This sinking air spreads out at the surface where it is influenced by the spinning motion of the earth which in the northern hemisphere has the effect of deflecting the air to the right. Thus, air moving towards the equator is deflected to form the north-east trade winds while the air moving towards the pole is deflected to form the westerly and south-westerly winds of temperate latitudes. Air flowing outwards from the Polar high is similarly deflected to give generally north east winds, and the boundary where these meet the warmer tropical air is known as the polar front. The fact that the British Isles lie close to the polar front accounts for many of the main characteristics of our weather. The pattern is still further modified by the effect of the great land masses which heat up and cool off much more quickly than the oceans and which, in the course of a season, can establish pressure systems which distort the general circulation. In winter the intense cooling of the atmosphere over the cold areas of Canada and Siberia causes high pressure systems to develop in these areas within the temperate low pressure belt.

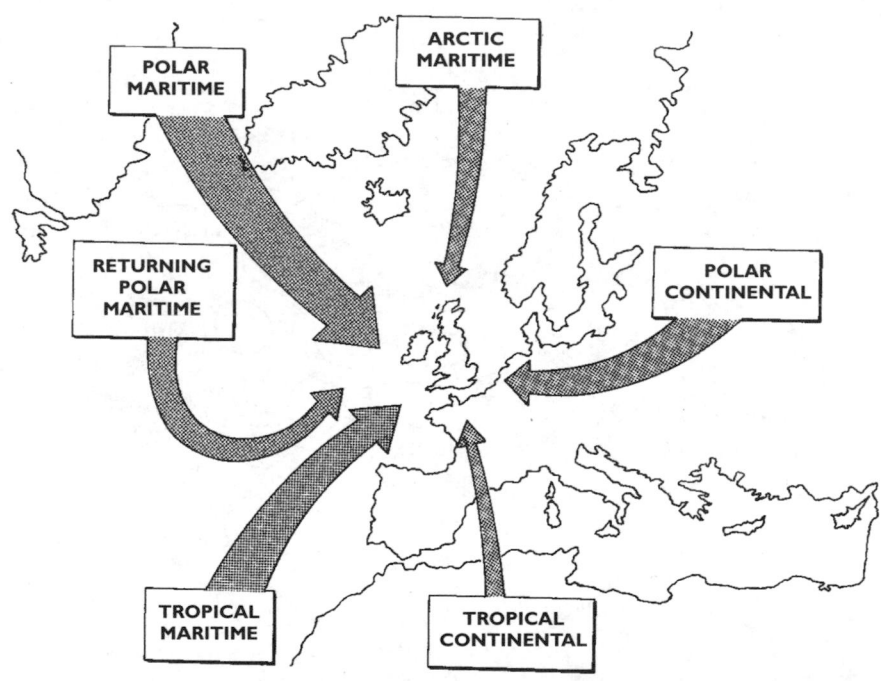

Fig. 87   *The main air streams which affect the British Isles. The width of the arrows is proportional to the frequency of occurrence.*

Airmasses and Airstreams

Air that remains in contact with a part of the earth's surface for a prolonged period of time gradually acquires the properties of that surface, notably temperature and humidity. Such stagnant oceans of air or "air masses" are usually to be found in the polar and sub-tropical high pressure belts. From these source regions the air flows out gently as air streams which themselves are modified by contact with the land or sea. A maritime airstream will tend to become saturated, especially in its lower layers in contact with the ocean surface. A continental airstream on the other hand is likely to be dry. Polar or arctic air moving south is warmed from below and therefore tends towards instability; in other words it has a tendency to rise and if moist enough to form clouds and possibly rain. Tropical air moving north is cooled from below and tends to become more stable; that is to say it is inclined to stay where it is and resist vertical movement. It is clear then that airstreams from particular source regions have fairly distinct characteristics and it is possible to deduce the general weather pattern associated with each of them by considering the properties of the original air mass and how it is modified during its migration from the source region. But take care. Few airstreams follow such an idealised pattern and many have characteristics which fall somewhere between the standard types.

WEATHER MAPS

The fronts which are shown on some of the charts, using the symbols which are familiar from television and press reports, represent sections of the polar front where there is pronounced interaction between warmer and cooler air masses. The fronts show the position on the surface of the boundary between these air masses. The lines which appear on all the charts are "isobars" or lines joining points of equal atmospheric pressure at sea level.

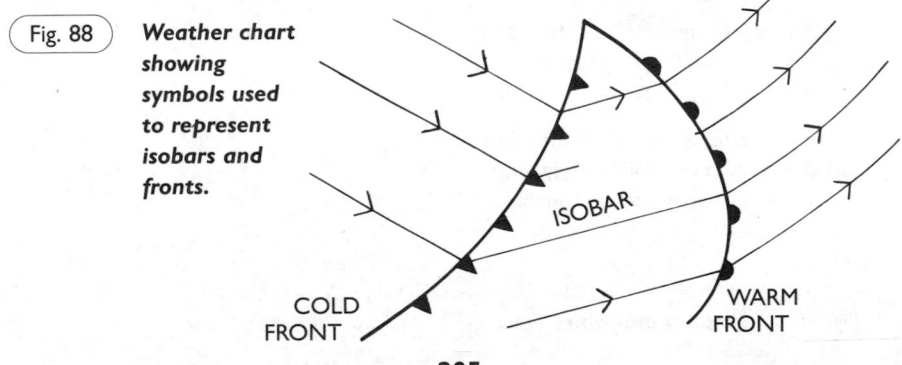

Fig. 88 *Weather chart showing symbols used to represent isobars and fronts.*

ISOBAR

COLD FRONT

WARM FRONT

You might expect the winds to follow a direct course from high to low pressure areas. In practice, because of the earth's rotation, the winds are deflected to the right in the northern hemisphere so that they tend to blow along the isobars with low pressure always on the left hand side.

WEATHER ASSOCIATED WITH THE MAIN AIRSTREAMS WHICH AFFECT THE BRITISH ISLES

In the following diagrams the meteorological situations associated with each of the six main airstreams which affect the British Isles are illustrated, together with a brief resume of the type of weather to be expected in winter and summer in Britain.

Polar Maritime

SUMMER: Heavy showers, thunder storms in mountains.

WINTER: Heavy showers in west, snow in mountains. Clear skies in east at night giving frost. Dry in lee of mountains.

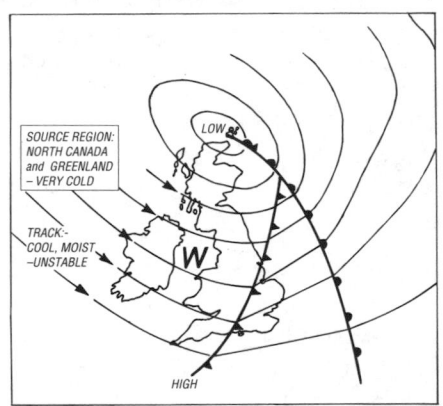

Fig. 89   *Polar maritime, Pm.*

Tropical Maritime

SUMMER: South-west winds. Warm and sunny inland. Low stratus clouds round west coast, perhaps with rain or drizzle.

WINTER: Stratus clouds/hill fog/drizzle clearing in north-east. Mild muggy with prolonged rainfall in westerly mountains.

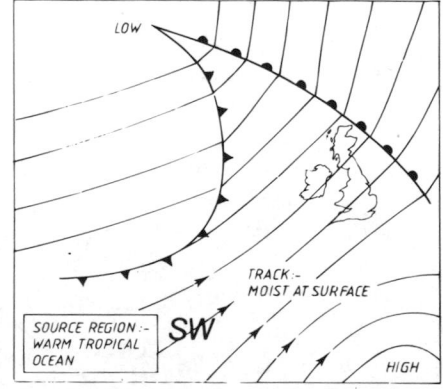

Fig. 90   *Tropical maritime, Tm.*

Tropical Continental

SUMMER ONLY: Heat-wave weather, hazy with occasional thunder. Fog on East Coast. Night time fog on eastern hills.

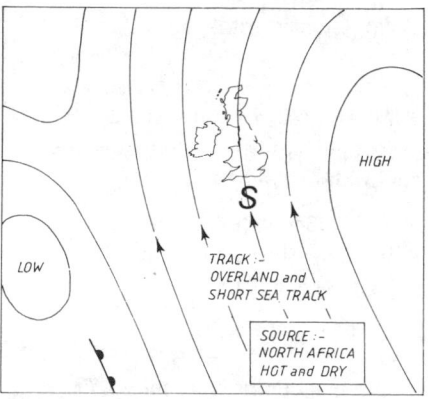

Fig. 91   *Tropical continental, Tc.*

Returning Polar Maritime

SUMMER: Very warm, stratus cloud in south-west. Equally showers and storms inland.

WINTER: Stratus cloud. Showers in mountains, particularly in the west.

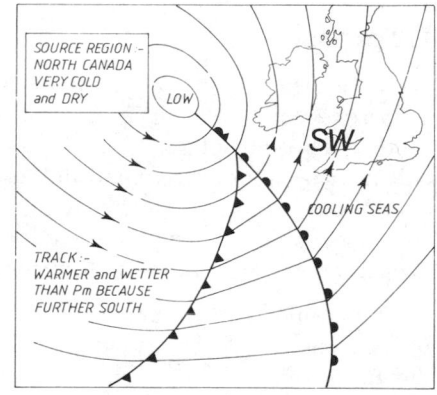

Fig. 92   *Returning polar maritime, rPm.*

Arctic Maritime

SUMMER: Cool with frequent heavy showers. Local thunderstorms.

WINTER: Very cold, strong winds from north and north-east. Heavy snow showers particularly in north and coastal areas. Cold and bright in Lake District and South Wales in lee of mountains to north.

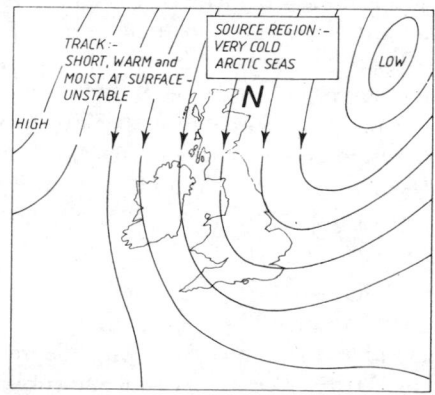

Fig. 93   *Arctic maritime, Am.*

Polar Continental

SUMMER: Warm and dry, cloud-free, except perhaps near east coast where cool with light showers.

WINTER: Snow showers near east coast. A few snow showers in west. Very cold and strong east winds.

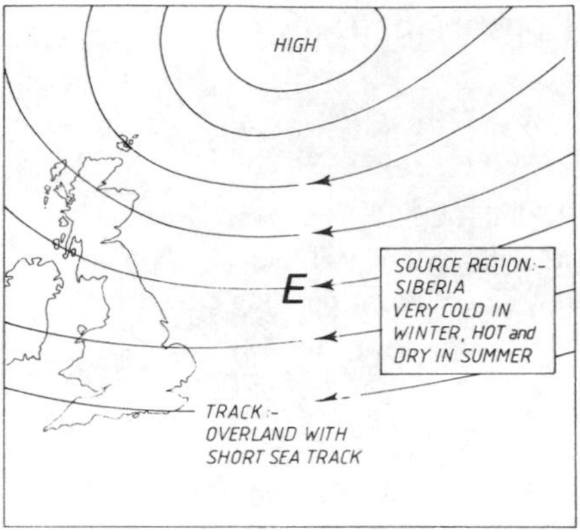

SOURCE REGION:- SIBERIA VERY COLD IN WINTER, HOT and DRY IN SUMMER

TRACK:- OVERLAND WITH SHORT SEA TRACK

HIGH

E

Fig. 94   *Polar continental, Pc.*

Depressions

We have seen how the polar front separates two air masses with contrasting properties; cold 'polar air' to the north and warm, moist 'tropical' air to the south. The line of this front is normally to be found across the North Atlantic, between Newfoundland and Iceland and it is here that the depressions, or low pressure systems, which dictate so much of our weather are born. Initiated simply as a wave in the polar front, a depression may deepen rapidly, developing a characteristic frontal pattern.

It is important to appreciate that a depression is not simply a surface phenomenon and Fig 95 attempts to illustrate its development in three dimensions.

Notice how three kinds of motion are involved: the cyclonic movement of air in an anticlockwise direction round the centre of the low pressure area, giving rise to the rule, 'that if you stand with your back to the surface wind, low pressure is on your left'; the upward movement of warm air drawn in at low levels (convergence) and spreading out a high levels (divergence); and the generally eastward movement of the whole system at a speed which varies between 20 km and 80 km per hour. Because the cold front moves somewhat faster than the warm front, it gradually catches up and eventually overtakes it so that the warm air is squeezed upwards by the colder and denser air behind the cold front.

The new front so formed between the two masses of cold air is known as an occlusion. This process continues until the depression fills. The extensive cloud and rain associated with depressions is caused by the forced ascent of the warm air which expands and cools, releasing the moisture which it can no longer hold. Occlusions are a common feature of weather systems over the British Isles. They tend to exhibit the characteristics of both warm and cold fronts and are often associated with prolonged periods of cloud and rain. (Fig. 99)

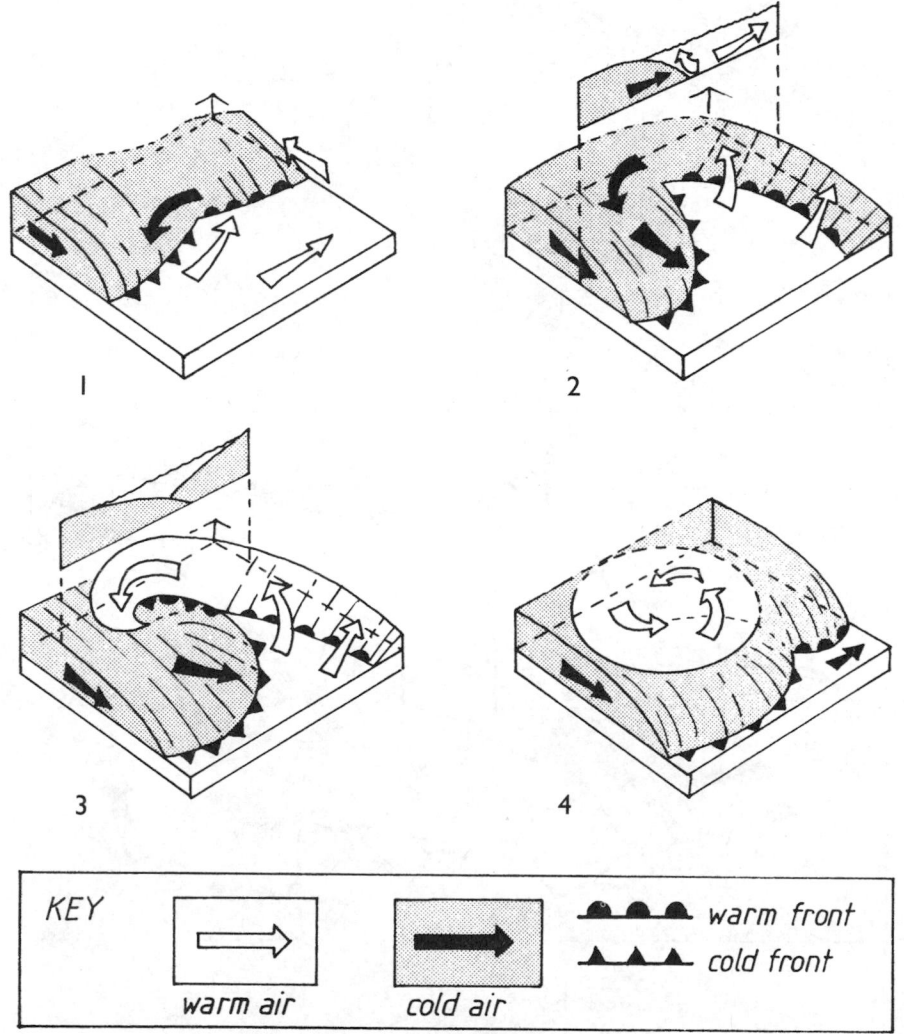

KEY

⇨ warm air

➡ cold air

� warm front

▲▲▲ cold front

Fig. 95 *The development of a depression showing the vertical dimension, based on an illustration in Mountain Weather for Climbers, by D. Unwin.*

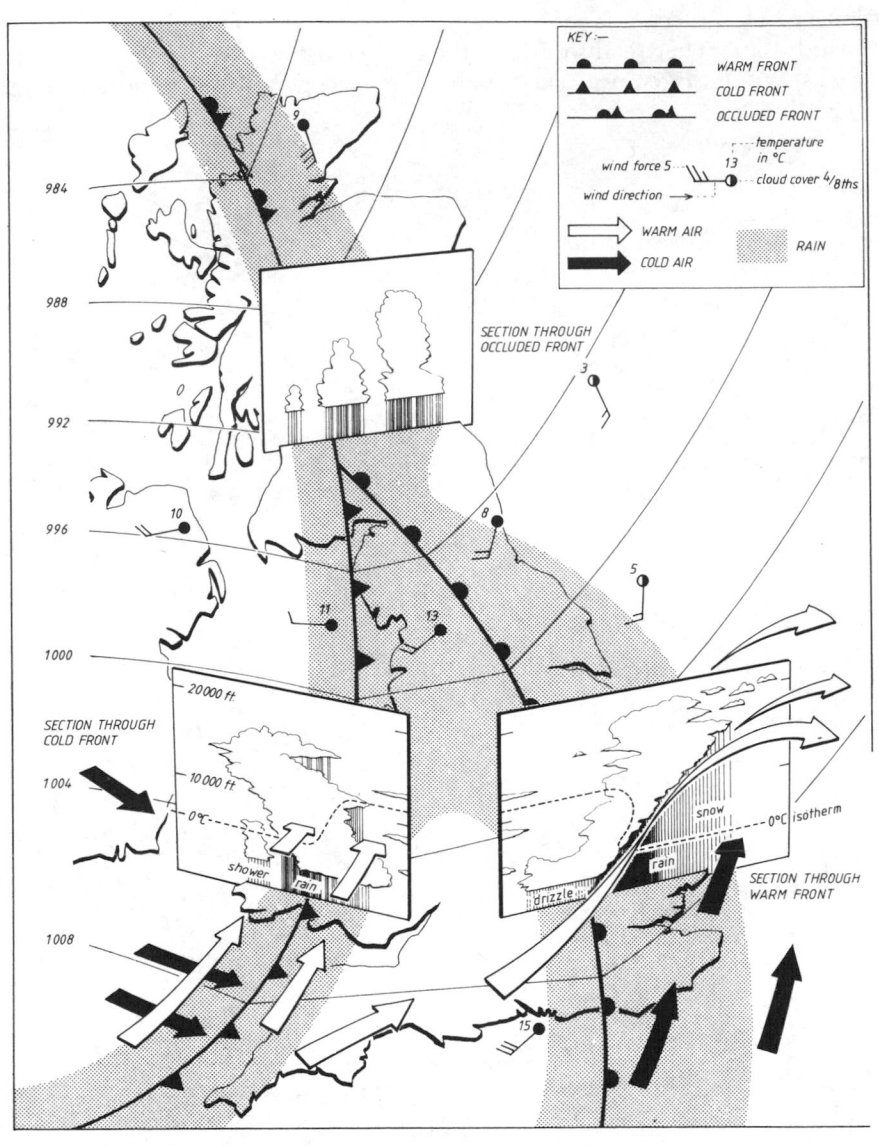

Fig. 96 — *A depression crossing the British Isles - based on an illustration in Know the Weather.*

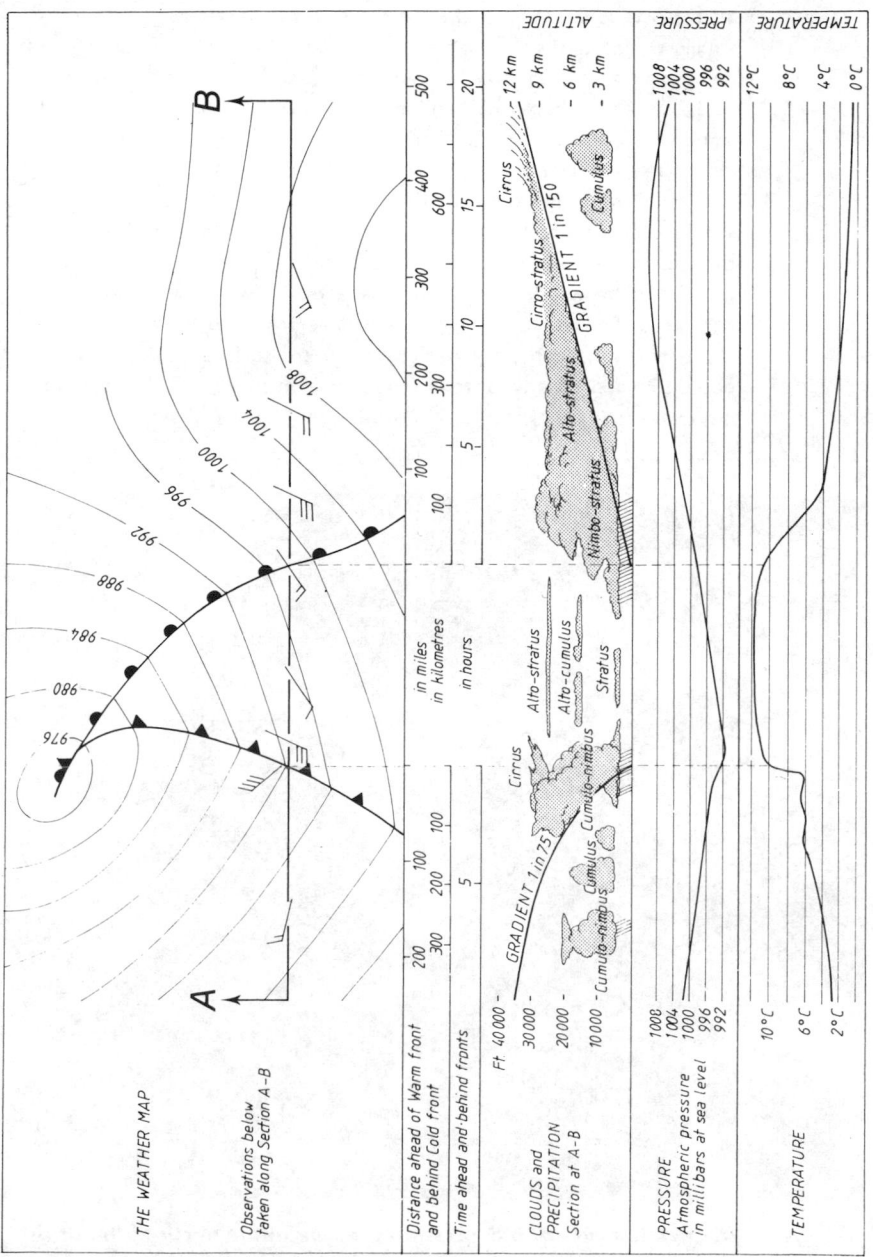

Fig. 97   *Description overleaf.*

Fig. 97 ***Weather associated with the passage of a depression.***
An illustration of the weather pattern associated with a 'typical'
depression moving eastwards at an average speed of 25mph. The width
of the system is almost 1,000 miles, so it takes 40 hours to pass over a
stationary observer. The vertical scale of the section along AB showing
clouds and precipitation is greatly exaggerated in relation to the
horizontal, with the result that the slope of the fronts appear much
steeper than they really are. In fact, the gradient of the warm front in
this example is 1 in 150, a slope of less than half a degree. One effect of
this is that the first high clouds on the leading edge of the warm front
may be seen by an observer many hours before the onset of rain
associated with the passage of the front at the surface. It should be
noted that depressions range in size from about 150 to 2,500 miles and
can travel at speeds of up to 50mph.

Fig. 98 ***A satellite's view of a depression crossing to the north of the British
Isles. Note the secondary depression already well established in the
trailing cold front of the primary.***

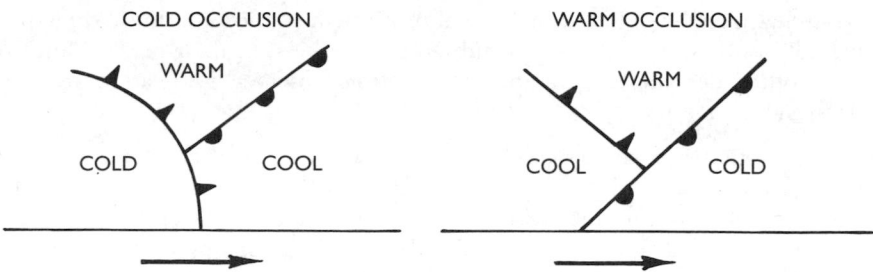

Vertical sections through a cold and a warm occlusion.

Such is the life-cycle of a typical depression and it follows that certain more or less regular patterns of weather are associated with its various phases. In looking at these patterns it must be remembered that no two depressions are exactly alike. Not only do they vary in depth and character but their track in relation to the observer may be very different.

CROSSED WINDS RULES

We can distinguish between the lower wind which corresponds to the movement of the lowest clouds, roughly parallel to the isobars, and the upper wind as indicated by the movement of the highest clouds. It is the upper

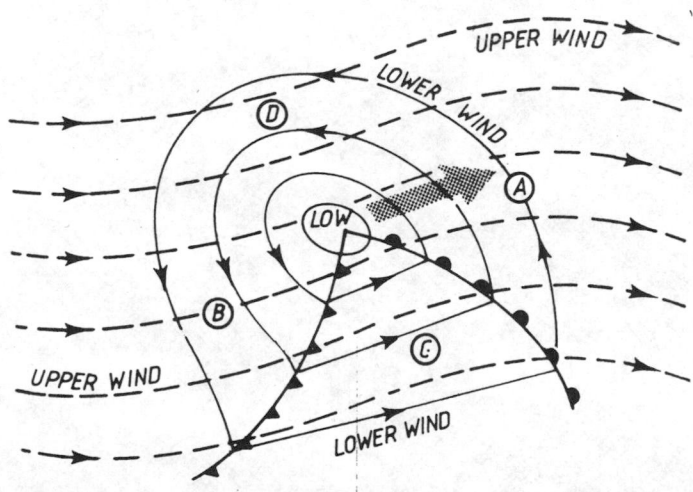

Fig. 100   *Weather map showing isobars for both upper and lower winds associated with a frontal depression.*

wind that is responsible for the general movement of the depression. Fig 100 includes isobars for both these winds and it can be seen their relationship to each other depends on the position of the observer in relation to the depression.

At position A, if the observer stands with the back to the lower wind ,the upper wind is blowing from the left. At B, with the back to the lower wind, the upper wind is from the right. At C the winds are parallel and in the same direction while at D they are parallel but blowing in opposite directions. Provided you can distinguish between the upper and lower winds it is possible to tell where you are in relation to the centre of the depression and therefore to anticipate the next sequence of weather.

The crossed winds rules can now be stated:

(a) If you stand with your back to the lower wind and the upper wind comes from your left then the weather is likely to deteriorate. (Observer A in Fig 100).

(b) If you stand with your back to the lower wind and the upper wind comes from your right then the weather is likely to improve. (Observer B in Fig 100)

(c) If you stand with your back to the lower wind and the upper wind is behind you or ahead of you then there is likely to be little immediate change in the weather. (Observers C, D in Fig 100)

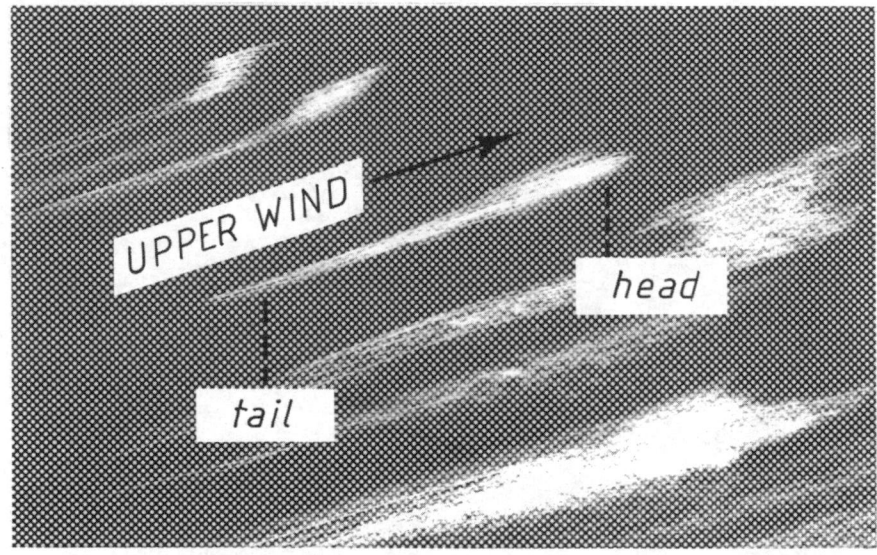

Fig. 101   *Cirrus clouds streaming in the upper wind at about 10km altitude.*

The wind at the surface in the vicinity of a depression blows at an angle of between 20-30° to the lower wind in the direction of the lowest pressure. So to find the lower wind turn 25° in a clockwise direction from the surface wind.

The upper wind is more difficult to gauge but can be estimated by reference to medium and high cloud layers. Cirrus clouds are particularly useful indicators since they normally herald the approach of a warm front. Remember that the tails or fall-streaks stream behind and below the heads.

SOME GENERAL POINTERS IN ANTICIPATING THE MOVEMENT OF DEPRESSIONS

In winter the polar front moves south, to lie roughly on a line between the eastern seaboard of the USA and the British Isles which are therefore close to the track of depressions.

If the Azores high extends northwards it pushes the polar front in the same direction. This results in warmer weather in the British Isles.

As a general rule, the centre of a depression will move parallel to the isobars in the warm sector and at the same speed as the wind in the warm sector.

A wide warm sector means that the depression is likely to continue to deepen.

Small developing depressions move quickly and tend to follow the main air streams.

Depressions move from areas of rising pressure tendency to areas of falling pressure tendency.

Depressions tend to follow the flow of air round large stationary anticyclones.

Families of depressions tend to follow the parent one, each new one starting further south than its predecessor.

A secondary depression tends to move with the main circulation round the primary.

Generally speaking, the future movement of a depression is an extension of its previous track, but intense depressions often move to the left.

A warm occlusion tends to follow the line of the warm front.

A cold occlusion tends to follow the line of the cold front.

As an occlusion progresses, the depression slows down and its movement becomes more erratic and may even cease altogether.

Anticyclones

An anticyclone is a region of relatively high pressure, with light winds circulating in a clockwise direction in the northern hemisphere round the centre of high pressure. Two main types are recognised: cold anticyclones where the cold dense air is confined to surface levels, and warm anticyclones where the cold air is to be found at higher levels.

We have already seen that a semi-permanent cold anticyclone forms over Siberia in winter due to intense surface cooling.

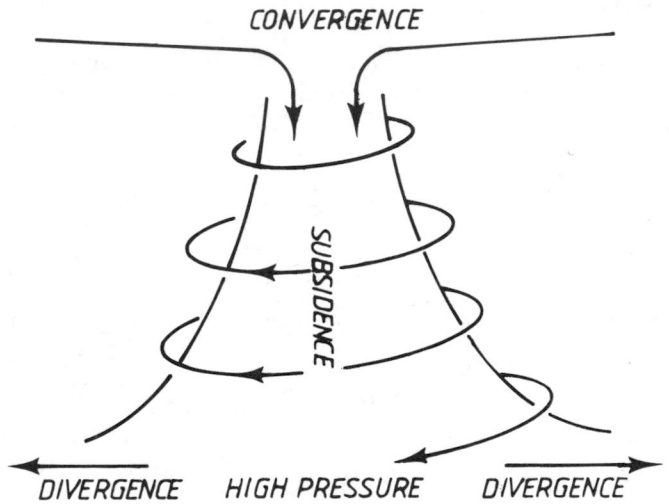

Fig. 102   *A model illustrating the main characteristics of an anticyclone.*

The cold dense air sinks and spreads out at the surface (divergence) while replacement air is drawn at high altitudes (convergence). When this system extends to the British Isles it can bring bright cold weather to inland areas, although low cloud may persist round the east coast and further inland, especially in the north. Transitory cold anticyclones or ridges of high pressure commonly occur between a succession of depressions bringing a short respite from the normal pattern of frontal weather. In winter they may become established for longer periods if they extend over cold land surfaces.

Warm anticyclones are systems within the sub-tropical high pressure belt resulting from persistent convergent winds at high level. In contrast with the cold anticyclone the subsiding air within the system does not undergo any appreciable surface cooling. The Azores high is one such system and its position in relation to the British Isles has a profound effect on the type of weather we experience. In general a warm anticyclone is a stable, slow moving system, consisting of warm dry subsiding air and bringing long periods of fine clear weather. Temporary warm anticyclones can develop as extensions from the sub-tropical high or, more often simply as a development of a cold anticyclone where warming due to prolonged subsidence overcomes surface cooling.

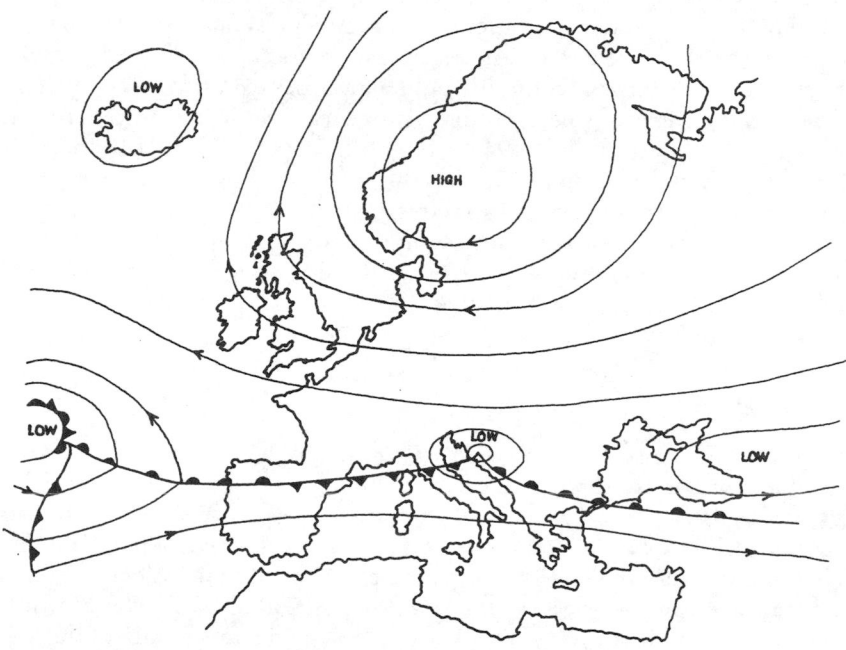

Fig. 103　*A 'blocking' high over Scandinavia which deflects the polar front and its associated depressions to the south of their normal track.*

Some Effects of Mountains on Weather

One of the very few reliable long term records of mountain weather in this country was compiled over a period of 21 years at the observatory on the summit of Ben Nevis, from 1883 to 1904. It is instructive to compare this record with similar recordings made at sea level in nearby Fort William. On average Ben Nevis summit was 8.6°C colder, had only two-thirds of the sunshine and more than twice the rainfall. All this within a distance of 7km.

Combine this with an average daily wind speed of 48kph and you have one of the most hostile environments in the world. So there is no doubt that mountains can and do have a profound effect on the weather.

ATMOSPHERIC PRESSURE

Air pressure, or atmospheric pressure, is caused by the weight of air at any given point. It varies with altitude; the higher you go, the less the weight of air above and therefore, the less the atmospheric pressure. It also varies according to the prevailing weather system. A depression means less weight of air and therefore a lower than normal pressure reading. If you did not take the weather system into account it would appear that you had gained height! Pressure is measured in millibars (mb) and at sea level in the British Isles is found to vary between about 940 mb (low pressure) and 1,040 mb (high pressure). With increasing altitude the pressure falls off at a rate of approximately 1 mb for every 10 metres. So, if the pressure at sea level is 1,013 mb (ie average or standard pressure) it will be 913 mb at a height of 1,000 metres. It should be noted that all the data shown on weather maps relate to conditions at sea level – this applies also to temperature and wind speed readings.

TEMPERATURE

As a parcel of air rises or is forced up a mountainside, it expands because of the reduction of atmosphere pressure. Energy is required to effect this expansion and the parcel cools as it ascends. The rate at which it cools is known as the lapse rate and on average this is - 1°C for every 150m of altitude. When the air is dry the lapse rate is greatest, - 1° per 100m. When the air is saturated, ie cloudy, it is least, - 1° per 200m. A feature of the weather over the British Isles is the sharp contrast between the mild temperatures of the low lying west coast and the nearby cold mountain areas.

Thus, if we follow our parcel of air up and over the mountain, it cools as it rises until it reaches the dew point, the temperature at which the water vapour in the air condenses into droplets. From this point upwards the air is saturated and it cools at the slower rate, possibly shedding moisture as it goes in the form of rain. Going down the lee side the air is dry and warms up as it expands at the dry lapse rate. The net effect of this passage over the mountain is that the air is both drier and warmer on the lee side than on the windward side. In the Alps the difference may be substantial, but even in the British Isles the 'Föhn' effect can result in the air temperature being up to 4°C warmer on the east side of the highlands when a moist south-west wind is blowing.

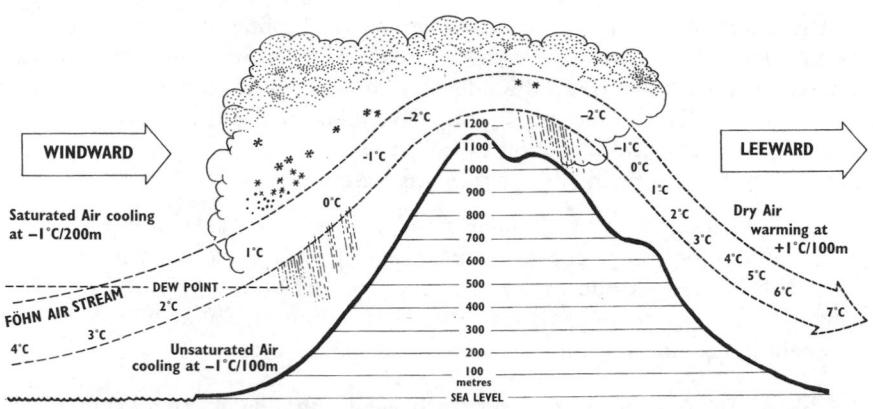

Fig. 104 *The Föhn effect. Because of the different lapse rates for saturated and unsaturated air, the air on the lee side of the mountain range is warmer than the air on the windward side. In the Alps this warm dry wind is known as the Föhn and is often associated with the onset of a wet avalanche cycle.*

WIND SPEED

Records from the automatic weather station on the summit of Cairngorm indicate that wind speeds are on average three times those in the adjacent Spey Valley. Wind in the mountains is indeed a force to be reckoned with, but it is not possible to establish any hard and fast relationship between altitude and wind speed. Much depends on the local topography, the direction of the wind and the atmospheric conditions prevailing at the time.

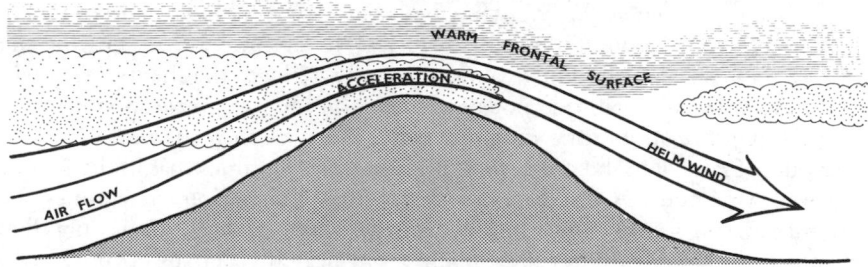

Fig. 105 *The acceleration of air flow over a mountain barrier caused by the squeezing of air between the mountain top and the ceiling created by a warm frontal surface.*

A range of mountains constitutes a barrier to the flow of air, particularly if it is orientated at right angles to the airstream. The air has only two options, to rise up and over the top of the range, or to flow round the obstacle. Both have the same effect: an increase in wind speed because of the 'overcrowding' of the air. If the airstream is stable, it will tend to flow round; if it is unstable, it will tend to rise over the range. (See page 205).

The funnelling effect of mountains and valleys is well known in the Lake District and other groups of hills, giving rise to greatly enhanced wind speeds particularly at the valley heads. Perhaps the best known example of this is the 'Mistral', a wind which blows down the narrow Rhone valley between two mountain blocks and out into the Mediterranean (Fig 106).

Fig. 106   *'The Mistral', a strong northerly wind, captured by the mountain barriers on either side of the Rhone and funnelled into its valley.*

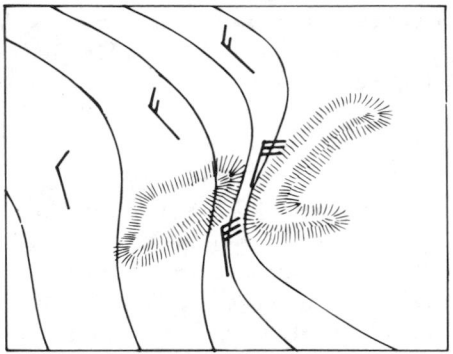

PRECIPITATION

You could be excused for thinking that Fig 107 is a simple contour map showing the high ground in the British Isles. In fact, it is a map showing the average annual rainfall which almost exactly reflects the main mountain features. Increase in altitude not only means an increase in the frequency of rainfall, but also an increase in its intensity. For example, the yearly average of hours of rainfall in the north-west highlands is four times that in the Moray Firth area on the east coast. However, within this period, nine times the amount of rain actually falls. In other words, in the mountains not only does it rain more frequently but also much more heavily. Perhaps a more valid comparison can be made between the 4.35m of rain which falls on the summit of Ben Nevis and the 2.05m which falls at Fort William. In this case it is estimated that more than half the precipitation on the summit falls as snow.

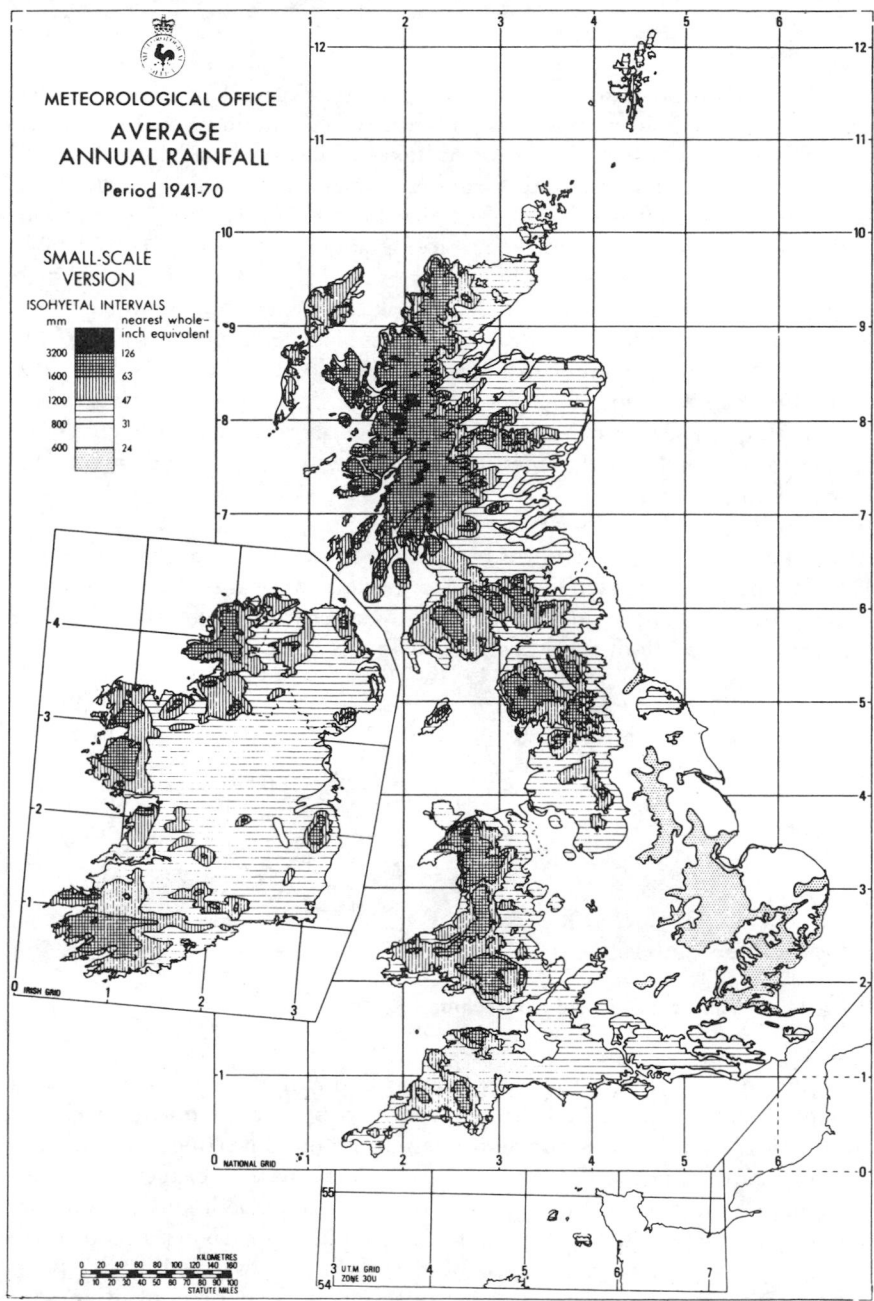

METEOROLOGICAL OFFICE
**AVERAGE
ANNUAL RAINFALL**
Period 1941-70

SMALL-SCALE
VERSION

ISOHYETAL INTERVALS
mm   nearest whole-inch equivalent

mm	nearest whole-inch equivalent
3200	126
1600	63
1200	47
800	31
600	24

Fig. 107 *Meteorological Office map showing the annual rainfall, 1941-70. Reproduced with the permission of the Meteorological Office Crown Copyright.*

The fundamental reason for the increase in rainfall with altitude is that moist air is lifted in its passage across a range of hills and in so doing is cooled to the Dew Point where condensation takes place and cloud forms. If the cloud is thick enough raindrops form, encouraged by turbulence within the cloud itself. This apparently straightforward process is, in reality, much more complex and local conditions and topography can have a considerable influence on the distribution and intensity of rainfall. A number of areas, such as the head of Borrowdale in the Lake District, are renowned for exceptionally heavy rainfall due to the convergence of air currents in the valleys leading to the mountain heartland. As we have seen the converse is also true when air, spreading out and subsiding after crossing a mountain range, can give rise to warmer conditions and clearer skies. When a cold front crosses the mountains and comes into contact with this warmer air, thunder storms with sleet and hail may be expected because of the heightened contrast between the two air masses. Following the same reasoning, a warm front would be weakened as a result of reduced contrast. In winter, the air in the lee of a mountain range tends to be colder because of clear skies and overnight cooling by radiation. Thus, more severe weather can be expected from the passage of a warm front and less severe from a cold front.

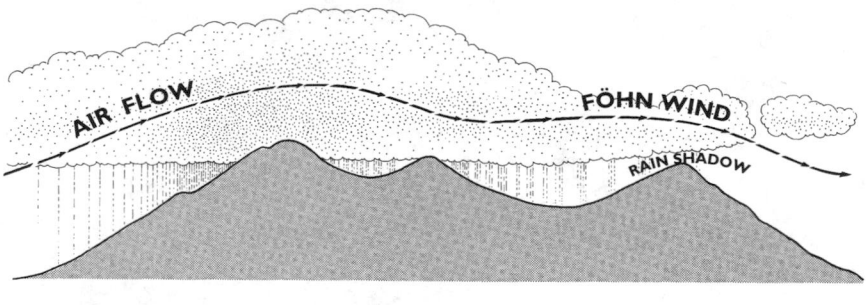

(Fig. 108) *Rain shadow and Föhn wind.*

Quite often there appears to be a slowing down of a front as it crosses a mountain barrier, particularly if it happens to be a slow-moving occluded front. When this happens rainfall is likely to be more prolonged and intense on the windward side of the front than would otherwise be expected. Finally, it should be mentioned that under certain favourable conditions areas of low pressure can form in the lee of mountains. Unlike normal depressions these 'orographic lows' are characterised by descending air warmed by the Föhn effect and are therefore likely to give rise to warm dry conditions in summer and cold frosty conditions in winter. They form most readily in the lee of the more substantial mountain ranges of Europe.

SNOW

Weather conditions giving rise to snow are much the same as those which bring rain. If it is sufficiently cold precipitation will fall as snow and in the mountains a greater proportion of the enhanced precipitation is likely to fall as snow. This is especially so in late autumn, winter and early spring when small differences in temperature are likely to be critical. The presence or absence of snow is of vital importance to the mountaineer and one needs to be aware that a forecast of rain or sleet in the valley can mean a blizzard on the tops.

BATTLING AGAINST THE WIND

Battling against a strong head wind greatly increases energy production and may lead to the early onset of exhaustion. It is not generally realised that a wind blowing against an object exerts a force roughly proportional to the square of its velocity. In simple terms, if the wind speed increases by a factor of 3 from say, 10mph to 30mph, then the force exerted by the wind increases by a factor of 9.

LOCAL HEATING AND COOLING EFFECTS

Air is warmed or cooled by contact with the ground. If the ground is warm, as it would be on south facing rocky mountain slopes on a hot summer day, the surface air tends to rise relative to the colder free air at the same level. This causes a gentle upslope breeze from the valley known as an anabatic

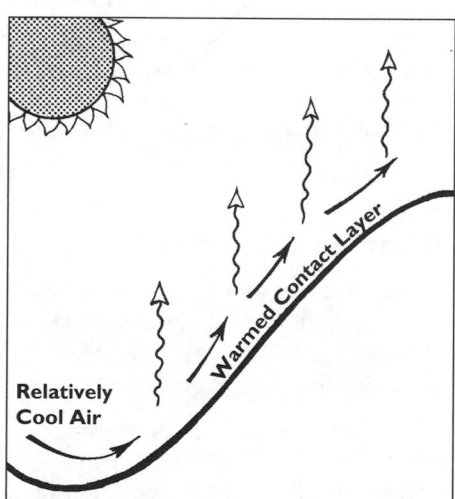

Fig. 109 *Anabatic winds caused by intense solar heating during the day.*

Warmed Contact Layer

Relatively Cool Air

wind. Sadly, such winds are not frequent or of much significance in the mountains. (Fig 109)

Of much greater significance are the cold winds which pour off the mountains, usually at night, when surface air is cooled by contact with the cold ground which has lost heat by radiation into clear skies. In favourable circumstances these katabatic winds can attain gale force although in the British mountains speeds in excess of 5mph are uncommon. Even very gentle down-slope movement of cold air is sufficient to cause it to accumulate in valley bottoms and hollows where the temperature may well reach many degrees below that on the hillsides above. These are the frost hollows and fog belts which the camper avoids to ensure a comfortable night.

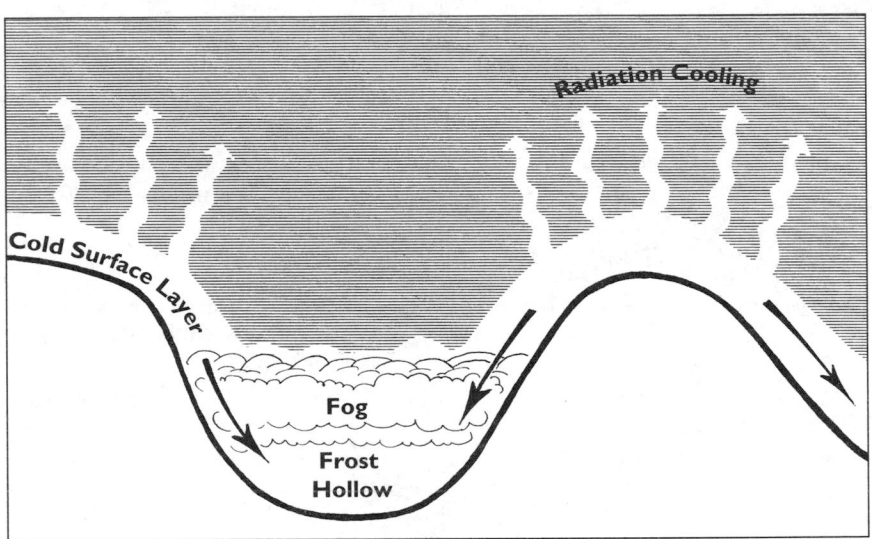

(Fig. 110) *Katabatic winds pouring off the snow covered hills at night filling the valleys with cold air and causing intense frost and morning fog.*

Weather Forecasts

There are many sources of weather information and the user should be aware of the limitations of the various methods of presentation.

Press Forecasts

These are unsuitable for up to date forecasts for upland localities and are only useful if they include weather maps giving the broad-scale synoptic pattern ie location of high and low pressure weather fronts etc. Better quality newspapers give forecast synoptic charts for the day of publication and area forecasts for lowland regions. However, by the time you see a chart in a paper new developments may have occurred in the time lag since the information was produced.

Television Forecasts

Again these can give only generalised forecasts for relatively large areas. However recent developments in television forecast presentation do mean that forecast synoptic charts and accompanying general outlooks are now available at certain times, which could help planning ahead to take advantage of settled spells or to avoid severe weather conditions.

Radio Forecasts

Weather forecasts are broadcast regularly in the various BBC services. On the whole they are for short periods only, mainly designed to give general guidance and certainly not applicable to mountain areas without careful interpretation and supplementary data. However a few specialised outdoor activities forecasts are broadcast by BBC Radio Scotland at weekends. The shipping forecast, which is broadcast on BBC Radio 4, is exceptional in that it provides detailed information including actual observations from coastal stations, from which is possible, not only to draw up a synoptic chart with isobars covering the whole of the British Isles, but also to draw a similar forecast chart for 24 hours ahead. This forecast situation can then be used to provide the base from which it should be possible to develop a clearer idea of what is likely to happen in the mountains.

Recorded Weather Forecasts

These are regional or local forecasts which can be obtaining by dialling a number which is linked with an automatic answering service which supplies a pre-recorded forecast for a specific area. Most of these services are charged at a premium rate so it is important to ensure that sufficient money is available. All are on 0898 or 0836 prefix. Where appropriate a phone card can be useful. Specialised 'mountain' forecasts are available in some areas – be wary of lowland forecasts which may be unsuitable. In some areas, such as the Lake District, there is still a special dial-the weather service for walkers and climbers charged at local call rates. Even so, mountain forecasts should always be supplemented by further information if there is any element of doubt.

In some districts, such as the Cairngorms, mountain activity and climbing centres display forecasts which have been issued by the regional Meteorological Office for the particular district. These forecasts can be very helpful, but it must be remembered that there is an inevitable time-lag between the weather chart(s) on which they are based, and the time when they go on display, so that the forecast becomes more and more out of date as each hour passes. When the weather situation is reasonably straightforward this is usually not very important but, during periods of unsettled weather and rapidly developing weather systems, a check should always be made if the forecast appears to be going awry.

The Met Office is now installing automatic weather stations in remote areas, including some mountain tops, which should assist in improving mountain forecasts.

Local On-the-Spot Sources of Information

Local people who have lived in a mountainous district for some time and whose daily activities take them out of doors, learn a great deal about local peculiarities of the weather. Their advice should always be listened to, especially when combined with an up-to-date appraisal of the synoptic weather chart situation as given by a Meteorological Office forecaster.

Lightning

Lightning can hardly be regarded as a major mountain hazard yet every year it claims the lives of two or three mountaineers. Like the winter avalanche it is commonly regard as an Act of God and the very impartiality with which it chooses its victims encourages a fatalistic outlook among climbers and walkers. The actual physical process is now fairly well understood and this emphasises that there are certain simple precautions which can be taken to avoid a strike.

The first thing to realise is that to be struck by lightning is by no means always fatal. True, a direct hit is likely to be so, but more often than not the victim receives only a part of the stroke, either by induction, because of proximity to the strike, or through the ground in the form of earth currents which dissipate, like the roots of a tree, from the source. Such partial shocks need not be fatal though they could, of course, cause death indirectly if the climber should fall off or be rendered incapable. The stroke itself is a variable quantity, being the product of a very large current (thousands of amps) and a very short time (thousands of a second). In many cases a much smaller current in contact for a few seconds could cause considerably more damage.

Fortunately, there is usually some advance warning of the approach of an electrical storm and avoiding action can be taken, but once in the firing line decisions tend to be taken out of your hands. Anyone who has experienced the literally hair-raising preliminaries will vouch for this. Ice axes hum and spark, the skin tingles and local projections glow with a bluish light.

Lightning is usually associated with the towering cumulonimbus type of cloud which heralds the passing of a cold front. The occasional flash followed by a roll of thunder should be warning enough that an electrical storm is on its way. The sound will travel at a speed of 1km per 3 seconds, so by timing the interval between the flash and the thunder you can estimate your distance from the storm.

During a storm, strikes tend to be concentrated on mountain tops or other natural projections from the general surroundings. At the same time, since such points 'service' a fairly wide area, there tends to be a shaded or relatively safe zone associated with them.

The peak must be at least 7m high and the relatively safe zone is of the same order horizontally. (Fig 111) Note that it affords no protection to be tucked in against the cliff or peak itself since in this position you are likely to receive earth currents shed from the peak.

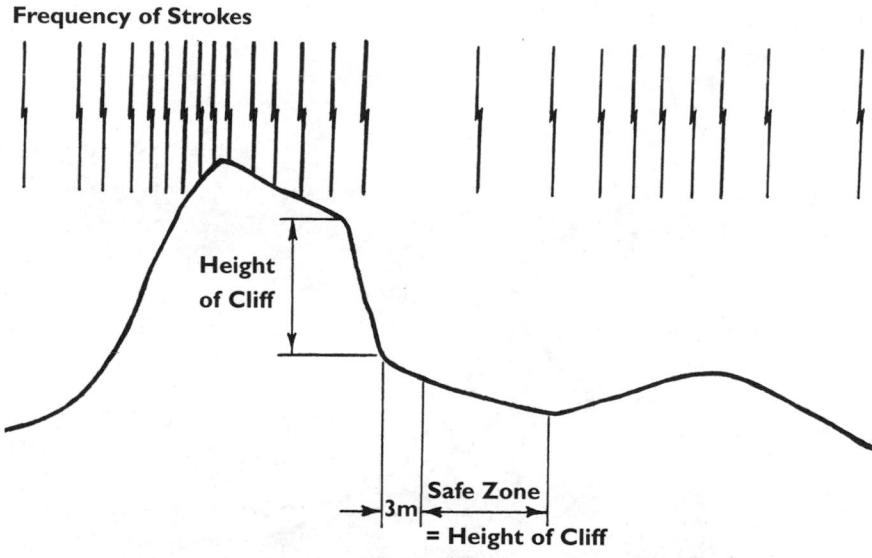

Frequency of Strokes

Height of Cliff

→3m← **Safe Zone** = **Height of Cliff**

(Fig. 111) *Frequency of lightning 'strokes' in mountain area.*

The natural inclination in a really violent storm is to seek shelter, especially if rain is driving down. Unfortunately, this is quite the wrong thing to do unless you can find a cave which gives you at least 3m head room and 1m on either side. Caves and hollows in the rock are often simply local expansions of natural fissures. These in turn are the likely conduits for earth currents, especially if they hold water and by sheltering in them you are offering yourself as a convenient alternative to the spark gap. (Figs 112 and 113)

Exactly the same argument applies to sheltering under large boulders. With reasonably waterproof clothing, remaining dry should not be a major problem and it is much safer to sit it out in the open. Try to find a broken scree slope, preferably in a safe zone and sit on top of a dry rope or rucksack with your knees up and your hands in your lap. (Fig 114) Do not attempt to support yourself on your hands or by leaning back. The object of these precautions is to keep your points of contact with the ground as close together as possible in such a position that a current flowing along the ground would tend to pass through a non-vital part of the body.

On a cliff face sit out the storm on the nearest ledge, but avoid chimneys and fissures of any kind. If a belay is necessary, try to avoid using the wet rope as a natural lead from a vertical crack to your body. On an exposed peak or ridge your position is much more vulnerable and it is normally advisable to make some attempt to get at least part way down, even at the height of the storm. Abseiling in an electrical storm is a risky manoeuvre, but it is normally preferable to a position on the lightning highway of an exposed ridge. In any

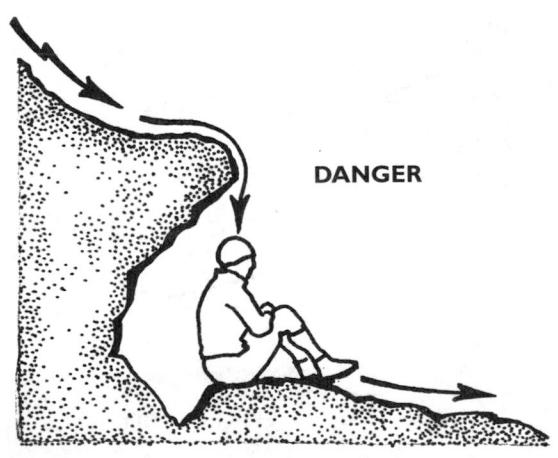

DANGER

Fig. 112 *Spark gap.*

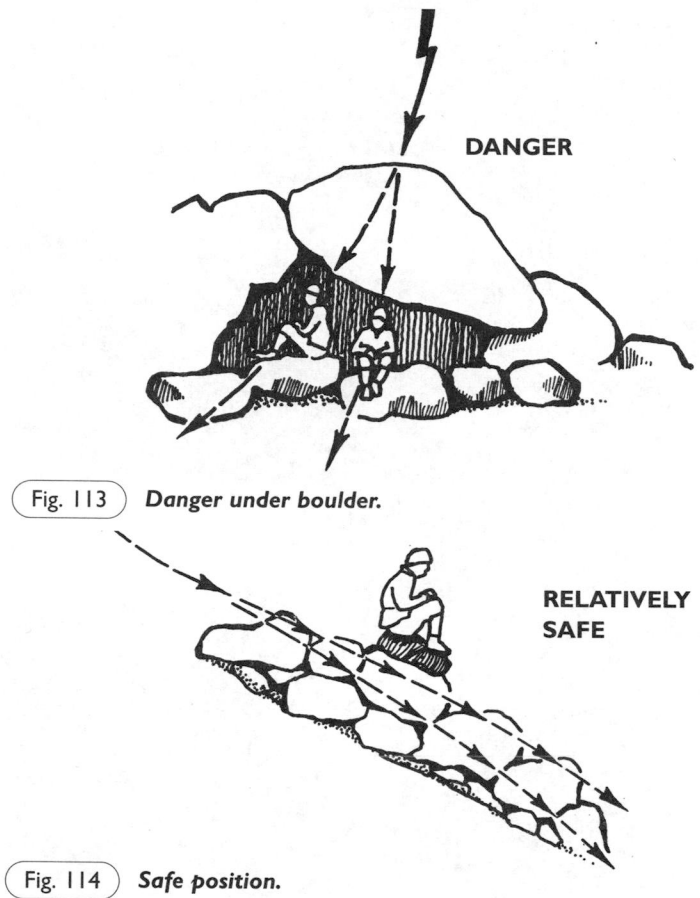

(Fig. 113) *Danger under boulder.*

DANGER

RELATIVELY SAFE

(Fig. 114) *Safe position.*

event, one or two rope lengths may well take you to a position of relative safety. If you do abseil, use a dry rope if you have the choice and use a safety rope. Fatal accidents have occurred following a non-fatal strike which, in the first instance, has merely stunned the victim.

It is fashionable, too, to discard pieces of extraneous equipment; cameras, rucksacks, crampons and even ice axes, under the mistaken impression that they 'attract' lightning. They do not, any more than you do yourself. The electrical resistance of the average axe between head and spike is almost five times that of the human body. If it is humming and sparking it may be prudent to lay it down carefully beside you, but no more. The axe is too valuable a tool to be tossed away in a storm. It may well be needed to deal with icy rocks on the retreat.

9

Mountain Hypothermia

Causes and Avoidance

Mountain hypothermia is the name given to the condition which arises when the vital core of the human body is cooled as a result of exposure to adverse conditions in the mountains. Formerly the complex of symptoms was known as 'exposure', but this term is more properly applied to exposure to the environmental conditions which give rise to hypothermia.

It is a topic which has aroused a great deal of interest and research over the years, stimulated by a number of tragic accidents to young people involved in officially sponsored expeditions. On the whole, the young are particularly vulnerable to hypothermia. Their physical and mental reserves are less than adults and for this reason great care must be taken in the planning and execution of any expedition to ensure that they are not overstretched. There has been a welcome decline in the number of reported cases of hypothermia and some of the credit for this must go to those who have worked to increase the awareness of leaders of the dangers to groups of young people exposed to wet cold conditions on the British hills and moors. Such conditions are commonplace and can be every bit as lethal as the more obviously cold, dry arctic conditions, particularly when coupled with exhaustion. Improvements in the design and quality of clothing has also had a beneficial effect and it is fortunately rare nowadays to see parties setting out for the hills inadequately clad. Indeed, the converse is sometimes the case, with groups labouring under an unnecessary burden of 'emergency' gear, sufficient to ensure that it will almost certainly be needed.

Man is a homeotherm and so endeavours to maintain a constant body temperature irrespective of the temperature of the surroundings. In a cold climate this is achieved by a combination of heat production and heat conservation, both processes being controlled partly by involuntary and partly by behavioural mechanisms.

The human body may be conceived as consisting of an inner 'hot' core surrounded by a cool outer shell. The core consists of the brain and other vital organs of the body, including the heart, lungs, liver, kidneys etc, contained within the skull, chest and abdomen. The temperature of the core is maintained at a constant 37°C. The shell is what is left; the skin, fat, muscle and limbs and is normally found to be 3°C to 5°C cooler than the core.

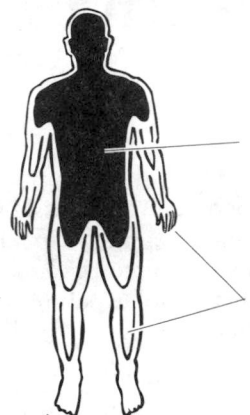

The CORE consisting of brain, lungs, heart, and other vital organs.

The SHELL consisting of the limbs, skin fat, muscle.

(Fig. 115) *The core and shell concept of heat regulation in the human body.*

In a cold environment, therefore, the shell may be regarded as a buffer zone between the core and the outside world protecting the organs of the body which are necessary for survival from any potentially catastrophic fall in temperature. It is helpful to visualise the boundary between these two areas as an elastic arrangement whereby in cold conditions the core contracts and in warm conditions the core expands into the shell.

Hypothermia is the name given to the condition which arises when there is a progressive fall in core temperature which, if not checked, leads on to unconsciousness, respiratory and cardiac failure and death. One of the quickest ways of cooling the human body is to immerse it in cold water and it is common knowledge that survival at sea in cold arctic water without special insulation can be measured in a matter of minutes. In the mountains the situation is different. Here, cold alone rarely kills, but combined with physical exhaustion it can kill just as surely as the arctic ocean. It may take longer, but the end result is the same.

It is the combination of exhaustion, cold, anxiety or mental stress which is especially dangerous. The elements in this combination will vary greatly with the individual, as will the individual's susceptibility to some or all of these factors. In considering exposure to cold, it is well to bear in mind the words of the late Mr. D. G. Duff, F.R.C.S, a mountaineer and rescuer of long experience. "It is, I consider, the additional factor of physical exhaustion over and above cold which kills quickly. Death has overtaken whole parties who, thinking they must keep moving at all costs, have bashed on instead of resting in some shelter before exhaustion supervened. The essential is always to preserve a sufficient reserve of energy in severe conditions of cold and high wind."

As a rider it may be added that, as in the case of an injured and immobilised climber in the mountains, cold may kill a person who is not, as such, physically exhausted. In this condition, however, the climber would certainly be suffering from shock and would therefore be much more susceptible to the effects of cold. Everything should be done to minimise shock and to reassure the patient. It is emphasised that the risk of death from hypothermia is a real, and often unrecognised danger among those, particularly the young, undertaking mountain expeditions in severe weather conditions.

Causes of Mountain Hypothermia

The causes of mountain hypothermia may be considered in two categories: those factors which relate to the individual and those which relate to the environment.

ENVIRONMENTAL FACTORS

Windchill

In the dry cold environment the factors to be considered are air temperature and wind speed, the combined cooling effect of which is known as wind chill. For any given air temperature the cooling effect (wind chill factor) increases rapidly with increasing wind speed. This is most marked at lower wind speeds, so that, in the range 0 - 15 m.p.h. even small changes in wind speed can have a profound effect on the degree of cooling. At wind speeds above 15 m.p.h. the factor changes more slowly. This does not mean that high winds can be discounted in other respects. A great deal more energy is required to fight against a 60 m.p.h. wind than a 15 m.p.h. one.

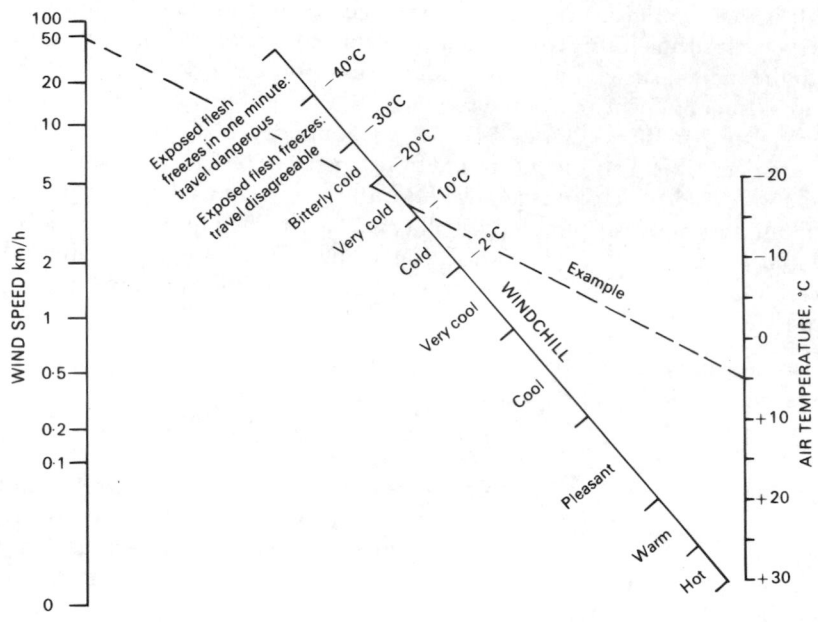

Fig. 116 **Nomogram showing effect of wind speed and air temperature on wind chill.**

Fig. 116 illustrates the cooling effect of different combinations of air temperature and wind speed on a normally clad hillwalker. The degree of windchill is represented by the subjective sensation of cold experienced by the walker. In the example given, when the air temperature is +5°C and the wind speed 50 k.p.h. the windchill is described as "very cold".

This can be expressed in a different way by calculating how cold it would have to be if there was no wind at all, to achieve the same cooling effect. In other words the equivalent temperature in still air. These still air temperatures are shown on the chart opposite the descriptive classification. In this example, the temperature in still air would have to be - 12°C to have the same cooling effect as +5°C in an 80km/h (50 m.p.h.) wind.

Charts such as this, however, should not be taken too literally. They serve to remind us that even a gentle breeze can have a dramatic effect on how cold we feel. Good, windproof clothing is therefore essential if the worst effects of wind chill are to be avoided.

Wet Cold

But protection from the wind alone is not enough. Most cases of exposure in the mountains of the British Isles occur in wet cold conditions and it is astonishing that in a country with such a high annual rainfall more attention has not been directed towards remaining dry. Even the best clothing suffers an enormous loss of its insulating efficiency when it becomes saturated, and in a wind, heat loss is further accelerated by convection and evaporation. Complete water-proofing brings its problems, but these can, at least in part, be overcome by good design.

INDIVIDUAL FACTORS

Insufficient or Inadequate Clothing

It follows from the above that clothing should offer a reasonable degree of independence from the environment. A waterproof anorak (and therefore also windproof) is a 'must' and there are many well designed, inexpensive 'cagoules' on the market. Sweating can be a problem, but the design should allow for a considerable degree of ventilation: this keeps condensation to a minimum and at the same time allows for a complete weather seal in severe conditions Careful regulation of pace uphill and of the amount of clothing worn helps to avoid discomfort. Breathable material such as Goretex which is waterproof but which allows the outward passage of water vapour is readily available and, though expensive, does provide a partial solution to one of the most intractable problems for the mountain walker: how to keep out the rain and avoid getting wet from condensation at the same time. What you wear underneath your anorak is largely a matter of personal taste provided you have enough to afford the right level of insulation to match the conditions. The fundamental principle is that these underlayers should trap a layer of warm air between your body and the outer shell. On the whole it is better to wear several layers of thin sweaters rather than one thick one. This allows you to ring the changes to suit the conditions as well as providing a kind of air sandwich which improves insulation. Next to the skin long johns and vest made from an efficient wicking fabric will help to keep the skin surface dry and comfortable.

A comprehensive range of clothing and equipment for different expeditions in summer or winter is given in Appendix 3. It is however worth drawing attention to the fact that an enormous amount of heat can be lost from the thighs and also from the head, both parts of the body that are all to commonly ignored as far as adequate cover is concerned. Some fashion trousers provide minimal protection when wet. The range and design of protective clothing nowadays is such that it is inexcusable for groups to set out inadequately clad. It is the leader's responsibility to see that each member of the party is wearing or carrying sufficient clothing to afford adequate protection in the event of bad weather.

It is important to realise that the clothing of growing children is rarely of comparable quality and fit to that of adults. Due allowance should be made for this and clothing and boots carefully checked before departure.

Exhaustion

This may be caused either by attempting too much or by not replacing the energy used by eating sufficient food. Exhaustion in itself is a dangerous condition since it implies that the body is quite unable to mobilise any further reserves of energy either to do physical work, in other words to carry on, or even to maintain normal body temperature against the sapping of the environment. A man engaged in heavy manual work expends something between 16.8 and 18.0 megajoules (MJ) per day (1 MJ = approximately 250 kilocalories (kcal)). The mountain equivalent of this is a 20km walk involving 750m of climbing.

Quite clearly, an expenditure of the order of 16.8MJ (4,000 kcal) of energy per day is going to require good training and an adequate food intake, especially if this level of output is to be maintained for any length of time, as on an expedition, for example. This does not include any allowance for difficult terrain, weather and load carried, all factors which could add substantially to the total energy demands. There are, of course, energy reserves in the body but you cannot go on drawing on them indefinitely. Sooner or later they have to be topped up by a period of rest and recuperation. Over a period of time, routes and expeditions should be planned so as to avoid making excessive overall demands, especially on young people whose working capacities may be as little as 50% of those of adults. Start in a modest way with expeditions in the 8.4 MJ (2,000 kcal) range or less and gradually build up to more ambitious projects. Exhaustion is always a possibility, but it becomes a probability if routes demanding more than 18.9 MJ (4,500 kcal) are tackled without adequate preparation and training. Know the individual capabilities or your party and plan accordingly.

Mention has already been made of the importance in time and distance calculations of making due allowance for weather, terrain, load carried and the general level of fitness of the party (Navigation; pages 40-43). These variables can be accommodated in the chart, Fig.117 (Aldridge, Waddell, Tranter) which offers a convenient method of estimating both the energy demands and the total time taken for expeditions of varying lengths. Note that it also provides a rough guide as to what is beyond the capabilities of parties with different levels of fitness.

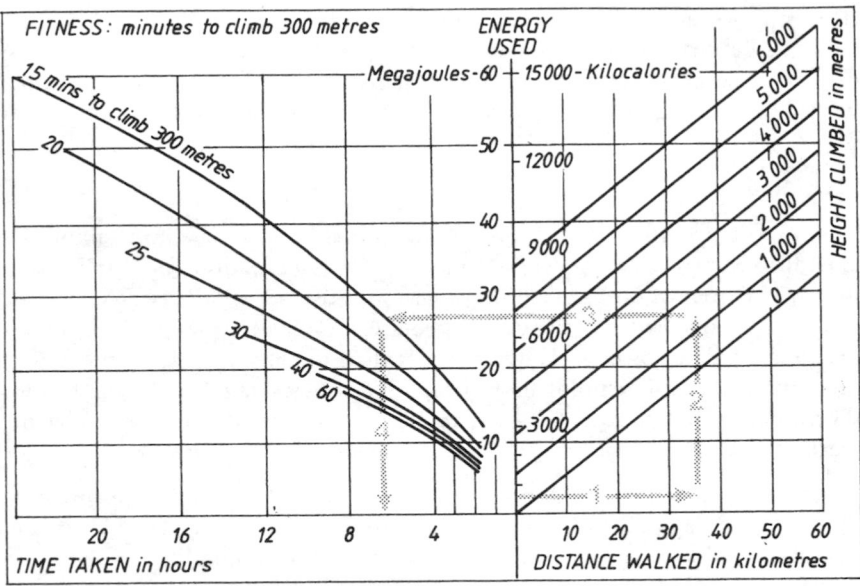

(Fig. 117) **Expedition time chart.**

How to use the chart:

First of all establish which condition line matches your level of fitness. Condition lines represent different fitness ratings as measured by the time taken to climb 300m in 800m horizontal distance at a normal pace. 15 minutes is super-fit and 50 minutes is unfit.

Start at the bottom right-hand side of the chart with the 'corrected' distance, i.e. the total distance across country plus three-quarters of the total distance on roads. Follow the arrow vertically until you intersect with the line representing the total height climbed. From this intersection move horizontally towards the centre line and read off the energy expenditure. Continue leftwards to meet your particular 'Condition' line; adjusted, of course, to take account of load, terrain and weather (See "Corrections to Naismith's Rule" page 42). If you run out of 'Condition' lines or if you do not meet your line because it stops short the trip must be regarded as too arduous. From this point descend vertically to the base line to read the estimated time in hours.

Sex and Physique

It is a fact that on the whole women are able to tolerate the effects of exposure better than men. This is due in part to better insulation provided by a thicker layer of subcutaneous fat and also to greater tolerance of physical stress. To a certain extent these advantages are offset by the fact that a woman's working capacity is, on average, some 30% less than a man's. Thin people and those with a poor strength-to-weight ratio are susceptible to hypothermia.

Lack of Training and Conditioning

The importance of training and of a gradual build up towards more ambitious expeditions has already been stressed. Overestimation of fitness and underestimation of time are all too common causes of accidents. Where large groups are concerned it is obviously better to arrange people into fitness groups according to their condition times than to cater for all on the basis of the lowest common denominator. The latter policy, apart from being bad for the morale of all concerned, leads to the dangerous situation whereby the weak can be pushed too far and the strong barely kept at 'tick-over'.

In addition to improving the physical performance of individuals, training should be designed to familiarise the group with the range of difficult conditions which may be expected and in this way condition them to a certain extent both mentally and physically against hardship and discomfort. Such conditioning is of proven value in cold climates and there is no doubt that it helps to maintain a high level of morale in our own.

Dehydration

Perhaps because water is so plentiful in Britain we tend to ignore the fact that it is a vital ingredient of our diet. Normal consumption is about 2.5 litres per day, but in a hot climate and when engaged in hard physical work it can rise to five times this amount. There is a general reluctance among walkers and climbers to drink water on the hill. This seems to be due to vague fears of pollution, stomach cramps and other debilitating effects, most of which are imaginary. Water is required and the more work done, the more water is necessary. Roughly speaking about 0.5 litre is required for each 1,000 kcal of energy expended in winter and about double this in summer. The 20km mountain walk involving 750 m of ascent previously referred to demands an expenditure of 4,400 kcal and a water requirement in summer of 4 litres. It is of course possible to go into water debt and replenish stocks at the end of the day, but if the expedition is a long one this could be a dangerous policy. It is better to keep pace with the needs of the body and drink when the opportunity presents itself, 'little and often' being the best maxim to follow. On a long expedition, salt lost through sweating should also be replaced to avoid muscle cramp. Serious dehydration leads to a decrease in physical and mental efficiency and lowers resistance to exhaustion.

Morale

This is something of an unknown quantity. Certainly it cannot be measured and yet it is one of the most significant contributory factors to exposure. Apprehension, fear and a spirit of hopelessness can induce a state which, if not checked, can spread through a party like a bush fire. Apprehension itself is of some short term benefit in meeting a difficult situation, since its effect is to increase the activity of certain organs of the body, including the heart. However, if this keyed-up condition is sustained for a long period, it drains the energy resources of the body and leads to exhaustion. Furthermore, the improved peripheral circulation results in cooled blood being returned to the core, and in this way accelerates the loss of body heat. Confident and cheerful leadership should be the keynote with a wary eye and ear for the first sign of depression or panic. This does not mean that in a tricky situation the leader should pretend that nothing is wrong but rather that he should inspire the confidence and the willingness to co-operate within the party that is necessary for a successful outcome.

Illness, Injury

A recent illness, such as an attack of 'flu, or even feeling a bit off-colour, predisposes a person to hypothermia and such people should not be put at risk. A period of running-in is essential before the full working capacity can be regained. Shock is present to some degree in each case of injury and it is important to treat the patient for this as well as for any injuries. Any person in a state of shock is much less able to combat the effects of cold and maintain body temperature. They are in fact half-way towards hypothermia already and must be protected from the rigours of the environment by all means at your disposal.

RECOGNITION AND TREATMENT

Symptoms of hypothermia

It would be foolish to regard everyone who felt a bit cold or tired in the mountains as suffering from hypothermia. Nevertheless, the symptoms are ordinary enough at first, becoming more pronounced and easily recognisable as the condition becomes more severe. As the severity increases, so it becomes more difficult for the exposed person to be rational about the situation and take the necessary steps to halt the downward spiral. It is critically important to be able to recognise the early stages of hypothermia and take immediate action to reverse the process, even if that involves a delay or a change of plan. The more thoroughly the leader knows the individual members of the party, the more likely the identification of the genuine from the exaggerated and the recognition of the warning signs for what they are.

At first, then, it is a matter of feeling cold and tired with perhaps some numbness of the hands and feet and intermittent bouts of shivering. Shivering is an involuntary response of the body to increase its heat production by a series of rapid oscillatory contractions of groups of muscles. None of these symptoms are in themselves particularly significant, but if left unattended they could progress towards true hypothermia. Continued exposure brings on more general and sometimes uncontrollable shivering. This is an indication of a more serious state of affairs and one or more of a range of other symptoms are now likely to appear:-

The casualties body feels "as cold as marble" and, in particular the armpit feels profoundly cold.

Unexpected and apparently unreasonable behaviour, often accompanied by complaints of coldness and tiredness.

Physical and mental lethargy, including failure to respond to or to understand questions and directions.

Some slurring of speech. There is not necessarily early failure of speech and the victim may speak quite strongly until shortly before collapse.

Violent outbursts of unexpected energy with possible physical resistance to succour. Violent language. Failure to appreciate that something is wrong.

Lack of muscular co-ordination leading to erratic movements and falling.

Failure of, or abnormality in vision. It should be noted that some failure of vision, such as difficulty in focusing, is a very usual symptom, and when this does occur, the condition should be regarded as very urgent.

It should be stressed that not all of these symptoms may be noticed, nor necessarily in this order. Other symptoms which may sometimes be observed are muscle cramp, extreme ashen pallor, light-headedness and occasionally a fainting fit.

SYMPTOMS OF DEEP HYPOTHERMIA

If left untreated the victim drifts into a deepening stupor. Shivering stops altogether and it becomes impossible to elicit any response. At this stage both pulse and respiration are feeble. Further cooling of the core leads inevitably to unconsciousness, coma and death. The time scale of these events varies but from recognition of the first serious symptoms until death occurs may be as little as two hours. It should, however, be borne in mind that it can be almost impossible to tell whether the victim is actually dead or not, since virtually all signs of life, including the pulse, may be absent in severe hypothermia. Cases have been recorded of complete recovery following one hour's total cardiac arrest. It is safest then to assume that even an apparently dead person may be revived by resuscitative treatment.

Early Treatment on the Mountain

An observant and attentive leader should be able to recognise the early symptoms of hypothermia. Prompt action before the point of no return is reached may allow a retreat to be made in good order while the patient is still able to help. The immediate necessity is to seek shelter from the worst of the weather in the nearest convenient place. Once out of the wind every effort should be made to prevent further heat loss by changing out of wet clothing into dry spare clothing. Get the patient into a sleeping bag inside a bivouac sack and provide insulation from the ground with anything which is available, rucksacks, etc. A hot drink and something to eat complete the treatment at this early stage. The remainder of the group should huddle round to provide additional shelter, natural warmth and moral support. Recovery may be rapid, but is unlikely to take less than half an hour, even in ideal conditions. Insist on a proper rest period and do not proceed unless and until you are sure that recovery is complete. Dr Ieuan Jones has suggested a simple way of testing this. Ask the patient to subtract aloud 7 from 100 and then 7 from the remainder and so on until 2 is reached. This mental arithmetic should take about a minute or less. If it takes much more than this or the test is failed altogether then suspect the early stages of hypothermia. Even if recovery is apparently total, there should be no question of pressing on. Remove the patient's rucksack and take the quickest and easiest route off the mountain.

THE DILEMMA

It is unfortunately the case that mountain hypothermia is often the final episode in a chapter of errors. It occurs when people are stretched beyond endurance, exposed to vile weather conditions and in all probability struggling to reach an objective that they are not confident of finding at the end of a long, hard day. It is all too easy to give sensible advice on what to do in such a situation and, alas, all too difficult to put into practice. The temptation to press on is very strong indeed, fuelled by the thought of a night out in an exposed situation without proper bivouac equipment. The leader of such a party is in an unenviable position, having to choose between two equally hazardous alternatives. The moral is surely obvious. Do not allow yourself to be trapped into such a situation.

Rewarming on the Mountain

However, let us assume the worst. You have diagnosed mountain hypothermia in a member of your party and they have not responded to the initial treatment. You decide that to attempt to move the casualty down the mountain would be too risky and therefore you must summon help and do what you can with what you have on the spot. The essential and immediate treatment is to prevent further heat loss by providing comprehensive insulation round the casualty. Given really good insulation, protection from the weather and rest, all but the most severe of cases will survive. Any positive contribution that can be made to the heat balance can be regarded as a bonus.

The body itself acts to maintain core circulation and temperature by restricting the flow to the exposed periphery so that core blood is not cooled at the surface. In any treatment, therefore, the importance must be realised of not increasing peripheral circulation unless there is minimal loss of heat at the skin surface. Further heat loss from the core must be avoided at all cost. Sudden local surface warming such as may be produced by hot water bottles, rubbing or alcohol intake could be disastrous.

Methods will vary according to conditions and the equipment immediately available. An outline of what should be done, if at all possible is:

Find the most sheltered spot in the vicinity or a place where some form of shelter could be constructed or a tent pitched. This is just the sort of situation where a bivouac tent which can accommodate the whole party is worth its very insignificant weight in gold.

First get the casualty into a plastic bag and then into a casualty bag or sleeping bags , not forgetting to provide insulation below as well as above. The plastic bag will prevent the clothes from wetting the sleeping bag which will therefore retain its insulation properties. The casualty should lie in the 'foetal' position with the head downslope. It is usually impracticable to remove wet clothes and a considerable amount of body heat may be lost in the process.

If there is room enough, put a fit companion into the sleeping bag to give additional bodily warmth.

There should be a windproof and waterproof covering (eg polythene) around the bag and the victim. Adequate insulation from the ground is most important.

Meanwhile, get the rest of the party to pitch a tent over the victim to provide more comprehensive shelter. Get as many people inside as possible and light a stove if one is available, ensuring that there is adequate ventilation.

If the victim can still take food, sugar in easily digestible form (eg condensed milk or in solution) may be given. A hot sweet drink may be prepared later if available.

If respiration falters or ceases altogether, perform artificial respiration continuously by mouth to nose/mouth method.

Be alert for failure of the heart (no pulse, blue lips, dilated pupils). It is important to continue artificial respiration and this can be administered by a second person at the rate of one inflation after every five compressions.

There will then normally ensue a period perhaps of some hours duration, before the rescue party arrive. Sometimes a casualty will make what appears to be a miraculous recovery and may even insist on getting down under their own steam. On no account should this be permitted. The symptoms which prompted the diagnosis of hypothermia in the first place could easily reoccur with more serious consequences. The casualty should be treated as a stretcher case and the full normal rescue procedure enforced. During this waiting period, once the patient has been insulated, a brew-up should be started and hot beverages and food should be given that is acceptable to the patient. Food and hot drinks should also be taken by the remainder of the party whom it is safer to regard as themselves suffering in some degree from shock and exhaustion.

Evacuation

The stretcher party, when it arrives, should of course preserve all the insulation around the patient during the carry. It is important that the face and mouth should be protected to minimise heat-loss, without interfering with ventilation and ease of breathing. It is imperative that in descent the patient should be evacuated in the head down position and that someone (not a stretcher bearer) is detailed to watch for signs of vomiting and respiratory or cardiac failure. The evacuation is a critical phase of the whole operation and great care must be taken in handling the stretcher, particularly in the case of an unconscious patient.

If a case of hypothermia occurs in a very distant and isolated spot, and the delay before the arrival of the rescue party is likely to be inordinately long, the leader may face the very difficult decision as to whether to start moving the casualty towards the rescuers and safety. But before any such attempt is made, all the measures of immediate treatment in the field, as outlined above, should be taken. Only if considerations of time, distance, and bad weather then clearly make it less of a risk to carry the patient towards safety, than to stay put where insulation and care can be provided, should the risk of a long carry be accepted. On no account should improvised carrying techniques be used which keep the patient in an upright or semi-upright position (eg pick-a-back). The improvised stretcher should be made as rigid as possible and the patient evacuated in the head-down position with as little movement as the terrain allows.

If, on the other hand, there is a good possibility of getting the patient to hospital within one or two hours, such as would be the case in a helicopter rescue then evacuation should be carried out immediately without any attempt being made to undertake treatment in the field, other than the provision of dry clothing and plenty of insulation. The sophisticated rewarming techniques available at a hospital make recovery of the severely hypothermic patient, who has been kept alive by resuscitative techniques, more likely. Until the treatment, the low body temperature due to hypothermia will keep the demand for oxygen by the brain and other vital organs to a minimum.

Treatment at Base

It must be emphasised that an unconscious victim of mountain hypothermia is in a critically ill condition. If at all possible, treatment should be undertaken by qualified medical staff in hospital. However, since such facilities and expertise are not always available it is important to understand the rewarming process so that the correct and safe procedure can be followed.

The need to avoid any measure which causes relatively warm core blood to flow through the cold outer shell of the body and so cool the core still further has already been mentioned. In the past, rapid rewarming by immersion in a hot bath, circa $40°C$, has been the treatment of choice and still is for patients suffering from rapid-onset immersion hypothermia. For the victim of mountain hypothermia the hot bath treatment involves some degree of risk and the more serious the condition the more likely "rewarming collapse".

After removal of the patient from the cold environment there is usually a continued fall in core temperature for a period of 10 – 20 minutes. This is the so called "after-drop". Its significance lies in the fact that the core temperature may fall to the lethal zone. It is therefore essential, whether rewarming is spontaneous or imposed, that someone should remain with the patient at all times to monitor breathing and pulse which may, in a severe case, be hardly perceptible. In the event of respiratory failure, the first priority should be to provide standard expired air ventilation (mouth to mouth resuscitation). Chest compressions should ONLY be started if:

1 there is no carotid pulse after feeling in the correct place for at least 1 minute, and

2 cardiac arrest has been observed or is likely to have occurred within the previous two hours, and

3 there is a reasonable expectation that effective CPR can be provided continuously until the casualty reaches hospital.

This important topic is discussed more fully in Chapter 11, First Aid.

Once cardiac functions have been restored, slow rewarming, preferably in a warm room and bed but without hot water bottle or pillow, is the treatment of choice.

Recovery can sometimes be quite dramatic. Insist on complete rest and examination by a doctor as a matter of urgency.

METHODS

The Hot Pack

The International Commission for Alpine Rescue, IKAR, recommends the use of a "Hot Pack" on hypothermic patients, both on the mountain and at base. The treatment involves making a thick pad out of a sheet or items of clothing, soaking the inner surface of this with hot water and placing it on top of the patient's underwear to cover the chest and abdomen. The compress is itself covered by more articles of clothing and the whole trunk then enveloped in foil or a space blanket leaving the extremities uncovered. Finally, the patient is wrapped up tightly in blankets, tucked in securely round the neck and placed inside a sleeping bag. The Hot Pack should be renewed after one hour. The removal of clothing which this method entails and the necessity to have hot water available, make it unlikely to be the treatment of choice on the mountain. However, it is a proven lifesaver and is the preferred treatment at the camp or bothy or whenever conditions make it a practicable proposition.

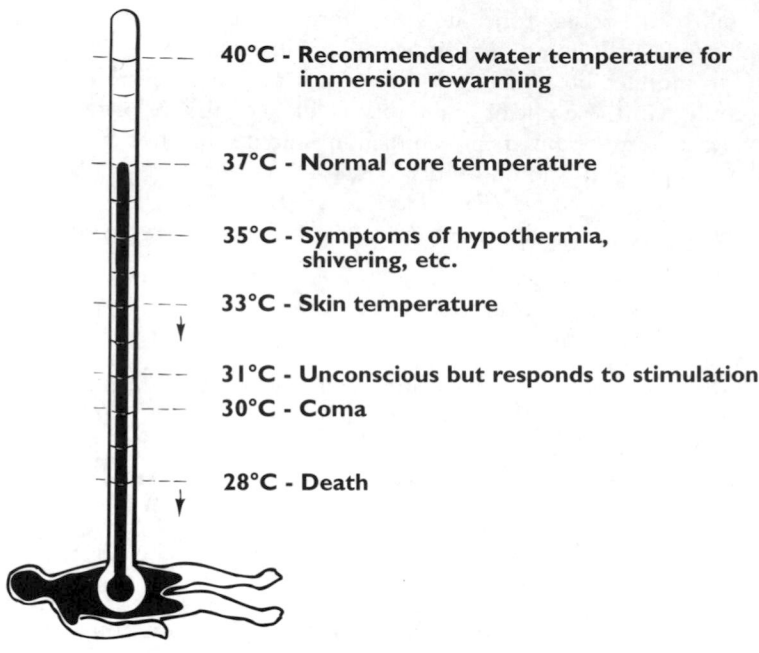

40°C - Recommended water temperature for immersion rewarming

37°C - Normal core temperature

35°C - Symptoms of hypothermia, shivering, etc.

33°C - Skin temperature

31°C - Unconscious but responds to stimulation

30°C - Coma

28°C - Death

Fig. 118 *Core Temperature in Hypothermic Patients.*

Hot Bath

Rapid rewarming by immersion of the patient in a bath of hot water kept at 40°C is an effective treatment for the early stage of hypothermia. It is not appropriate for severe cases, or for the unconscious, the very old and the very young or for those who for any reason are frail or unwell.

Strip or cut way the outer garments and immerse the patient in the bath taking care to exclude any frostbitten part which should be dealt with separately. The legs and arms should be left out and the trunk maintained in a horizontal position with the head held just out of the water. The bath temperature will fall immediately and therefore hot water should be added at regular intervals and the water agitated to maintain the temperature at 40°C. After 20 minutes or when sweating starts, remove the patient in the prone position to a previously warmed bed.

Airway Insulation

Heat lost through the expiration of warm moist air forms a substantial proportion of the total heat loss in a cold environment. A simple device allows both heat and moisture to be exchanged from expired to inspired air – even a loose scarf over the nose and mouth can help, provided the airway is not compromised.

Conclusion

It is said that Eskimos, immersed in cold Arctic water, will die from hypothermia just as quickly as the rest of us. Their ability, not only to survive, but to live comfortably in a hostile environment is almost entirely due to the fact that they keep fit, dress well and are highly experienced in avoidance. This, perhaps slightly unfair comparison, sums up all that is necessary to know as regards prevention. Better by far that you should know how to avoid getting a case of exposure then to treat one. Therefore:

See to it that the equipment and clothing worn by the party is sufficient for the route chosen and takes cognisance of sudden and unexpected changes in conditions. Water-proof clothing is a must whether it be worn or carried in the pack. It is effective even when worn over wet clothes as it reduces the windchill/evaporation effect.

Adequate food and water should be taken before and during any mountain journey.

A minimum of emergency food and equipment must be carried by the party. In winter time, at high level, this should include a lightweight bivouac tent sufficiently large to accommodate the whole party.

Progressive training is important as is the careful regulation of pace throughout the day. Arrange large groups according to their fitness and capabilities.

Loads in excess of 40lbs are unnecessary, as well as being heavy. As a rough guide on a camping expedition loads should never exceed one-third of the body weight of the individual.

Good morale means increased safety.

Safety first – seek shelter or turn back in good time.

Good leadership involves good planning.

Finally, it must be said that good leadership is also an awareness on the part of the leader of each member of the party as an individual; an awareness amounting almost to a premonition of possible hazards and dangers that may arise and above all the ability to take avoiding action before circumstances dictate their own terms.

Remember the words of Dr Duff. "It is the additional factor of exhaustion over and above cold which kills quickly. Death has overtaken whole parties who, thinking they must keep moving at all costs, have bashed on instead of resting in some shelter before exhaustion supervenes. When the bodies of the victims are finally recovered, it is not uncommon to find that they carried the means of survival with them to their deaths; tents, sleeping bags, spare clothing, food. The essential is always to preserve a sufficient reserve of energy in severe conditions of cold and high wind."

10

Effects of Heat

It is often said that man is a tropical animal, and it is certainly true that in general it is a good deal easier to lose heat than to conserve it. However, in a cold climate, heat conservation is achieved by the relatively simple expedient of improving the insulation, whereas, in a hot climate, heat loss is largely controlled by physiological adjustments which are outside the control of the individual. It is easier to wear an overcoat than a refrigerator. Exposure to heat is, in any case, a rare phenomenon in this country. However, cases of quite serious sunburn and mild heat exhaustion have been known, and the mountain leader should be familiar with the main heat disorders and their avoidance.

WATER REQUIREMENTS

Since most of these disorders are due to water depletion, rather than the direct effects of heat, an appreciation of the water requirements of the body is necessary. As a rough guide, 2½ litres may be taken as the average daily requirement, broken down as follows:

	ml per 24 hours
Urine	1400
Respiration	400
Insensible perspiration	600
Faeces	100
Total	2500

This requirement is greatly increased by hard physical work, especially in hot weather, when an additional 750 ml may be required for every 4.1 MJ (1,000 kcal) of energy expended. Most of this water is evaporated as sweat and in this way serves to cool the body surface. The evaporation of 1 litre of sweat results in a heat loss of about 600 kcal. In really hot climates the water requirement may be as much as 8 litres/24 hours.

SALT REQUIREMENTS

Normally our salt intake is a good deal more than our actual requirement, but prolonged sweating can lead to substantial salt losses, particularly in those who are unacclimatised. For every litre of fluid lost, 2 grams of salt is lost. Fortunately, acclimatisation to salt depletion in a hot environment takes place fairly rapidly and the immediate effects can be countered by the simple expedient of taking salt, solid or in solution, and by cutting down on water intake.

ACCLIMATISATION

Very little is known about long-term adaptation to heat and one is left with the impression that, as with the eskimo in the cold environment, experience in avoidance is the best protection against the harmful effects of a hot climate. There is no doubt that short term adjustments take place in a matter of several days of exposure to heat and these include: a less marked increase in heart rate when working, a lower skin and deep body temperature, greater efficiency of the sweating mechanism (sweating is more rapid in onset), a reduction of salt in sweat and urine and a marked increase in tolerance of the conditions.

SUNBURN

This can be very severe particularly to those with sensitive skins. In addition, sunburn can interfere with sweat secretion and lead to further heat complications. It is usually caused by sudden and prolonged exposure to sunlight without adequate protection. The length of exposure should be carefully regulated to build up a protective tan and initially, at any rate, an efficient barrier cream used which does not interfere with sweating and which cuts out most of the harmful ultra-violet radiation. In applying the cream it is important to remember the lips and also those areas of the face which receive a lot of reflected light from the ground or snow; under the nose and ears, chin, etc. Sunburn can be effectively treated with calamine lotion.

Today there is increased awareness of the dangers of excessive exposure to the sun and there is concern that the depletion of ozone in the upper layers of the atmosphere may lead to an increase in the amount of harmful radiation reaching the earth's surface.

EFFECTS OF GLARE

Snow blindness is considered briefly in the winter section (page 427). Here we are concerned with discomfort and strain, as a consequence of inadequate protection of the eyes. The remedy is simple; wear sunglasses. These must be of good quality and reduce the amount of ultra-violet without cutting down too much on the total transmission of light. In snow conditions, especially at high altitudes, it is essential to shield the eyes as well from light entering round the sides of the lenses.

HEAT DISORDERS

Prickly Heat

This is an irritating rash of tiny blisters, usually caused by constant sweating in a hot climate. The only real cure is to get out of the sun and rest, although various measures can be adopted to relieve the symptoms.

Heat Syncope

Unacclimatised people exposed to heat frequently suffer periods of acute fatigue associated with fainting or a feeling of giddiness. This is a common condition and it can be counteracted effectively by rest.

Heat Exhaustion

When due to water depletion this can be a very serious condition, leading ultimately to death. The symptoms include, thirst, fatigue, giddiness, a rapid pulse, raised body temperature, low urine output and later on, delirium and coma. The only remedy is to re-establish water balance.

When due to salt depletion, similar symptoms are manifest though without any marked rise in body temperature, but almost always associated with severe muscle cramp. It can be serious if not treated by the addition of salt to the diet. There is no such thing in humans as a craving for salt and therefore the victims are unaware that they are suffering from a deficiency.

Heat Stroke

Mistakenly referred to as sunstroke. This is by far the most serious of the heat disorders and is caused by a failure of the body's temperature regulating system. It is associated with a very high body temperature and absence of sweating. The skin is hot and dry to the touch. Early symptoms show a remarkable similarity to the symptoms of hypothermia, such as aggressive behaviour, lack of co-ordination and so on. Later on the victim goes into a coma or convulsions and death will follow unless effective treatment is given.

In the field, the treatment consists of sponging down, or covering the patient with wet towels, accompanied by vigorous fanning. It is imperative to begin treatment immediately, unless of course, the shortage of water is so acute that other lives may be endangered. When facilities permit, immersion in a cold bath (10°c) is the treatment of choice.

PRECAUTIONS

It is wise to remember that it is not possible to acclimatise to a low intake of water. A certain minimum quantity is required for survival. Most of the recommendations, therefore, concern conservation of water:

Keep fit. Fitness is very important, especially when travel is involved.

Do the minimum of work consistent with the achievement of the expedition's aims.

Keep out of the sun as far as possible and certainly during the hottest part of the day.

Drink more than you need when water is readily available; a little and often being the best maxim to follow. Thirst is a poor indicator of your actual requirement and a reserve will be useful on a long journey.

Don't hoard water till collapse is imminent.

Be prepared to collect rainwater by tapping as large a surface area as possible e.g. with a polythene sheet. A plastic straw can be used to extract water from rock pools.

A high calorie diet, short on protein, is desirable.

Wear loose, lightweight clothing, permeable to sweat and light in colour. Also a shady hat and sun glasses. On no account labour uphill in hot conditions wearing fully waterproof clothing.

If salt tablets are taken they must be dissolved in a sufficient quantity of water; 1,500 gram tablet per litre.

11

First Aid

This chapter assumes basic competence in first aid and is designed to help adapt these skills for practical use by a walking party leader in the environment of the British hills, the most notable aspects of which are remoteness (up to six hours from the road) and wet, cold and windy weather. The application of first aid skills in any extreme situation is fundamentally different and must be viewed in context. Any illness or injury is potentially more dangerous and more difficult to deal with than in a normal environment. Isolation usually means that it will be a long time before help arrives or the patient reaches safety and proper medical care. Transport may be slow, dangerous and rough. First aid equipment is limited, and the incident may have taken place in a dangerous and exposed situation.

Traditional first aid relied heavily upon details of bandages, knots and minor injures. Now first aid teaching focuses on areas where first aiders can make a major difference in critical situations, saving lives and limiting further damage and suffering. In this chapter I have included a brief recap of these important topics. However, I have omitted the practical details of how to do cardio-pulmonary resuscitation (CPR). This and how to clear an airway are best learnt from an instructor by demonstration and practice.

This book is for people who want to go to the mountains and return without mishap. The risks faced, however, are not only from accidents and cold, but also from illnesses such as asthma, epilepsy or a heart attack. Included are sections on some of these illnesses not usually taught in first aid, but which are common and life-threatening, and are specially important when in a remote area, where you may be the only form of medical care for many hours. Depending on the type of activity you are planning and the composition of your group, the risks from these illnesses may actually present the greatest risk to your party.

Death from injuries can be divided up into 3 time periods, the first being at, or immediately after, the time of injury and is due to devastating injury. The second time period is the next 4 hours or so, when death is due to a blocked airway, bleeding, etc. The third period is over the following days and weeks where death may be due to kidney failure, infections, etc. It is during this second time period, i.e. the 4 hour period, that first aid and medical intervention can make a major difference and save lives. It has been estimated, for example that 40% of deaths during this time period are mainly due to a blocked airway, a problem often solved by simple and basic first aid.

BEING PREPARED

A high level of proficiency in first aid is vital. Although this may seem an excessive precaution if you have made countless trips without serious mishap, in a critical situation it can avert disaster. The level of first aid competence which could reasonably be expected of a mountain leader would be, for example, recent completion of a course of two or three days or its equivalent.

First aid equipment to be carried in a rucksack must include only the basics. Take just what is familiar to you. Balance taking commonly-used items for minor problems such as antiseptic creams, with the rarely used life-saving items such as a plastic airway. Light rubber gloves, to reduce transmission of infection, should be high on your list. Many emergency equipment items have first aid applications and vice versa. Select items with this in mind, for example, tape, bandages, plastic bags and a torch. Items should be versatile and multipurpose. Adaptation and improvisation is the key.

No matter how much you learn, or what equipment you take, you can always be presented with a situation that you feel it is well beyond what you can cope with. You must then do what seems best and most sensible. This applies to everyone, from the basic first-aider to the casualty department doctor.

Before setting out it is important to find out if anyone in your party has any disabilities, any long standing illnesses such as diabetes, or is taking any medication. Be sensitive and ask about their special needs and try to accommodate them if you can. Be sure they understand what the task ahead involves, and be sure it is realistically within their ability. Be aware of the pressures on an individual to do what the others are doing. Ensure they have their usual medication and some extra in case of emergency, such as an unplanned night on the hill. Certain conditions are made worse by the cold, these include exercise induced asthma, high blood pressure and angina (heart pain on exercise).

INCIDENT MANAGEMENT

The management of a medical problem in the mountains not only involves providing first aid, but also involves management of the overall incident, with its wider implications for the patient and the rest of the group. This can be compared with the management of any other incident in the mountains, where a single problem or event, such as loss or breakage of a vital piece of equipment, has wider implications. Even a small problem can be exacerbated by other factors, or be the trigger for a further sequence of events, for example, a twisted ankle in a tired group in fading light. Once one person in the group becomes a patient, the level of danger rises for all. Your decision making must be a risk balancing exercise for all concerned. Sometimes the best decision may seem harsh, for example moving a patient with a painful injury.

Approach an incident with the following plan. Firstly remove everyone from immediate danger. Then quickly assess the patient using the first aid "ABC's" (airway, breathing, circulation) and give life-saving treatment, such as clearing the airway. Once in a more controlled situation examine the patient thoroughly, and then provide any further treatment needed such as splinting fractures.

This is conventional first aid so far, but now you must go on to manage the incident as a whole. Stand back and view the situation as if through a wide angle lens. In a complex situation decide priorities. Don't rush. In the time scale of mountain rescue a few minutes extra spent in this vital decision making is well spent. Start by clarifying in your mind a brief summary of the patient's problem. You must now put this in the context of your particular situation. Consider these factors:

Are you in a dangerous spot?

How is the weather, and how much daylight is left?

How far are you from help, where is there shelter,
how far to vehicle or helicopter pickup points?

What equipment do you have, what can you improvise?

Consider the other party members: how strong and able are they,
their clothing, their emotional state, injuries, etc.

Two important decisions you will have to make are whether to split up the party, with one group going for help, and whether to move the patient. Moving the patient a short distance may be advantageous in order to gain safer ground, to find shelter, or to move to an area where you will be more easily found. If you are sending for help, starting to move the patient towards a pickup point such as a road head, before help arrives, may be the quickest way of getting everyone off the hill and getting the patient to more expert medical help.

However, the advantages of moving the patient must be balanced against the many possible difficulties, including rough and dangerous terrain. Movement may be too painful or liable to cause further injury. Insufficient manpower and carrying equipment may make movement difficult or impossible.

EXAMINATION, DIAGNOSIS AND REPORTING

The purpose of examination is to collect information in order to make a diagnosis. It is essential in an isolated setting, where the time scale is long and your actions may greatly affect the outcome, that you gather all the information you can by careful examination and by enquiring about symptoms. Most important of all, make sure you miss nothing major. Your diagnosis can be anything from a broad diagnosis, such as 'ankle injury', to a more precise diagnosis, such as 'fractured tibia'. In a difficult situation and with limited skills expect only to make a fairly broad diagnosis. Your diagnosis needs only to be as precise as required to enable you to decide what you are going to do in the practical situation. In some situations a more precise diagnosis is important, where the detail does make a practical difference. For example, with chest pain it is important to try to differentiate between heart pain and other pain in order to decide the urgency of evacuation (see section on chest pain).

Examination of a patient on a cold mountain side is notoriously difficult. You may feel under pressure to be quick, and the temptation is to cut corners. Your hands may be numb. How much do you unwrap the patient for examination? It is important both physiologically and psychologically to avoid cooling the patient, either by removing or loosening clothing or by thrusting in a cold hand, but this must be balanced against the importance of proper thorough examination. Proper examination is particularly important where the diagnosis is unclear and there is potential for missing something major. This is especially so in confused or unconscious patients, and after injuries such as a fall.

There are some tricks you can use to get round the unwrapping problem. The face and neck are always accessible and provide a substantial amount of information: the skin colour for shock, the pupil size for head injury, the side of the neck for pulse, the expression for pain and shortness of breath, etc. In a conscious patient, pressing your hand through the patient's clothing may be enough to identify injured areas which you can then explore further. For monitoring the patient's condition after the initial examination, prepare easy access points for relevant important checks.

The way you approach making a diagnosis of the patients problem should be determined by the circumstances. For example if you find an unconscious climber at the side of a river, consider both hypothermia and drowning. Also look for other clues, such as finding pills or documents in the patient's pocket.

For the seriously ill, and for those who may deteriorate, regular monitoring and a written record of the patient's condition is essential. This information may be of vital importance for later treatment, for example the timing of surgery in head injuries. The regularity of recording and what you record should be determined by the patient's condition and how quickly this is changing. Generally, record pulse, respiratory rate, how he/she looks and feels, and then other details relevant to the problem such as level of consciousness and size of pupils for head injuries. To save time it may be sufficient to monitor regularly only a relevant indicator of the patients condition, such as the heart rate in shock. To test the pupils reaction to light (daylight or torch light), hold the eye closed with your finger for a few seconds and then opening it, watch the response to the light. Record size and light response in both eyes. To find heart rate, count the pulse for six seconds and multiply by ten. It does not need to be exact. Comparing the recordings to your own or another member of the party may be useful if you are unsure of what normal is. You can also compare the patient's right and left, for example to assess pupils, or limb circulation in fractures.

If you are reporting the incident by messenger, the message must be written. Provide as much information as possible. Whoever receives the message and must organise the rescue has many complex decisions to make. Give details of location, time, etc., and the patient's condition. Include relevant recordings and their times. Include normal recordings if it is relevant to the patients condition, for example a normal heart rate in spite of blood loss is important as it shows blood loss has not been severe. Unless you are certain of medical terms, use layman's terms, for example instead of confusing a femur with the fibula, call it a thigh bone. Similarly, if transmitting the message verbally (only if you have no pen and paper), put this in terms the messenger understands.

PATIENT TRANSPORT

Your options for transporting a patient are basically those of carrying the patient (by improvised stretcher, piggy-back, etc.) or by the patient walking, with assistance if necessary. For speed, walking is usually the quickest in terms of both movement across the ground, and in minimising set-up time and organisation. The walking patient can be assisted and speeded along by helpers, in relays if possible, for example by putting the patient's arms over their shoulders.

Patients unable to weight bear due to pain or because of the risk of causing further injury, need to be carried. Similarly their injuries may not permit piggy back carrying. Stretchers can provide a 'whole body splintage effect' when the patient is fixed to the stretcher with firm, multiple point strapping. This minimises movement at the injury site, which is fundamental for spinal and neck injuries. This also benefits many other injures, especially those near the centre of the body such as fractured pelvis and fractured femur.

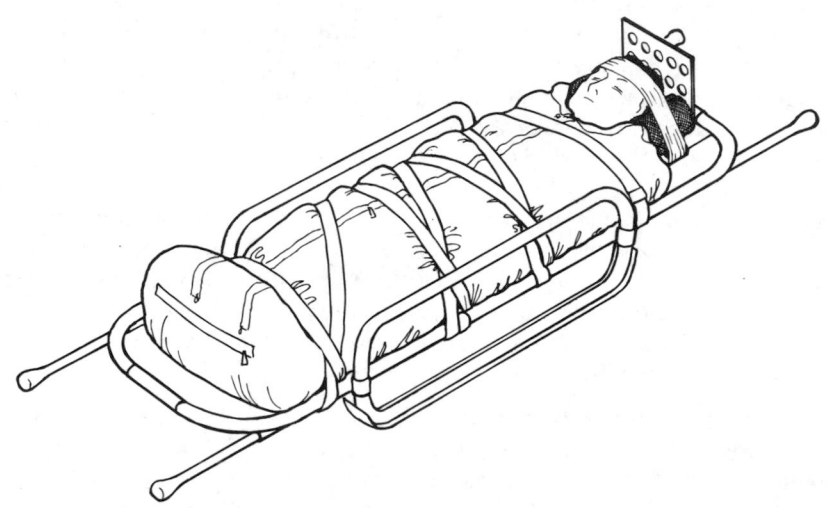

(Fig. 119)   *Firm multiple point strapping for the 'whole body splintage effect'.*

Patients suffering from any severe life threatening conditions such as severe hypothermia, shock, unconsciousness, etc., need stretcher transport. This is because they will be unable to walk and in many of these conditions the upright position is detrimental. Stretcher patients should travel feet first. This is psychologically more comfortable, and when going downhill generally more comfortable and obviously safer. Some conditions, however, have special needs as to patient position (see the sections on each condition). Shocked patients should be placed on a slight head down incline. If this is not possible then at least raise the legs. Unconscious patients must be transported in the recovery position. Patients short of breath should be transported in the sitting position. Severely hypothermic patients (severe enough to effect conscious level) who are already lying down should not be brought to the vertical position, and should be transported horizontal or head down. Patients with painful injuries generally should be kept in the position they find most comfortable.

When choosing the method of transport, also consider what terrain lies ahead, what carrying equipment you have or could improvise, how able your party is to carry the patient and to what degree speed is a priority. Speed of transport is often a major priority, both to remove the patient and others concerned from further danger, and to get the patient to medical care as soon as possible. Speed however, must be balanced against safety and careful handling in order to limit further damage and suffering. When considering transport, consider above all whether you should try to transport the patient at all or whether you should wait for the rescue team.

Once on the move, reassess the situation. With painful injuries, and with injuries where further damage may be caused by movement, watch carefully to see where any movement is occurring and adjust straps and padding if necessary. Because of the long time scale of mountain transportation do not forget to monitor the patient's condition from time to time. Pay particular attention to minimising heat loss, especially through the underside of the stretcher where clothing will be compressed flat by the patient's weight, and from the patients head.

GENERAL FIRST AID TREATMENT

General first aid treatment means attending to basic problems common to many conditions, including attending to psychological needs, pain management, keeping the patient warm, positioning and comfort, and giving food and drink. These general measures may be all that you can provide, if you are lacking equipment or are able only to make a general diagnosis.

The psychological needs of the sick or injured patient are important but are often overlooked. Keep the patient informed and tell him the plan. Be truthful, keep his trust and establish a good rapport. Avoid setting goals which are not met. Avoid whispering in pessimistic tones near the patient.

Pain is a problem common to many conditions. Strong pain killers such as morphine are only carried by Doctors and mountain rescue teams. However mild pain killers such as aspirin or paracetamol are surprisingly effective, and much better than nothing for severe pain, but do not exceed normal recommended doses. Pain is more bearable, and more easily dealt with by the patient, if other discomforts and stresses are removed, so pay careful attention to details of general comfort, warmth, and psychological support. Also, the meaning of the pain can make pain seem worse or better. For example, if the patient thinks he is going to lose his leg or die in the mountains as a result of a broken leg, the pain will seem worse. Again provide psychological support and information.

Cold is commonly a significant factor in many mountain deaths. The importance of providing as much protection from the cold as possible cannot be over stressed, and is vital for the following reasons. Firstly, the effects of cold add to the patients overall problems. This is particularly so if the patient is shocked or injured. Secondly, an injured or sick person will become cold more quickly than a normal person in the same environmental conditions, with the same clothing. This is due to circulatory and metabolic changes. It is therefore necessary to provide more cold protection than you would for an uninjured person in the same circumstances. Remember also that compared to an erect walking person a person sitting or lying is no longer producing heat generated by exercise, and if in contact with the ground, clothing will be compressed flat and may get wet and heat will be lost by radiation and conduction to the ground.

Food and drink, especially if hot and high in calories, provides heat, refuels the exhausted patient and has great psychological benefits in providing comfort and making the patient generally feel better. Cold but calorific food and drink still provide all of these benefits but to a lesser degree. (Although ingested cold, the calories still provide heat during digestion and when burnt in the muscles.) Do not give food or drink to patients with certain conditions, including abdominal injury, those with vomiting or nausea, and obviously to those who are unconscious. Patients requiring surgery and therefore an anaesthetic should not have anything to eat or drink for at least four hours before the operation to allow the stomach to empty (this takes longer the more sick or injured they are). The likelihood of the need for an operation in the near future, which is difficult for you to decide, must be balanced against the beneficial effects of giving food and drink.

THE UNCONSCIOUS PATIENT

Unconsciousness can result from a wide spectrum of conditions. It can result from a direct injury to the brain, as in a head injury or a stroke (a stroke is caused by a blockage or bursting of one of the blood vessels in the brain). A lack of oxygenated blood reaching the brain also causes unconsciousness, and this may be caused by insufficient blood flow, for example in severe shock or cardiac arrest, or by insufficient oxygen in the blood which occurs for example in severe lung conditions. Hypothermia causes unconsciousness by extreme slowing of brain function. After an epileptic fit the patient usually remains unconscious for about 15 to 20 minutes until brain function slowly returns. Unconsciousness can result from a severe change in blood chemistry caused by a variety of conditions, including a low blood glucose (see section on diabetes), poisoning (including alcohol), and many slowly developing conditions such as liver or kidney failure. So unconsciousness often occurs as one of the end results of many serious conditions.

An unconscious patient must therefore always be considered as having a life threatening condition, the only exceptions to this being perhaps a brief period of unconsciousness after a minor blow to the head, or after a straightforward epileptic fit.

Consciousness and unconsciousness are the endpoints on the spectrum of conscious levels, ranging from normal, to drowsy, to just unconscious, to deeply unconscious (sometimes referred to as a coma). Of course the deeper the unconsciousness, generally the worse the patient's condition. Therefore making an assessment of the patient's conscious level is very useful for assessing their condition, and needs to be done regularly to see if they are getting better or worse. Once the patient arrives in hospital a written record of conscious level can be of vital importance, for example in the timing of surgery in head injuries.

Assessment of conscious level is done by observing how the patient responds to your voice and to pain. Lightly unconscious patients will respond to your voice by opening their eyes, moving or speaking, just as if they were sleeping. Patients more deeply unconscious will not respond to your voice, so then you must see if they respond to pain (this may seem cruel but it is very important to assess conscious level). Place a pen or similar object across the base of the finger nail and press hard. A response to pain but no response to your voice means they are not too deeply unconscious. No response to pain means they are deeply unconscious. Test all limbs, to make sure they can feel and move all limbs, and record the results. As with all sick patients, also record pulse, breathing, pupil size and reaction, etc.

When treating an unconscious patient start as usual with the 'ABC's'. If a pulse and breathing are present, use the recovery position and keep the airway clear. Since the patient will be unable to tell you about symptoms and the condition is likely to be serious, you must carry out a meticulous examination. Look especially for the cause of the unconsciousness which may be obvious, for example a blow to the head, or may not be. Indeed, unconsciousness due to an unknown cause is a fairly common problem in patients arriving in Casualty Departments. Specific treatment may be needed to deal with whatever is causing the unconsciousness, such as shock. Since an unconscious patient is helpless, you must not only keep a clear airway but also make sure that there is ample cold protection, and that there are no pressure or rubbing points.

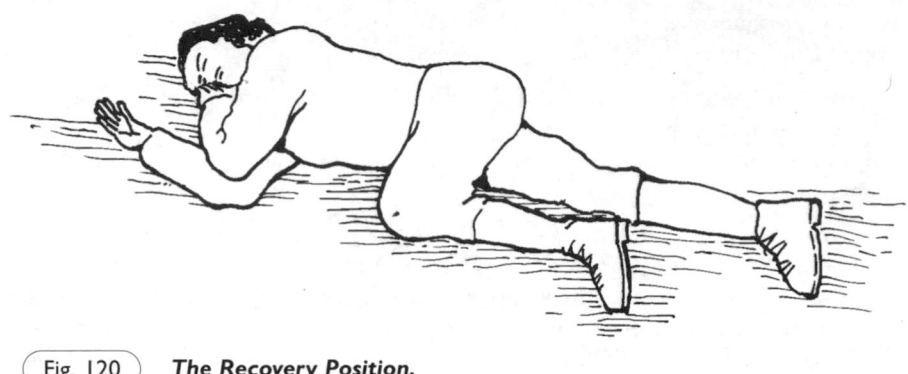

Fig. 120   *The Recovery Position.*

Head injury is one of the most likely causes of unconsciousness you may have to deal with in the mountains. The deeper and longer the unconsciousness, the more severe the injury. Very bad signs are progressively deepening unconsciousness and one or both pupils becoming dilated.

The real killer in head injuries is brain swelling which leads to increasing pressure inside the skull. Brain swelling is made much worse if the airway is not kept clear. This is because if it is not kept clear the amount of air breathed in and out is reduced, resulting in a build up of carbon dioxide which in turn causes dilation of the blood vessels in the brain, leading to more swelling. Therefore, in head injury it is of paramount importance to keep the airway as clear as possible.

Many head injuries are accompanied by neck injuries. If the patient is unconscious they can not tell you they have neck pain. Therefore take great care when moving the neck, especially when moving or rolling the patient, or when trying to clear the airway. A blocked airway however takes priority, so if you have to move the neck to clear the airway, move it.

THE AIRWAY

The importance of attention to the airway cannot be overestimated. Most blocked airways can be cleared with simple and basic manoeuvres, but tragically it is still one of the commonest causes of death in patients unconscious after an injury, or unconscious as a result of other illnesses such as a stroke, epilepsy etc. Therefore, clearing a blocked airway is probably the single most important lifesaving action a first aider can take.

The airway is the way the air goes between the mouth or nose and the lungs. The airway can be blocked at any point along this path, and blockage may be due to any of a number of causes. By far the commonest cause, however, is unconsciousness.

When conscious, we automatically maintain a clear airway and also cough violently if any foreign bodies enter the upper trachea (windpipe). With decreasing levels of consciousness, muscle tone and the cough reflex are progressively lost. Reduced muscle tone allows the tongue, and the jaw to which it is attached, to slide back until the base of the tongue presses against the back of the throat, blocking the airway. This can occur with the patient lying in any position, but is more likely with the patient lying flat on their

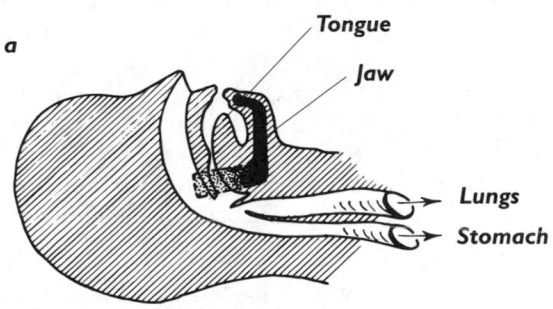

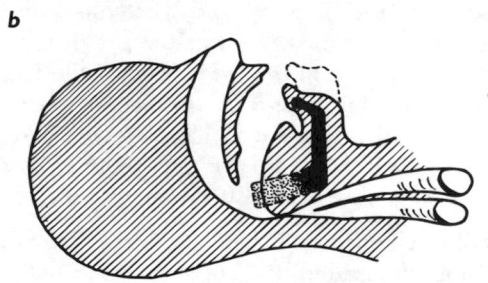

Fig. 121   *The Airway:*
            a Normal, and b when unconscious the tongue and jaw may slide back.

back as gravity will pull the tongue and jaw back. A reduction in cough reflex means that foreign bodies (including vomit) are not coughed up.

So in the lighter levels of unconsciousness, for example when asleep or drunk, the airway can become partially blocked. This causes the familiar snoring noise. In deeper levels of unconsciousness, for example after a severe head injury, the airway can become totally blocked, and the cough reflex completely lost. So when caring for an unconscious patient, make sure the airway is kept clear, and put them in the recovery position to stop vomit going into the lungs.

Vomit rarely causes complete blockage of the airway, but may if the patient is left lying flat on the back and large amounts of vomit are inhaled or lie in a pool at the back of the throat. The big problem with vomit is the effect of the acid it contains on the lungs. The acid may have a devastating and sometimes fatal effect over the following hours and days, almost digesting the delicate lung tissues. As little as half a cupful can be fatal.

To assess whether the airway is clear, place your palm in front of the nose and mouth and feel for air movement and listen for the snoring noise of partial obstruction. Watch the patients chest to see if they are trying to breathe, if not they need mouth to mouth resuscitation. A clear airway and good breathing effort is indicated by free air movement felt on your hand. Also look at the patients colour. (A blue tinge especially on the lips, known as 'cyanosis' means there is not enough oxygen in the blood. This can be caused by a blocked airway, by the patient not trying to breathe or by severe heart and lung problems.)

If the airway is blocked or partially blocked, clear it using the three airway clearing manoeuvres. These are best learnt by practical demonstration (Fig. 122). They are: 1 tipping the head back, 2 chin lift, and if necessary, 3 jaw thrust. The difference between the last two is that the chin lift uses the straightforward hinge motion of the jaw, while the jaw thrust slides the whole jaw forward as if it was a drawer in the lower part of the face. It takes two hands to do the jaw thrust, and quite a lot of force: grip the corners of the jaw with your finger tips just in front and below the ears and put the heel of your hands on the cheek bones and then tighten your grip, pulling the jaw forwards. The jaw thrust is only needed for the rare difficult cases.

The majority of blocked or partially blocked airways are easily cleared with the chin lift and tipping the head back. These can both be done at the same time by simply hooking your fingers under the chin and pulling up. While doing this you can also feel for air movement by holding the palm of the same hand in front of the nose and mouth. This then is a good position to be in.

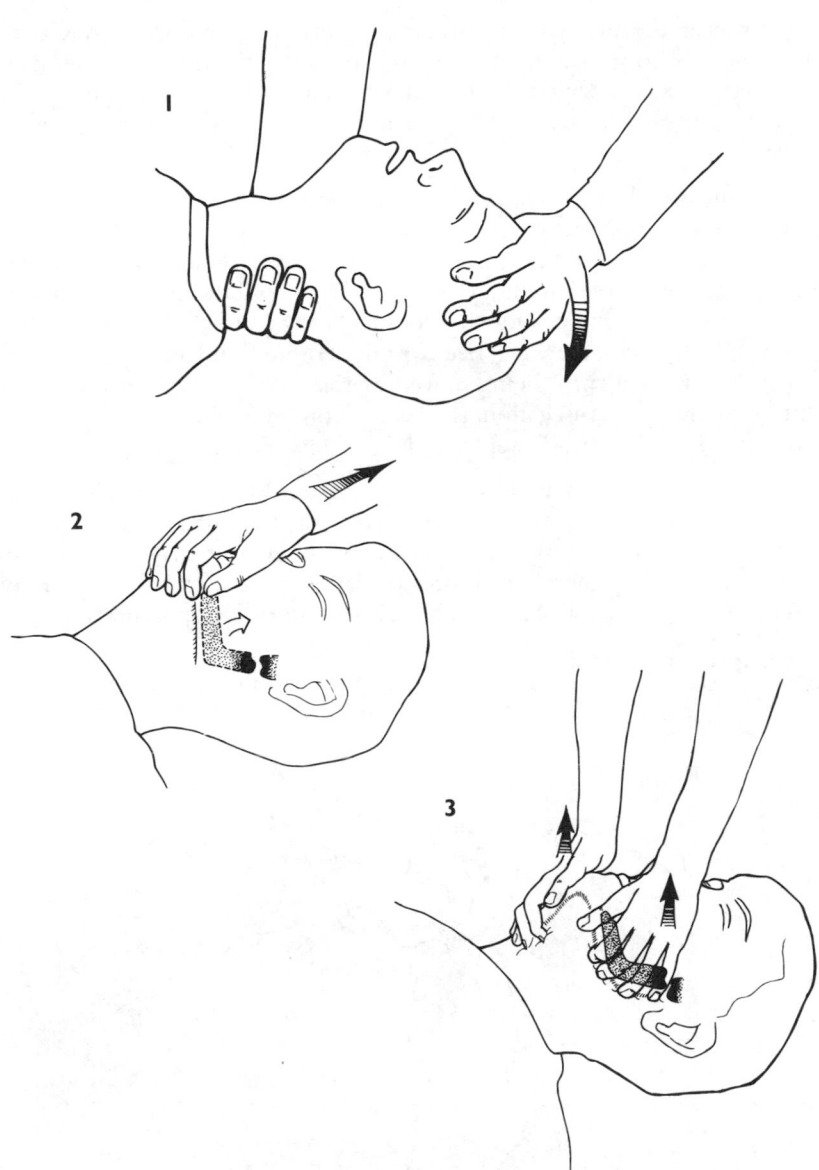

Fig. 122   *The three airway clearing manoeuvres:*
  1 Tipping the head back.
  2 Chin lift.
  3 Jaw thrust.

You can keep the airway open and monitor breathing and the airway all with one hand, leaving you fairly free to do other things. As you do the manoeuvres, see in which position the air moves most freely. Even if you think the airway is clear try the manoeuvres to see if this improves air movement.

Tipping the head back, and other movement of the neck should be avoided unless absolutely necessary to clear the airway if there is the possibility of a neck injury. All of these three manoeuvres can be done with the patient on their side or on their back. You may have to hold the airway's position for some time, for example until the conscious level rises. A patient with an airway which keeps blocking needs uninterrupted and full time attention, especially if the patient is being moved or transported. Do not forget that if mouth to mouth resuscitation is needed you may also have to use these manoeuvres to clear the airway in order to blow air in.

A plastic airway is a valuable piece of first aid equipment which can be used in addition to the normal manoeuvres in cases where it is difficult to keep the airway clear. Also, when used on its own, it may keep an airway open which would otherwise require constant attention. There is a variety of these plastic airways available through some of the larger pharmacy stores.

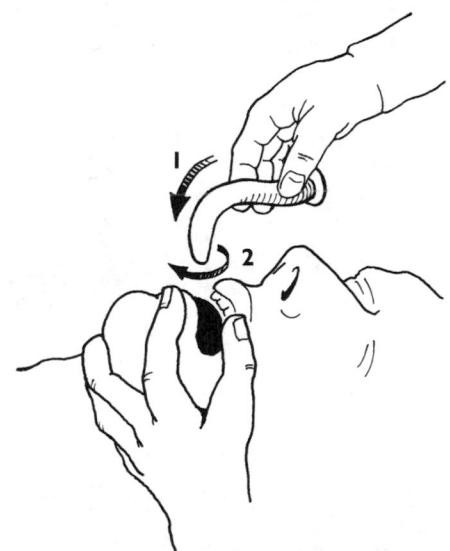

Fig. 123   *Inserting a Plastic Airway. This type is a 'Guedel Airway' and is recommended.*

SPINAL INJURIES

The spine is made up of 25 individual vertebral bones and the moving joints between them. It runs from the base of the skull to the pelvis. The vertebral bones enclose a central canal within which the spinal cord is protected. The spinal cord is made up of fragile nervous tissue, similar to that of the brain. An injury to the spine may result in fractures or dislocations to the bones and the joints of the spine. This may or may not be accompanied by spinal cord damage, which depends on the degree of disruption to the canal in which it lies. Damage to the spinal cord may be reversible or irreversible; often there are elements of both. The higher up the spine the injury is, the worse the long term consequences.

Damage to the spinal cord most often occurs at the time of injury. However, further damage can be caused after the injury by movement, if movement of the fracture impinges upon the cord. Spinal, and especially neck fractures, are often unstable. Movement in any direction can cause further damage, including rotation or flexion in any direction. There is no way of telling whether your patient has an injury which if moved will result in cord damage, and since the results of cord damage are so devastating all cases must be handled with meticulous care.

In an isolated and difficult setting, dealing with a serious spinal injury is a formidable task. The main difficulties arise when the injury is accompanied by other problems and secondly when transporting the patient.

Since spinal injuries are usually the result of an accident involving large amounts of force, for example a fall from a height, they are often accompanied by other injuries such as chest, abdominal and head injuries, and fractures. When treating a patient after this sort of accident, and with these more obvious injuries, always remember to roll the patient over to examine for signs of spinal injury. (Look for swelling, tenderness, deformity or steps over the spine. Reduced sensation and movement in the arms or legs are a symptom of cord damage.)

The combination of spinal injuries, and especially neck injuries, with unconsciousness and airway problems is particularly difficult to deal with. Clearing the airway may be difficult without neck movement, and they will need to be rolled onto their side to prevent inhalation of vomit. When placing the patient on their side, use ample padding and a head support to keep the spine straight and prevent any movement.

Traditionally, any movement of patients with suspected spinal injury is forbidden. However, there are certain situations where the benefits outweigh the risks. Patients with multiple injuries need to be rolled over to be properly examined. Unconscious patients must be kept on their side. In cold or wet conditions, or if the patient is lying on a rough surface or in a contorted position, they should be moved to lie flat on their back on a waterproof mat padded for comfort and cold protection.

When rolling or moving these patients you must minimise spinal movement. When rolling the patient use the 'log rolling' technique (Fig. 124). Several people roll all parts of the body simultaneously with one person carefully holding the head. Similarly, when lifting the patient lift all parts simultaneously to minimise movement.

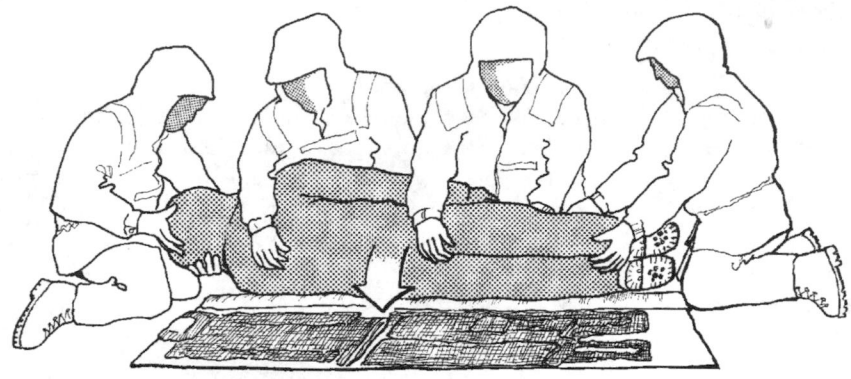

(Fig. 124)   *"Log rolling".*

To splint a neck injury a rigid collar can be improvised, for example by using a piece of camping mat carefully cut to shape and adjusted on another party member of similar size. When applying these collars take great care not to cause neck movement. The neck must be splinted in the 'neutral', i.e.

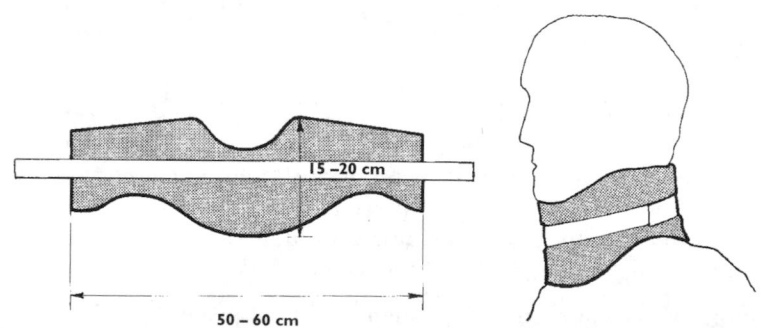

(Fig. 125)   *A neck collar can be improvised from camping mat, folded newspaper, etc.*

normal, position. Often it may be better to simply support the head on each side with the patient lying flat and wait for the mountain rescue team who carry special collars.

Attempting to transport a patient with a spinal injury with improvised equipment should only be considered in the most extreme situations where moving the patient is imperative. Unless there is some other overriding priority, do not hurry and do not attempt to transport the patient yourself but wait for the rescue team to bring expertise and a proper stretcher.

A good stretcher is vital for transport. Use multiple point, firm strapping for the 'whole body splintage effect' (page 258). The flat on the back position is easily the best position, both in terms of ease of application and good immobilisation. Always use this position unless the patient is unconscious. For neck injuries immobilise the whole patient and splint the neck by using firm padding at either side of the head and secure the head to the stretcher using adhesive tape wrapped around the top of the stretcher and across the forehead.

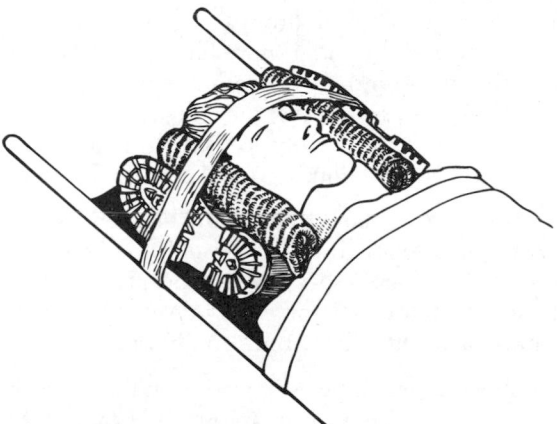

(Fig. 126)   *Neck immobilisation using adhesive tape.*

Always pad the stretcher well, especially if sensation is reduced since the patient will be unaware of pressure and rubbing points. Once on the move, watch carefully to see if there is any movement between the patient and the stretcher. Straps and pads may need adjusting. Monitor the patients condition and especially look out for pain at the site of injury which is associated with stretcher movement. Signs of further damage to the cord, for example an increase in the area of reduced sensation, could mean that you are causing a disaster. Stop and rethink.

BLEEDING AND SHOCK

Loss of blood causes shock. Shock is a state of low blood pressure and the accompanying physiological responses which try to restore blood pressure back up to normal. The term 'shock' is also used by some laymen to describe the state of psychological distress following a stressful situation. This is of course completely different and the use of the term in this context should be avoided.

Adult blood volume is approximately six litres. Loss of 1 litre causes moderate shock, 1.5 litres severe shock and over 2 litres usually causes death. To give an idea of rate of blood loss, complete division of the artery at the wrist would cause loss of about one litre in one minute. Rapid blood loss, as in this example, causes more severe shock than slow blood loss, this is because there is time for some of the physiological responses to have an effect and bring the blood pressure back up towards normal.

Shock is much more easily understood and remembered if its physiology is explained. The arteries can be thought of as a tree shaped elastic container. When blood is lost the blood pressure drops. Compensatory mechanisms are then activated: heart rate rises to pump more blood into the arteries and the small blood vessels (the twigs on the tree) constrict to slow the flow of blood out of the arteries. Blood vessel constriction in the skin causes pallor, the patient's hands and face most noticeably looking "ashen white". Sweating accompanies blood vessel constriction, so that the skin feels cold and clammy.

More severe shock causes confusion and agitation as blood pressure becomes too low to pump enough blood through the brain. Breathlessness and mild cyanosis (a blue tinge, especially on the lips) occurs when blood pressure becomes too low to pump enough blood through the lungs. Patients with these symptoms have a life threatening condition.

The severity of shock can then be estimated from the symptoms described above. Further assessment can be made by measuring heart rate and by feeling the pulse: as shock worsens the pulse fades from the periphery towards the centre. This is useful for grading severe shock. The wrist pulse goes first (this indicates severe shock), then the pulse at the front of the elbow goes (this indicates near death). The pulse at the groin and the side of the neck are the last to go. When these go, it indicates cardiac arrest. To remind yourself where these pulses are, feel for them on yourself. The heart rate usually goes up to about 120 to 150 before the pulses start to fade.

For treatment of shock, the vital action you must take is of course to stop bleeding as soon and completely as possible. The source of the bleeding may be obvious and easy to stop, as in some straightforward limb injuries, using the

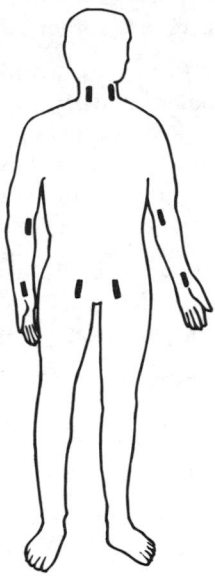

Fig. 127 *Pulses fade from the periphery inwards as shock gets worse.*

old principles of pressure and elevation. However the source of bleeding may be less obvious and may be more difficult to stop. It may indeed go unnoticed until shock develops. After an abdominal or chest injury it is impossible for all but the surgical expert to tell if there is internal bleeding by examining the injured area. However the lack of tenderness to firm pressure on the abdomen usually excludes bleeding there.

Bleeding and shock are usually associated with injuries. However massive bleeding from stomach ulcers is a common cause of shock. In the case of internal bleeding or bleeding from an ulcer there is nothing you can do to stop it. It may stop on its own.

What you can do as a first aider beyond the vital job of stopping the bleeding is limited. Lie the patient head down on a gentle slope (e.g. 10 to 20 degrees). If this is not possible at least raise the legs. This empties blood towards the more vital areas. Institute general measures (see that section) and treat other injures.

A shocked patient will slowly improve if the bleeding stops and the shock was not too bad. Severely shocked patients, and those where bleeding continues, need intravenous fluids as soon as possible to replace lost blood. If internal bleeding persists emergency surgery is also needed.

If the patient's condition is serious, avoiding further blood loss is vital. Moving such a patient could be dangerous. Internal bleeding can be exacerbated by movement. Pelvis and limb fractures, particularly femoral fractures, may bleed badly if the patient is moved before adequate splintage is applied. Take care to protect any bleeding wounds from knocking or rubbing as this may aggravate bleeding, or move pressure bandages.

A good quick check for regular monitoring of shock is simply to assess heart rate by feeling the neck pulses and watch facial skin colour. In severe shock also watch for fading pulses and the conscious level.

FRACTURES

The main and most common problem caused by fractures in the mountains is pain and the difficulty this causes in moving the patient.

For initial treatment, most fractures need no more than simple splintage and pain killers (even aspirin helps). The function of splintage is to reduce movement between the fractured bone ends. This reduces pain and bleeding around the fracture, and reduces further damage to adjacent nerves and blood vessels. The more unstable (wobbly) a fracture is, the more splintage is important. Splints also give protection from pressure and knocks.

Effective splintage can often best be achieved by strapping the fractured limb to another part of the body. For example, in upper arm fractures, strap the arm against the side of the chest and support the forearm in a sling. This technique can be combined with the use of improvised splints, for example for lower leg fractures use splints and padding, and strap the two legs together. Ideally splints should extend well above and below the fracture site to 'immobilise the joint below and above'. A stretcher serves an important splintage role (page 258).

A fractured limb is usually best splinted in the position in which it is found, accommodating the limb shape using ample padding. Straightening is painful and may cause damage. However, straightening should be considered in a few uncommon situations. These are:

1. If the limb is grossly deformed or very difficult to splint and transport in its present position.

2. If the bone ends are nearly breaking through the skin (look for the skin tenting outwards over the bone ends and looking white).

3. If there are marked signs of impaired circulation (see later).

The further you are from medical help the more important it is to straighten the limb, as the damage caused by impaired circulation and the bone ends pressing up under the skin gets worse with time. The decision whether or not to straighten the limb is difficult. If in doubt don't.

To straighten the fracture pull along the axis of the limb to pull the bone ends apart and then gently attempt to straighten it. It may be bent or twisted. Try one pull and correction lasting a few seconds, hold gently in place and reassess. The manoeuvre may need to be repeated. Don't aim for perfection, just try to improve it. Sometimes the bone ends are well jammed together and large amounts of force are needed to straighten the limb. This should only be done in hospital under an anaesthetic. A first aider should only attempt to straighten a limb using moderate but firm force, using a maximum of about 5 Kg pulling along the limb. Unstable fractures are much easier, less painful and less damaging to straighten. Once the fracture has been pulled straight, hold it gently in position, and get someone to splint it.

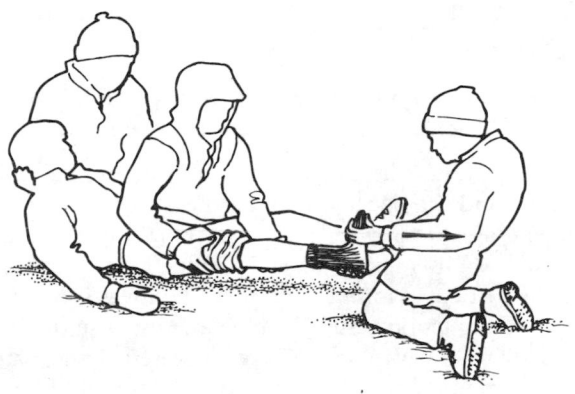

Fig. 128   *Straightening a fracture.*

If the bone ends are nearly breaking through the skin, and you can not correct this by straightening the limb, pad the area generously with a doughnut shaped pad to protect from pressure and rubbing. If the skin overlying the fracture is broken, apply some antiseptic solution or cream and cover carefully with a sterile dressing if available. If the skin is broken they may well need surgery and therefore an anaesthetic, so avoid giving them food or drink.

Fractures can impair limb circulation if an artery becomes compressed. However, this can also be caused by too tight splint strapping or clothing. A limb with severely impaired circulation looks white, it may also have a slight blue tinge, it feels cold and no pulses can be felt. Compare the limb to the opposite limb; if the circulation is seriously impaired there will be a striking difference. If you can not remember where to find the pulses look for them on yourself.

Cooling of a normal limb also causes a reduction in the limb's circulation. This occurs as a result of the small blood vessels constricting in response to the cold, the function of this being to reduce heat loss. It may therefore be difficult to decide whether reduced circulation is due to the injury or just due to cooling. The two of course can add up.

A limb with reduced circulation due to an injury is at a greater risk of developing frost bite, so be meticulous with insulation in cold conditions. Re-assess circulation and the tightness of the strapping regularly, as swelling may progress and the fracture or strapping may move. Make an easy access point to facilitate this.

FRACTURED FEMUR

A fractured femur (thigh bone) deserves special mention because it presents serious problems, particularly in a mountain environment.

Femur fractures are usually unstable, and this combined with its position between the body and the size and mass of the lower leg (causing the two to move in different directions with patient movement) make immobilisation with improvised splints particularly difficult. Furthermore, good immobilisation is particularly important as the femur is surrounded by a large mass of muscle and big blood vessels, so bleeding into the thigh, and pain, can be severe. Bleeding and pain are greatly increased if the patient is moved without adequate immobilisation. As much as one litre of blood or more can be lost into the thigh. Muscle spasm of the large thigh muscle is usual and may cause shortening of the leg as the bone ends overlap and angulate at the fracture. This also increases pain and bleeding. The only treatment for spasm is longitudinal traction (that is a steady pull along the limb), this also immobilises the fracture well. To provide longitudinal traction special splints are needed. (Fig. 129) These special splints are usually carried by Mountain rescue teams, but would not be expected to be carried by a walking party.

Improvised traction splints are very difficult to make using ski poles or ice axes. Applying such splints may result in excessive fracture movement, causing more harm than good. For these reasons they cannot be recommended.

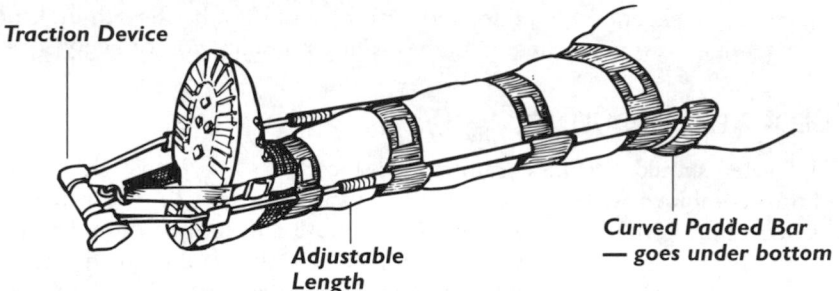

Traction Device

Curved Padded Bar
— goes under bottom

Adjustable
Length

(Fig. 129) *A traction splint for a fractured femur.*

The best first aid treatment is to immobilise the fracture using improvised splints. These should be long, ideally being from the armpit to the foot. Use two walking poles fixed together for example. Avoid strapping over the fracture as circulation may already be compromised through the fracture site. Strap the legs together using lots of padding. The whole body splintage effect of a stretcher (see section on transport) helps greatly with immobilisation, especially if you are using improvised splints.

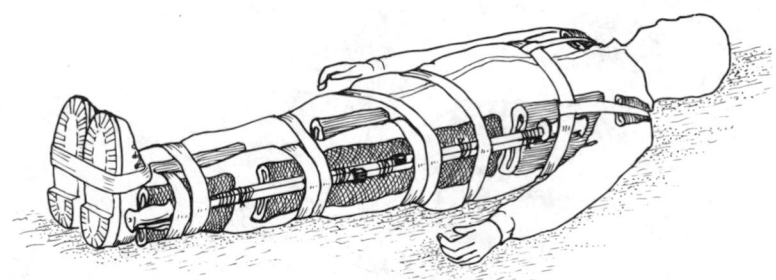

(Fig. 130) *Improvised splint for a fractured femur.*

Fractures of the upper femur can easily be confused with other injuries including hip, pelvis, or even lower spinal fractures. All of these injuries may cause severe and widespread pain, and may be accompanied by internal bleeding. In any case use long splints and a stretcher for all of these injuries.

In summary, a fractured femur is a severe injury, difficult to splint for evacuation and fares badly if moved before proper splints are applied. For these reasons a patient with a fractured femur should not be moved until the rescue team arrives unless there is an overriding consideration of safety.

DISLOCATED SHOULDER

A dislocated shoulder is the commonest dislocation. It is extremely painful and this, combined with the frequently awkward position the arm is left in, make transport particularly difficult. To diagnose a dislocated shoulder, feel both shoulders simultaneously and feel for asymmetry. If dislocated, the tip of the shoulder feels very prominent and a hollow can be felt below this where the top of the upper arm bone should be. This appearance is often described as a 'squaring off' of the shoulder.

An attempt at putting the joint back into place is worthwhile, even though the method below works in less than 50% of cases, since it results in a great relief of pain and reduces damage to the joint . Lie the patient face down on

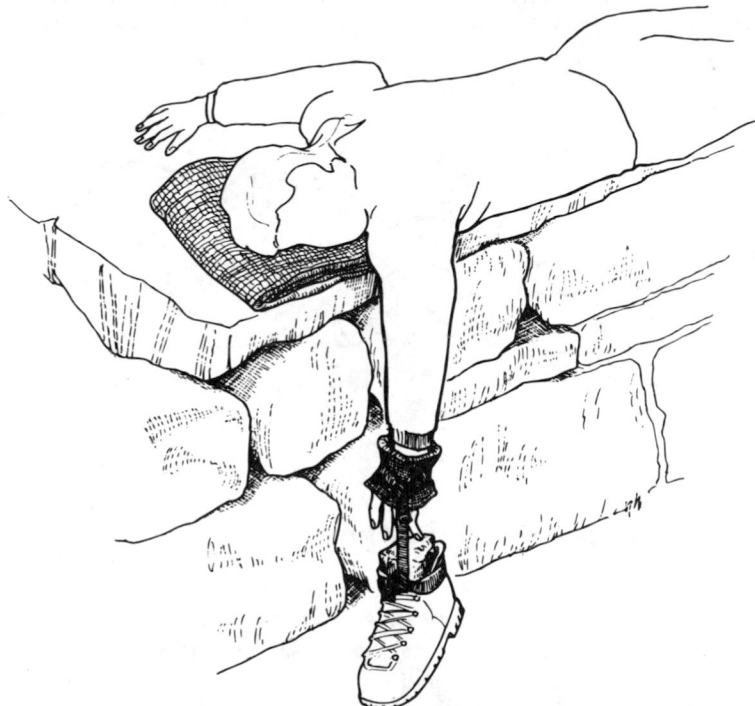

Fig. 131   *Traction and relaxation to put a dislocated shoulder back into place.*

a rock or on a ledge with the injured arm hanging vertically downwards. Attach a weight of about 2 kg to the wrist using ample padding. A stone in a polythene bag or in a boot make an effective weight. Encourage the patient to relax, then wait. If it works they will feel the joint going back into place. It is probably worth waiting for half an hour or so, depending on your circumstances, to see if it does go back in. Other methods involving more force should be avoided, as you may in fact be dealing with a fracture and not a dislocation, and you may then cause damage. Some people have a recurrently dislocating shoulder. The more often it has dislocated the more sure you can be that it has happened again, and the more likely it is to go back into place with this method.

When transporting a patient with a dislocated shoulder (which would not go back into place), support the arm in its most comfortable position, if necessary using large pads such as a rolled up sleeping bag tied up under the armpit. The patient may then be able to walk.

Fig. 132   *Support a dislocated shoulder in the most comfortable position.*

BURNS

Minor burns are a fairly common camping accident, often resulting from accidents with stoves and fuel, or spilt hot liquids. The areas most commonly burnt are the hands and the face (on the face usually superficial burns caused by fuel flare-ups). The main problems caused by minor burns are pain and the difficulties associated with the dressings and heat loss in a cold isolated setting. Burns to the face and hands are painful and may cause serious scarring and disability if they are deep. Large burns endanger life.

Partial thickness burns (previously called first and second degree) do not involve the full thickness of the skin. They are often blistered, have a wet weeping surface, and they are painful and are sensitive to touch. They usually heal well if treated correctly. Only the most superficial of these burns do not leave scars. Areas of full thickness burns (previously known as third degree) have a white leathery or dry cardboard like surface. They are not painful initially and are insensitive to touch. They often need skin grafting and leave scars.

For treatment, the immediate action is to throw cold water onto the area as quickly as possible, i.e. within seconds. Do not delay to remove clothing. This cools the skin and so stops burning continuing. The traditional treatment is then to cover the burn with wet dressings. However this has lead to hypothermia, even in the relative warmth of an ambulance. The treatment recommended now is to cover the burn with 'cling film' or a clean plastic bag, and hold it in place with loose bandages. If the hand is burnt, put the whole hand in a plastic bag and secure with a bandage round the wrist. Plastic does not stick to the burn, is comfortable and reduces heat loss and evaporation. If you have no suitable plastic covering, then a dry material dressing is second best. After dressing the burn, carefully cover the area with the patient's clothing to reduce heat loss.

Even simple pain killers such as aspirin or paracetamol help to reduce the pain. Avoid the application of creams or ointments (except for the very minor burns, where antiseptic cream is a good treatment). Avoid trying to pick off adherent burnt clothing or anything else stuck to the burn.

Large burns have severe generalised effects on the body, including the effects of the large fluid losses from the burn surface. These effects can lead to many serious and life threatening problems over the following days such as kidney failure and infection. The larger the total area burnt (partial plus full thickness), the greater these effects. Burns covering an area bigger than about 15% of the body surface (equivalent to one whole arm), are a serious problem in this respect, and require urgent evacuation and medical attention (to

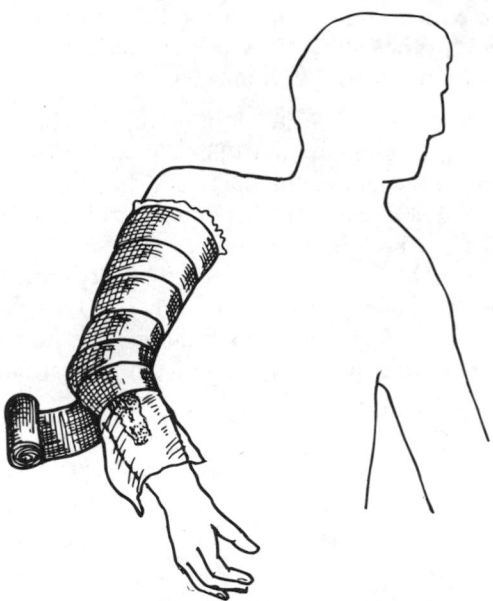

Fig. 133   *Cover the burn with plastic and bandage lightly.*

administer pain-killers and to give fluids through a drip). One surface of the patient's hand with the fingers held together equals one percent of body surface area. Hypothermia is a real risk in patients with large burns and protection from the cold must be thorough.

COLD DEATH AND CPR

Many practical aspects of hypothermia are covered in chapter 9. Here we are concerned with some medical aspects of hypothermia, in particular diagnosis of death and cardio pulmonary resuscitation (CPR) in hypothermic patients.

Hypothermia is defined by convention as a core temperature below 35°C. When the body's heat conserving and heat producing mechanisms can no longer keep up with heat loss, core temperature starts to drops below the normal 37°C. As temperature drops there is progressive slowing and malfunction of all body systems, but most importantly the brain and heart. The effects on the brain start to appear in mild hypothermia, and on the heart in severe hypothermia.

In mild hypothermia, brain cooling causes the many well known subtle symptoms such as slow thought, slurred speech and poor judgement. As temperature drops these progress to confusion and drowsiness, and eventually loss of consciousness occurs below 32°C. Once unconscious, death can result from a blocked airway or inhalation of vomit.

Many other conditions also cause the symptoms of mild brain malfunction (slow thought, confusion, drowsiness, etc.). These may then be confused with hypothermia, and include low blood glucose in a diabetic, severe shock, head injury and exhaustion. Exhaustion and hypothermia often coexist, and the treatment is then to provide both protection from cold, and hot calorific food or drink. Symptoms of mild hypothermia may also be confused simply with normal mood changes, so watch for this particularly in teenage groups. Heat exhaustion also gives rise to the symptoms of mild brain malfunction, and can surprisingly be confused with hypothermia. It can occur if far too much clothing is worn during exercise.

Cooling of the heart causes irregular heartbeats initially, but as cooling progresses these may worsen until they eventually lead to cardiac arrest. Irregular heartbeats usually start to occur below 30°C and cardiac arrest may occur below about 28°C. Cardiac arrest can occur suddenly and without warning.

Cardiac arrest can easily be triggered by the rough handling of hypothermic patients with a core temperature of less than 28 degrees C. (At this temperature they will usually be unconscious or at least drowsy.) If they are unconscious, avoid rough handling including jolting the stretcher, sudden pulling of a limb, etc. Do not attempt to move a prone patient into a sitting or standing position as this causes blood to pool in the legs resulting in a drop in blood pressure or even cardiac arrest. If it is imperative that you have to lift the patient up then do it slowly.

In near death cases of hypothermia the diagnosis of cardiac arrest is much more difficult than in a patient with a normal temperature. Since all body systems slow with cooling, signs of life are less obvious and may even appear absent. Breathing is slower and the breaths are smaller, movement and reflexes slow, pupils may be dilated and joints become stiff. Heart rate can slow and become irregular. The pumping action of the heart becomes weaker so the pulse is harder to feel. The hands may be cold and numb. Always feel for the pulse at the side of the neck carefully and for at least a minute.

The absence of a pulse at the side of the neck under normal circumstances means you should start CPR immediately. However, hypothermia is a special case for the following reasons. Firstly, since the pulse is so hard to find you can never be certain it is absent. Secondly, CPR will make things worse in cases where there is still a weak heart beat. This is because CPR, even when correctly applied may result in serious injuries such as bruising of the heart.

Also, CPR can actually cause cardiac arrest, particularly in hypothermic patients. CPR is never as good as a weak heart beat at pumping blood round the body. Finally, you should only start CPR if it can be maintained continuously until the patient reaches hospital or other medical facility. This is because once CPR has been started, cardiac arrest will probably not be reversible until the patient is re-warmed and expertise, drugs, monitors, etc. are available. Clearly, providing CPR for prolonged periods during evacuation from an isolated locality is in most cases not possible, and may endanger others. So if in doubt, do not give CPR. Remember, "above all, do no harm".

Hypothermic patients are able to survive a surprisingly long period of cardiac arrest before CPR is started. This is because cooling results in slowing of all body systems and thereby a reduction in the rate that oxygen in the body is used up. Delay in starting CPR on a hypothermic patient may be caused by difficulty in diagnosing cardiac arrest, or if there is delay in reaching the patient. Similarly, patients who have been immersed in cold water or buried in an avalanche may be both hypothermic and have had a cardiac arrest (here the cardiac arrest may be due to severe hypothermia or due to asphyxia). Survival after total immersion in icy water, of up to 40 minutes has been recorded.

Mouth-to-mouth resuscitation, known also as expired air resuscitation (EAR), is of course part of CPR. In contrast to full CPR, EAR alone is fairly harmless. EAR provides both oxygenation and warmth, since exhaled breath contains oxygen and is warm. So EAR alone can be used safely and with confidence in cases of hypothermia where you think breathing has stopped, but you are not confident enough to start full CPR.

CHEST PAIN

Chest pain is a common symptom, accounting for about one in 25 of all casualty department attendance's. It can be caused by disorders in any of the organs in the chest and even the upper abdomen, but most notably the heart.

Chest pain is a symptom which should be taken very seriously. Once one of your group complains of chest pain, regardless of the cause, you must abort your expedition. The only question is, how urgent is evacuation. You may have to decide, for example, whether or not to split your party in order to send someone off to raise the alarm. Generally, if the pain is due to a heart problem, this signals greater danger to the patient than if the pain is coming from elsewhere. However, it must be stressed that since reliable diagnosis on the hill is not possible one must always assume that the pain is caused by a potentially life-threatening condition and act on this assumption.

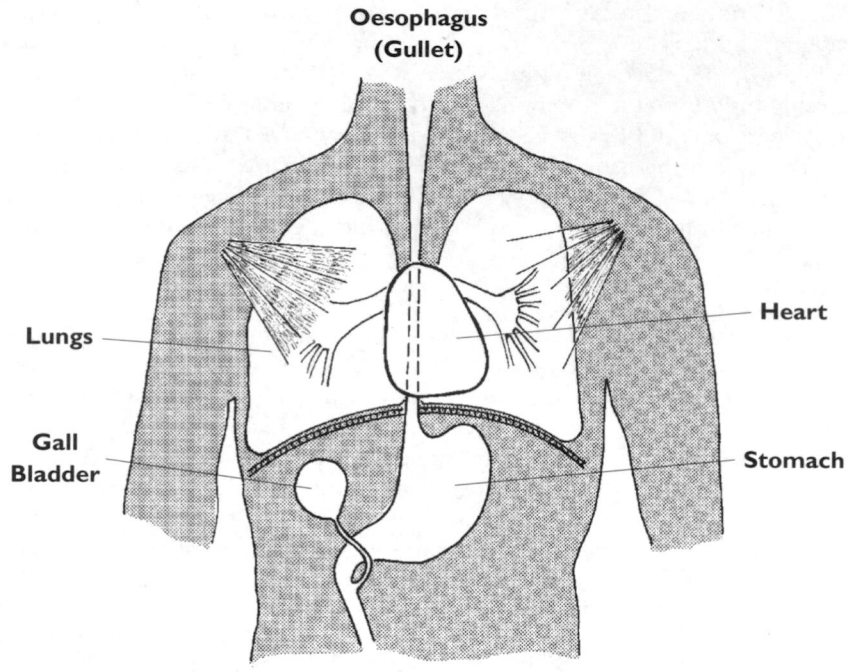

**Oesophagus
(Gullet)**

Lungs

Gall
Bladder

Heart

Stomach

<table>
<tr><td>Fig. 134</td><td>Chest pain can originate from any of these organs.</td></tr>
</table>

Chest pain originating from the heart is caused by angina or a heart attack. Angina is heart pain caused by exercise. It is often made worse by the cold. It is frequently a long term ongoing problem, and the patient usually carries a supply of tablets to put under his tongue which generally work in minutes. A heart attack means death of part of the heart muscle. Both of these conditions give rise to the characteristic heavy, crushing pain which is felt over the front of the chest or as a tight band around the chest.

If the pain is associated with breathlessness, this suggests a heart or lung problem. Pain originating from the lungs is usually sharp, "like a knife", and changes with breathing. Pain originating in the chest wall muscles increases with shoulder, arm or body trunk movement. Pain originating in the upper abdomen is usually felt there, but may occasionally also be felt up into the chest. To find out if the pain is originating from the abdomen feel firmly for tenderness. Chest pain can also be experienced as a symptom of anxiety alone, i.e. there is nothing physically wrong with the heart, lungs, etc. Typically these patients are younger, of an anxious predisposition, and are also hyperventilating. They need to be reassured and calmed down. Chest pain commonly occurs in those who have had it before and can recognise the symptoms. They are therefore able to tell you what the problem is.

Crushing chest pain which is prolonged and severe suggests that it is of cardiac origin and that the patients life is in serious danger. Significantly, the patient may appear agitated, anxious, pale and sweaty, and looks generally sick. Evacuation and early medical attention is extremely urgent. Monitor the patients condition continuously as unconsciousness and cardiac arrest may occur.

Patients with chest pain, especially if it is suspected that it is originating from the heart and is severe, must not exert themselves as this may aggravate their condition. If at all possible they should be carried.

ASTHMA AND SHORTNESS OF BREATH

Shortness of breath is a fairly common symptom, distressing for both patient and those in attendance. Apart from the important general measures outlined at the end of this section, there is little specific treatment you can give.

In younger patients sudden and severe episodes of shortness of breath are usually caused by asthma. Asthma is a common illness, affecting about one in 20 of the population, although many of these in a mild form. Exercise, pollen, dust and psychological stress can be triggering factors. Exercise induced asthma may be made worse by cold air.

Most asthmatics are well in tune with their condition and its treatment. Problems arise when their inhalers can not cope with the attack, and they become unable to inhale enough to get the medication into their lungs. Sometimes the inhaler is simply forgotten and left at home. Those liable to have severe life threatening attacks are often already on several different medications, have had previous hospital admissions with asthma, and may have had increasing symptoms in the preceding days. Severe attacks are very dangerous and require urgent medical attention.

In older patients, episodes of sudden and severe shortness of breath are usually due to heart problems, and so is often associated with chest pain. Shortness of breath can also be caused by anxiety alone, and may be accompanied by chest pain (page 281).

Signs of a life threatening condition in any patient short of breath are the development of a blue tinge, especially on the lips and becoming unable to speak due to breathlessness. They become confused, agitated and drowsy. Further deterioration leads to unconsciousness and may be followed by cardiac arrest. The blue tinge is known as "cyanosis", and is caused by a lack of oxygen in the blood. Unconsciousness, confusion etc. are caused by insufficient oxygen reaching the brain.

Patients short of breath become understandably very anxious and agitated, and are then difficult to handle. They may fight to get out of the tent or snow hole, 'to get air'. This helps psychologically as does loosening the clothing round the neck. They may also insist on the sitting position which makes breathing easier, as it allows the diaphragm to move freely without the weight of the abdominal contents pressing up on it as it does when lying down. Providing psychological support is important. Try to get them to relax and reassure them. Transporting these patients is often very difficult. They will be unable to walk if the problem is severe. They will want to sit up, and may be agitated and confused. Altogether it is a difficult problem.

DIABETES

Diabetes is caused by a lack of insulin which is normally produced by the pancreas gland, and results in a high blood sugar. There are two distinct types of diabetes, one requiring regular treatment with insulin injections which usually starts at a young age, i.e. as a teenager or in the early twenties. The second type which can normally be treated with tablets and by eating less sugar, starts at an older age, usually over forty. In the insulin-treated type, the blood sugar level can fluctuate more quickly and more severely and so is much more likely to cause problems, especially in the hill-walking situation. I shall therefore discuss this condition only.

Most diabetics are fairly knowledgeable about their condition and manage it carefully and sensibly. Problems arise however, when the blood sugar either goes too high or too low. The blood sugar falls during exercise as it is used up in the muscles, and after an insulin injection. Food causes the blood sugar to rise. Diabetics adjust their insulin dose and food intake to achieve a balance, allowing them to exercise and keep their glucose level within normal limits. Unfortunately in the hill-walking situation there are many factors at play which can upset this balance. They can under or over-estimate the possibly unaccustomed exercise factor. Food may not be available at all or at the right times. The food may be unfamiliar resulting in incorrect estimate of its sugar content. The upset to daily routine generally is important. You must give the patient the opportunity to take regular meals and allow time for insulin injections, without making them feel that they are holding others back or are a liability.

The main problems likely to be encountered are a low blood sugar level and, more rarely, a high level. The symptoms of both are unfortunately quite similar, so they are hard to tell apart. These symptoms are of increasing confusion which may progress if severe to unconsciousness, then coma and death. There are, however, two fairly reliable ways of finding whether the blood glucose has gone too high or too low. These are:

1. Find out how much insulin, exercise and food the patient has taken over the preceding twelve hours or so. A common cause of low blood sugar is taking a regular dose of insulin, then missing breakfast and then walking all day. When symptoms arise from high blood sugar it results from grossly insufficient insulin e.g. none for two days. This is why a high glucose is much less common.

2. Consider the length of time over which symptoms have been running. Low blood sugar symptoms usually develop quite rapidly over a period of minutes, but symptoms of high blood sugar usually develop much more slowly, sometimes even over a period of days.

Treatment of the more common low blood sugar is to give fluids or foods with a high sugar content by mouth. The treatment of high blood sugar levels is complex and requires urgent medical attention in a hospital. If the incorrect diagnosis is made, and you give sugar to someone with high blood sugar, this surprisingly causes little further ill effects. In contrast, giving insulin to someone with low blood sugar can rapidly prove fatal. So the message is always to give sugary foods never insulin, to avoid the fatal error.

Episodes of slightly low blood sugar, known as 'hypos', are quite common. The symptoms are usually mild confusion and tiredness. Sometimes hypos lead to irrational and aggressive behaviour, so don't mistake this for mood changes. Diabetics usually recognise these symptoms early and know to correct this quickly themselves by eating sugary food (they should carry sweets on them for this purpose). If they don't do this quickly blood sugar may drop further, confusion will increase and then they will be unable to help themselves. You must then help them to eat or drink sugary foods before they become too confused and drowsy to swallow. The best way of giving sugar to a drowsy patient is to dissolve about six heaped teaspoonfuls of sugar in warm liquid. Usually there is a marked improvement over 10 to 15 minutes, but sometimes they improve more slowly after a severe episode, in which case you may need to give them more sugar. Once recovered there is little danger to the patient, as they will be able to take control again, realise their error and readjust their food and insulin intake.

So, to summarise always give sugar. A diabetic who is confused and drowsy and does not improve with sugar is in danger. An unconscious diabetic may easily die. Treatment is urgent. Time is critical, especially in the quicker moving low blood sugar problem, so the rescue priority is to get the patient to a doctor or a doctor to the patient as soon as possible.

EPILEPSY

Epilepsy is a common condition affecting approximately 1 in 200 of the population. It is particularly likely to be a problem in school parties. Some epileptics are well controlled by their medication and may not have fits for years, others have frequent fits, some even daily in extreme cases. One of the commonest causes of fits, however, is the patient simply not taking the drugs, for a number of reasons. In a school group this is particularly likely to happen. With the upset to normal daily routine and the lack of normal supervision, they may forget to take a dose, or simply forget the drugs and leave them at home. Omitting a single dose puts the patient at risk of having fits for the following day or two. If the patient does have a fit and then admits to having missed taking a dose within the last twenty four hours, the missed dose should be taken straight away. If there is any uncertainty then a dose should be taken anyway.

An epileptic fit is caused by an uncontrolled electrical discharge travelling through the brain. During a fit the patient loses consciousness, falls down and then usually the limbs, body and face muscles go into spasm for a few seconds. This is followed by jerking motions and the patient may become incontinent. When the fit stops the patient will slowly regain consciousness over the next 10 minutes or so, after which they will be very confused. The confusion may be distressing to others around them as they may not even recognise relatives or friends at first. This slowly resolves over half an hour or so, at which time you can enquire as to any missed drug doses, etc.

During a fit you must try to protect the patient from injury when they fall and then during the jerking phase when they may strike objects. While unconscious the airway may become blocked or they may inhale vomit, so keep the airway clear and put them in the recovery position. Reassure others in the group, and also the patient when awake. Keep things calm.

The great majority of fits surprisingly occur without any injury or mishap. Once the patient has recovered from a straightforward fit, there is little cause for concern except that whatever caused the fit will still be there, and so another fit may occur. The usual cause of a fit is insufficient anti-epileptic drug in the blood. A missed dose taken after the fit takes a few hours to be absorbed from the stomach and become effective. Because of this it is best to abandon your expedition. The patient should then see a doctor.

A fit may occasionally last for longer than the normal 10 to 20 seconds, with continuous jerking and spasm lasting for sometime. Similarly, the patient may have a series of fits in quick succession without regaining consciousness in between. This is much more dangerous than a normal fit. Uninterrupted attention to the airway and patient position is vital, and medical help and evacuation must be arranged urgently.

Epileptic fits may occur rarely as a result of other causes (that is other than the usual cause of long-standing predisposition). Thus fits may occur in life threatening conditions due to their effects on the brain. These include the severe head injury, very low blood glucose in a diabetic, and conditions where grossly insufficient oxygen is reaching the brain (including severe shock, cardiac arrest and extreme breathing and lung problems). In these extreme life-threatening conditions try to treat the underlying cause, and as before, put the patient in the coma position and keep the airway clear.

EYES

The eye problem you are most likely to encounter is the watering 'red eye', which is usually caused by conjunctivitis or a foreign body.

Conjunctivitis is a common infection. It has a slow onset over hours or days and the eye often feels gritty. The gritty feeling may make the patient think there is a foreign body there. Check for foreign bodies in any case. It is not a serious condition but the patient needs to see a doctor for antibiotic cream.

Foreign bodies often enter the eye when the wind is blowing things about, or when looking up on a rock climb or hammering in a piton. Metal to metal hammering may cause small metal fragments to fly off and penetrate the eye. This is a serious condition. Usually the patient is aware of the foreign body going into the eye and may be able to indicate where it is. Investigate by gently pulling the lower lid down with your finger tip and ask the patient to look up and then look left and right. Repeat for the upper lid. If you see a foreign body try to remove it by touching it carefully with just the corner of some absorbent material such as a paper handkerchief. Tears will be wicked up by the handkerchief and the foreign body may then stick to its surface. Never attempt to remove adherent or penetrating foreign bodies. After removal there may still be a gritty sensation due to the raised edges of the small scratches remaining, or there may be another foreign body, so look again.

Severe cases of 'red eye', except those responding to the above treatment, require an eye patch, regardless of the cause. To improvise an eye patch place a folded handkerchief or something similar over the closed eye and hold it in place with tape. The aim is to apply just enough pressure to keep the eye lid shut. This reduces irritation and scratching caused by blinking. Check that the eye is kept closed by peeking under the patch as the patient blinks.

BLISTERS

There are dozens of remedies for blisters. Here is another based on a scientific approach. Foot blisters are caused by friction on the skin surface, where the boot is pressing and is moving in relation to the foot. The solutions are:

1. Adjust your boots, lacing, socks, etc. to reduce the combined effects of friction and pressure on the area.

2. Stick smooth shiny-surfaced tape over the area. This ensures that the plane of movement is on the tape's slidy surface and not on the skin's surface. The smooth surface further ensures that the tape is not rubbed off by the sock, as a rough surfaced tape would be. The key is good adhesion to the skin. To achieve this first clean the skin, ideally with an alcohol based liquid to remove the oils from the skin surface. Dry, then apply the most adhesive tape available (one inch elastoplast on a roll is good). On top of this stick the shiniest surfaced tape available. The purpose of the first tape layer is to give the shiny tape something easy to stick to. Bursting the blister slightly increases infection risk if it is not kept clean, but reduces the prominence of the area thus reducing friction on the tape surface.

12

Mountain Rescue

Not long ago there were no organised mountain rescue teams, no helicopters, and fewer people walking and climbing in the mountains. If an accident occurred there was no professional organisation ready to sweep into action as soon as the alarm was raised. Mountaineers had to rely on their own resources to get themselves out of trouble and if, for any reason, this was not possible then they had to call on such help as was available from other parties walking or climbing in the neighbourhood. It is a tradition of self-reliance and mutual support that is well worth preserving, even in this day of sophisticated rescue aids. It is a mistake in principle to rely on others to come and sort you out should things go wrong. Leaders should set out on the clear understanding that they are in charge of independent, self reliant groups, able to deal competently with most eventualities and ready and willing to offer assistance to others should this be required.

Today, with greatly increased numbers of people taking to the hills such a system of self-help is no longer sufficient. It has, of necessity, been reinforced by a more professionally orientated organisation comprising local mountain rescue teams which are well equipped, efficient and are supported by the mountain rescue teams and the search and rescue helicopters of the RAF. Inevitably, such a service brings with it the danger that we may come to rely on always having a back-stop should things go wrong. This is a dangerous attitude of mind which may encourage those who have it to overreach themselves. When conditions are really bad, helicopters cannot fly and even efficient rescue teams are greatly restricted in what they can do on foot.

The mountaineer attempts to be self-reliant in attitude and, as far as possible, self-sufficient in terms of equipment and skills. Accidents happen, often when they are least expected, and mountain leaders should be confident that they can make the right decisions and act on them competently. Accidents in the mountains have a nasty habit of escalating. A relatively minor mishap and a subsequent series of wrong decisions can, and often does, develop into an incident involving possible threat to life. Making the right decisions at an early stage in an incident is of paramount importance. To do this a leader needs a cool head, the right quality of experience and a liberal dose of common sense.

ACCIDENT PROCEDURE

In the event of an incident, do not rush. It is essential that you keep a grip of yourself and assert your control over the party at an early stage when your concern for the casualty may encourage you into precipitate action. Keep other members of the group back and give them instructions to do something useful. Approach with caution and never from above if there is a chance of slipping or dislodging loose rocks onto the casualty.

Make a rapid examination of the casualty checking for life threatening conditions; failure of breathing, no pulse, arterial bleeding. A leader should be familiar with methods of resuscitation and life-saving first-aid (Chapter 11).

See to it that no immediate danger threatens the casualty or the rest of the party. If it does then the first priority may be to move to a safer area nearby where you can render first aid treatment as required. Remember that no treatment is better than unnecessary meddling. Make the casualty as comfortable as possible and provide warmth and shelter as far as circumstances and equipment allow. Be particularly careful to provide adequate insulation from the ground. If there is no spinal injury it may be advantageous to move to a more sheltered site provided this can be accomplished without undue discomfort or aggravation of injuries. If you decide not to move the casualty build a shelter with whatever materials are to hand, but remember the first rule of casualty care, "do not move unless you have to".

Plan of Action

This is a critical stage in the whole operation, so take your time and do not be rushed into making over-hasty decisions. Decide whether the incident can be handled using the resources of the party or whether outside help will be needed. In either case work out a detailed plan taking into account the following factors:

The nature of the casualty's injuries: Few injuries require immediate evacuation as an absolute priority, although there are one or two conditions where such action would be justified, eg acute appendicitis, diabetic coma.

On the other hand, there are some where the specialised expertise of a rescue team, probably with a doctor in attendance, would be virtually essential, eg head and spinal injuries, severe internal injuries, heart attack, stroke, severe hypothermia.

The state of the party: It is very understandable, but nevertheless a mistake, to focus all the attention on the casualty. The leader has a responsibility for the rest of the party who may be particularly vulnerable to cold and anxiety at this time. Failure to attend to them may well lead to additional casualties. Discuss the situation frankly, but optimistically, with party members and consult them before finalising your plan of action. As far as possible keep them busy and involved in providing succour to the casualty - organising protective equipment, setting up some form of shelter, talking encouragingly to the patient, monitoring breathing, pulse and colour.

The time available: There is very rarely enough time to do all that has to be done. Time spent in making the casualty comfortable is time well spent. Make sure that everyone, including the casualty, understands what you intend to do. Make an estimate of the time required to complete each of the possible alternatives taking account of the fact that part of the rescue operation may have to be conducted in darkness.

The weather: Bad weather conditions are frequently associated with accidents. It may be so bad that immediate evacuation to a lower, more sheltered, location overrides all other considerations. In winter, snow conditions underfoot may rule out the possibility of evacuation using improvised material and techniques.

The availability of assistance: Sometimes, with the support of other groups walking or climbing in the neighbourhood, it may be practicable to evacuate the casualty. Advice on how to attract attention is given in the next section. Familiarity with the location of the nearest mountain rescue post and the most convenient place from which the rescue services can be summoned is part of the essential information a leader should have before taking a group into the hills.

The terrain: Determine the best route out for the messengers who may be sent to summon help and give careful consideration to the composition of such a party.

Finally, you must evaluate the human and material resources available at the accident site and decide whether or not the party has the capability of evacuating the casualty without outside assistance.

SIGNALLING

(Table 13)   *Signals used in Mountain Rescue.*

Message	Flare Signal	Audible Signal	Light Signal
HELP REQUIRED	RedFlare(s)	6 blasts etc. in quick success, repeated after a 1 minute interval. SOS: Three short, three long, three short blasts etc. in succession repeated after a 1 minute interval.	6 flashes in quick succession, repeated after a 1 minute interval. SOS: Three short, three long, three short flashes, repeated after a 1 minute interval.
MESSAGE UNDERSTOOD	White Flare(s) (also used for illumination).	3 blasts etc in quick succession, repeated after a 1 minute interval.	3 flashes in quick succession, after a 1 minute interval.
RETURN TO BASE	Green Flare(s) A prolonged succession of blasts etc.	A prolonged succession of blasts etc	A prolonged succession of flashes
POSITION OF BASE	White or Yellow Flare(s) Continuous light		Continuous light.

NB. FIXING POSITION. As soon as a signal is seen (or heard) a compass bearing must be taken on it. Two such bearings, if taken from different positions, will give a reasonably accurate fix on the position of the signal.

Whatever you decide to do it is likely that you will want to attract the attention of other parties in the area to seek whatever help they can offer. There is an internationally recognised code of signals, both audible and visual and this is summarised in the table above. It should be borne in mind that a single signal can easily be missed so keep repeating it until it is acknowledged. Severe weather can render all signalling except radio worthless.

There are really only two options available. Either send for help or evacuate the casualty using whatever assistance can be mustered at the accident site. It is possible, of course, to leave one or more of the group with the injured person and lead the rest down to safety yourself.

SENDING FOR HELP

Deciding who to send for help is a most important issue for mountain leaders. We can make the assumption that the party is not experienced enough to be on the hill by themselves or they would not need a leader with them. In these circumstances it would seem foolish to send any member of an inexperienced party off to get help. They will undoubtedly be under considerable stress and in such a situation the role of the leader will inevitably become more authoritarian, not one of delegation of greater responsibility to the party.

There are obvious riders to be made to this statement as there are many variables in the circumstances in which help has to be obtained. The first consideration is the condition of the casualty and of the rest of the party. The priority must be to keep the casualty alive and if this means that the leader cannot leave, then all future decisions have to be taken with this limitation in mind. The rest of the party will, as already stated, be under a certain amount of stress and what they do and how they cope must be the responsibility of the leader.

Other factors to take into account when deciding who should be sent for help are the weather conditions, the terrain to be covered and the distance involved. The difficulty of the navigation must be borne in mind as it would be pointless sending someone for help only for them to get lost.

If the casualty or an inexperienced party is to be left on their own, and it must be stressed that only in the direst of emergencies should a casualty be left alone, they should be told to stay put at all costs. If they move, a comparatively simple treatment and recovery operation could be transformed into a major search. They should be given all the spare clothing and food and be provided with a whistle and torch if these are not required by the messengers.

Make the target as large as possible by laying a rope at right angles to the probable line of approach of the rescue party or construct some other linear feature such as a line of footprints in the snow or a line of small cairns. Remember that the rescue team may have to find the location in the dark or mist. An unconscious patient should not be left alone. In a party of two, it is safer for the uninjured person to render first-aid and assistance and to try to attract the attention of other climbers. Only as an absolute last resort should a casualty be left alone and in that event they should be tied securely to the rock if in an exposed situation and a note left explaining what action has been taken and when. It is worth remembering that an injured person on regaining consciousness will sometimes attempt to untie themselves.

As a final word, remember to tell anyone left behind the possible time scale of the rescue. It often takes far longer than first imagined for a rescue team to be assembled and for help to reach a casualty.

It may be that the best person to go for help will be the leader and groups will have to be left with the casualty. It should be appreciated that inexperienced mountaineers may well be in less danger left in a safe location and told not to move.

Whoever goes for help should carry a written note with at the very least the following information:-

The precise location of the accident including a 6 figure grid reference.

A description of the location.

A description of the accident and the time it occurred.

The name of the casualty and his/her next of kin, if known.

The nature of the injuries sustained.

An outline of the plan of action, including details of the other members of the party.

Any relevant information about the terrain and the best approach route.

The messengers should take note of the terrain on the way out as they may have to lead the rescue team back in the dark. At the first opportunity they should contact the police who co-ordinate all land-based rescue and are empowered to mobilise all services. If the message is to be relayed they should remain by the telephone to be interviewed by the leader of the mountain rescue team.

SELF HELP

At the outset it should be emphasised that improvised carries and stretchers are of limited short range value. It is exhausting and possibly dangerous to the casualty, to attempt a long evacuation by such methods. The main use of them is for moving a casualty to a more sheltered position or for evacuating someone with relatively minor injuries or, of course, if evacuation is preferable to leaving the casualty on the mountain. Any sort of improvised carry is likely to aggravate injuries, cause additional pain, and increase shock, anxiety and the risk of hypothermia.

A number of different techniques are illustrated in the following pages, some of which look deceptively straight forward to improvise. They all need practice to become fully aware of the limitations of each method in terms of material, manpower and effective range and, more important still, to increase awareness of the physical limitations of rescuers.

Four Hand Chair

Two people form a simple seat by gripping each others wrists. This method is only suitable for short carries of less than 50 metres. It is strenuous and extremely awkward for the carriers.

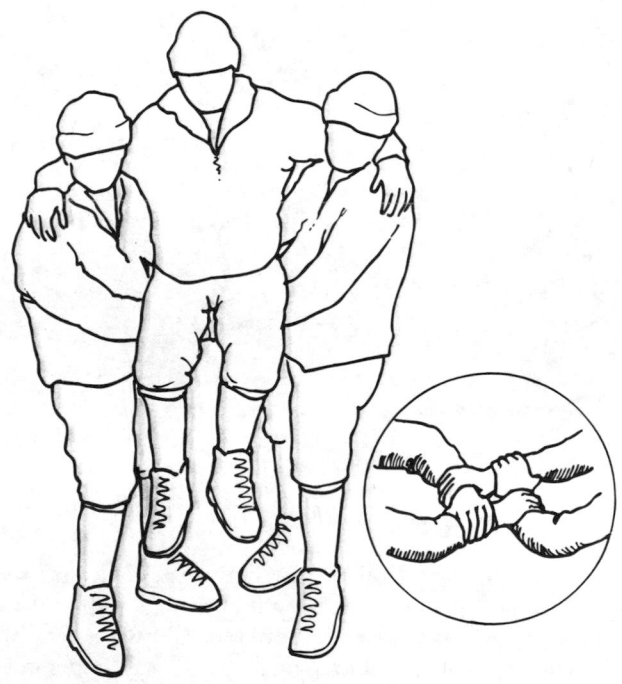

Fig. 135   *Four hand chair.*

Rucksack Carry

The casualty sits on the carriers back with the legs through the rucksack straps which should be padded. Adapt the method to suit the type of rucksack and the physique of the carrier and casualty. It is strenuous but can be effective over short distances.

*a **Casualty sits
   between rucksack
   and carrier.***

*b **Casualty sits on top
   of rucksack.***

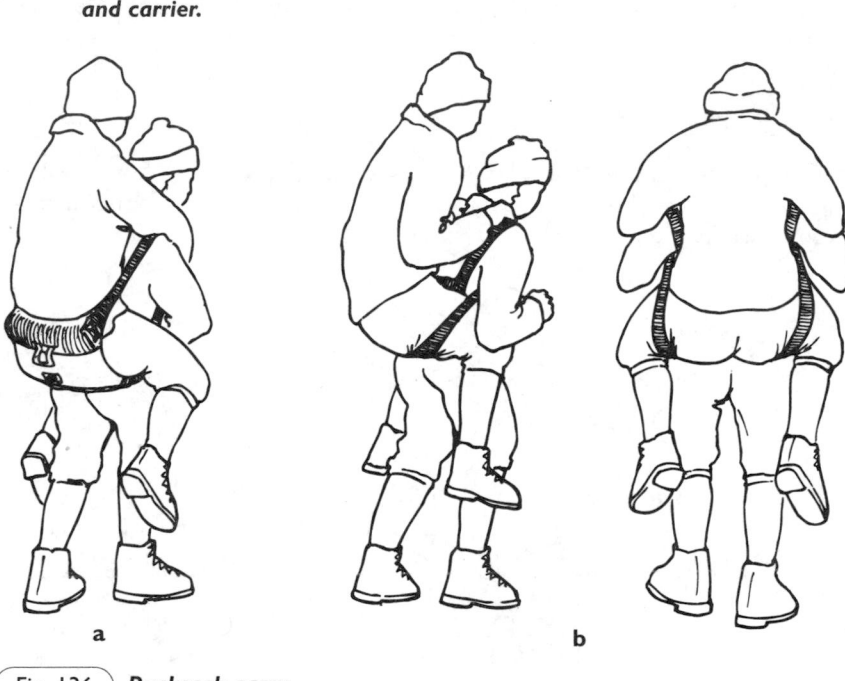

a   b

Fig. 136   *Rucksack carry.*

One-person Split Rope Carry

The carrier wears the split coiled rope like a rucksack and the casualty sits piggy back with the legs through the split coils which should be padded. To prevent coils falling off the carrier's shoulders the two halves of the rope can be linked across the chest with a strap or sling. This is moderately comfortable method so long as the coil length is correct. It is not too exhausting with a small casualty.

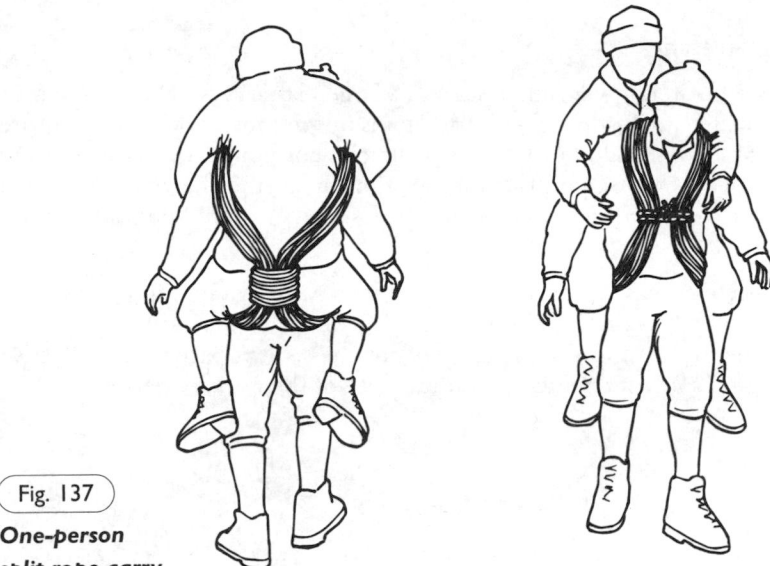

One-person split rope carry.

Two-person Split Rope Carry

The rope is split as in the 'One Person Carry' and the coils taken over the outside shoulders of the two carriers. The casualty sits on the padded rope between the carriers. The method is not good enough for rough terrain or narrow paths.

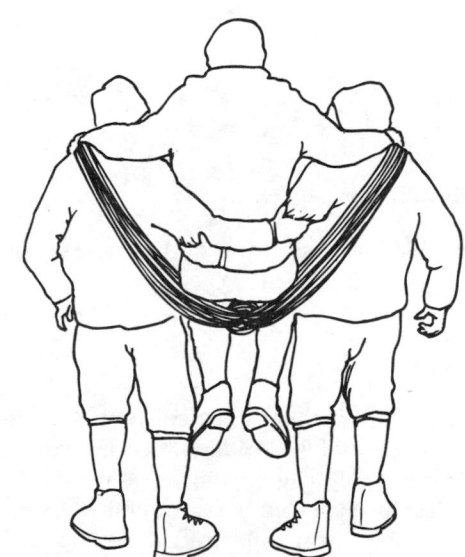

Fig. 138

Two-person split rope carry.

Poly Bag Stretcher

Any sheeted material will suffice such as a large plastic survival bag, a tent or flysheet or similar. 6 or 8 soft compact items (gloves, spare socks, hats etc) are required to act as handles or to provide attachment points for carrying straps or slings. These items are placed in position under the sheet and each one secured with a clove hitch. The bed of the stretcher should be padded with spare clothing.

This stretcher has the great merit of simplicity. It is a bit fragile so care is needed on rough ground. Although it is uncomfortable in wet weather it is undoubtedly the best of the improvised stretchers. It is particularly effective for sliding on snow if conditions and the state of the casualty permit.

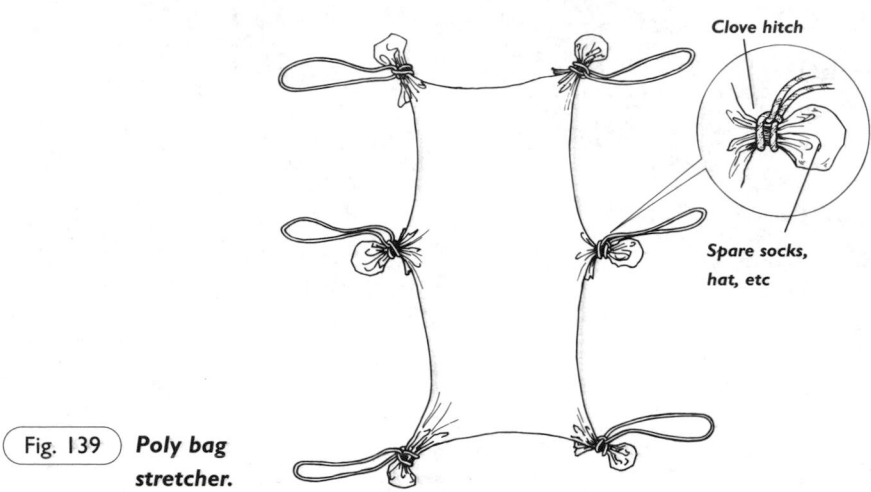

Clove hitch

Spare socks, hat, etc

(Fig. 139) **Poly bag stretcher.**

The Thompson Knot

This provides a reliable and easy to tie body harness which can be used for lowering a casualty (Fig 62, page 163).

ROPE STRETCHERS

It takes a lot of patience, time and practice to make a useful rope stretcher. Unless they are well made and well padded they are worse than useless. Their one saving grace over a poly bag stretcher is their durability. The original Piggott stretcher has been extensively modified and the two methods illustrated are considerably easier to tie and adjust.

Roscoe Rope Stretcher

1   *Find centre of the rope.*
2   *Leave enough rope for a carrying loop (to go over head and shoulder of carrier).*
3   *Make a loop with one of the ends using an overhand knot.*
4   *Make a slip knot in the rope on the opposite side.*
5   *Thread the loop through the slip knot, then pull the slip knot inside out, to form a sheet bend. (The end of the loop should be long enough to tie a half-hitch, once the stretcher is finished, and be used as a small handle.)*

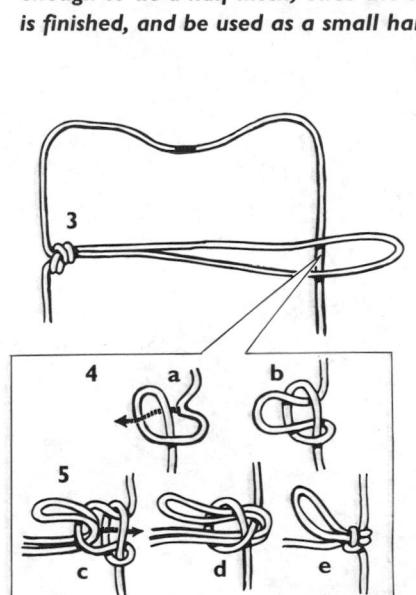

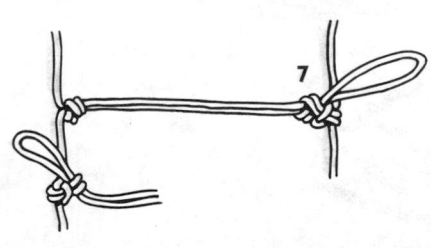

6   *Repeat this, taking loops from alternate sides, until the stretcher is the required length. The knots should be about 4" apart at weight bearing parts of the stretcher (where shoulders, head and hips will be); if short of rope they can be further apart on legs.*
7   *Adjust width of stretcher to fit patient. Tie off ends of loops with half-hitches. (These can then be used as small handles.)*
8   *Tie ends of rope to form a carrying loop at foot of stretcher. Pad stretcher before loading patient.*

(Fig. 140)   **The Roscoe rope stretcher.**

Clove Hitch Stretcher

From the centre of the rope lay out eight loops on either side to form the bed of the stretcher. The arrangement of the loops should approximate to the size of the casualty. The rope on each side is then used to tie a clove hitch at the end of the each loop, leaving a small end of the loop protruding. When all the clove hitches have been tied the remaining rope is threaded through these small loops, round the perimeter of the stretcher until it is all used up. The threaded rope can now be pulled up tight against the clove hitches and the two ends of the rope tied off.

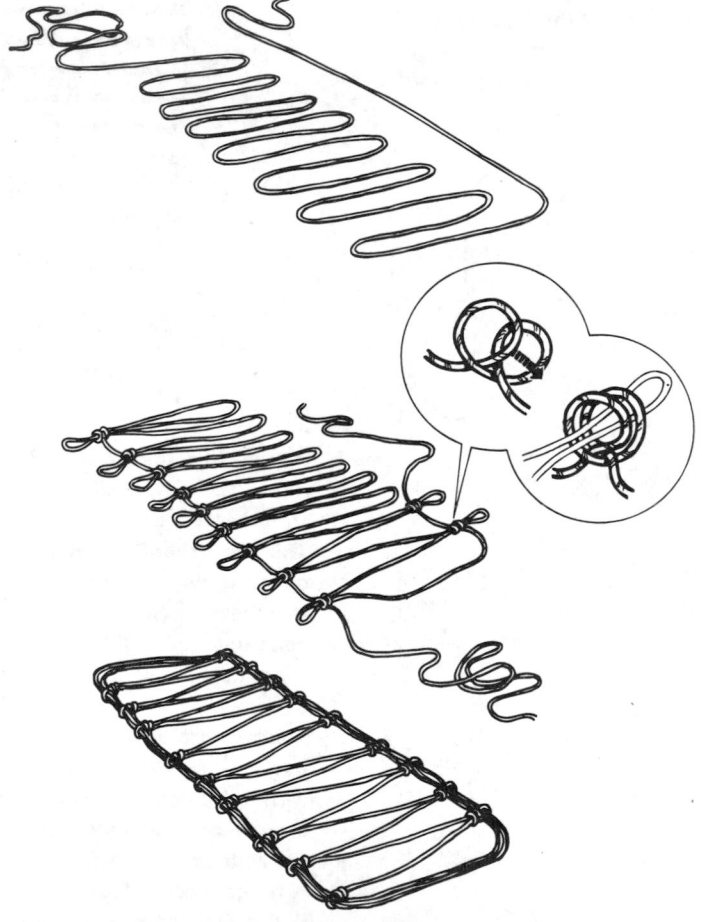

Fig. 141) *The Clove Hitch Stretcher.*

Both types of rope stretcher need to be well padded with any suitable material which is to hand: clothing, camping mats, rucksacks. But no matter how well padded the casualty is certain to have a rough ride. For this reason no one with a suspected serious spinal injury should be transported by these methods.

BIVOUAC TECHNIQUES

There is a world of difference between a planned bivouac and an unplanned one. If you deliberately set off with the intention of spending the night out you can, to a large extent, choose when you will bivouac and also ensure that you have with you the means to spend a reasonably comfortable night: a down jacket or a sleeping bag, a piece of mat for insulation, a change of underclothes, some food, a stove to make a hot brew and a bivy-sac or polythene bag to provide protection from the wind and rain. In an emergency situation you may have none of these things and you will have to make do with what you normally carry on a hill walk.

To what extent, then, should you 'be prepared' to deal with and survive an unexpected night out? There is more than a grain of truth in the observation that if you burden yourself with all the gear required for a comfortable 'emergency' bivouac you will almost certainly ensure that you have one. What is carried in the way of emergency gear is very much a matter of judgement, taking into account the nature of the expedition, the composition of the party and the likelihood of being caught out. The obligation on the leader of a party of inexperienced people to adopt a fail-safe approach is clearly much greater than on a similar party of independent experienced hillwalkers. The possibility of an emergency must be considered seriously and some provision made in the equipment to be carried among the party. Individual protection from the wind and rain is the primary requirement and this can be achieved by each person carrying an 8' x 4' polythene survival bag. Some condensation is inevitable, but for a single night it is surely a tolerable alternative to exposure. A group bivy-sac, large enough to accommodate six to eight people, is a very satisfactory alternative allowing all to benefit from sharing body warmth as well as the companionship of being under one roof. The amount of spare clothing to be carried will depend on the season and circumstances but an extra sweater and a spare pair of socks (which can double-up as spare mitts or even a hat) should normally be carried in reserve. An emergency ration, over and above the day's supply, is a sensible addition, as much for its psychological as for its nutritional value.

'Howffing' may be defined as the art of making oneself comfortable with the natural material to be found in the wild. To some it is an end in itself to others a means to an end, but there is no doubt that necessity is the mother of invention and inventiveness is the foremost attribute of the howffer. A range of survival skills come into play, but the most important of all is likely to be maintaining the morale of the party, especially in an emergency situation where the shortage of time is likely to preclude all but the most rudimentary preparations. In winter conditions an emergency bivouac is a much more serious proposition where the risk of frostbite and exposure is very real. A bivouac under these circumstances should not be contemplated unless there is no other possible alternative.

Mountain Rescue Teams

There are about 100 mountain rescue teams established in the British Isles. The work of the teams is co-ordinated by the Mountain Rescue Council through its various regional associations and by the Mountain Rescue Committee of Scotland and the Northern Ireland Mountain Rescue Co-ordinating Committee. These committees work closely with the Police and with the RAF mountain rescue teams and rescue co-ordinating centres. Detailed lists of teams and posts are contained in the Mountain and Cave Rescue handbook published by the Mountain Rescue Council each year. You should be familiar with the general contents of this and be aware of the teams and the location of rescue posts in the area.

Mountain Rescue Posts and Equipment

The first mountain rescue posts were established in Britain over 50 years ago to serve as locations where mountaineers in distress could obtain the minimum of equipment necessary to administer first aid and evacuate a casualty. Today, rescue posts in England and Wales have been disbanded. Their functions have been largely superseded by effective rescue teams. However, in other areas of the country, particularly in parts of Scotland and Ireland where there are fewer rescue teams, or where the centres of mountaineering are more scattered, rescue posts are still regarded as an essential part of the service.

Mountain leaders should be familiar with the locations of rescue posts and their equipment. In all cases local knowledge should be obtained where possible, as ordnance survey maps, and even the Mountain and Cave Rescue Handbooks, are soon out of date. Posts are moved, closed and even at times vandalised, so that to rely too much on their being available could be a costly mistake.

Table 14	*Authorised List of Equipment.*

1 or more stretchers (with head shield for selected posts).

2 rucksacks, including one medical rucksack.

1 casualty bag and one large polythene bag, 2m long.

1 Thomas splint or equivalent

6 triangular bandages. 12 x 15cm Dommette bandages.

2.5cm zinc oxide strapping

7.5cm elastic adhesive bandage

2 straight aluminium arm splints or Kramer wire splints.

1 inflatable leg splint, 1 inflatable arm splint. (For selected posts)

1 Airway Brooks, Hewit's or modification (Ambu respiratory apparatus for very busy posts only).

1 protective helmet (for selected posts)

1 container of antiseptic powder or liquid

6 factory dressings or equivalent

1 packet gauze.

1 ¼lb cotton wool.

1 pair surgical stainless steel dressing scissors.

2 dozen safety pins.

1 electric hand lamp (for selected posts).

3 cups, including 1 feeding cup.

2 Thermos flasks.

1 pair stainless steel dressing forceps.

1 packet disposable gloves.

1 packet Jaycloths.

For Selected Posts

Sphygmomanometer (Anaeroid blood pressure apparatus)

Vitalograph suction apparatus (with Yankaver disposable suction end)

Plastic water bottle

1 Non-stretch rope

The decision whether or not to use Post equipment will depend on the circumstances of the accident and your assessment of the groups capability to carry out a successful rescue operation without calling on the resources of the local mountain rescue organisation. Do not make the mistake of underestimating the difficulty and sheer physical endeavour required to evacuate a casualty over rough terrain. It is almost certain that help will be needed, although much can be done while this help is on its way. If Post equipment is used it is vital that the Post Supervisor is informed immediately afterwards so that arrangements can be made for its return or replacement.

RADIO COMMUNICATIONS

All teams are now equipped with portable transceivers. Most of these are on the Mountain Rescue frequency, but call signs should be checked before departure and procedure established, including time on and off the air. Good communications can be a tremendous asset in any search and rescue operation, but their maintenance should not so dominate the conduct of affairs that other vital considerations, such as speed and efficiency of search, are neglected.

It is important to be aware of the limitations of radio communications in the mountains. Broadly speaking VHF transmission is only possible between stations within line of sight of each other and therefore communication across intervening ridges and hills is not practicable. It is possible, of course, to position an operator on the intervening feature and relay messages from one side to the other. In some areas a 'relay' station has been permanently sited on top of some strategic high point which automatically relays transmissions over a wide area.

A mobile phone is basically a radio transceiver linked into the telephone system. There are areas of the country where they can not be used and, like radios, they suffer from 'dead zones' where communications is limited or impossible. Nevertheless, they are increasingly being used by organised parties and on occasion have resulted in the early arrival of the rescue team.

STRETCHERS

There are four types of stretcher in common use: the Thomas, the MacInnes, the Bell and the Ogwen. Assembly of these is normally self explanatory but if the opportunity to practice with one presents itself you should make use of it. The main features of each type are described briefly.

Split Thomas

This stretcher splits in two sections for easy carrying. The carrying straps serve as rucksack-type straps. The stretcher bed is made from either plastic coated wire mesh or canvas duck. The shafts are telescopic and the complete stretcher

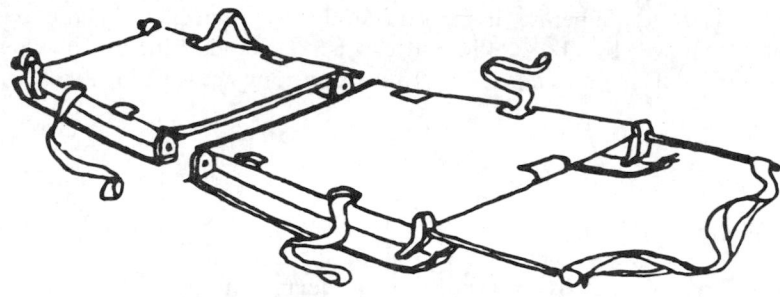

Fig. 142) **Split Thomas stretcher.**

weighs over 18kg (40lbs). The two sections are locked together with a bolt. A mesh head guard is also available. This stretcher may be fitted with a Thomas splint which enables a fractured leg to be immobilised under traction. If you are unfamiliar with this technique use some other method, such as an inflatable splint, Kramer wire splint, wooden slats etc. to immobilise the limb.

MacInnes

The Split model is based on the design of the folding model, but with the two sections being held together with stainless steel pins and locking plates. The alloy patient bed is covered with closed cell foam. There are four side-bearer straps, a patient stirrup and a long patient wrap-round security tape. The shafts are telescopic and lock into position. The transport which is secured by four hook bolts and is fitted into a heel brake. The complete stretcher weighs 22kg (48lb).

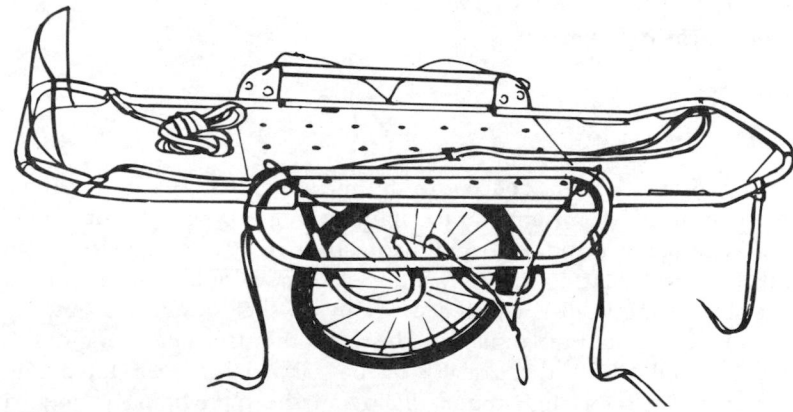

Fig. 143) **The MacInnes Superlight.**

The MacInnes Superlite has been developed especially for use with helicopters. It weighs 11kg (24lb) and can take a standard transport wheel. The two ends of the stretcher fold in to make a compact load for carrying.

Bell

The Bell Split Rescue Stretcher is supplied in two halves, each with its own carrying pack frame. Assembled and with the hinged handles inboard it measures 2m x 60cm. It is constructed from square section stainless steel tube and weighs approximately 20kg when ready for use. Plastic ski runners and a headguard can be fitted as and when required. The patient bed is of reinforced steel mesh strengthened by cross wires.

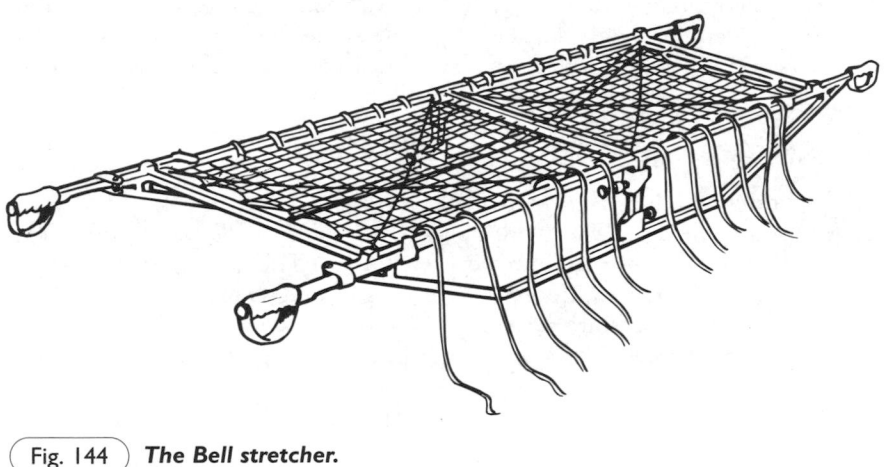

(Fig. 144)   *The Bell stretcher.*

Ogwen

This is a radically different concept to the previous stretchers in that the bed is a stretcher in it's own right and the frame only need be used for extended carries. The bed is made of a rigid nylon sheet covered by a nylon envelop with handles and securing straps sewn on. The casualty lies on the sheet and when the securing straps are fastened the nylon sheet assumes a gutter like shape and folds around the casualty. This gives the stretcher a longitudinally rigid shape and allows the casualty to be carried, or even lifted into a helicopter. The frame fits around the nylon sheet providing runners and carrying handles when necessary.

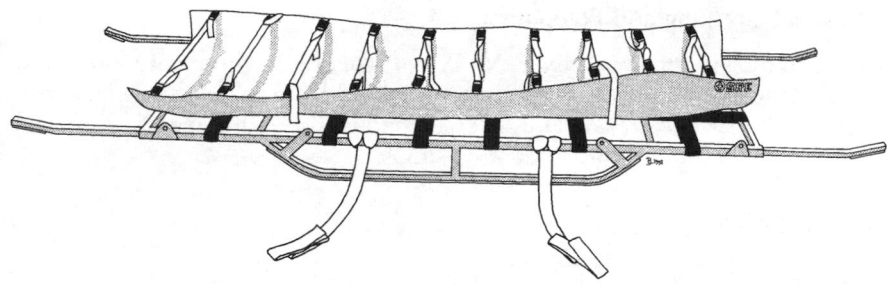

(Fig. 145) *The Ogwen stretcher.*

Securing Casualty to the Stretcher

Different types of stretchers have different means of securing the casualty, but the essential elements are:

The casualty should be warm and comfortable. The use of a casualty bag makes the whole process very much easier.

The casualty should be securely attached to the stretcher by adjustable straps which can be positioned to avoid pressure on injuries.

There should be support such as a foot stirrup or chest harness. A decision will usually have to be taken on the use of this before the casualty is placed in the casualty bag.

The casualty should be provided with head protection if necessary. Most stretchers have some sort of head guard.

OTHER ITEMS OF EQUIPMENT

Casualty Bag

Most posts and teams are equipped with specially designed casualty bags incorporating sleeping bag, mattress and carrying handles. Their main advantages are that they allow minimal handling while getting the patient into the bag, they provide a convenient method of transport to and from the stretcher and they offer excellent insulation from the ground or on the stretcher itself. A sleeping bag with an all-round zip should be carried by teams not equipped with a casualty bag, although it will be appreciated that it can be exceedingly difficult to get a severely injured person into a bag which does not have a full length side zip.

Personal Clothing and Equipment

Refer to the kit list, Appendix E, but be particularly careful to ensure that you have adequate lighting. A pocket torch or head lamp may last less than one hour so take spare batteries. Long life cells should be used, three of which will usually last a winters night when used singly.

Lightweight Tent

This is not part of the official post equipment but it could prove a life saver especially if the casualty is suffering from exposure. On wide scale searches in bad conditions a tent with each search party is a must. Some teams have a complete bivouac unit which will accommodate the whole party including the casualty.

Search Lamps

At night each team should carry at least one search lamp capable of providing wide and narrow beam illumination continuously for at least four hours. It must be backed up by first class personal lighting and, if available, by illuminating flares. Some teams may have a portable generator on a packframe powering a 12 volt spotlight.

Signalling Devices

Rockets, maroon, miniflares and so on may be of use in favourable conditions. The agreed code is as follows: Red – help wanted here; Green – recall to base; White – message understood. Do not rely on a single flare. Release several at intervals till acknowledged. A thunderflash or other loud noise will help to attract attention before releasing flares. These should only be used by people authorised and trained to use them. They should never be left in the rescue sack but stored in a 'fire store'.

Food and Drink

Adequate supplies of food and hot soup or other liquids should be carried to meet the needs of both rescuers and rescued. If the search is likely to be a long one then a stove, fuel, billies and the necessary material (tea, sugar, etc) may be the preferred option.

Specialised Equipment

Depending on the circumstances of the accident certain items of more specialised equipment may be required such as climbing ropes, crash helmets, pitons, slings, karabiners and so on. In any event at least two ropes should be carried by each team since these may be required to deal with a host of unforeseen problems.

ORGANISATION OF SEARCH

It is not expected that mountain leaders should be concerned with the organisation of a major search. This is a very specialised area of rescue work and should be left to the best qualified rescue team in the area. Many areas will have search organisations made up of experienced personnel from a number of teams and associated bodies.

It is probable that the mountain leader will have contact with a major search in one of two situations. Either that of being the leader of the party which has lost one or more of its members, or as a responsible mountaineer offering his or her services to the rescue organisation. Whichever is the case there are several principles which need to be borne in mind.

The speed of success of a search decreases as the subject has time to move away from the point last seen. Therefore the urgency with which action needs to be taken cannot be overemphasised.

The concept of the 'point last seen' (PLS) is vital to the conduct of search. It is not a static position and may well change as more information becomes available. The search area is an expanding area centred on the PLS. As time increases then the area to be searched becomes larger and the ability of the lost individuals to attract attention to themselves and their plight diminishes. Speed, therefore is essential provided it can be achieved without loss of efficiency.

Thus, in addition to calling out the rescue services, an initial search should be carried out by the first individuals to hear of the lost party. What kind of search and where to search depends on the resources available and the area to be covered but it should be borne in mind that close contact line searching is a technique which is expensive in terms of both manpower and time and is almost certainly inappropriate to an initial search. Some sort of quick corridor search along the probable lines of travel by small, highly mobile parties is generally more effective.

The other factor to bear in mind, if you are involved in a search before the rescue services swing into action is the concept of confinement. It has already been stated that the size of the search area is dependent on time and if this area can be confined then the chances and speed of success are increased. It makes sense, therefore, to patrol roads and tracks and to station parties at cols and the heads of valleys in order to contain the area to be searched. Obtaining the assistance of hostel and hotel staff, the police and any other parties in the area may also be of great value. The leader of a party which has got into difficulties is certain to be influenced by thoughts of undesirable publicity and perhaps criticism which may be directed against them at a later stage. Try to put all such thoughts out of your mind. Your first responsibility is to those who are lost. Actions or decisions based on avoiding publicity are only likely to make matters worse.

SEARCH METHODS

It may seem at first that the obvious way to search for a lost party is to get all available people to stand in a line and to walk through the area to be searched until you find them. In practice this is not likely to achieve success, for a number of reasons:

It is a very slow method, and as we have already seen the search area is likely to be an expanding one.

It requires a large number of people, not a resource likely to be available until the victim has been lost for some time.

It ignores other more effective search methods such as dogs and aircraft.

It can only ever cover a small area and there is no guarantee that the lost party is in that area.

Having said that line searching is ineffective at the initial stage of the search, what should the mountain leader do?

1. Apply the principles of confinement wherever possible.

2. Use whatever limited resources are available to search the most likely corridors of travel. This only needs very small parties.

3. Make a record of where the lost party was last seen, any clues found, areas searched and action taken. This will be of great help to the search manager later.

4. Write down any information available on the lost party: names, clothing, equipment, ages, experience etc as all of this will be required if the search becomes a full scale operation.

5. Inform the relevant authorities, usually the police, even though you may not want them to take action at this stage.

As a search progress then the party leader will have less and less control of the process. Well thought out action at an early stage will pay dividends later.

Search and Rescue Dog Association

S.A.R.D.A. was founded by Hamish MacInnes in 1965 when the first training course was held in Glencoe. Now the Association has handlers and dogs in all the main mountain areas in the British Isles whose services can be called upon to assist in the search for missing persons and to locate people buried in avalanches in winter.

The dogs and their handlers attend a selection course and if successful, a follow-up course at which 'novice dogs' are selected. The dogs are reassessed after a year, qualifying as 'Search dogs'. Search dogs are retested every 3 years.

The requirements in Britain are quite different from those in Alpine countries in that large tracts of mountain country may have to be searched both in summer and winter conditions. Dogs may have to operate at some considerable distance from their handlers in order to cover as large an area as possible. In the Alps dogs are primarily used at close quarters to search avalanche debris for buried victims.

To make the best use of a trained dog it should be allowed to search the most likely areas before large parties of searchers move in. If a dog is not immediately available the search must be pursued using whatever resources are available. Wherever possible dogs should be allowed to work into the wind where any scent will be carried towards them. They rely very little on sight and indeed one of their great advantages is that they will operate equally well at night, when other search work is greatly curtailed. As a very approximate guide a trained dog is capable of doing the work of twenty searchers and in some conditions, such as after a fall of new snow, considerably more. Nevertheless it should be borne in mind that dogs can not work miracles, but when used properly and in good time they can be an invaluable asset in a search operation.

Helicopters

Helicopters are frequently used in rescue operations and have been instrumental in saving many lives. However, it is important that their use is seen as being complimentary to the mountain rescue teams, not a substitute for them. There are many situations where the deployment of a helicopter is difficult or impossible, such as in dense cloud, darkness or in very severe weather conditions. Under these circumstances the ground team is the only reliable source of help. When lives are at stake, sympathetic consideration is always given by the Service authorities to a request for a helicopter, although it should be appreciated that Service requirements must have first priority. Any such request should be made through the police who will contact the Rescue Co-ordination Centre.

Signalling from Ground to Air

If you have to communicate with a helicopter or other aircraft from the ground there is an internationally recognised code of signals, making use of whatever materials are to hand, to convey simple messages.

GROUND-AIR VISUAL CODE FOR USE IN EMERGENCY BY SURVIVORS:

| REQUIRE ASSISTANCE | REQUIRE MEDICAL ASSISTANCE | PROCEEDING IN THIS DIRECTION | YES OR AFFIRMATIVE | NO OR NEGATIVE |

IF IN DOUBT, USE INTERNATIONAL SYMBOL **SOS**

GROUND-AIR VISUAL CODE FOR USE IN EMERGENCY BY SEARCH PARTIES:

OPERATION COMPLETED   WE HAVE FOUND ALL PERSONNEL

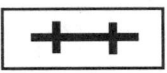  

WE HAVE FOUND ONLY SOME PERSONNEL   WE ARE NOT ABLE TO CONTINUE. RETURNING TO BASE   NOTHING FOUND. WILL CONTINUE TO SEARCH

HAVE DIVIDED INTO TWO GROUPS EACH PROCEEDING IN THE DIRECTION INDICATED   INFORMATION RECEIVED THAT AIRCRAFT IS IN THIS DIRECTION

Notes: *1. Symbols should be at least 2.5 metres long (8 feet) and should be as conspicuous as possible.*
2. Symbols may be formed by any means such as: strips of fabric, parachute materials, pieces of wood, stones or such like material, marking the surface by trampling, staining with oil etc.
3. Attention to these signals should be attracted by other means such as radio, flares, smoke, reflected light etc.

AIR-GROUND SIGNALS

1. The following signals by aircraft mean that the ground signals have been understood:
    a. During hours of daylight – by rocking the aircraft's wings.
    b. During hours of darkness – by flashing the aircraft's landing lights ON and OFF twice or, if not so equipped, by switching the navigation lights ON and OFF twice.
    Lack of the above signals indicate that the ground signal has not been understood.

(Fig. 146)   *International Ground/Air Visual Signals. (ICAO ANNEX 12)*

Normally the pilot will select a safe area to land. The clothing of the ground party should be sufficient to attract attention, but if a marker of any kind is used it should be firmly pegged or weighted down in the centre of the landing area. Clear away any loose debris and stamp down dry snow. The aircraft will approach into the wind, so assemble your party well clear and to windward of the landing area.

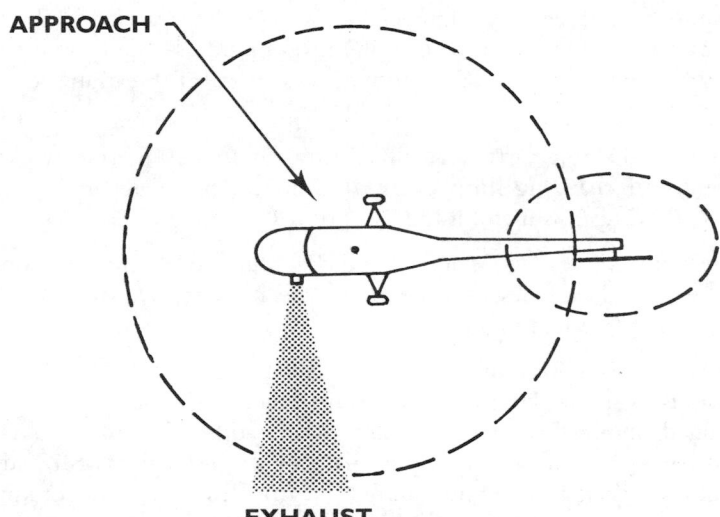

APPROACH

EXHAUST

(Fig. 147) *Approaching a helicopter.*

Safety Precautions

Do not approach the helicopter until you are signalled to do so by the pilot. When you do, proceed with caution in the direction indicated, usually from the front and on the pilot's right hand side, so that you remain in sight at all times. Do exactly as you are told by the crew.

Evacuation of the Victim

With the main party, proceed to the scene of the accident at a steady pace. Do not rush, as the time is being put to good use by the advance party in making the patient comfortable and rendering the necessary first aid. Remember that there may be a long carry back and energy must be conserved. If there is the prospect of a very long carry make arrangements for a support party to bring food and drink.

On the way in examine the ground for the best evacuation route and mark it if necessary.

The arrangement of the victim on the stretcher will depend on the nature of their injuries and the type of stretcher in use. Freedom from pain on the move should be the aim. Remember that a helmet may be necessary if steep ground or screes have to be crossed. Be particularly careful in the case of suspected spinal injuries to avoid any movement of the spine itself. A rigid stretcher is absolutely essential for the safe evacuation of such cases.

Unconscious, or seriously injured casualties are best carried in the three-quarter prone position with the head tilted to one side. Someone must always be in attendance in case of vomiting, cessation of breathing or other emergency.

A stretcher-bearing party normally consists of 16 - 20 persons working in two teams and changing shifts every 10 minutes or so depending on the terrain. A third team is useful if the carry is to be a long one.

If the route is not obvious and has not been previously marked, someone should be sent ahead to select and mark the best line. This is, of course, particularly important at night.

It is the responsibility of the Police to give information to the Press. If asked, the facts should be given, but on no account should any information be divulged about the victims, their names, addresses and so on. Even apparently harmless information about place of work, relatives or friends may be used by the media to identify injured persons before the next of kin have been informed. These details will be given at the proper time by the Police.

Report to the Rescue Controller on return to base.

The Mountain Rescue Council and the Mountain Rescue Committee of Scotland keep a record of all accidents in the hills. It is important that a full report on every incident is submitted to them.

ACCIDENT REPORT FORM

There are two types of accident report. The first is the written message from the leader of the party to alert the rescue services. The second is the formal report submitted to the mountain rescue organisation after the rescue operation has been completed. The detailed form of this varies from district to district.

The comprehensive report form shown opposite is intended only as a guide to the sort of information which the rescue services may find useful. Some of it is essential, such as the location of the incident and some of it less so. What is included will depend very much on the circumstances and the time available.

Table 15 **Accident Report Form.**

ACCIDENT REPORT	Date		Time	AM	PM
LOCATION	Nat Grid Ref:				
	Exact Location (include marked map):				
	Terrain: Snow Heather	Moor Easy	Forest Moderate	Rock Steep	Path Other
COMPLETE DESCRIPTION OF ACCIDENT			Ascending Roped Rock Fall Avalanche Equipment Failure	Descending Unroped Illness Cold	
	Witnesses:		Other:		
INJURED PERSON	Name:		Age:		
	Address:		Male	Female	
	Phone:				
	Whom to notify:		Relationship:	Phone:	
INJURIES	Overall Condition:	Good Unconscious If yes, length of time:	Fair	Serious Yes	Fatal No
	Injury 1	Location on Body: Nature of Injury:			
	Injury 2	Location on Body: Nature of Injury:			
	Other Injuries	Location on Body: Nature of Injury:			
	General:	Bleeding Stopped Artificial Respiration Treated for Shock	Shelter Built Warm Fluids Given Evacuation		

Table 15   *Accident Report Form — continued.*

FIRST AID TREATMENT	Injury 1
	Injury 2
	Other Injuries:
ON-THE-SCENE PLANS	Will stay put Will evacuate to road Will evacuate a short distance to shelter Will send some members out Others:
PERSONNEL	Numbers: Inexperienced Intermediate Experienced Advanced Capability for a bivouac: Yes No
	Attach the pre-trip prepared LIST OF PARTY MEMBERS including names, addresses and phone numbers to the ACCIDENT FORM BEING TAKEN OUT.
EQUIPMENT AVAILABLE	Tents Sleeping Bags Flares Ice Axes Hardware Stove and Fuel Ropes Other:
WEATHER	Warm Moderate Freezing Snow Wind Sun Mist Rain Other:
TYPE OF EVACUATION RECOMMENDED	Lowering Operation Carry-out Helicopter Rigid Stretcher None until specialised medical assistance Specify:
PARTY LEADER	Name:
MESSENGERS SENT FOR HELP	Names:
FURTHER INFORMATION IF ANY	

13

Party Leadership

One of the unavoidable illusions created by any handbook of this type, is the impression of a mass of material all in watertight compartments, any one of which a leader may be required to recall from time to time. What such handbooks cannot easily convey, is the need for all these items of skill and knowledge to have been so well absorbed that they no longer exist in isolated compartments. It is necessary for them to have meshed with all the others in an integrated manner similar to the way in which tapestry threads interweave to form a pattern or picture. This mingling of threads underlines the fact that each of them has a relationship with all the others. The nature of these interdependent relationships must be understood by the leader so that when situations are faced requiring leadership skills, the interaction of all the factors will have occurred almost intuitively and spontaneously to the point where the key factors influencing the situation are identified. Identifying the key factors in a situation is a crucial leadership skill for it is these factors which influence judgements and subsequent decisions. The ability to scan them analytically and quickly select the appropriate skills from the armoury to deal with a situation should be an important aim for all aspirant leaders.

This handbook cannot tell you how to 'get it all together' so that all that has been learned can be applied in the right sequence; pitched at the right level; delivered at the right moment in the manner most appropriate for a group in the course of a day in the hills. Depending on one's experience and point of view it is either a very simple or a very complex business.

The notes in this section attempt to give some impression of the nature of the task when the job of leading is actually being carried out.

AIMS AND VALUES

In the hills with a group of people, the party leader has one big paradox to resolve - the management of risk! The right balance has to be found between what seems dangerous and therefore exciting, and what is safe and perhaps dull. This is, admittedly, oversimplifying the situation but the problem lies at the heart of the most fundamental questions: "Why are you doing it?" "What is it all for?" "What are you hoping to achieve?" "For what overall purpose is the group really being taken out into the mountains?" The answer to these questions requires an answer to the hardest of questions, "What am I all about?"

In leaders who have not really attempted to sort out and find an answer to these mysteries for themselves, there will be something lacking in the way they approach both their group and the mountains. It should be emphasised that awareness of these conflicting values will shape all subsequent behaviour and actions in the leading situation. No one else can give the answers either. Discussing and exchanging opinions about them will help, but the final amalgam of ideas must necessarily be of the leader's own making.

The leader has an ever present practical problem – to maintain the right balance between apparent danger and safety. This requires finding the balance between, on the one hand, excitement, pleasure, interest, spontaneity, enjoyment and freedom; and on the other hand, excessive discipline, regimentation, monotony and the sterile rigidity that comes from over-planning and over-preparation. The leader should always try to be aware if the balance is being tipped in one direction or another – either through over confident arrogance, optimistic inexperience or anxious lack of self confidence.

A leader has to know when it is permissible to prevent the considerations of safety from intruding too strongly on the party to the point that they detract from the experiences intended for the party. A leader needs to control the safety factors so that they are a discrete background framework of good practice working to ensure feelings of excitement, interest, curiosity, exploration, adventure, achievement and a general enjoyment of the hills.

The mountain leader scheme does not set out to teach the aspirant how to become infallible. It cannot give a set of rules and procedures that will provide the right answer for every situation. It can only offer a set of techniques during training and show how they might be used in specific instances. How they might be used in other circumstances can only be learned through experience. Developing a comprehensive awareness of the total mountain context within which a group is placed provides a way forward towards finding answers to these questions.

Experience helps here so that the leader is able to weigh up all the various factors and come up with the right answer, for a particular party, in a specific situation.

It should be obvious that the quality of a leader's own personal experience is going to be a crucial factor. Considerable demands may be made on powers of judgement and decision-making at times. To be effective, it is necessary to be able to call upon a sound foundation of solid personal experience.

PERSONAL EXPERIENCE

There is no substitute for actual personal experience and there are no short cuts to the gaining of it.

If going into the hills is done merely to gain sufficient experience to scrape through an assessment course rather than because of the inherent attractions of hills, then it is necessary to think very deeply about whether or not to continue with it. The chances of becoming an effective party leader are greatly reduced unless a considerable amount of time is spent on acquiring experience. It will be adequate when an extensive background of personal experience will enable accurate assessments to be made of most situations and therefore the sound decisions regarding action to be taken. These assessments and decisions must then be tempered by knowledge of what the group can take or is capable of doing. If it is a new group about which knowledge is scanty and less certain, safety margins must be greater.

Amongst other things this means that:

Leaders must be able to distinguish between real and apparent danger.

Leaders need to know what their strengths and weaknesses are on the mountain so that they can recognise and avoid situations where they will be more concerned for self than the party. Risks taken with the party in such situations may also be unjustifiable.

Leaders need sufficient depth of experience to enable them to recognise those exceptional situations when the text book answer should be disregarded because it is unsuitable to a particular set of circumstances. It then becomes a question of using past experience to help judge what needs doing, what should be guarded against and applying intelligence as to the best way of doing it with the means available. Mountaineers have a rather vague term for this. They call it having "mountain sense". There are times when it is intuitive and almost subconscious in nature and other times when it is strongly conscious and insistent. It probably has its roots in past experience.

LEADERSHIP STYLES

'Leadership' is a complex topic of many widely differing interpretations. The resultant confusion tends to hinder a proper understanding of the subject which is only briefly dealt with here in a very basic, simple manner. Some leadership styles are easily identifiable.

- There is leadership by example – a force pulling the group along from the front. Unless care is taken the tail end may suffer. If leaders are highly skilled and competent they may be so far removed from the level of skill in the party that they are unaware of, or unsympathetic to, any difficulties the party may be experiencing. Being at the front, they will tend to take all the decisions all the time. The group will hardly be involved in the experience and will tend to be tagging along blindly. They will have no real idea of what is happening, or why, where and how.

- There is leadership from the rear of the party – a force pushing the group from the back. The concern here may be to allow those at the front to feel they are involved and exercising some initiative in the shape of the day. There is also present a humane concern to encourage the weaker ones who tend to be in the rear. The danger here is the leader's loss of control at the front unless some thought has been given to the problem. First hand knowledge of the ground is necessary so that the need to return to the front to cope with any tricky sections of the route can be anticipated. Knowledge of the party needs to be good enough to be able to rely on them not moving beyond the contact range of eye, ear or voice, as necessary to the situation. Recognisable points can be set at which the front should halt to allow the rear to catch up. A more experienced party may be content to go at the pace of the slowest but techniques need devising to cope with the impulsiveness of novice groups. The skill is to maintain enthusiasm and enjoyment without losing control. To regard the leader's role as one of maintaining control without killing enthusiasm is a negative way of approaching the situation.

- There is leadership from the middle of the group. This style tends to work democratically, helping, but not generally dictating to, the group to resolve their different impulses and inclinations, to decide for themselves, to adapt and carry through their plans. The group is helped to lead itself as far as it is judged capable of doing so. The leader is watchful to give support, encouragement, sympathy, guidance or advice to those individuals who need help. Modern ideas about leadership advocate a flexible combination of all of the styles mentioned above. The leader will only be authoritarian or military in style at those times when the occasion or situation demand it. This style will be used sparingly, perhaps only in emergencies or when physical safety is threatened by ignorance or fool-hardiness in the group. The leader can be at the front, centre or back according to the indications picked up from the physical environment and the group. The leader should be tuned into signs of discomfort, stress or anxiety and alive to possibilities that will arouse interest in, enthusiasm and reverence for, the mountain environment. The leader is at once consultant, counsellor, guide, mentor, chaperone and a source of information, knowledge, skill and experience. The leader is not so much a leader in the traditional sense, but more a person whose experience and resources are at the service of the group.

LEADERSHIP AWARENESS

Leading a formal party in the hills is a very different 'game' from the 'walking informally with friends' situation. With friends of equal ability, responsibility and decision-making is shared in a casual almost carefree way. Each is tacitly understood to be self responsible (and for adults this is the legal interpretation too), each having the skill and experience to know and observe personal limits. If one of the party has a problem it is assumed that it will be brought to the notice of the others.

Once the business of leading a formal party is embarked upon, a different world is entered of hill-walking with a new, extra, second dimension containing an additional set of factors to become aware of and to take into account. These factors are mostly to do with managing people and maintaining good working relationships.

- Although there is a group the leader will be virtually walking 'solo' in the sense that there may be no other person with whom in extremity, the responsibility of decision-making and navigating can be shared - unless of course the leader is fortunate enough to have a second adult along as a designated assistant. The group may be encouraged to participate in these activities, but still the onus will be on the leader to check they are correct or acceptable. The leader is the one held accountable.

- The whole group is dependent on the leader to the extent that, in the final analysis, their enjoyment, comfort and safety is the leader's responsibility.

The leader:

- may have to do all the thinking for each and everyone of them - especially if they are novices.

- may not assume that what the leader can do, the group can also do.

- may not even assume that personal ambitions will coincide with their desires and aspirations. This is one aspect served well by the democratic style of leadership which keeps channels of communication open and gives vital feedback on how the group reads the situation.

- may not assume that because the leader feels comfortable, relaxed, confident, at any given moment, it is how they feel. For all that can be known, they are quite likely to be, too hot, too cold, thirsty, hungry, out of breath, miserable, over-awed, anxious, tense, bored, fed-up or plain tired. Watch for 'signs and signals'. Be aware of the group. Safety should be more a matter of good practice used discreetly so as to detract minimally from enjoyment.

LEADERSHIP ATTITUDES AND APPROACHES

To deal successfully with the factors outlined in previous section, an attitude and approach must develop that is rather different from the hill-walker who climbs for personal satisfaction and pleasure. Refer again to the first section about aims and values.

- Leaders need to have examined their personal reasons and motives for wanting to take groups into the hills and to have clarified for themselves why they are wanting to do it at all, and to what ends. There needs to be a clear realisation that the responsibilities of leadership impose a discipline that allows very little room for personal wishes, ambitions or aspirations. Leadership in this context is a state of mind that is largely selfless.

- Leadership used for selfish ends is empty, non-creative and sterile. Leadership used to inflate the ego, such as needing to demonstrate expertise and 'superior' powers to the group, is a destructive exercise without value to the group. The group should be approached with humility rather than arrogance. Leaders should not assume they will always know what is best for the group or think they understand their needs so well that there is not need ever to consult them or ask for opinions. Leaders could not otherwise ever hope to pitch things at the group's level of expectation, motivation, interest and capability.

- A leader's interest in mountains should not over-shadow interest in the group. If getting into the hills means more than leading a group, a leader should think twice before taking it on. If personal satisfaction is derived primarily from personal reasons such as so many miles covered or peaks ascended, a leader is going to be a disappointed, frustrated person who is unsympathetic to the group and a bad leader. Very rarely will the motives, ambitions, interest and capabilities of the group coincide with those of the leader.

- The leader's concept of the role should not consist solely in imparting as much technical know-how to the group as possible. There is more to mountains than teaching the skills and techniques of mountain-craft. These things are essential aids and tools, but a day so spent may be too clinical, too mechanical, and so without life. The essential nature of the mountain experience may be missed. Under the mass of time calculations, distances, bearings, conventional signs, contour lines, do's and don'ts, the mountains may be so obscured that they never have the chance to reveal their inherent attractions to the group. If the garnering of the leader's own experience was a chore, it will never be possible so to generate an atmosphere in which a love and feeling for mountains can be transmitted to the group. Time should be given for the aesthetic and yes, even spiritual feelings, to impinge on the awareness of those in the group for whom such things will have meaning and great importance.

- Colour, light and shade, shape and form, textures, sounds and scents are all part of the mountain scene. Sometimes they will work their own magic unassisted, at other times the leader may find it possible to heighten the group's awareness of them. The ability to interpret the mountain scene is of enormous value, for walking can become a monotonous business for many young people. They usually need to have been exposed to the hills a number of times before they come to appreciate that a good deal of the charm of mountains lies in their contrasts and infinite variety. Any snippet of information about flora, fauna, natural and man-made features, is grist to the leader's mill. Curiosity starved often dies quickly. Feed it and the results are often very surprising and fruitful.

- Because of the serious nature of a leader's responsibilities, the approach to the leadership situation must be systematic. The 'woolliness' of the 'walking with friends' situation will no longer suffice. All the detailed factors relating to good practice, comfort and safety, must be identified. In this context of safety there must be a reason for everything done or said. The reason must be conscious. There will be many things the leader learned in early hill days by experience which are now done unconsciously without thought. For example, the way to walk and pick a way up or down a hill. All these things now have to be brought, as it were, from the back of the head to the front and consciously stored ready for use.

In those areas which relate to safety and comfort, leaders must be able to justify in every minute detail everything they do or choose not to do.

This implies a very articulate grasp of the mountain situation which only a process of reflective self-analysis and self-questioning about a leader's own experience, mountain and otherwise, will give. It is not enough to know the right thing to do. A leader must know why it is right and what the consequences will be if it is done incorrectly or differently.

LEADERSHIP SKILLS

All the foregoing sections may seem to present a formidable challenge to an aspirant leader. But there are a number of trainable skills which can be acquired to assist the leader. Indeed, the attempt should be made so to develop these skills that they become ingrained habits rather than skills.

Insight

One of your most invaluable aids in coaching and supporting will be the ability to recall clearly past experience, particularly feelings as a beginner. It will enable you to appreciate and to be more acutely aware that if there are occasions now which you feel are personally extending in the slightest bit, there will be some in the group in whom these feelings will be greatly magnified. This awareness is 'insight'. Possible examples are when negotiating sections of rocky scrambling, narrow paths across steep slopes, steep descents, feelings of cold, hunger, thirst, fatigue to which you are more likely to be acclimatised than they are.

Planning and Forethought - Anticipation

This is a skill which will enable leaders to meet difficulties in a state of greater preparedness. It will often provide you with a ready made course of action when emergencies arise and mean that the necessary resources to meet them are to hand. It is, of course, undesirable to go about continually expecting crisis after crisis. But it is wise to be ready for them when they happen and have a plan of action already prepared to meet them. Typical examples would be, "If someone had an accident here, what would I do?". "If something happened to me could the group cope?" "If I had to take this group down there, how long would it take and who would be the ones to watch?" "Where is the point of no return on this trip?"

Checking

This skill should be cultivated until it becomes a habit.

Check that both self and party have the necessary food, clothing and equipment before setting off. In their concern for others leaders should beware of forgetting to check that their own gear is complete. It happens sometimes. Check that any instructions given are heard, understood and obeyed. This may be obvious but it is often neglected, particularly in the informal, fluid circumstances that are characteristic of mountain parties. Noise from strong winds, rain on anorak hoods, river noises, all affect the hearing quite considerably.

Check how things are going with the party. With practice this becomes a 'sense' that is always switched on. If the leader is at the front, there should be frequent looking back. It is too easy to forge on unaware of the mounting chaos behind.

Observation

This skill is supplementary to the skill of checking. The ability to perceive things varies greatly in people. Work to improve yours.

It is mainly by observation that a leader will get to know the characteristics, strengths and weaknesses of each member of the party. Although there may be a lot of chat exchanged with the group, it is the non-verbal signals, facial expressions and body signals that will tell the leader much of what is needed to be known. It is mainly by observation that leaders will become aware of signs of tiredness, boredom, low morale, tension, anxiety stresses, personality conflicts, acute discomforts, feelings of insecurity, lack of a sense of balance, lack of powers of co-ordination, sloppy, energy consuming footwork and so on. All these and many others, leaders will often have to discern for themselves, for the members of your group will tend not to want to mention them. The pressure of a group on the move is a palpable thing and may cause people within the group to feel reluctant to slow it down or stop it. Leaders may have to find out by asking direct questions and a good leader will give them an opening by making it clear that their comfort or enjoyment is just as important as pushing on.

The environment should be observed continuously so that its implications for the party can be assessed in terms of enjoyment and pleasure, danger and effort. Assess which routes offer most interest, protection from head winds, reasonable footing, etc. They may not always be footpaths, which may be badly eroded. Watch out for changes in the weather, greasy rocks or unbridged streams requiring to be crossed.

Decision-making

A wise leader will normally contrive to get the group participating in as many decisions as is consistent with safety. The group members should be given the chance to say what sort of things they would like to see or do on a particular day. Feedback from such a discussion will be invaluable to the leader. This may not be feasible with some novice groups. But much more can be done by skilful prompting to help them identify their expectations and feel involved. More experienced groups are quite likely to have ideas on the subject which will be useful, not only for gearing up their sense of commitment, but for providing, often incidentally, feedback on their assessment of themselves and of what they feel capable.

One of the difficult problems to resolve always is whether the make-up of the group should be determined by the target hill or whether the nature of the hill to be climbed should be determined by the structure of the group. Group discussion about the objective for the day should facilitate the resolution of this problem in the early stages of planning. During the traverse of the route, there are many decisions in which the group should be encouraged to participate such as, when to stop for lunch, where to go next, identifying landmarks, and even whether to go on or not.

But it is the emergency/crisis decisions that are particularly the concern of leader. If the skills and habits already outlined have been developed strongly enough, the business of decision making will already be half accomplished. For the big important decisions relating to the party's safety, the relevant factors will have been already observed or anticipated. It is then a question of using past experience to assess all the factors for and against, and picking out the best course of action from a number of possible alternatives.

CONCLUSION

Thus we return again to the quality of this all important previous personal experience. Wise leaders learn about their own limitations before ever leading parties and get to know not only themselves but themselves in mountains. Beware against anxiety causing an acceleration of pace whilst navigating in mist. Learn beforehand what it is like to be lost temporarily; what it is like to be out in foul conditions; how to handle different types of terrain in ascent and descent; what it is like to be out at night - try a planned bivouac.

There are many other skills which should be mentioned, but space does not permit covering them more fully here. They are mostly skills which contribute to the quality of working relationships in the leadership situation: the art of dealing with and relating to people; the skills and intricacies of communication; the relieving of tension, of using humour; of understanding the dynamics of group life and encouraging the full development of the individuals in your group; of fostering self sufficiency, confidence and self determination in people.

Although for most of the group the aim for the day may well be in getting to the top and enjoying the experience, it is hoped that the leader has a broader awareness of the potential of the outdoors as a marvellous medium for helping people to develop their capacities to the full. The leader's job should be to provide the atmosphere and the setting for this to take place. Whilst a leader's responsibilities, in order of priority, may be the safety, comfort and enjoyment of the party, the members should feel it happening in exactly the reverse order for most of the time.

14

Technique on snow and ice

Snow has a purifying effect on mountains, eliminating the signs and artefacts of man. Artificial boundaries vanish beneath the white mantle, footpaths disappear and a general stillness contributes to a feeling that the original wilderness has returned. Travellers are thrown back on their own resources and skills to make a trail through this suddenly virgin country. It is exhilarating and there are few mountaineers whose pulses do not quicken at the first snow fall. It is also a challenge and, as the list of accidents each winter shows only too clearly, some are ill prepared to meet it.

Those who graduate from summer hillwalking to winter mountaineering sometimes underestimate the potential ferocity of conditions, particularly in the Scottish Highlands. Snow is often propelled by gale force winds into gullies and corrie headwalls where it accumulates in thick, potentially hazardous, slabs topped by overhanging cornices. Although temperatures rarely fall below –15°C they fluctuate within a wide range and with disconcerting rapidity, with the result that a mountaineer can sometimes be wading through soft slush in the morning and cramponing on hard boiler-plate in the afternoon. High winds, zero or sub-zero temperatures when combined with a damp air mass are a heat-sapping combination and create a high risk of exposure, particularly when coupled with tiredness and inadequate clothing. Winter days are short; as little as 6 hours of daylight, and it is easy for even experienced mountaineers to underestimate the time required to overcome the difficulties of a descent in poor light when the party is tired. A high proportion of accidents are 'slips while descending'. The penalty of making such a slip is likely to be far more serious in conditions of snow and ice than in summer. What could result in only a grazed knee and a certain loss of dignity on a grass slope in summer could, on that same slope in winter, mean a long uncontrolled slide with the possibility of a much more serious outcome.

The demarcation between scrambling and rock climbing is more obvious than that between winter hillwalking and snow and ice climbing and it is easy for the winter hillwalker to stray onto hazardous terrain without really being aware of doing so. Indeed, the transition may well be due to factors outside human control such as a sudden fall in temperature causing the snow to become hard. It is for this reason that the winter hillwalking leader must be familiar with all the techniques which form the basis of the winter climber's skill; the use of the ice axe for step-cutting, cramponing, ice-axe braking, belaying on snow and careful route choice. A leader must learn through experience a fine sense of what is appropriate in particular situations: when to put on the rope, what type of protection is suitable for the prevailing conditions, what route to follow to make the most of the conditions and how to recognise and avoid dangerous slopes. This quality of judgement is only acquired as a result of considerable experience. To quote from the syllabus for the Winter Certificate: "To lead a party into the Scottish Mountains in winter conditions is a serious undertaking. Demands are made on the leader which are far in excess of the responsibilities normally carried in summer".

Equipment and Clothing

The subject of clothing has already been discussed in Chapter 2. Winter weather conditions in the British Isles, particularly in the Scottish Highlands, provide a most searching test of the effectiveness of clothing. Inner warmth is essential and this is best provided in several layers, starting with polypropylene long johns next to the skin followed by a long-tailed shirt, and a couple of sweaters or a fleece. Various combinations are possible for the outer layers, for example a vapour permeable outer with an inner synthetic fibre liner, but it is important to be aware of the problem of overheating. Moving up a long snow slope is hard work and can generate a great deal of perspiration. It must be possible to respond by removing one or more of the outer layers. This is particularly important if the outer layer is not vapour permeable because this can give rise to condensation, which soaks the inner clothing. When the activity ceases, cooling is accelerated by the evaporation of all this moisture. The anorak should be long enough to cover the buttocks but no so long that it interferes with leg movements. Nylon anoraks and overtrousers can be potentially dangerous if they have a very smooth finish which offers little friction against the snow in the event of a slide. Acceleration is very rapid even on quite gentle slopes. For the legs and trunk salopettes are more practical than breeches or trousers which can leave the midriff exposed. If woollen breeches are worn waterproof overtrousers should be carried which can be put on and taken off with the minimum of difficulty. Overtrousers are essential in winter but are best not worn with crampons unless they can be tucked into knee length gaiters which fit snugly round the boots and calves. Other essential items include some kind of warm head protection. Ski hats are adequate and can be used with a silk/polypropylene balaclava in really bad conditions. A short absorbent wool scarf is a useful barrier against getting spindrift, ice chips and melting water down the neck. Hands are probably the most difficult part of the anatomy to protect because they have to be used for tasks which are better performed without gloves. Apart from making your hands cold, continually taking your gloves off makes them wet. There is no complete answer, but for warmth wear a pair of thick preshrunk woollen mitts, possibly over thin gloves and carry at least one spare pair of woollen mitts or gloves. It is important to become proficient at undertaking tasks with the gloves on.

Boots for winter walking and climbing must have certain characteristics to make them suitable for the job. Accidents have been caused by people making use of their lightweight summer walking boots for a winter expedition. Unfortunately, boots for winter use are not cheap. Plastic boots with a separate inner boot are often preferred for winter use. A comfortable fit is essential to avoid cold penetrating into the foot, but loose boots make using crampons wearisome. The design of the boots must accommodate the use of crampons. Leather boots need to be of first quality and made from unsplit leather to provide the required degree of water resistance, insulation, stiffness and general durability. The sole should be stiffened to enable the boot to be used for kicking steps in hard snow and to provide a stable platform for crampons. A mid-height boot is probably best and to avoid cold feet they should not be too neat a fit. Allow plenty of room for the toes.

The Ice Axe

There is probably more controversy surrounding the ice axe than almost any other item of equipment and this is in spite of the fact that it is a very ancient instrument which has remained remarkably unchanged since it was first used by shepherds in Alpine regions centuries ago. It has become the basic tool of the winter mountaineer, an indispensable aid to safe progress across snow and ice covered terrain. A modern ice axe is illustrated in Fig 148. The head is usually made in chrome molybdenum steel with an adze at one end and a gently curved pick at the other. It is attached to a hollow metal shaft covered in a rubber or plastic sheath to improve grip and provide insulation. The length of the shaft is determined by the use to which it is to be put. For general winter mountaineering an axe of 55-65cm is a good functional length, suitable for most purposes, although the final choice will be determined by personal preference. For the winter leader an axe that is long enough to make cutting steps in descent easy, will be found very useful. The axe length should also permit the axe to be used for support well down the slope when descending. The axe may be fitted with a sliding wrist loop or with a long tape threaded through the hole in the head and adjusted so that it is taut when the axe is gripped just above the spike.

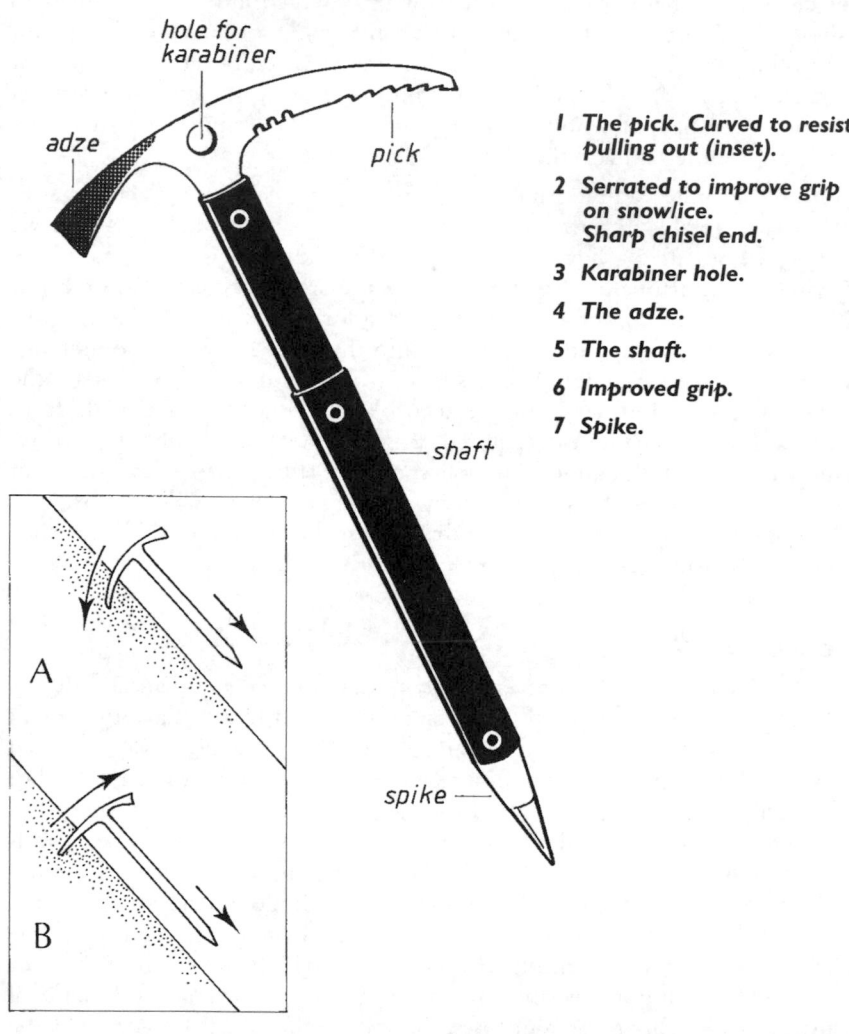

1 **The pick. Curved to resist pulling out (inset).**

2 **Serrated to improve grip on snow/ice. Sharp chisel end.**

3 **Karabiner hole.**

4 **The adze.**

5 **The shaft.**

6 **Improved grip.**

7 **Spike.**

Fig. 148 *Modern Axe.*

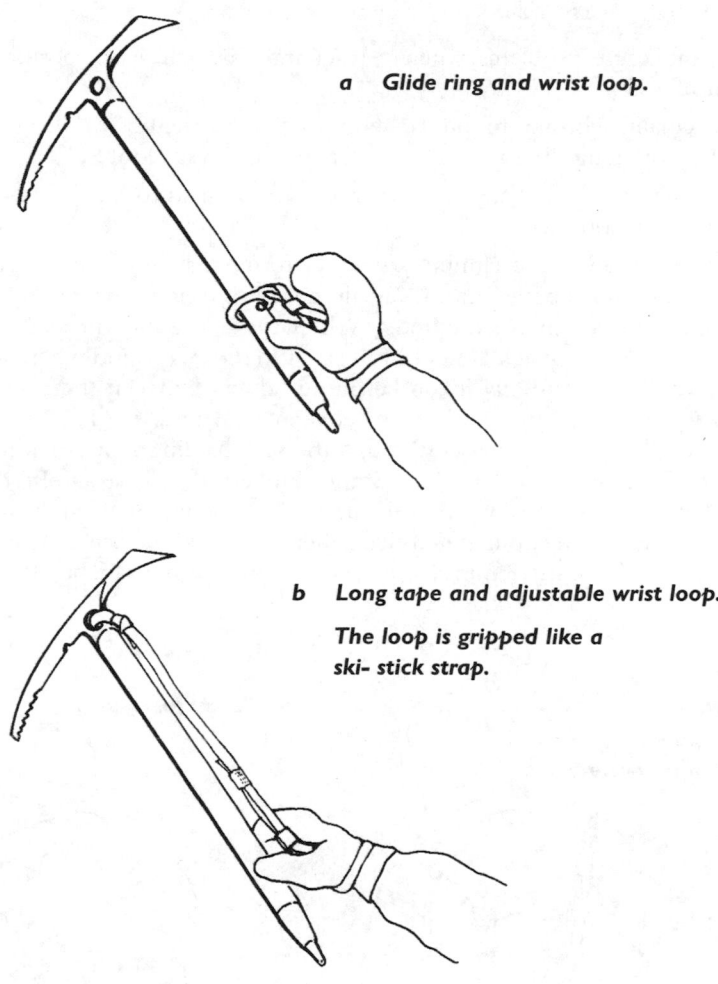

a Glide ring and wrist loop.

b Long tape and adjustable wrist loop.
The loop is gripped like a
ski- stick strap.

(Fig. 149) *Ice axe wrist loops.*

Whether or not to use a wrist loop is open to debate. The advantages of a wrist loop are:

if the axe slips from the hand it remains securely attached to the wrist;

it can relieve some of the strain on the arm when pulling up on the axe;

the axe can be suspended from the wrist freeing the hand for other tasks.

The disadvantages are:

it can cause problems when getting into the self arrest position in the event of a slip;

it remains whirling round dangerously close to the body during a fall - in this case the long sling is probably safer than the wrist loop;

it is necessary to change the wrist loop from hand to hand every time you change direction.

For more advanced climbing whether to use a sling or nothing at all is a matter of personal preference. Each climber must weigh the pros and cons and adopt the most suitable method. When the axe is not needed it can be strapped to the rucksack as in Fig 150 (a). On mixed ground where it is likely to be used intermittently it can be pushed down between the back and the rucksack, making sure that it goes between the straps, see Fig 150 (b). For extra security it can be passed through the sack hauling loop; then it will not fall off when the sack is taken off. Some climbers like to use a holster attached to a belt but this is really only suitable for a short axe or hammer-axe. As a general rule it is recommended that when on snow and ice covered ground the axe should be carried in the hand at all times. An accidental slip is, by its very nature, totally unexpected.

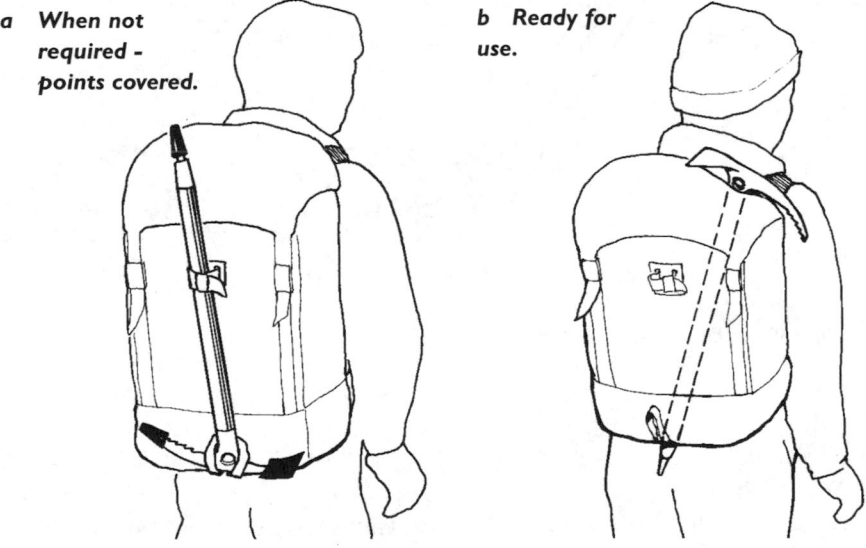

a   **When not required - points covered.**

b   **Ready for use.**

(Fig. 150)   *Carrying the axe.*

Technique on Snow

For convenience the techniques used on snow are described separately from those used mainly on ice. On the mountain snow and ice merge imperceptibly with one another so that it is difficult to define at what point one begins and the other ends and techniques which are appropriate for ice climbing may also be adaptable for use on hard snow.

CARRYING THE AXE

It is not a matter of great moment whether you carry your axe with the pick or the adze pointing forward. What is important is to hold it so that it is not likely to damage yourself or others and to have it available for support and as an aid to balance, ready to bring into use as the situation requires. Those who advocate carrying it pick forward claim that you are less likely to puncture yourself and that it is more comfortable to have the heel of your palm resting on the flat of the adze than on the narrow blade of the pick. Those who advocate carrying it adze forward point out that this is the natural position from which to move directly into the self arrest position. Generally, it is best for the climber to be fully prepared for a slip – and therefore the axe should be carried in such a way that it can be deployed instantly.

KICKING STEPS

Steps are simply kicked into the snow, either straight up or in a series of diagonal zig-zag traverses. The harder the snow the more vigorous the kick has to be and the smaller the step that results. Economy of effort is important because kicking a long line of steps can be very tiring, especially on the calf muscles. Swing the lower leg from the knee and allow its momentum to work for you. The step should, if possible, be large enough to take the ball of the foot as far as the instep and it should slope down into the hill to provide a secure platform. A step kicked in this fashion tends to become more secure as following members of the party use it. Shallow, outward sloping steps soon become degraded causing difficulties for the tail enders. Support and balance are obtained from the axe which is held like a walking stick in whichever hand is closest to the slope ie on the uphill side.

As the slope steepens a zig-zag ascent is often less tiring, with the axe being driven in like a stake for security. A rhythm soon develops: two steps, drive in the axe, two steps and so on. The axe should be moved when the body is in a stable position, with both feet firm and secure and the inside foot in front and above the outside one. To change direction turn, face to the slope, with

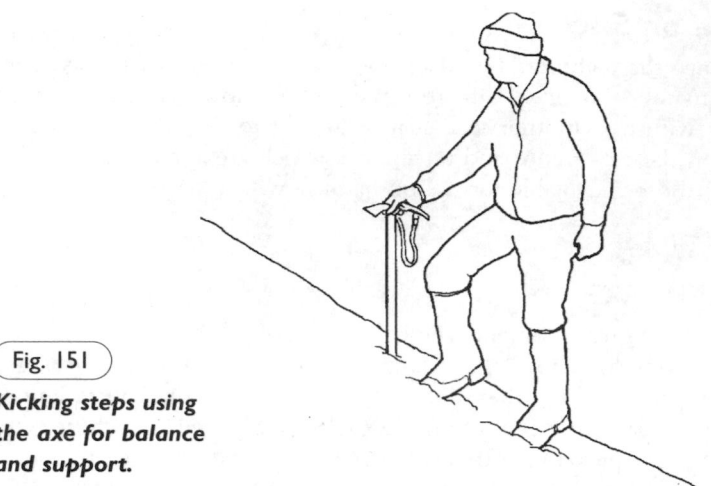

Fig. 151

Kicking steps using the axe for balance and support.

a 3 step movement instead of the usual two and continue on in the new direction. This technique is particularly effective on hard snow where a slicing kick with the side of the boot can provide a small but adequate foothold. Such small holds are inadequate if a retreat has to be made and they are quickly degraded by those following unless each member of the party tries to improve and enlarge them by repeating the kicking action of the leader. Steps should, where possible, support the whole length of the foot to the heel, and at least one-third of the width of the boot. Anything less and it is time to start cutting slash steps with the axe.

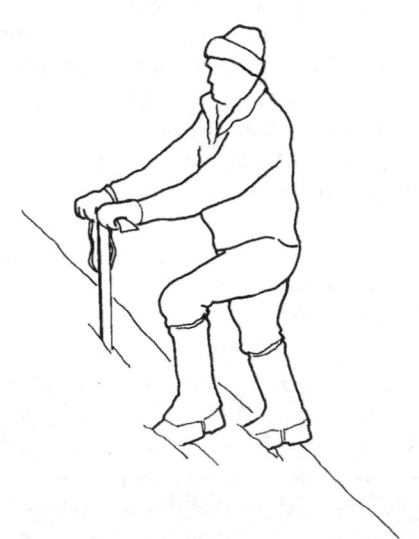

Fig. 152

For greater security the axe can be driven in two handed. This technique is commonly used when changing direction on a zig-zag ascent.

As the slope steepens further it becomes necessary to increase your security by driving the axe shaft further into the snow. In harder snow the axe may only penetrate a short distance and in this case a two-handed grip is to be preferred, one hand on the head and the other low down on the shaft, against the snow surface, to reduce leverage and provide a firm hold.

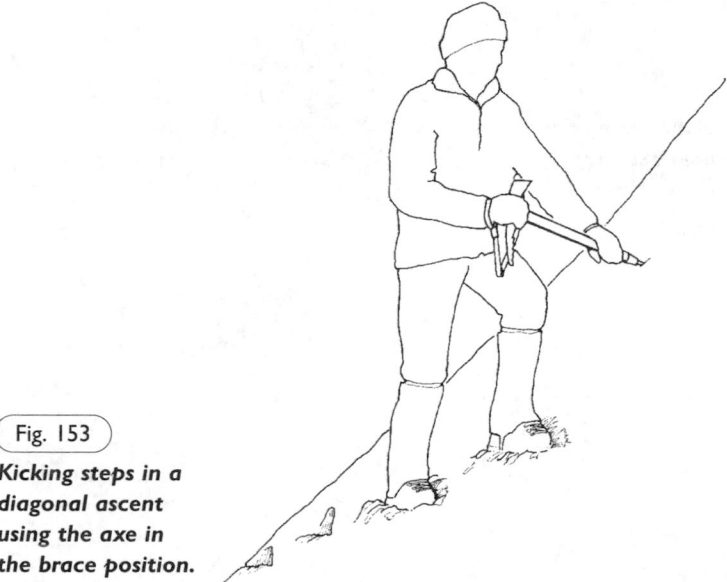

(Fig. 153)

Kicking steps in a diagonal ascent using the axe in the brace position.

As the slope steepens still further (45°) and especially if the snow is too hard to take more than a few centimetres of the shaft, the axe can be held across the body in the 'brace' position with the outside hand on the head and the inside hand on the shaft as close to the snow as possible. This is not as secure a technique as driving the axe in vertically and at this point it is worth considering whether to cut steps. Any decision will be influenced by the hardness of the snow and the degree of responsibility that is being taken for the party. A line of good steps is very useful if it is intended to descend the same slope later in the day.

Descending a steep snow slope is a serious undertaking. On steep firm snow face the slope, thrust the axe in as far below you as you can comfortably reach and then kick steps straight down. As the slope eases turn to face the valley and walk down. This is a technique that should be approached positively. Lean forward so that the whole body weight is brought to bear on the heel that is being driven, stiff-legged, into the slope below. Security is provided by reaching down and driving the axe vertically into the snow every two or three steps – a long axe is useful in these circumstances. As the slope eases the axe can be held in the walking or self-arrest position. The sense of exposure that is experienced on an unbroken open snow slope tends to make the less confident climber lean backwards into the slope. This only provides an illusion of security while actually making a slip more probable. As far as possible keep the centre of gravity vertically over the feet.

a   On steep slopes face in and use the whole axe shaft for support., either single handed as shown, or two handed.

b   On moderate slopes make plunge steps by applying the whole body weight to the heels. The axe should be held in the self arrest position.

Fig. 154   *Descending a snow slope kicking steps.*

c **On gentle slopes walk straight down using heels to make firm steps. The axe is held in the walking position.**

STEP CUTTING

It is sometimes said that step cutting is a dying craft and certainly, now that the majority of climbers are using crampons with front-points and two axes, the need to laboriously cut lines of steps is less common. Nevertheless, there are many occasions, particularly with a party of novices, when a line of well cut steps can make the difference between a safe passage and unjustifiable risk. For general hill walking without crampons cutting steps is as essential a technique as knowing how to brake with the ice axe. A competent mountaineer is well practised at both.

Cutting steps is a skill which requires regular practice and since it involves swinging the axe with one or sometimes two hands good balance is critical. Always cut while standing in a stable position, with the inside boot above and in front. Develop a steady rhythm: chop two steps, thrust in the axe, move up, chop the next two steps, take out the axe and plant it higher up, move up and so on. On snow try to chop into the hole made by the previous cut. See Fig 156. The size and spacing of the steps will depend on the angle of the slope and the experience of the party. As a general rule cut generous sized steps that will support as near to the whole foot as possible and keep the interval between them as small as convenient. Widely spaced steps are tiring to use and can be extremely awkward in descent if a party has to use them later in the day.

Fig. 155 *Step cutting in diagonal ascent. Two steps cut from a stable position before moving up.*

If the snow is slabby make a Vee-shaped slash with the pick and then chop-out inside the Vee. On ice the same basic rules apply though it takes more skill and effort to cut good steps with the pick. It is normal to cut steps in a series of zig zags. On easier slopes a single line of steps will usually suffice but as the slope steepens it becomes difficult to bring the inside leg through and at this point two parallel lines are better, one for each boot.

If the consistency of the snow is right it is often possible to cut a slash step with a single blow of the axe, using the adze, just long enough and wide enough to accommodate the side of the boot. It is much easier to develop a good rhythm with this method and a diagonal line of steps can be cut either up or down in a fraction of the time it would take to cut full steps. Careful route choice should be made to take advantage of ground on which this technique is applicable as it is a fast and relatively secure means of ascent.

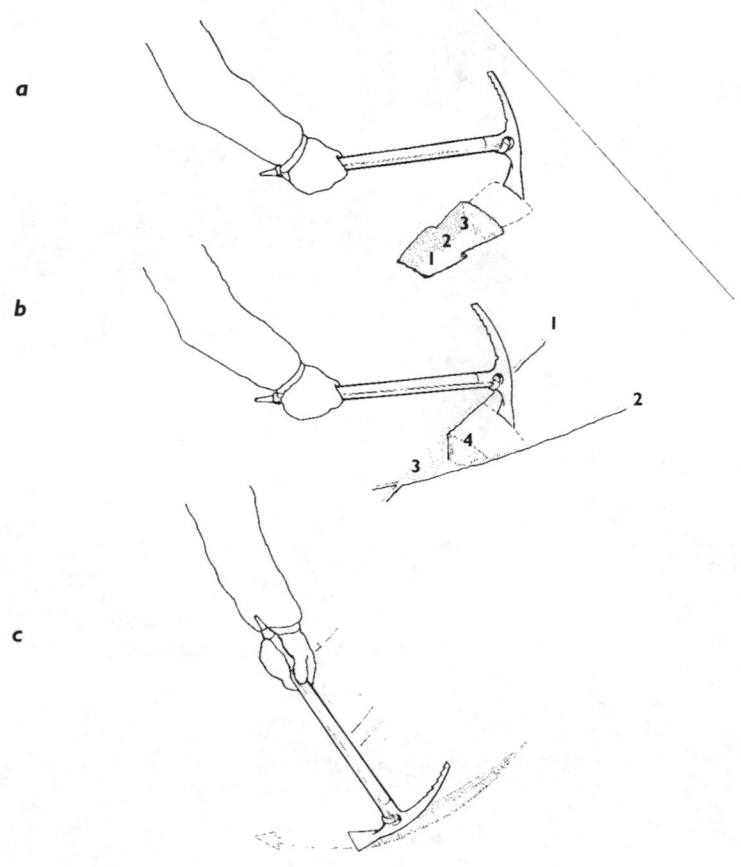

(Fig. 156)   **Cutting a step in snow.**

a   **with the adze - always cut away from the first chop.**

b   **with the pick - in slabby snow make two slashes with the pick (1 and 2) and then chop out the angle between them with the adze (3 and 4).**

c   **slash steps with inside arm.**

341

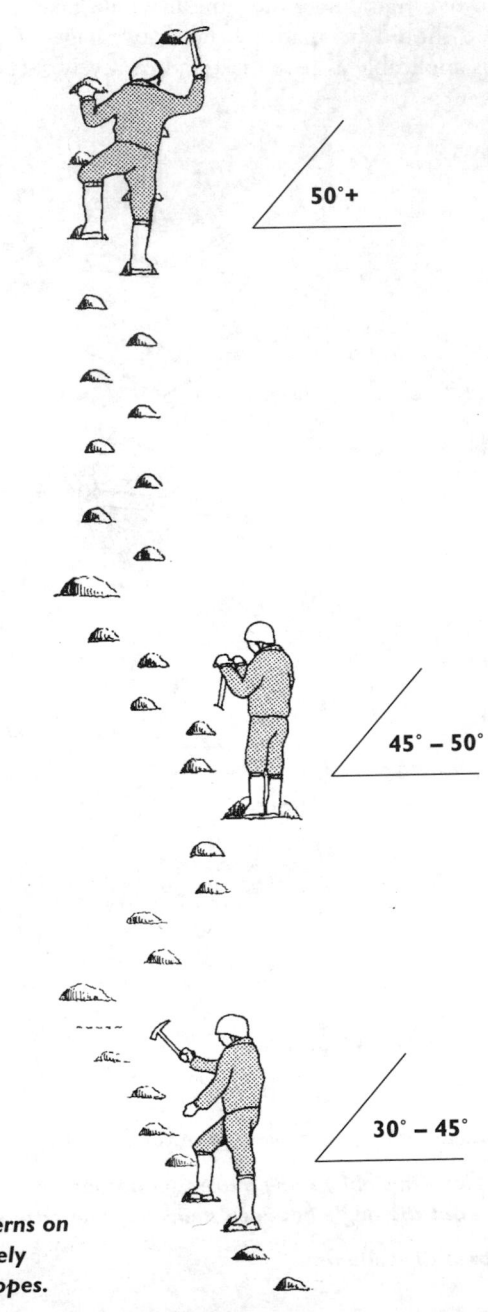

50°+

45° – 50°

30° – 45°

Fig. 157 *Step patterns on progressively steeper slopes.*

On the steepest slopes a direct frontal approach is best, cutting a ladder of steps straight up. This is extremely hard work, especially on ice, so make the interval between them as long as it is comfortable to step up and cut at least two steps above shoulder height before moving up. Since the steps may be used for both hands and feet it is helpful to fashion a small lip on each step with the adze to serve as a jughandle. When moving up the axe is used for additional support and to assist balance by driving in either the adze or the pick.

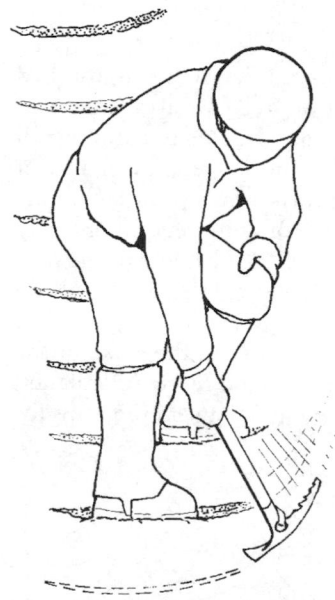
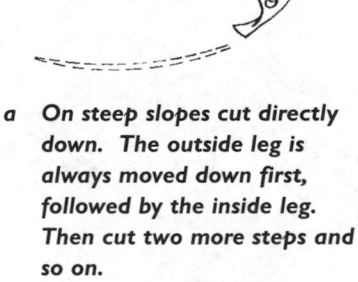
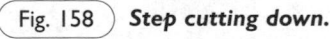

a **On steep slopes cut directly down. The outside leg is always moved down first, followed by the inside leg. Then cut two more steps and so on.**

b **On moderate slopes it is possible to cut a double line of steps diagonally down. Cut two steps at a time from a stable position.**

Fig. 158   **Step cutting down.**

Cutting steps down can be awkward, the more so with a short axe. It is best to cut a ladder of steps directly down the slope, usually one-handed, cutting one step at a time. Face right if you are right handed and move down in such a way that your right foot (outside leg) is always lower than your left (inside leg). In other words always step down with the lower leg first and on no account attempt to step through. In the right snow conditions a single line of slash steps can be cut. Reach down, cut a step and move the lower foot on to it. Bring the upper foot onto the step just vacated; and so on. On a less steep slope it is possible to descend on a diagonal line, cutting two steps at a time from a stable position (inside leg ahead and above). On very steep snow or ice often the only sensible means of descent is by abseiling using rock or snow anchors.

GLISSADING

Glissading can be exhilarating but like scree running, it has to be approached with caution and common sense. The slope must be free of avalanche hazard and it must be possible to see the whole of it including the run–out area which should be free of boulders and other obstacles. The danger lies in loss of control which can be caused by all sorts of things other than poor technique such as a sudden change in the texture of the snow, or an unseen irregularity in the slope. To be ready for any emergency the axe should be held in the self-arrest position. The actual technique used will depend on the nature of the snow and the angle of the slope. The simplest is to sit down as if on a toboggan controlling speed with the feet and by pressure on the spike of the axe in the snow to one side. The standing glissade is much more difficult and is really a form of skiing but on very short skis! It helps to spread the arms for balance but still keep a firm grip on the axe.

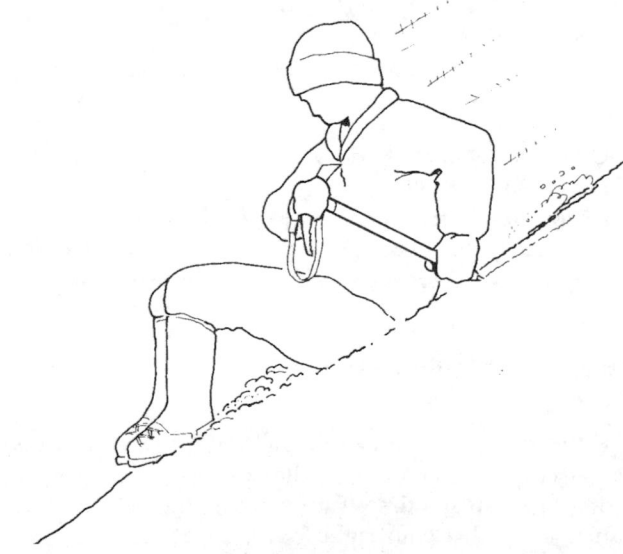

Fig. 159

Sitting glissade.

In general it must be said that glissading is not advised and it should not be introduced as a game to novices. It is a technique to be adopted by experienced mountaineers and even then with the greatest caution.

SELF BELAY

This is the term used to describe the state of readiness the climber should adopt when moving on any snow slope. It involves holding the axe in a position from which it can be thrust into the snow immediately a slip occurs and so prevent it developing into a dangerous slide. On a moderately angled slope the axe will be carried in the hand nearest the slope with the pick pointing to the rear. If a slip occurs the axe shaft is thrust into the snow as far as it will go while the other hand grabs the shaft at the snow surface and takes most of the weight. At the same time kick the toes into the slope to obtain additional braking purchase. Practice makes perfect. It is better to stop a slip starting than to risk making an unsuccessful arrest of a high speed slide. If an uncontrolled slide begins, the longer it takes to stop the less likely it will be that it will be halted by ice axe arrest techniques.

Ice Axe Braking

Since it is a relatively simple matter to slip on snow or ice and since the consequences of doing so can be serious, one of the essential skills to be learned by the winter mountaineer is to be able to stop a slide. Ice axe braking or self-arrest, is not a difficult technique to master but it needs practice and novices should be given the opportunity of doing so on the first suitable snow slope. A concave slope, free of protruding rocks and with a long, safe run out will ensure that in the event of failure to stop the novice will not be injured.

Sliding Feet First, Facing the Slope

The basic braking position is lying facing the slope with the axe held diagonally across the body, one hand on the head of the axe with the adze tucked in against the chest and shoulder and the pick directed into the snow. The other hand covers the spike. Keep the elbows well in to the sides and try to bring as much of your weight as possible to bear on the pick. During the slide try to pull up on the axe head and arch your back over the top of it, keeping the forehead close to the snow but with the face turned to the side away from the adze. Apply pressure on the pick gradually to avoid the axe being snatched out of your grasp. Keep the legs apart for stability and, as long as crampons are not being worn, the toes can be used to add to the braking effect of the axe. Having come to a stop kick a secure step in the snow before standing up and removing the axe. Most people brake with their right hand on the axe head. It is better to concentrate on perfecting this before practising with the hands reversed. However, since there is no guarantee which hand will be on the head of the axe at the time of a slip both techniques must be perfected.

a **As seen from the snow.**

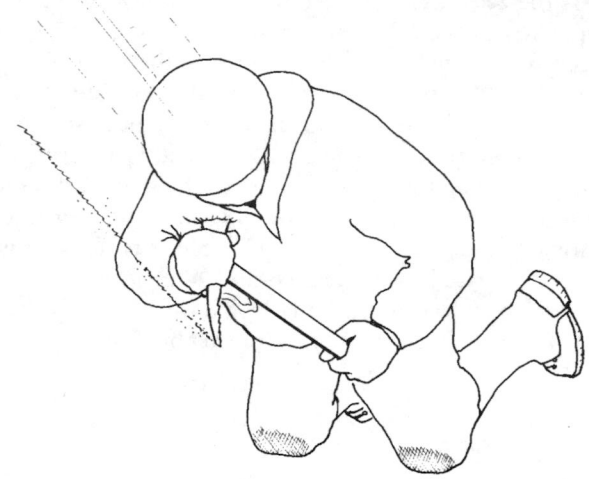

b **In profile.**

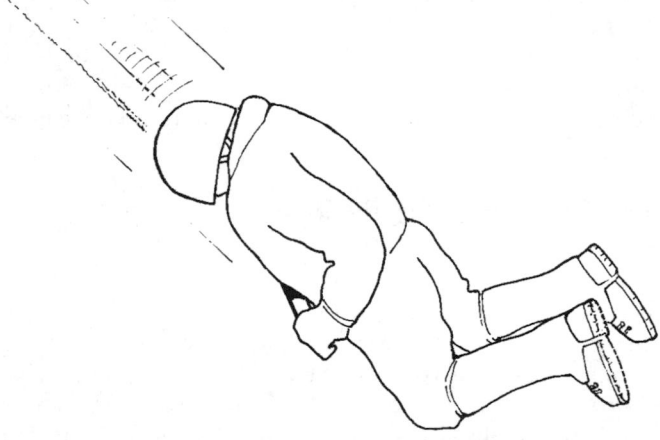

Fig. 160   *Ice axe braking.*

Sliding Feet First on the Back

To get into the braking position first roll your body towards the same side as the hand that is holding the axe head and gradually apply pressure on the pick. Do not roll towards the hand holding the spike which could easily dig into the snow first, with disastrous consequences.

Fig. 161 *Braking with the ice axe from a feet first slide on the back.*

Sliding Head First, Face towards the slope

Head-first slides are more difficult to control and the first action is to get into a head-uphill position from which the conventional self-arrest technique can be used. When sliding in this position the technique is to reach out horizontally with the pick as far as possible on the same side as the arm which is holding the axe head. Insert the pick into the snow and the braking effect on that side will cause the body to swing round past the axe into a head-uphill position. The body will then be in a position with the arms at full stretch. Arch the back, lift out the pick and place it below the shoulder and brake as described above.

Fig. 162

Braking with the ice axe from a head first slide, face towards the slope.

Sliding Head First on the Back

From this position the sequence of moves is first to insert the pick at hip level and as far out from the body as you can comfortably reach. Then, as the pick bites, pull up on it with a twisting movement of the upper body towards the axe head so that the shoulder and hip come to rest against the slope. At the same time throw your legs out on the opposite side and allow them to swing down and round while completing the body turn to face the slope. Lift out the pick and complete the normal braking procedure.

Fig. 163

Braking with the ice axe from a head first slide on the back.

Tumbling Fall

In a tumbling fall the first priority is to stabilise the position by spreading the arms and legs as widely as possible. Once in a stable position it is possible to adopt the appropriate braking method. When wearing crampons it is important that they should be kept well clear of the snow by bending the knees. This minimises the chance of a crampon catching and again throwing the body into a tumbling fall.

These descriptions and the diagrams which accompany them will make it abundantly clear that the techniques of self-arrest can only be mastered after a period of determined practice. Hopefully, they may never be required in a real emergency situation, but when they are, they must succeed first time. Speed of execution is as important as technique because of the very rapid acceleration of a sliding body on hard snow.

In circumstances when it can be seen that the consequences of failing to perform an effective self arrest is likely to result in injury, then it is time to start using the rope to provide additional security.

CORNICES

The formation of cornices is discussed more fully in the chapter on snow structure (page 398). In this section it is sufficient to note that they form in the lee of ridges or on the edges of plateaux and that they constitute a significant threat to climbers because of their inherent tendency to collapse and because they often pose a final obstacle at the end of an ascent, at which point the prospect of a retreat may be difficult to contemplate.

The moment of collapse of a cornice is difficult to predict, but indications of instability may be seen on neighbouring slopes. Warm conditions at any time during the winter spell danger and at these times it is wise to steer clear of routes with cornices overtopping them. The presence of a large cornice indicates the accumulation of potentially unstable masses of wind blown snow on the slopes below. The possibility of a sub–cornice avalanche must be considered and the degree of risk properly evaluated before proceeding.

Before attempting to break through a cornice a solid anchor, preferably rock, should be found well to the side and out of the way of the debris should there be a collapse. Cornices take a great variety of forms and vary widely in their hardness, but it will often be necessary to cut a trench or to tunnel through it. This requires strenuous and determined effort and can take up a considerable amount of time. The adze of the axe can be used as a scraper although much effort can be saved by the use of a snow saw or shovel.

Techniques on Hard Snow and Ice

Before the 50's it was unusual to see anyone wearing crampons in this country, even on 'The Ben' when plastered with snow and ice. Nailed boots were the order of the day and crampons were new fangled gadgets that some people, who did not know any better, used in foreign parts. But of course the wearing of nailed boots enabled the hillwalker to roam the mountains, if not in complete safety, at least in the confidence that a slip on a patch of hard snow or ice was unlikely. The modern hillwalker has to get used to the fact that vibram soled boots are not ideally suited for winter conditions. The practice of mountaineering calls for a keen awareness of where one may, and where one may not, tread. Crampons may not be an indispensable item of equipment but without them the climber is inevitably restricted in the range and quality of the expeditions which can be tackled.

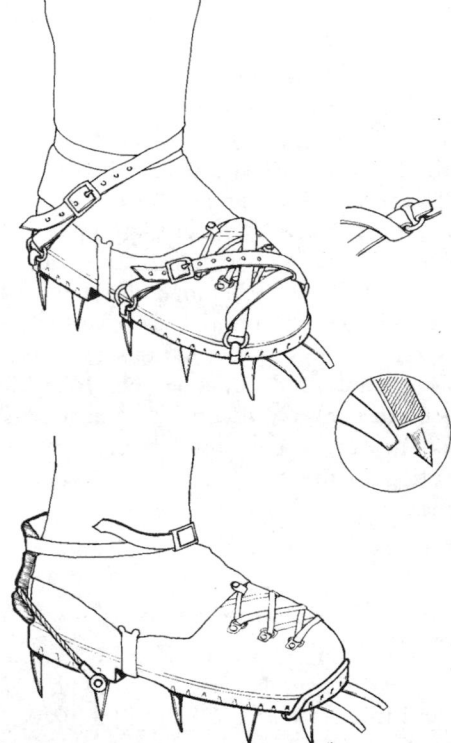

a **Note particularly the arrangement of the strap at the toe which ensures that the toe loop will not fall forward.**

b **Clip on. Boots must have a compatible heel and toe profile.**

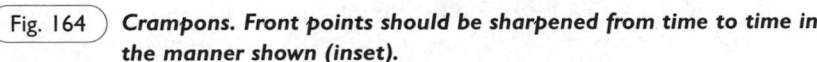

Fig. 164 — *Crampons. Front points should be sharpened from time to time in the manner shown (inset).*

There are several types of crampons: rigid crampons which can be adjusted for length but provide a rigid platform; articulated crampons where the toe and heel pieces are loosely connected by an adjustable bar and flexible crampons where the two pieces are connected by a flexible steel plate. Instep crampons are not suitable for winter mountaineering. As a general rule the more rigid the crampons the stiffer the boots must be to accommodate them. Although flexible crampons can be fitted to 'bendy' boots their use is not recommended. Most crampons have twelve points with the front pair directed forward as an aid to climbing steep snow/ice. These front points are not really necessary for winter walking and can in fact be a menace on untrained feet because of the danger of tripping up or catching the points on the trousers. This is the reason for advising the use of long close fitting gaiters when crampons are worn.

It is vitally important that crampons should fit the boots and be securely strapped on. It is better to have no crampons at all than to have ones that are badly fitting. The tales of crampons coming adrift at some critical stage of a route are legion. When buying a pair of crampons take your winter boots and gaiters to the shop and seek the advice of an experienced assistant. When they are properly fitted crampons should be a spring fit on to the boots, in other words they should stay on without straps even when the boot is shaken vigorously. There are two main types of binding: strap and clip-on. Clip-on crampons are popular because of the ease with which they can be put on or taken off. However, proper alignment is critical and they are only really suitable for rigid boots which have a compatible heel and toe profile. Strap bindings come in a wide range of designs. The important points are that the strap should be robust and not prone to freezing up (reinforced neoprene is satisfactory in this respect) and that the means of securing the strap should be simple to adjust and non-slip. Fig 164a illustrates how the strap should be threaded through the post rings to provide a secure fastening which will not slip off the toe. The strap should not be pulled so tight that it impairs circulation in the foot. This can lead to cold feet, blisters, and at worst frostbite.

Crampon Technique

Walking on hard snow or ice is made a good deal easier by wearing crampons but it is easy to trip or worse still to catch a gaiter with one of the front points. To avoid this get into the habit of walking with the feet about 30 cm (1ft) apart. Walking on gentle terrain with crampons is a precise technique, so concentrate all the time on placing the crampon onto the snow using all the points - and moving with a wide gait and the toes turned out.

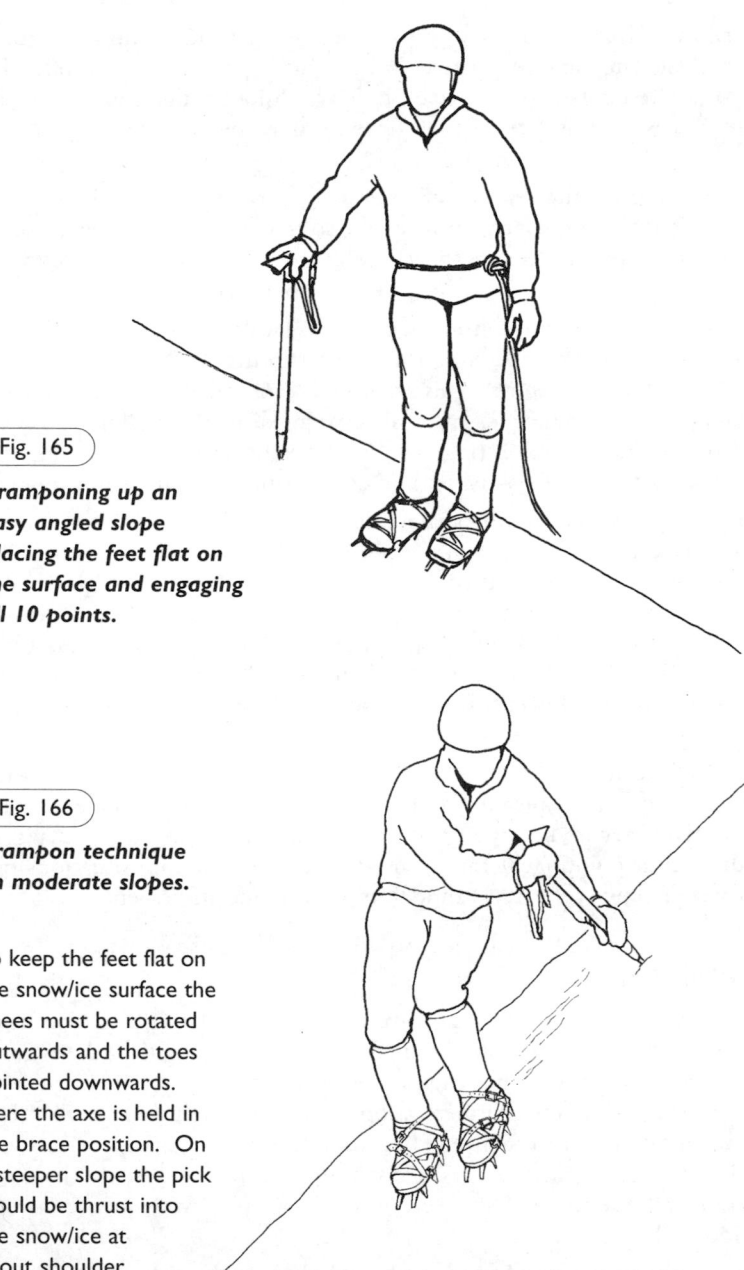

Fig. 165

Cramponing up an easy angled slope placing the feet flat on the surface and engaging all 10 points.

Fig. 166

Crampon technique on moderate slopes.

To keep the feet flat on the snow/ice surface the knees must be rotated outwards and the toes pointed downwards. Here the axe is held in the brace position. On a steeper slope the pick would be thrust into the snow/ice at about shoulder level.

If the snow is damp it can cling to the boots so that the crampons become completely 'balled-up' and ineffective. When this happens, every so often hit the side of each boot with the axe shaft to dislodge the snow. If these conditions persist for any length of time it may be best to remove the crampons.

When walking on the flat or on reasonably straightforward slopes keep your feet as flat as possible on the snow or ice so that all the points bite, except of course the front ones. Because there is a limit to how far you can flex your ankles a direct ascent must eventually give way to a diagonal one.

As the slope steepens it becomes necessary to face more outwards, turning the toes more and more downhill in order to maintain the flat-footed position and ten-point contact with the snow. It also helps to bend your knees. Axe support will depend on the slope angle, and will change from the walking position (Fig. 165) to the brace position (Fig. 166) and finally, on the steepest slopes it will be necessary to face the slope and go straight up using the front points.

On hard snow or ice it will be necessary to plant the pick or the adze, which has a larger surface area with a swinging blow of the axe above and ahead of you so that it can be used for support and balance while you make the next two steps. The inside hand grasps the axe head while the outside hand pulls gently out and down on the spike. It is a mistake to rest the spike of the axe on the snow. In practice, the shaft should remain roughly parallel to the slope in order to benefit from the positive hooking angle of the pick. (Figs.148, 168)

The 'French technique', as it is called, is difficult to master but it is worth persevering because it is a pleasing and graceful method when well executed. It is also relatively secure because of the 10-point contact and is less tiring in the end than front pointing. It can be used in a wide range of situations but is particularly effective on easy to moderate terrain and in descent.

FRONT POINTING

Front pointing is a rather more aggressive technique, tackling the slope head on, with the result that it is physically much more demanding than the French technique, particularly on the calves. Because it is easy to learn and immediately effective many climbers adopt it to the exclusion of all other techniques. This is short-sighted because there are many situations, particularly on mixed rock, snow and ice where front pointing is not the most appropriate technique to use. However, on really steep snow or ice it is a very effective method.

The front points are kicked firmly and squarely into the snow/ice with just sufficient vigour to obtain a good bite. The sole of the boot should be

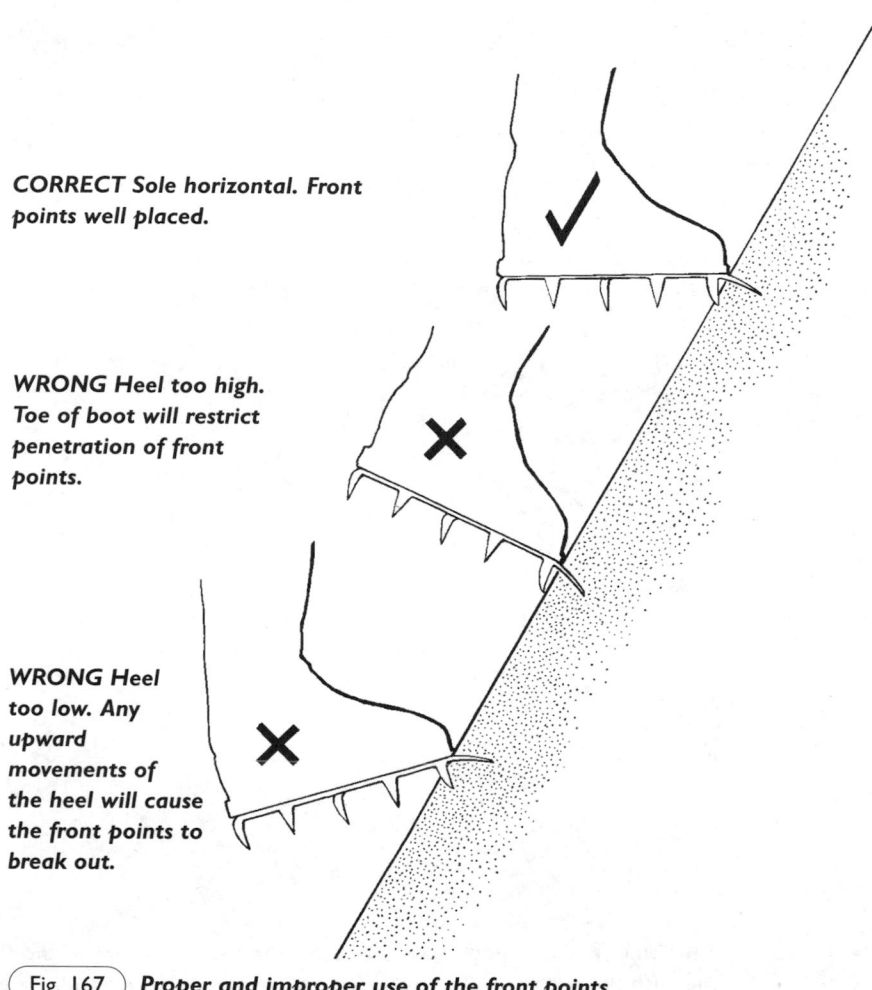

CORRECT Sole horizontal. Front points well placed.

WRONG Heel too high. Toe of boot will restrict penetration of front points.

WRONG Heel too low. Any upward movements of the heel will cause the front points to break out.

Fig. 167   *Proper and improper use of the front points*

horizontal and once planted, about hip width apart, the feet should remain still so that there is no tendency for the points to break out of the ice. (Fig 167) Depending on the angle of slope the axe may be used as a dagger, thrusting the pick into the snow/ice at waist level or up to full stretch above your head. At steeper angles and on ice it will be necessary to plant the pick with a single swing of the axe, using the wrist loop for support as you front point up. Since the pick has to be removed and driven in again higher up there is a period when there is no support from the axe and the climber is simply balancing on crampons alone. This is a limiting factor when using a single axe. (Fig. 168)

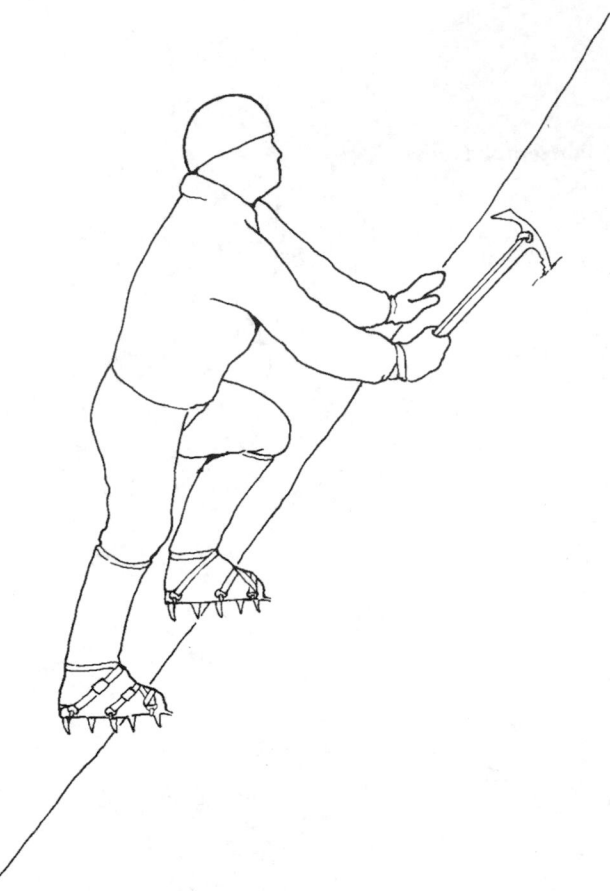

Fig. 168 — ***Front pointing with a single axe. Note how the spike is clear of the slope with the shaft parallel to it. The crampons are horizontal. The left hand can be placed on the axe head for additional support.***

It is now common practice for climbers to use a second short axe or hammer-axe in the other hand. By using this double axe technique even overhanging ice pitches can be overcome.

The danger of front-pointing for the novice mountaineer is that it is a deceptively easy technique to use in ascent but rather more difficult to use in descent. The over ambitious can be lured into climbing to a position from which descent is difficult. The maxim that you should climb only what your are reasonably confident of being able to reverse remains relevant on ice. It

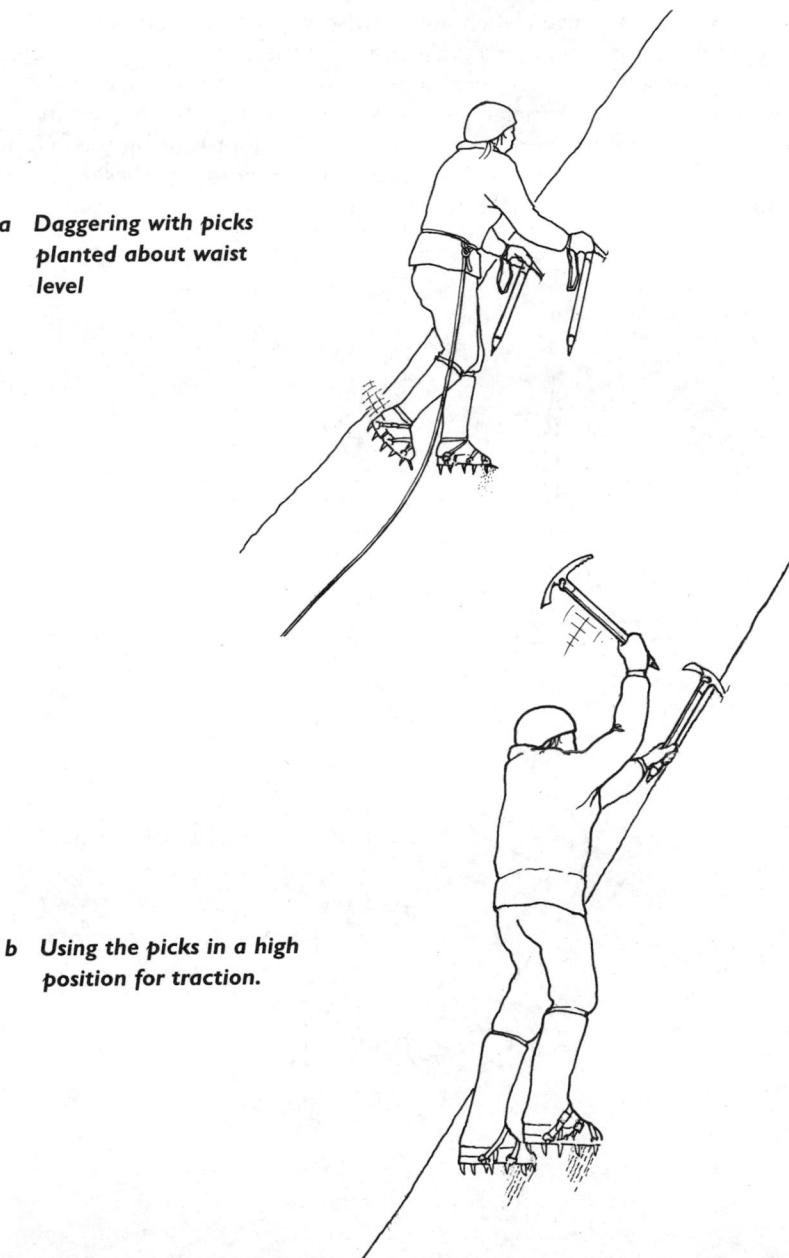

a *Daggering with picks planted about waist level*

b *Using the picks in a high position for traction.*

Fig. 169   **Two Axe Techniques.**

is possible to combine various techniques to solve particular problems. The French method can be combined with front pointing to produce an energy saving method of tackling long, steep slopes. The technique involves one foot front pointing while the other is placed out to the side, flat footed in the 3 o'clock or 9 o'clock position depending on which foot is being used. The technique can be very useful in situations when the climber wishes to relieve the strain on the calf muscles. (Fig. 170)

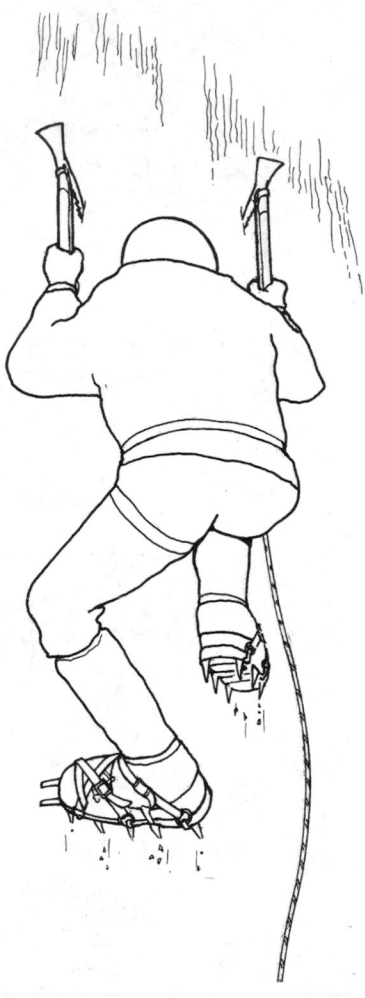

Fig. 170   *The nine o'clock position. This technique combines front pointing with flat footing and is less tiring than using the front points only.*

DESCENDING SNOW / ICE

The problem when descending steep snow/ice facing the slope is that it is difficult to plant the pick with a good swing of the axe. To be any good at all the pick must go in at about eye level which requires a grip about half way up the shaft. Furthermore, it is often difficult to ensure that the front points are well kicked in and that the boots are horizontal. The difficulties are compounded if the climber is only using one ice tool. For all these reasons abseiling down should always be considered as an option. As the angle eases it will eventually be possible to face sideways or outwards and descend in the 'French' manner; feet twelve to eighteen inches apart and flat on the surface with the toes turned out, knees well bent and with the upper body curved outwards so that all the weight is directly over the crampons. The axe can be used in whichever way gives the most positive support. This will either be in the brace position with the spike of the axe against the snow or with the axe held in a self belay. It is very important to be positive and confident in all movements. A tentative approach will almost certainly be counter productive.

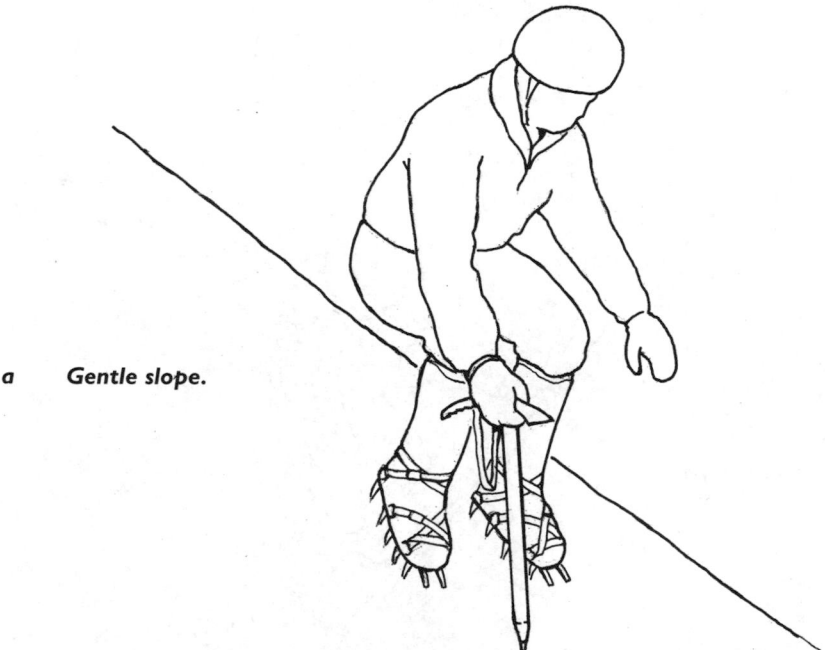

a **Gentle slope.**

(Fig. 171) ***Descending snow / ice. In each case note how the feet are flat on the surface with the body weight directly over them.***

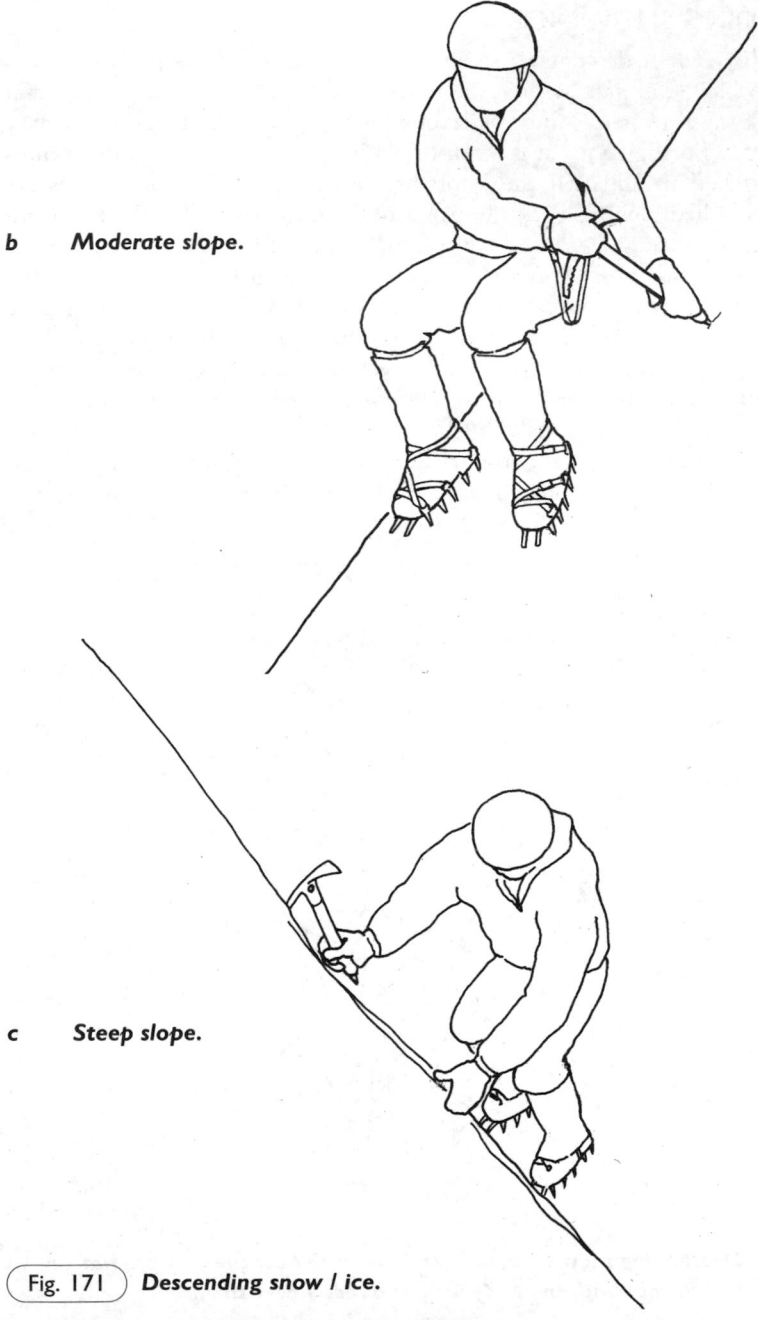

b   *Moderate slope.*

c   *Steep slope.*

Fig. 171   *Descending snow / ice.*

15

Security on Snow and Ice

Some mountaineers tend to adopt a particular technique and use it regardless of all other factors. Many techniques are available, each one suited to particular snow conditions. A leader must be aware of these different conditions and adapt the method used accordingly. All the techniques demand very careful application. A badly placed axe, an insecure step, an inadequate stance, a rope in the wrong place, can all give rise to problems. The ice axe is the most important tool and the mountaineer should learn through constant practice to use it instinctively so that if a slip occurs it is used appropriately without thinking. While climbing snow the ice axe is a portable anchor available to assist and to safeguard every move. If the anchor fails, or as is more likely, the climber fails to use it properly, it is important to have practised ice axe braking. This is a technique which is easy enough to understand but slips rarely occur exactly as they are described in the text-book or when the climber is fully prepared.

Belaying on Snow

Because one is dealing with a soft material as opposed to a hard one, security on snow can never have the certainty of security on rock. There is always an element of unpredictability about it. For this reason it is important to adopt a system of belaying which avoids shock loading the snow anchor. The indirect belay described on page 167 is satisfactory in this respect, because the belayer can provide a dynamic arrest by controlling the braking force applied to the rope. In so doing the load is spread over a period of time thus reducing the impact on both the belayer and the belay. Hopefully, the falling climber will be able to contribute to self arrest by braking with the axe. It is important to cut an ample and stable stance well down the slope directly below the anchor, since a pull on the anchor from the wrong direction could render it useless. A sitting position is sometimes preferred, with slots cut for the legs. The system for managing the rope is exactly the same as described for security on rock.

Fig. 172   *Hip belay on snow.*

SLINGS AND KARABINERS

Before discussing the subject of security on snow and ice it is necessary to introduce two items of special equipment which, although not absolutely essential, do make belaying a much more simple and effective procedure.

A sling is simply a length of nylon rope or tape tied with a double fisherman's or tape knot to form a loop (see Fig 173). It is useful to carry several of these made from lengths between 1.5 and 4.0 metres. They are normally used in conjunction with a karabiner to attach to an anchor, either to provide the main belay, or to provide additional intermediate protection, known as a running belay.

A karabiner is a metal snap link, usually made out of aluminium alloy, which combines lightness with strength. A wide range of models is available, but the basic principle is the same throughout the range. Strength is the most

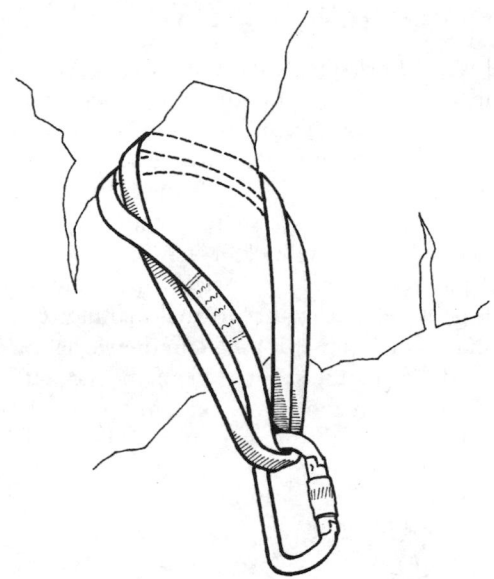

(Fig. 173) *Doubled tape sling with karabiner.*

important characteristic and in this respect the karabiner must conform to the standards laid down by the U.I.A.A. The gate is the weakest part and its design should include some arrangement for locking the gate in case the karabiner becomes loaded in a fall. A locking screw across the gate itself is a common device for ensuring that the gate remains closed while in use. The karabiner is a most versatile tool and is very often used in conjunction with a sling for belaying and as a waist or harness attachment. It has many other specialised uses which are beyond the scope of this chapter.

Inspect karabiners and slings regularly. Karabiner gates should open and close cleanly and smoothly. Check slings for signs of abrasion or cuts which could reduce their strength significantly.

Ice Axe Anchors

The axe can be used to give an acceptable form of belay in a wide range of snow conditions; generally the harder the snow the more secure the belay will be. The choice of method will depend both on the hardness of the snow and its structure. In nearly all circumstances a horizontal axe is to be preferred to a vertical one but before making a decision it is necessary to think carefully about how to take best advantage of the various layers within the snow cover.

HORIZONTAL AXE ANCHOR

The basic method is the horizontally buried ice-axe. First a slot is cut with the adze across the slope and to a depth of 20-30cm depending on snow conditions. A vertical slot from about one-third the way along is then cut downslope for about 2m. The upper end is the depth of the horizontal slot and it then tapers out towards the surface. It should be wide enough to take a sling which is attached towards the shaft of the axe with a clove hitch at about its balance point. This is roughly half-way in terms of surface area. The axe is then placed pick down in the horizontal slot with the sling in the vertical slot. The rope is belayed in the normal manner. Care must be taken to ensure that the sling is tied so that it pulls symmetrically on the axe and that the axe is placed hard against the front wall of the slot. It can also help to reduce swivelling if snow from above is packed into the horizontal slot round the axe, taking care not to disturb the structure of the snow below.

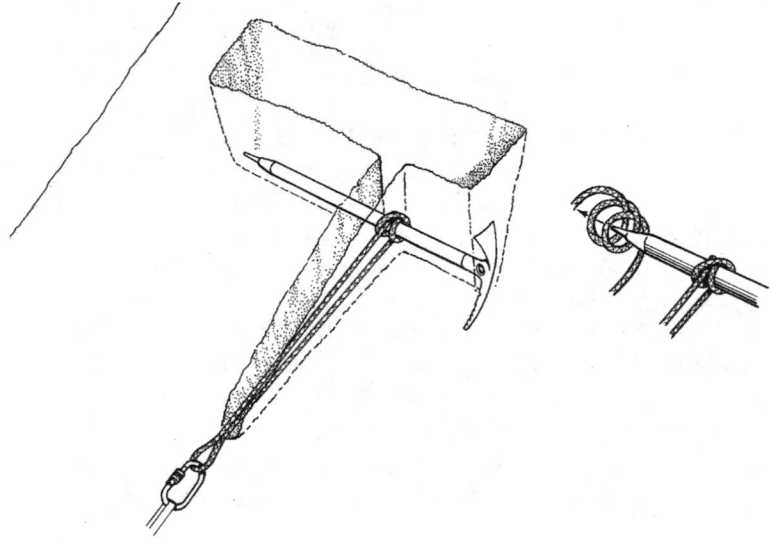

(Fig. 174) *Horizontal axe anchor.*

The axe is buried horizontally in the snow. The climbing rope or a sling is attached to the centre of the shaft using a clove hitch. Turn the clove hitch so that the knot is at the back of the axe, with the free ends wrapping round the shaft, one above and one below. This ensures that the knot will tighten if the anchor is loaded, and the sling is less likely to slip along the length of the axe shaft.

REINFORCED HORIZONTAL AXE

The horizontal axe can be reinforced by driving a second axe vertically into the snow immediately in front of the buried axe and through the sling. In this way any movement of the horizontal axe is resisted by the vertical one. This system works best where there is a layer of harder snow immediately above or below the horizontal axe.

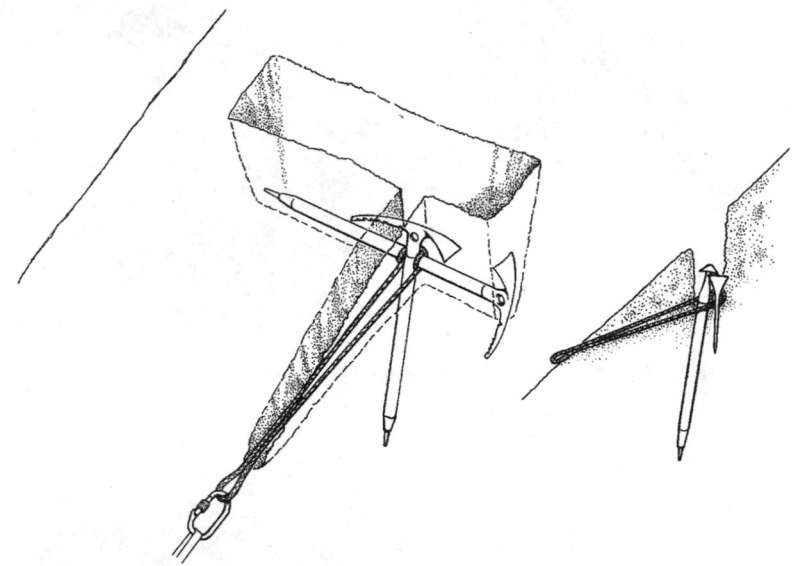

Fig. 175 *'Reinforced horizontal axe'. In this case the belay is to the horizontal axe.*

"T" AXE

The 'T' axe differs from the Reinforced Axe in that the rope or sling is attached to the vertical axe which is placed behind the horizontal one. The rope passes above the horizontal axe and down the slot to the belayer. It is important to make sure that the clove hitch is pushed as far down the shaft as it will go. This system is basically a vertical axe anchor reinforced near the surface by a horizontal axe or hammer or indeed any other appropriate object such as a walking pole. Its other advantage is that it is quick to set up and can be used where there is a firm layer to support the horizontal axe near the surface.

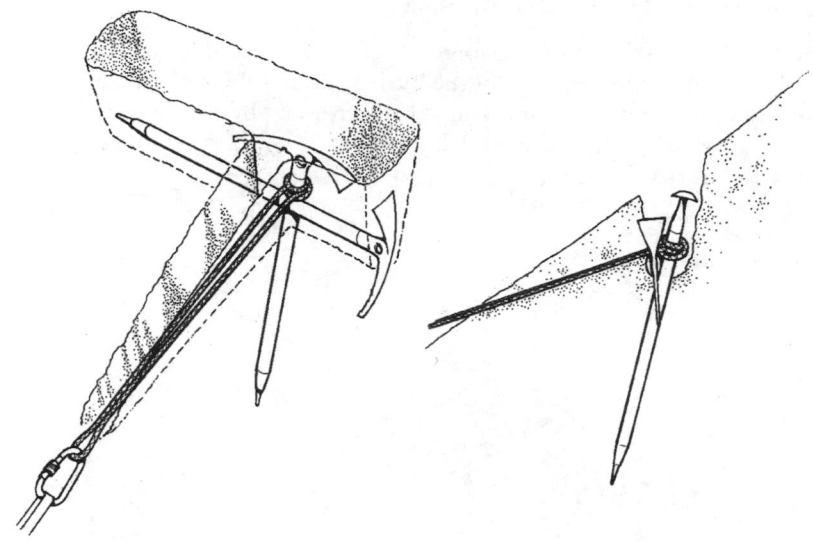

Fig. 176   **'T axe'. In this case the belay is to the vertical axe.**

VERTICAL AXE

This was the traditional, now largely discredited, method of belaying on snow. However, there are circumstances when the vertical axe anchor may be used to good effect. In the first place, the snow must be very hard, so hard in fact that the axe has to be stamped in. Secondly, it should be used as an indirect belay or as a back-up anchor, the climber taking the initial strain with a waist belay. Thirdly, the situation, exposure, run-out etc may justify a less than perfect anchor in the interests of speed if the consequences of a fall are not likely to be serious. As far as the mechanics of the belay are concerned it is important to see that the rope or sling is securely attached to the shaft of the axe at the surface of the snow, preferably with a clove hitch.

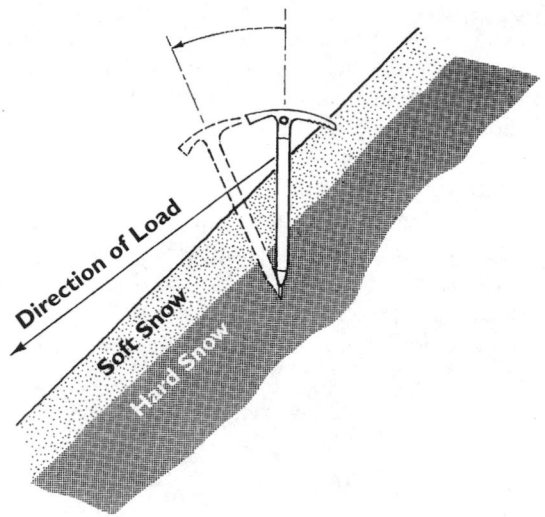

Fig. 177 · *A vertical axe embedded in typical snow cover has a tendency to pivot and break out in the softer surface layer.*

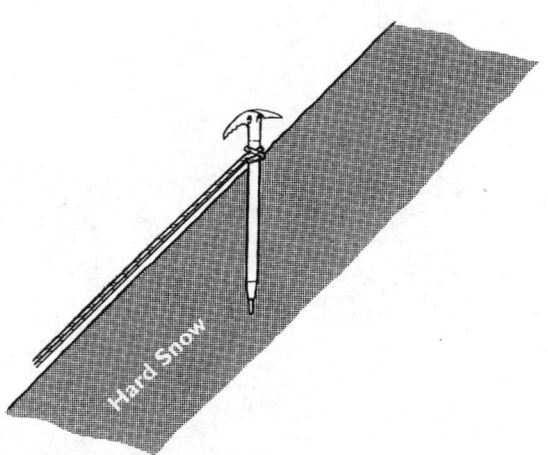

Fig. 178 · *Vertical axe anchor. Note that the rope is tied off at the snow surface.*

STANDING AXE BELAY

The Standing axe or Stomper belay is not suitable as a main anchor. It can be used to bring up a second in situations such as the top of a climb or on a straightforward snow slope where the full length of the axe can be pushed vertically into the snow. A locking karabiner is clipped into the eye in the axe head and the rope passed through this to the belayer who takes up a standing position facing outwards with one instep across the adze and the other across the pick. The rope is passed across the shoulder on the 'dead' side. Should a fall occur part of the load is taken by the axe and part is transmitted to the belayer causing downward pressure on the axe head which in turn increases its stability. This ingenious system needs to be practised thoroughly in a variety of situations.

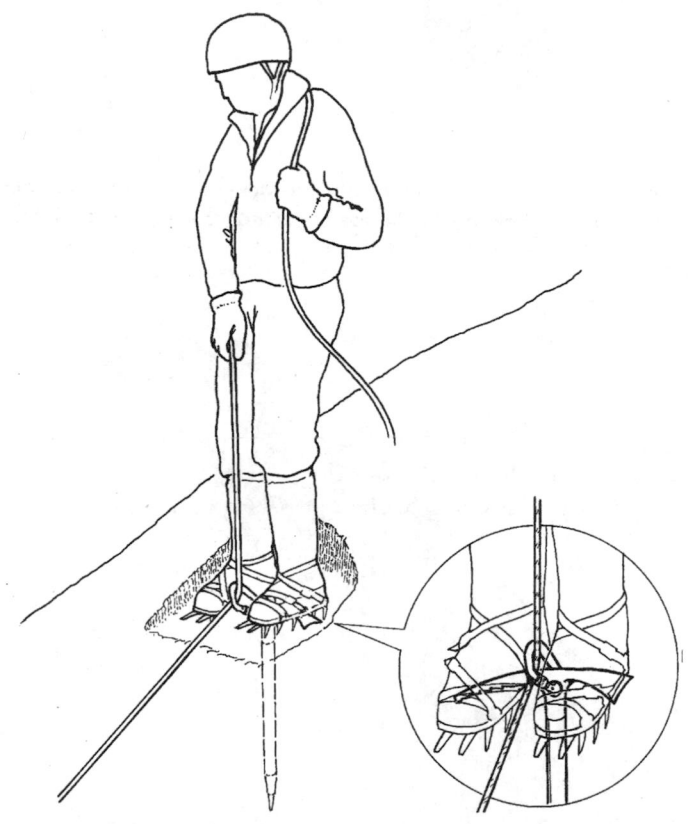

(Fig. 179) *Standing axe or Stomper belay.*

Dead Man Anchor

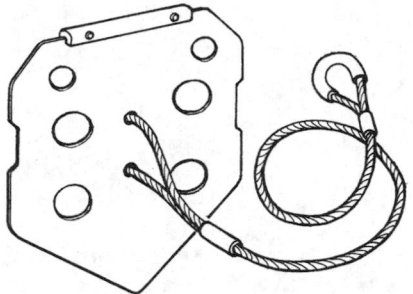

Fig. 180 · **Dead man.**

The 'dead man' shown in Fig 180 is a spade shaped alloy plate reinforced along the top with a wire or tape attached centrally. The principle is that the plate is embedded in the snow in such a way that its entire surface resists movement through the snow when a load is applied to the wire. This method has the merit of working in most kinds of snow, particularly in poorly consolidated snow where other methods offer little or no security. Careful placing of the dead man to avoid pulling out is absolutely vital and it must always be tested before use. This also has the effect of bedding the dead man in.

A horizontal slot should be cut in the snow at least 3m (10ft) above the stance, taking care to disturb the snow as little as possible in the immediate area. The dead man is inserted at the bottom of this slot in such a way that the plane of the plate makes an angle of approximately 40° with the snow surface. A convenient way to estimate this angle is to hold your ice axe at right angles to the slope just over the slot. Bisect this angle with the plate and then tilt it back a further 5° and push it home. Some ice axes have a lip near the spike and this can be used to tap the plate into the snow to a depth of at least 30cm (1ft). It is necessary to clear out a passage for the wire to prevent it hooking, as in Fig. . In this illustration a sudden load on the wire could jerk the dead man out of the snow.

The stance should be taken at least 3m (10ft) below the dead man. This will ensure that the internal angle between the plate and the wire does not exceed 50°. Clearly, a high stance will result in a dangerous increase in this angle. The climber belays to the dead man in the normal way, adopting a

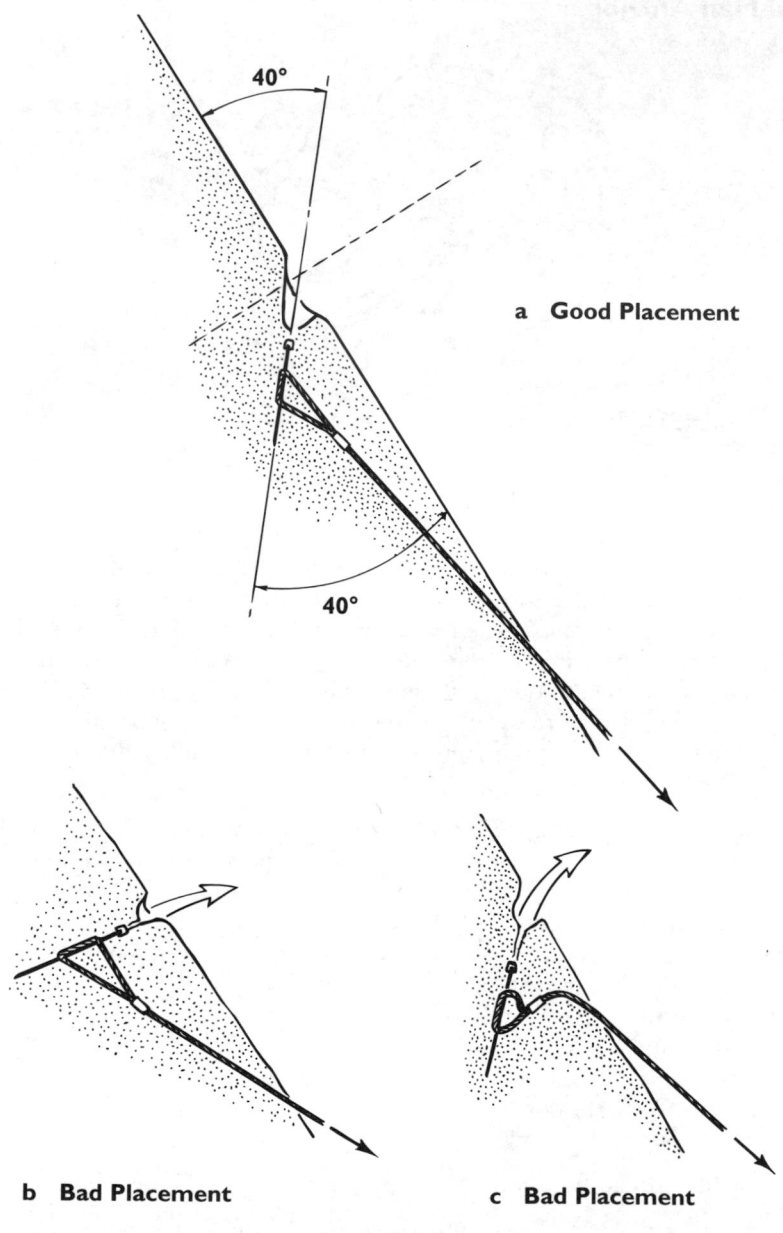

a   Good Placement

b   Bad Placement   c   Bad Placement

Fig. 181   *Good and bad placement of dead man.*

sitting position for maximum holding power, with the added benefit of reducing the dead man angle.

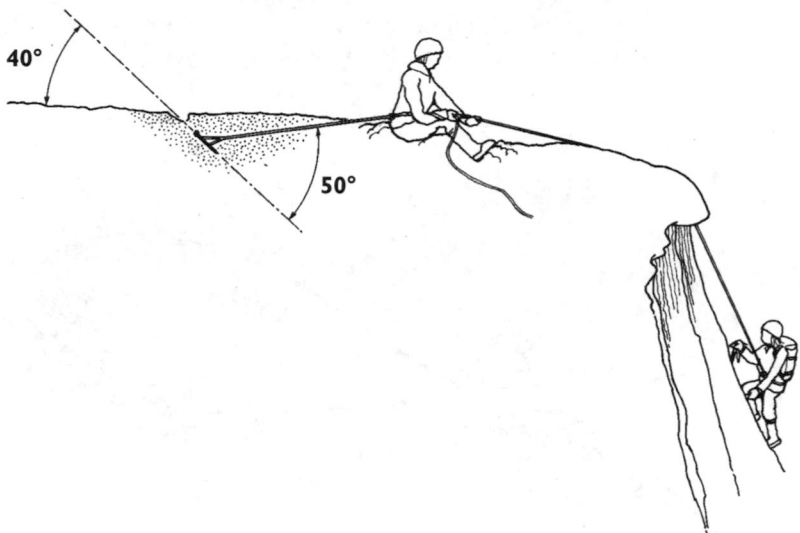

Fig. 182 *Horizontally placed dead man.*

Many winter climbs finish on flat ground, on a ridge, or at the edge of a plateau. It is often difficult to provide any satisfactory belay in such a situation. The dead man is just as efficient buried in a horizontal position as in any other and exactly the same rules apply for placement. The stance must be well back from any cornice and that means that the dead man may be as much as 10m (33ft) back from the edge. (Fig 182)

Since the dead man depends for its successful operation on the cohesion of the snow, it is particularly important that this is not disturbed in any way. Special care must be taken in slabby snow not to fracture the whole retaining mass of snow. The general rule is that if the snow has good natural cohesion, (e.g. old snow, wind slab, wet slab), disturb it as little as possible, but if, on the other hand, it lacks cohesion, e.g. powder snow, wet snow, then the whole area should be well stamped down.

Exercise great care in placing a dead man in snow which has a layered structure or icy crusts. Under load the dead man may penetrate into these layers resulting in failure. In this situation a 'T' axe may provide a superior anchor.

Snow Bollard

There is really no foolproof method of belaying in very soft snow. A well padded snow bollard is probably the closest you will get to finding a satisfactory anchor. It is a technique which is applicable to a wide range of snow conditions and requires little in the way of equipment.

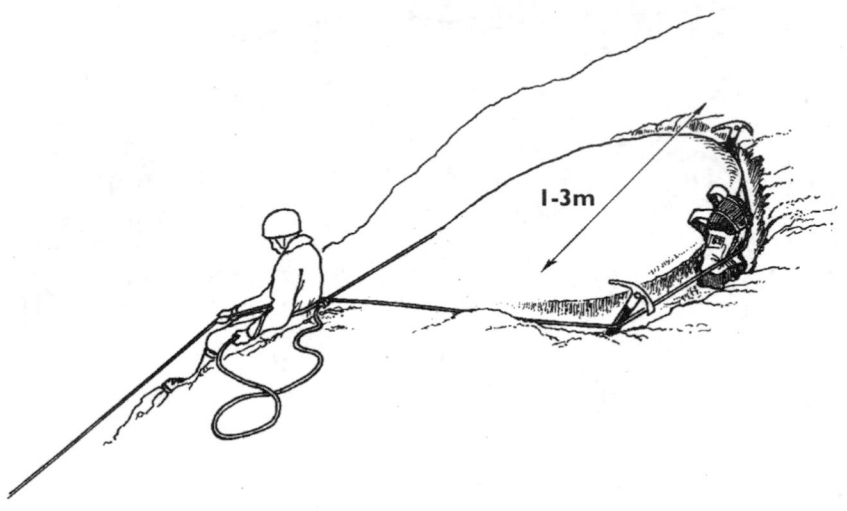

Fig. 183 **Snow Bollard. The channel should be cut so that the bollard is mushroom shaped.**

The size of the bollard is determined by the hardness of the snow and will vary from about 1m in hard snow to 3m in soft. In plan it should be horseshoe shaped rather than balloon shaped. In other words it should have a wide throat which should be left untrampled, particularly in slabby snow. The channel should be approximately 30cm (1ft) deep but this too will vary with the nature of the snow. The rope does tend to cut in so it helps to pad the back of the bollard with your rucksack and spare clothes. Any extra ice axes can be planted to provide additional support. If the air temperature is cold enough the groove may be warmed with the hand so that melting and refreezing reinforces the surface. In layered snow try to ensure that the rope rests in the middle of the firmest layer. A sitting stance is generally best taken well below the bollard and the rope belayed around the waist in the conventional manner.

Belaying on Ice

Taken in isolation this is one of the most specialised aspects of mountaineering demanding a great deal of skill and experience on the part of the climber. Ice can be found at some time on every mountain area in the British Isles and not just on graded climbs. The mountain walker must know how to cope with a short ice pitch on an otherwise straightforward ascent and must know how to handle ice glazed rocks, how to negotiate an icy section of ridge or an icy descent when late afternoon frost has turned slush into a sheet of ice. Ice is a frequent and not always predictable element of the winter scene.

Before the invention of ice screws and pitons one of the favoured methods of belaying on ice was to take a direct belay to the pick of the axe driven into the ice. Nowadays such flimsy protection would be seen for what it is, a psychological belay of the most misleading kind. Occasionally, a natural anchor can be found - the base of a giant icicle, a thread belay through ice frozen rocks, a boss or flake of ice which can be fashioned into a suitable anchor. Care is needed in working on these natural features not to fracture them through over-enthusiastic chopping with the axe.

ICE BOLLARD

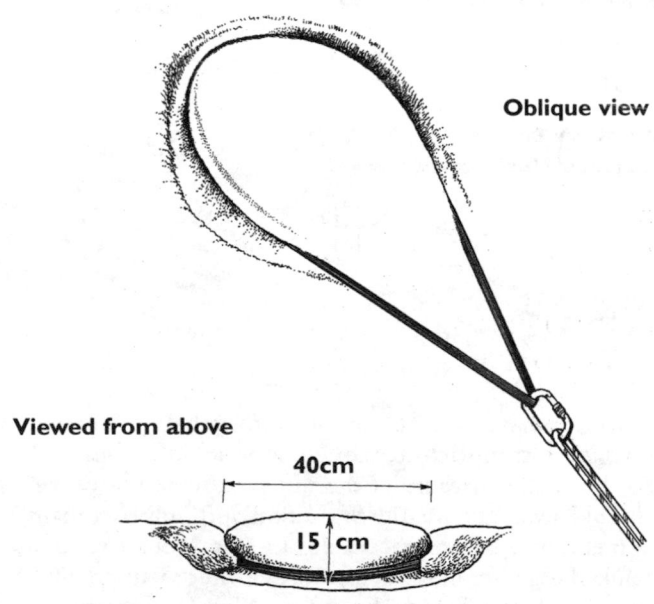

Oblique view

Viewed from above

40cm

15 cm

(Fig. 184) *Ice Bollard.*

This is one of the most effective anchors on ice and its only disadvantage is that it takes time as well as skill to make. For a single difficult pitch or an abseil the security it brings to the passage may be well worth the effort. The ice bollard is really a small edition of the snow bollard, measuring approximately 40cm (15ins) across and cut to a depth of 15cm (6ins), with a pronounced mushroom shape at the sides and back to ensure that the rope does not ride off. Choose a site where the natural formation of the ice, such as a bulge or change of slope, makes it easier to cut. The stance must be taken well below so as to apply a downward pull on the back of the anchor. Once again care must be exercised in cutting out the shape. If there is the slightest sign of fracturing, discard the bollard and start again.

ICE SCREWS

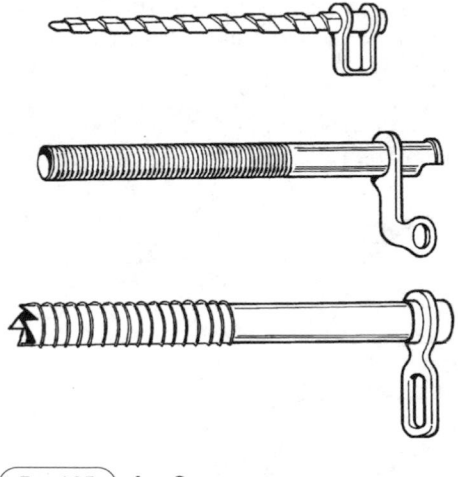

a   **Solid shaft.**
     Drive in, screw out.

b   **Tubular shaft.**
     Screw in, screw out.

c   **Tubular shaft.**
     Screw in, screw out.

Fig. 185   *Ice Screws.*

In general ice screws do not make satisfactory belays, not because of any defects in design or manufacture, though undoubtedly some makes are better than others, but rather because of the inherent weakness of ice. Ice screws therefore should always be used with caution and only as a main belay when alternative methods are not practicable. In this event two or more screws should be linked together in series to afford greater security. There are 2 basic types of ice screw: 'screw in – screw out' and 'drive in – screw out'. There are, of course, many variations within these broad categories and no one screw performs well in every type of ice. For this reason most climbers carry a selection, depending on the climb and the prevailing conditions.

The most versatile type of ice screw is the tubular variety which extracts a core as it is screwed into the ice. A shallow depression makes an ideal site for an ice screw which should be started in a small hole made with the pick. The screw should be tapped in with a hammer at an angle of about 10° above the perpendicular to the slope until the thread catches and it begins to turn as it is hit. It can then be screwed home using the pick or hammer as a lever if need be. The lug should lie flush with the surface but if this is not possible then a short sling should be tied to the shaft with a clove hitch hard against the surface. (Fig. 188) This greatly reduces the levering effect of a load applied to the screw.

Experience in using ice screws and pitons will reveal their limitations. The drive in-screw out type are prone to shatter the ice on the way in, while they can also obstinately refuse to screw out. In warm conditions the ice in contact with the screw can melt, thus destroying its anchorage. In cold conditions the core extracted by a tubular screw can freeze inside making it impossible to use again until it is cleared by warming the screw and pushing out the core. 'Shattering' or 'dinner plating' are two fairly common mishaps when placing screws or pitons in ice. If this happens take it out and try again somewhere else.

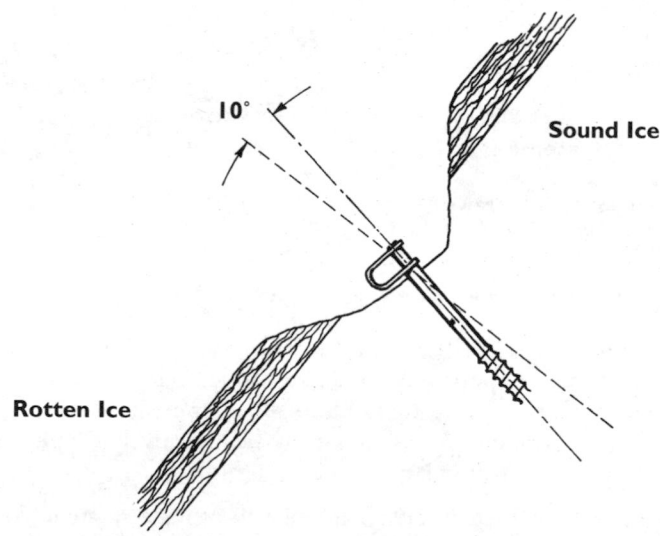

10°

Sound Ice

Rotten Ice

Fig. 186   *Good placement for tubular ice screw. Clear away rotten ice.*

375

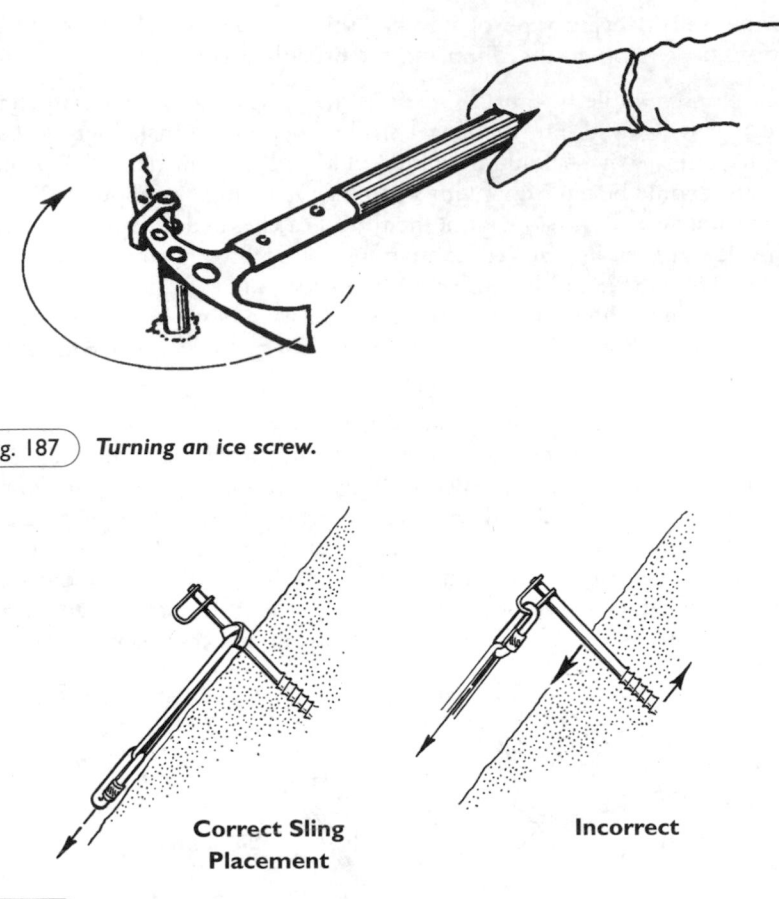

Fig. 187 *Turning an ice screw.*

Correct Sling Placement

Incorrect

Fig. 188 *Attachment to ice screws.*

ROCK BELAYS, CHOCKS AND PITONS

There are, in fact, very few winter climbs that do not have rock somewhere around which may offer an opportunity to take a natural belay. Rock belays are generally to be preferred. With the additional equipment likely to be carried in winter, slings, karabiners, nuts etc., it can be a relatively simple and speedy matter to construct a rock belay.

A sling can be used with a screw-gated karabiner to provide an anchor for the main belay. The anchor itself might be a rock spike or better still a thread of some kind where the sling is threaded through a natural hole in the rock or perhaps round a stone jammed in a crack. A threaded anchor is the most effective of all because it can withstand a pull from most directions. The 'nuts, chocks, and hexes', so much a part of the modern climber's hardware, are really a development from this basic idea. They are essentially artificial chockstones, of ingenious design and they come in every conceivable shape and size. The principle of operation is simple enough, but there are one or two guidelines for their use.

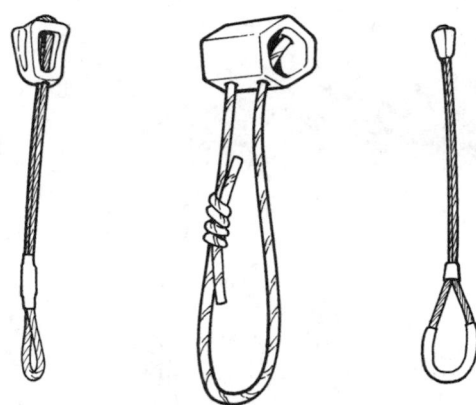

Fig. 189 *Different types of artificial chockstones, with wire, tape or rope slings attached.*

The chock may be attached to a wire, tape or rope sling. Wired chocks are easy to insert and remove and of course for its diameter, wire is much stronger than rope. However, being stiff, it can be lifted out by the movement of the climbing rope. Wire resists cutting and for this reason is preferred when there are any sharp edges around.

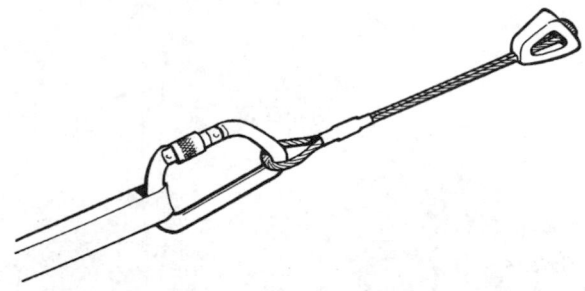

Fig. 190 *Clipping in to a wired nut.*

Chock slings are usually short and it may be necessary to extend them by adding another sling. Always link to a wired chock with a karabiner. The karabiner should be clipped in such a way that the gate will not be inadvertently opened by contact with the rock or the climbing rope. This usually means that the gate should be on the side away from the rock, with the opening at the lower end. The ideal chock placement is at a constriction in a crack where the expected load on the sling will tend to pull the chock further into the constriction. There is a considerable art in placing chocks and many ingenious placements can be devised.

Fig. 191 *A hex in a perfect placement in a vertical crack.*

A 'Friend' is an adjustable jamming device using spring-loaded cams to hold it in position in a crack. It is particularly important to place it so that the expected load is in line with the shaft of the 'Friend'.

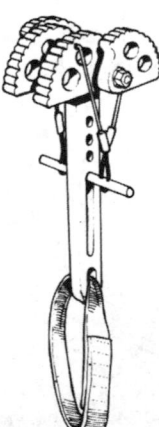

Fig. 192 *A 'Friend'.*
A system of spring - loaded cams for jamming in cracks.

ROCK PITONS

Today's climbers tend to limit the use of rock pitons to artificial rock climbs or winter routes. Modern aid equipment is such that chocks and friends and other devices yet to be invented can be used in situations which have hitherto required pitons. Even with the most careful placement and removal afterwards a piton leaves a scar and that is surely a matter of some concern. Nevertheless, from time to time there are likely to be situations where a piton is the only satisfactory anchor and this is particularly so on snow and ice climbs.

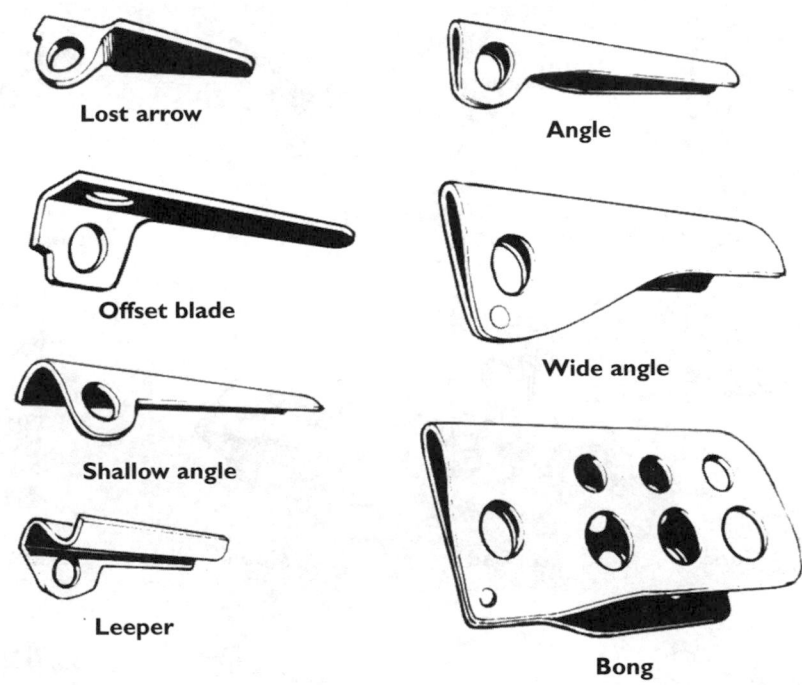

Lost arrow

Angle

Offset blade

Wide angle

Shallow angle

Leeper

Bong

Fig. 193 *Different types of pitons. A karabiner clips into the eye.*

Most modern pitons are of the chrome-molybdenum hard steel type and can be classified into three main groups: blades, angles, and those with a Z section called 'leepers'. Correct placement is very important to allow for the maximum mechanical advantage and torque. The piton should be placed in the crack to about half to two-thirds of its length by hand, then hammered home. The eye should be flush with the rock. If it is not, the piton should be tied-off with a short loop of tape using a clove hitch. It may also have to be tied-off if there is any possibility of the karabiner acting as a lever against the rock. Do not overdrive pitons. Both the resistance to the hammer and the rising ring of the piton as it is struck gives an indication of when to stop.

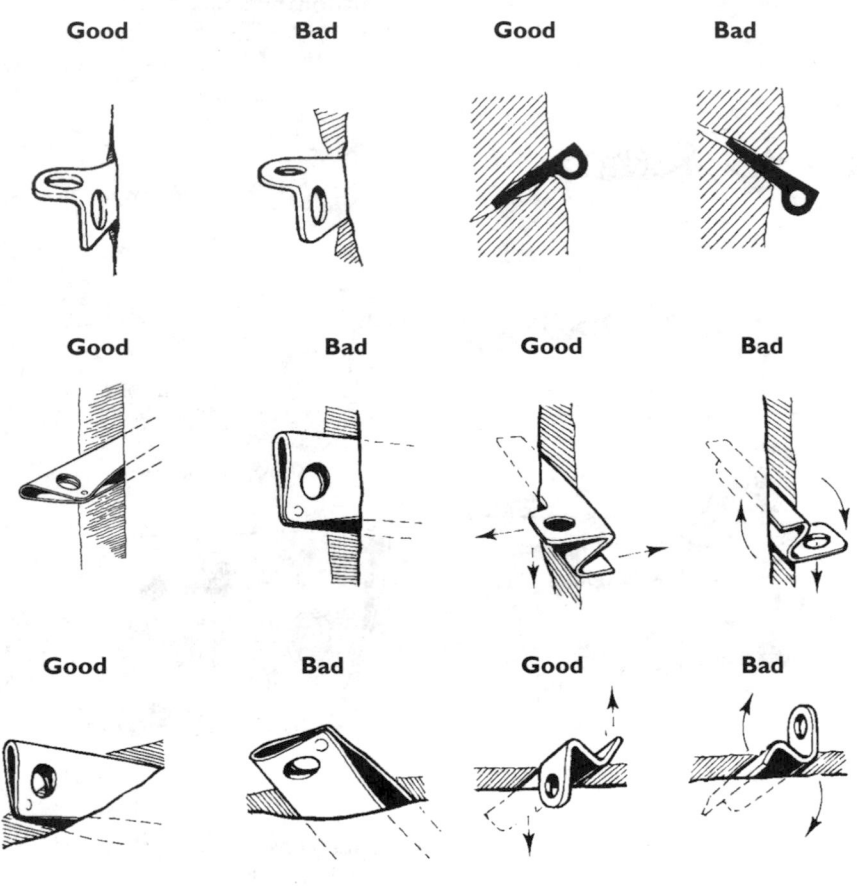

Fig. 194   *Good and bad placement of pitons.*

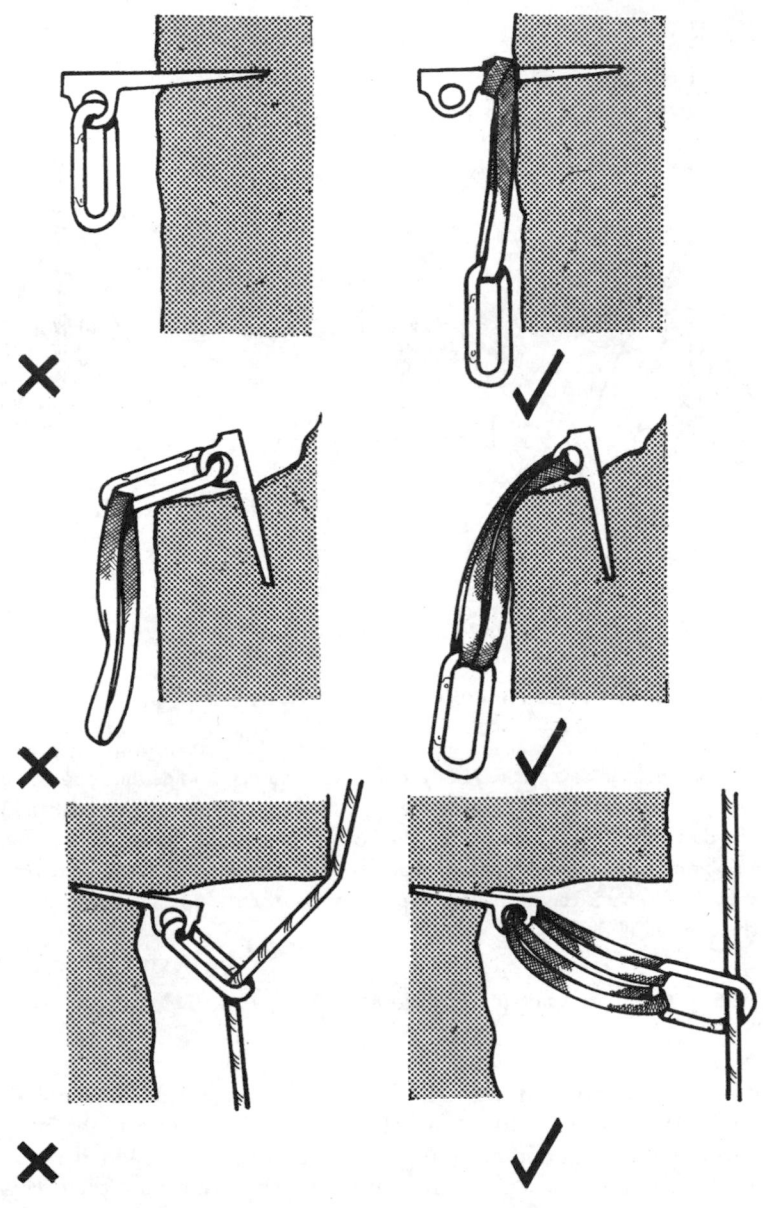

Fig. 195 *Some Do's and Don'ts when tying on to pitons.*

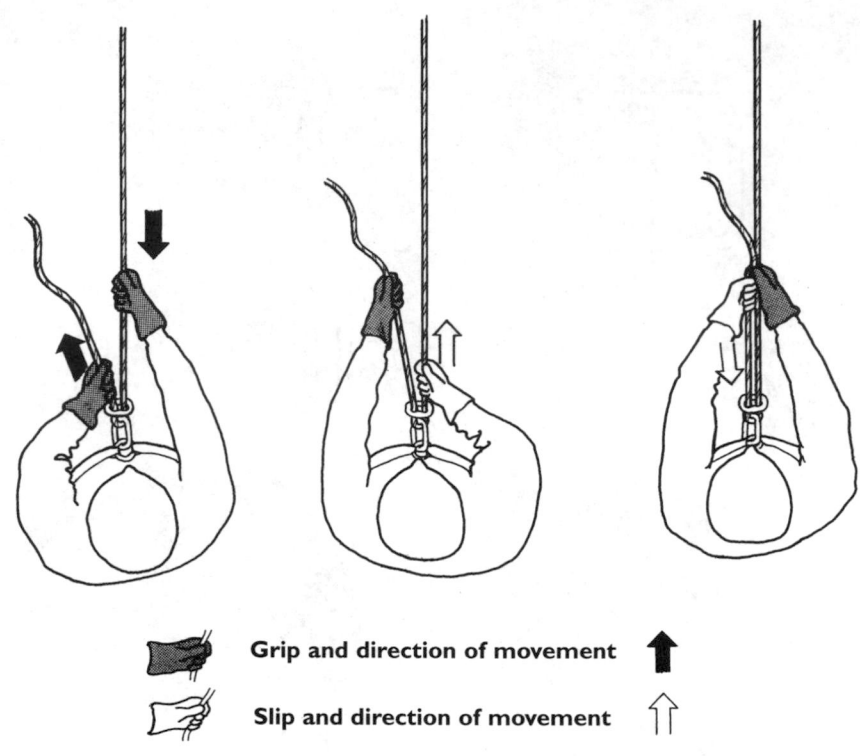

Grip and direction of movement

Slip and direction of movement

The live hand pulls in towards the body while the dead hand holds the rope and pulls out away from the body, thus drawing the rope through the plate. The live hand is then slid down the live rope away from the body until it is just past the dead hand, at which point it grips both ropes which allows the dead hand to be slid back towards the body. The cycle is repeated. It is important that the dead hand remains in contact with the rope at all times.

(Fig. 196) *Taking in, using a Belay Plate.*

In many situations in winter, belay plates may be a suitable, or even preferable, alternative to the waist belay. To use the plate a bight of rope is taken through the slot and put into a screw–gate karabiner which is attached to the front of the harness. As in the waist belay the live rope is the one which goes directly to the person climbing. To pay out the rope the live hand simply pulls the rope through the plate while the dead hand keeps a grip of the dead rope. This is easier if the ropes are held parallel.

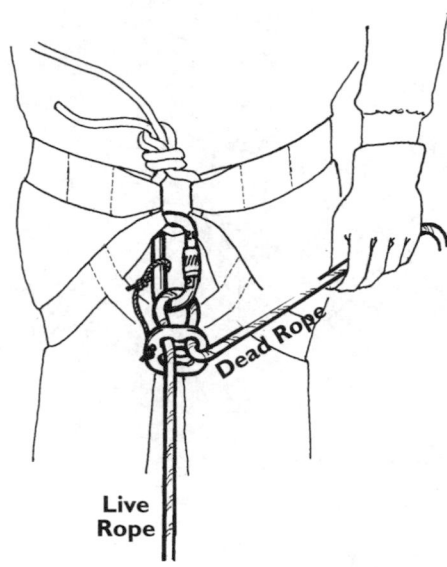

Live
Rope

To brake the dead hand is pulled back towards the side of the waist at the same time allowing the rope to run so that the braking effect is applied gradually.

(Fig. 197) *Belay plates.*

The advantage of the plate is that it is convenient to use and very safe. It saves the trouble of putting the rope over the rucksack as in the waist belay. However, it can be awkward to use with an iced up rope and it takes a lot of practice to let the rope slide intentionally through the plate in the event of a fall to give a dynamic arrest. For this reason it should only be used when the anchor is absolutely sound and capable of withstanding the sudden impact of a fall.

The figure of eight descendeur can also be used in this manner.

The Friction or Italian Hitch is a simple method of providing a dynamic belay without the need for a Belay Plate. All that is required is a locking karabiner, preferably of the pear shaped variety and a rope. The technique should not be used for belaying a lead climber. It could however prove useful in providing support to individuals descending an awkward icy step or snow slope.

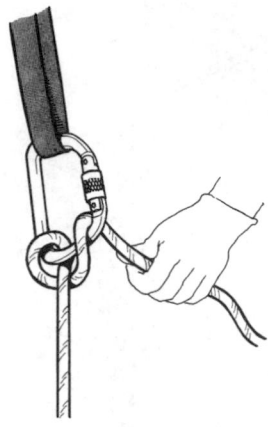

Fig. 198   *Friction Hitch.*

MOVING TOGETHER

If you are the most experienced member of a party it will be your responsibility to decide when to rope up. If there is a risk of serious injury to anyone as a result of a slip then it is certainly time to put on the rope, but you must be quite clear about the level of security it offers. Moving together roped is a recognised technique on glaciers and on terrain when it is possible to respond quickly to an emergency by improvising a direct belay or by using one of the belaying methods particularly suited to such circumstances. There are of course many expeditions when the rope is required intermittently and it may be sensible and save a lot of time to keep it on for the easy in-between sections.

The early use of the rope and practise in rope handling when moving together using the rope to provide an additional element of security on technically easy ground is a technique which is particularly suited to winter conditions. The short rope techniques described on pages 181, 182 are relevant. The consequences of a simple slip on quite easy terrain can be serious. A short rope from the leader gives a novice the confidence to adopt a upright body position and provides instant support in the event of a slip. Good judgement is needed on the part of the leader to decide when it is appropriate to use the rope in this way.

16

Snow and Avalanches

Mountains and Snow = Avalanches. It seems a simple enough equation, but it is one which has taxed some of the best scientific minds in those countries which possess the two basic ingredients of mountains and snow. Avalanche forecasting is about probabilities and it is very difficult to say that a particular slope will avalanche at a predicted time.

Whether the forecast is being made for public dissemination or by a mountaineer for his own on-the-spot guidance, information derived from a variety of sources is used. Direct observation of recent weather and snow conditions is necessary, along with an understanding of the mechanics of avalanche release.

Avalanches are common in the hill areas of Scotland, England and Wales and are not unknown in Ireland. The winter mountaineer would be unwise, who did not take cognisance of this. All the features described in this section have been observed in Scotland, although in differing proportion to the situation in Alpine regions.

SNOW CRYSTALS

Snow crystals form in the atmosphere. Although the basic structure of the crystal is hexagonal, the detailed form is infinitely varied and is determined by the temperature and degree of vapour saturation at the time of formation. Much has been written about the process of crystallisation, but from a practical point of view it is sufficient to know that the crystal form will have a profound effect on the subsequent changes which take place within the snow cover and on its propensity for avalanching. The behaviour of a layer of hail, for example, in which the individual crystals lack any cohesion, will be markedly different from a layer of stellar crystals whose delicate and complex structure is highly sensitive to change. Some of the main families of crystals are illustrated in Fig.199.

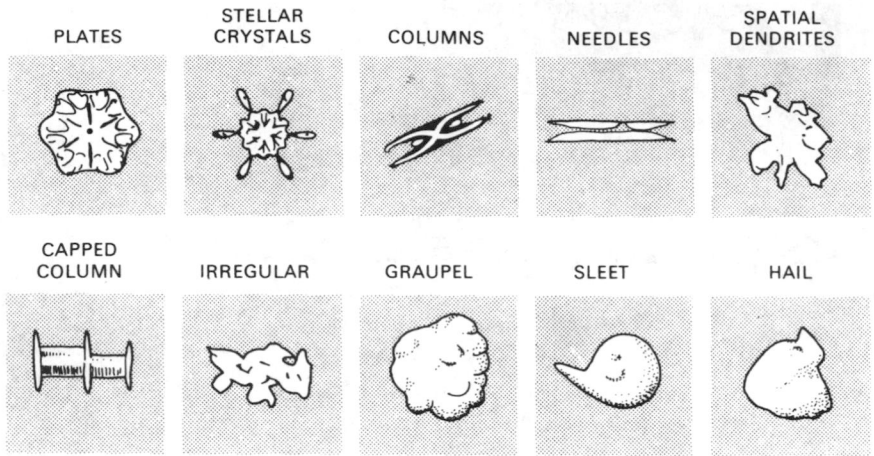

(Fig. 199) *The basic forms of solid precipitation.*

Metamorphism

No sooner have they formed than snow crystals start to undergo certain changes. These may take place as the snowflake falls through the atmosphere, drastically altering the original shape, such as by the addition of rime as the crystal falls through a moist layer, or they may take place as the snow accumulates on the ground. The nature and speed of these changes, which are collectively known as metamorphism, is determined by the prevailing temperature and pressure.

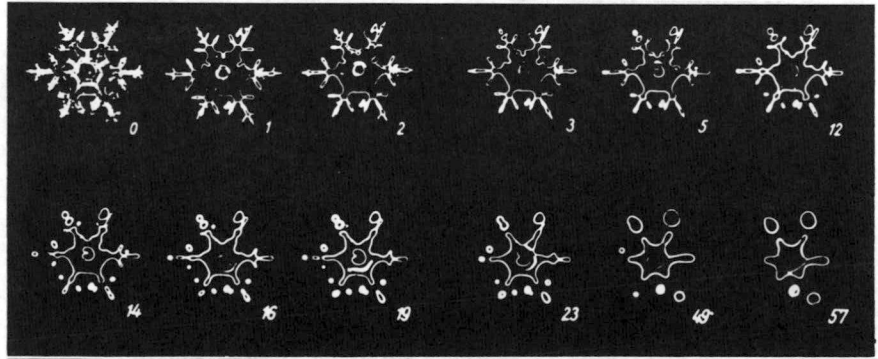

(Fig. 200) *Isothermal metamorphism in a single stellar snow crystal maintained at a constant temperature of - 5°C for period of 57 days. Note the gradual simplification and rounding of the crystal form.*

ISOTHERMAL(IT) METAMORPHISM

In the normal course of events this leads to a simplification of crystal structure with the establishment of strong bonds between individual crystals and a shrinking of the whole snow layer. This process is known as 'Isothermal (IT) Metamorphism' (formerly called 'Equitemperature (ET) Metamorphism' and in older textbooks, 'Destructive Metamorphism'). Its net effect is commonly known as 'settling' and it is accelerated as snow temperature rises towards melting point. It is clearly a process which has a stabilising influence on the snow pack resulting ultimately in the formation of a single compact layer of homogeneous ice crystals.

KINETIC GROWTH (KG) METAMORPHISM

Under certain conditions, usually in cold regions or at high altitudes where there is intense radiative heat loss from the snow surface, a steep temperature gradient exists between the relatively warm base layers in contact with the ground and the much colder surface layers exposed to the atmosphere. Under the influence of this gradient, water vapour moves upwards through the snow cover recrystallising at favourable localities within the snowpack.

The end product of this process of 'Kinetic Growth' (formerly called 'Temperature Gradient (TG) Metamorphism' and in older textbooks, 'Constructive Metamorphism') is depth hoar (KG crystals). Such layers are extremely fragile and may give rise to devastating avalanches when overloaded beyond their strength. Furthermore, because they are buried deep within the snow pack they can only be detected by digging a snow pit to ground level or by careful examination of the early winter weather records in order to identify those conditions which encourage their growth. In Scotland, KG crystals are less uncommon than previously believed and may sometimes be observed, particularly under surface crust in thin snowpacks early in the winter. However, avalanches running on layers of these crystals appear uncommon in Scotland, although the weakening effect of vapour loss upon layers of snow lower down in the snowpack, is believed to have been the cause of some incidents.

(Fig. 201)

A single crystal of depth hoar magnified twenty times, the product of Kinetic Growth (KG) Metamorphism. Note the hexagonal symmetry and cup like crystal form with characteristic striations.

MELT/FREEZE METAMORPHISM

In spring, the temperature of the whole snow cover may be just below freezing level. Because of radiation heat loss at night, the snow alternately freezes and thaws and this gives rise to the third process of change known as melt/freeze metamorphism. The effect of this is that the larger crystals grow at the expense of the smaller and that there is a very marked difference in the strength of the snow, depending on whether it is in the melt or freeze phase of the cycle. The danger lies in the melt phase when water (rain or melt water) percolates through the snow till it reaches the ground or an impermeable crust. Flowing at this level, it may completely undermine the anchorage of the snow to the underlayer, whether that be the ground surface or older snow, and provide an effective lubricant for any subsequent avalanche. It is important to distinguish this type of occurrence from the avalanche which results from a rapid thaw following a fall of fresh snow. In this case there is a genuine melting of the crystal fabric which precipitates a wet surface slide. A fall of wet snow turning to rain will obviously accentuate this danger. The effect of rain on old snow is less easy to predict, but avalanches may often be expected within one hour of the onset of heavy rain and up to 24 hours thereafter.

These then are the three fundamental processes of metamorphism which determine the nature of the snowpack and which give rise to the infinite variations of its physical and mechanical properties.

SURFACE HOAR

Feathery crystals of surface hoar may form on cold, clear nights, on any exposed surface, including the snow surface. They do not at this stage constitute a danger, but when covered by subsequent snowfall or drifting, may remain as a microscopically thin, but very fragile layer for some days. The fatal avalanche accident in Coire Cas of Cairngorm on 31.12.85, ran on a partly metamorphosed layer of surface hoar.

Surface hoar crystals are formed on cold, clear nights, when emission of long-wave radiation permits the snow surface to become cooler than the atmosphere. As may be seen from Fig 202, conditions of high relative humidity favour rapid crystal growth.

The time taken for buried surface hoar to stabilise is mainly a function of temperature and whereas in a thawing snowpack, it may be assumed that any risk it poses will decline very rapidly, in suitably cold conditions, its evolution may be similar to that of depth hoar.

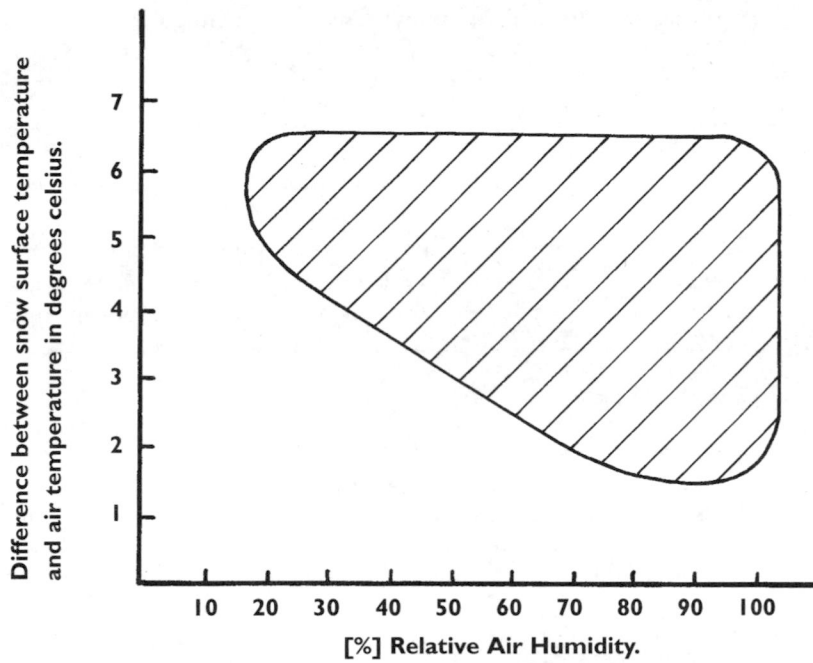

Fig. 202 *The range of conditions favourable for surface hoar development. Note that the formation of surface hoar requires that the snow surface temperature should be colder than the air temperature. (After H. Goblen).*

SNOWFALL

What is it that causes snow to avalanche? Well, first of all there has to be enough snow. The more there is and the faster it accumulates the more likely it is to avalanche and the larger the avalanche will be. Even 25cm (10in.) of snow can form an impressive slide. Most avalanches occur during or immediately after a heavy fall of snow, so this is a time to be particularly careful in the mountains. Evidence suggests that the rate of precipitation is as important as the total amount of snow which falls in a single storm. Precipitation intensities in excess of 2mm/hr (water equivalent) are usually regarded as hazardous. This is roughly equivalent to a fall of 2cm of fresh snow per hour. It will be appreciated that precipitation intensity is a measure of the rate at which a slope is loaded. New snow adds to the burden on the layers below and this can cause a failure in them. Indeed, the most common avalanche trigger is a fall of fresh snow.

The correlation between new snowfall and avalanching can be seen in the following figures from Switzerland:

New Snow Added in 3 Days	Observed Avalanches
Up to 10cm	Rare avalanches, mostly of loose snow.
10–30cm	Very occasional slabs, frequent sloughs (loose snow avalanches).
30–50cm	Frequent slabs on slopes 35°.
50–80cm	Widespread slabs on slopes down to 25°. (De Quervain, 1975)

ANGLE OF SLOPE

The slope must also be sufficiently steep to allow the snow to slide. Generally speaking, the steeper the slope, the more likely it is to avalanche, but on very steep slopes, say over 60°, the snow rarely gets a chance to accumulate, so avalanches on such slopes are infrequent. The most dangerous slopes are therefore those of intermediate angle, between 30°–45°.

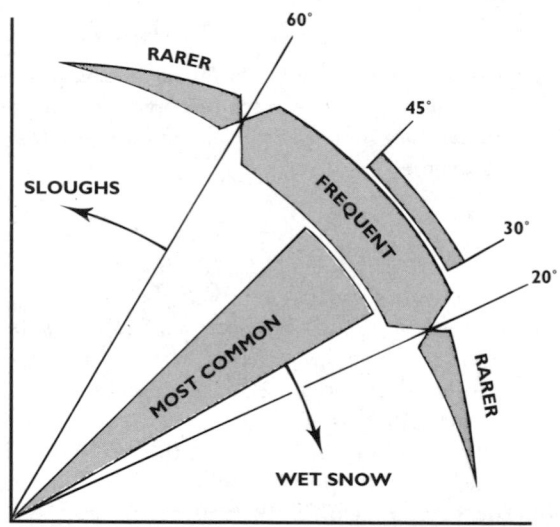

(Fig. 203) *The frequency of avalanches in relation to slope angle.*

Avalanches occur most frequently on slopes between 30 and 45 degrees. However, some of the most devastating avalanches can occur when slopes of lower angle do avalanche, due to the great depth of snow accumulation possible on these slopes.

STRENGTH v STRESS

These two factors of weight of snow and angle of slope are the main stress factors tending to move the snow downhill. They are resisted by the strength of the snow which, in simple terms, can be regarded as a function of the cohesion of the individual crystals and the adhesion of the various layers to each other and to the surface of the ground below. Theoretically, at least, when the stress factors exceed the strength of the snow, failure will occur. In practice affairs are a good deal more complex. Providing the overloading is not too sudden the snow may adjust by internal deformation (creep) or by the sliding of the whole snow layer along the ground (glide). These phenomena are well seen in the spring when the whole snow cover may become buckled and warped as a result of the plastic response of the snow to downslope pressure. It is the absence of such a response which allows the tension to build up to the point where slab fracture is the only way of restoring equilibrium to the system.

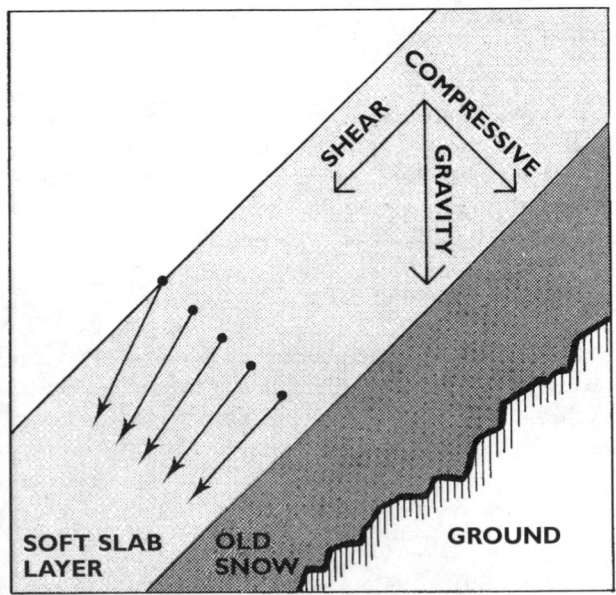

(Fig. 204) *The forces at work in an inclined slab of snow.*

The force of gravity can be resolved into shear and compressive components.
When shear stress exceeds shear strength slab failure may occur. In response to shear pressure the snow creeps and glides downslope. The higher the temperature the more rapid the deformation. The arrows represent the movement of a snow crystal at different depths within the snow layer.

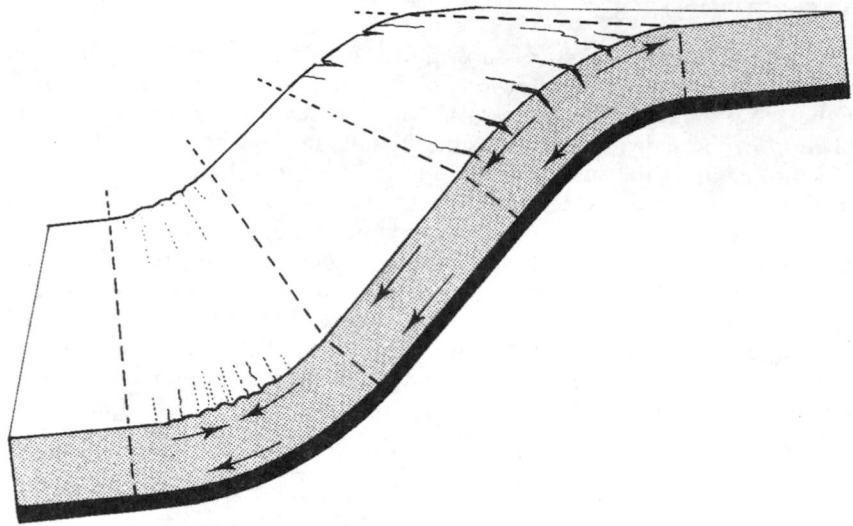

Fig. 205 *The tendency for the snow to creep and glide downhill under the influence of gravity creates an area of compression at the bottom of the slope where it is concave and an area of tension at the top where it is convex. It is in the convex part of the slope that an avalanche is most likely to be released.*

Types of Avalanche

An avalanche is a complex dynamic phenomenon which is not easily pigeon-holed into one category or another. Many of the larger ones defy classification comprising, as they do, a series of consecutive events each one triggered by its predecessor and involving one layer after another until the whole snow cover could be on the move. Nevertheless, it is possible to describe most avalanches by reference to a set of five criteria. This simple system, recognised internationally, is illustrated in Fig 206.

Thus, a particular avalanche might be described as 'unconfined, dry, surface slab avalanche, flowing'. Within this system it is possible to identify a number of recurring types which merit some further consideration.

LOOSE, DRY SNOW AVALANCHES (SLOUGHS)

These occur when new snow crystals lose cohesion due to rounding of crystals by the process of isothermal metamorphism. In very cold weather

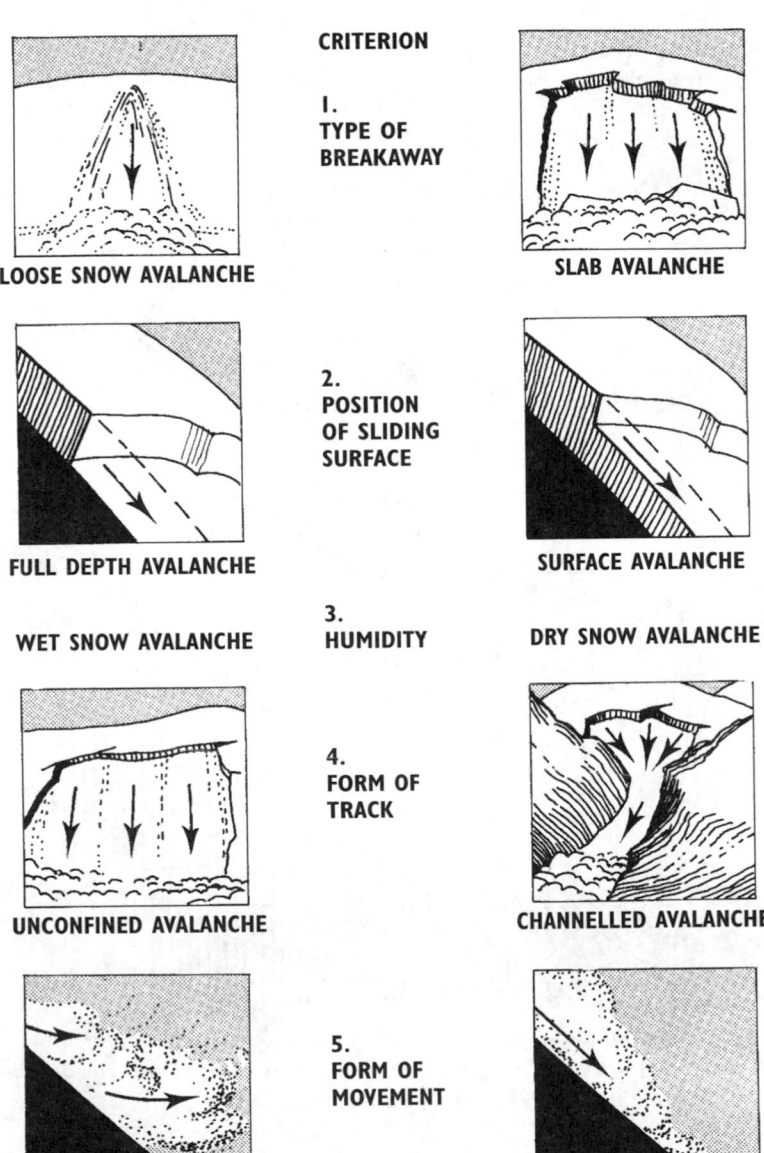

CRITERION

1.
TYPE OF
BREAKAWAY

LOOSE SNOW AVALANCHE

SLAB AVALANCHE

2.
POSITION
OF SLIDING
SURFACE

FULL DEPTH AVALANCHE

SURFACE AVALANCHE

WET SNOW AVALANCHE

3.
HUMIDITY

DRY SNOW AVALANCHE

4.
FORM OF
TRACK

UNCONFINED AVALANCHE

CHANNELLED AVALANCHE

5.
FORM OF
MOVEMENT

AIRBORNE POWDER

FLOWING AVALANCHE

Fig. 206 *Avalanche classification system. It should be noted that intermediate types are common, particularly with regard to form of movement where mixed motion avalanches are prevalent.*

with clear skies, particularly on north facing slopes, true "powder" snow may form by an accelerated vapour loss and rounding of crystals due to high gradient metamorphism in the soft surface layers. In these circumstances, avalanche risk may persist for considerable periods.

These avalanches are characterised by single-point release. They commonly occur up to three days after recent snowfall and may be quite large. Their motion is generally flowing at speeds up to 65-70 kph (40 mph). When this figure is exceeded, airborne motion may occur.

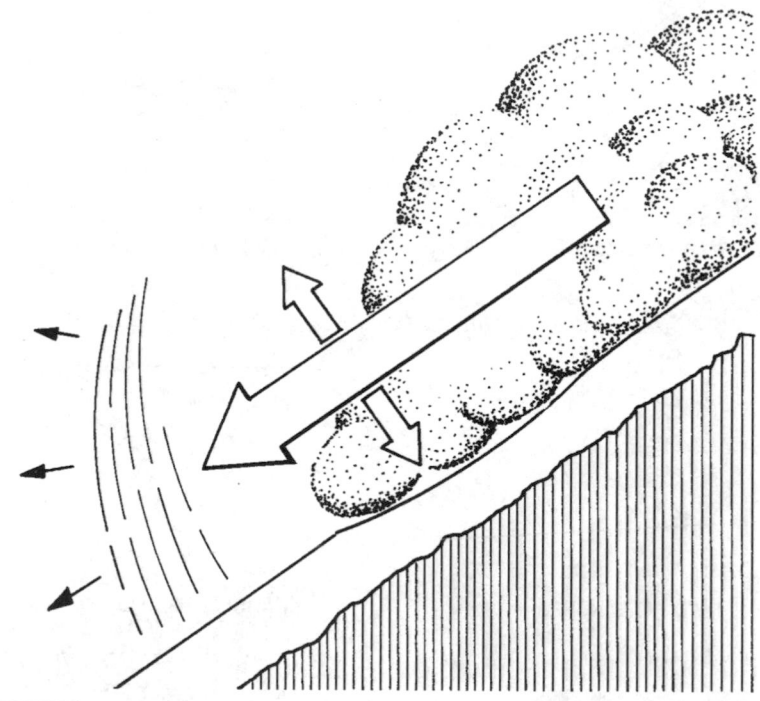

Fig. 207 *A large airborne powder avalanche may cause impact pressures from 5 to 50 tons/m2. The expanding snow cloud may travel at speeds up to 125m/sec (280 mph) and is preceded by a powerful air blast.*

As little as 20cm (8 inches) of snow in the starting zone can pose a threat although, as mentioned previously, the precipitation intensity is also of critical importance. As a rough guide, an accumulation rate in excess of 2cm per hour is a dangerously high value. Typical circumstances include: new snow falling on a surface crust or on a layer of surface hoar, or new snow falling after a period of cold weather.

AIRBORNE-POWDER AVALANCHES

These are amongst the most destructive and least-understood of all avalanche types. In Alpine regions they can be of enormous proportions, but several accounts including photographic records now exist of their occurrence in Scotland (on Ben Nevis, Lochnagar, Bheinn Bhan, Bidean nam Bian and Buachaille Etive Mor).

An airborne-powder avalanche may start as a normal, flowing, dry, loose-snow avalanche (dry slough). A critical speed threshold of about 65-70 kph (40 mph) must then be crossed for airborne motion to become possible. However, many powder avalanches start off as soft slabs, which disintegrate into a powdery mass. Equally, hard slab or even ice avalanches may, in the course of their fall, pulverise sufficiently and achieve high enough velocity for airborne motion to occur.

Airborne avalanches are characterised by turbulent clouds of snow dust, swirling outwards from the centre of the moving mass. Often, the motion is not completely airborne, some of the moving snow continuing to travel along the ground. This is known as 'mixed motion'. Airborne-powder avalanches travel at very high speed (Fig 207) and are preceded by a destructive air blast, which may flatten buildings or forests. The snow in such an avalanche is thought to combine with air to form a suspension many times heavier than air, perhaps combining with a 'ground-cushion' effect to permit rapid motion.

There is no known way of telling whether a slope that is disposed to avalanche will in fact produce an airborne-powder avalanche. Clearly, the longer and steeper the slope, the more likely it is that conditions as regards critical speed will be met. Large snow accumulations will also pre-dispose towards this.

SLAB AVALANCHES

Slab avalanches constitute by far the greatest potential hazard in the mountains in winter and they are, more often than not, quite impossible to identify merely by a surface inspection. Dangerous slabs can result from a variety of conditions but it is in the attachment of the slab to the layer below that we must look for the underlying cause. In extreme cases there may be no attachment at all, the underlayers having contracted away leaving the slab completely unsupported over a considerable area. This situation makes it easier to understand the often hair-trigger sensitivity of slabs.

More commonly, there will be some discontinuity between the slab and the layer below. This may take the form of a crust, or perhaps an intervening layer of weak unconsolidated snow or in Alpine regions it may be that an earlier firm anchorage has been destroyed by the growth of a layer of depth hoar. In the spring the attachment of the whole snow cover to the ground becomes of increasing significance. Smooth surfaces such as rock slabs or long grass offer little support.

Probably the greatest single factor in promoting the development of slabs is the wind. Under its influence, snow is transported and packed into 'windslabs' which can vary in hardness from no more than firm powder (soft slab) to a consistency more akin to concrete (hard slab). The later is associated with high windspeeds in excess of about 50 kph (30 mph). High atmospheric humidity is also conducive to the creation of hard, rather than soft slab.

(i) Soft Slab Avalanches

These are the most common of winter avalanches and are associated with the rapid accumulation of fresh snow on lee slopes under the influence of winds of 25-50 kph (15-30 mph). After heavy falls the danger may not be confined to lee slopes and all slopes should be treated with suspicion until the snow settles. This may occur in a matter of hours or it may take several days if conditions remain cold. Extensive small surface slides are a sure sign that settlement is taking place (but not that the slope is as yet in a stable condition!)

Although it may be released as a unit, the soft slab, by definition, pulverises in motion and if it is large enough may develop into a mixed powder avalanche. Initially, it involves only the surface layer of snow, although its release may trigger off other weaknesses within the snow cover. It is as well to remember the dictum that most soft slab avalanches are released by their victims.

Soft slabs are most easily recognised by reference to the weather conditions which favour their formation. Since they are surface phenomena it is usually possible in the field to dig through the surface layer and examine the attachment to the underlayer. In a suitable test location the slab will often respond to a kick with a boot or ski by breaking away in straight-edged pieces. The same kind of practical test on a larger scale involves 'test skiing' in safe locations, but which have a similar exposure to the avalanche prone slopes. It is important to remember that in the absence of fresh snow, drifting alone can build up soft slabs on lee slopes.

(ii) Hard Slab Avalanches

The hard slab presents one of the greatest hazards in the mountains, not because of its frequency, but because its deceptively solid surface gives a false sense of security to those passing over it. The combination of high winds (50 kph) and low temperatures favour the formation of hard slabs on lee slopes. If it remains cold, the danger can persist for some time and may be obscured by subsequent snowfalls. Any substantial new snowfall or drifting (typically 25-30 cm) might lead to the triggering of such an avalanche.

Release is much the same as for soft slabs and may be accompanied by a sharp cracking noise. In this case however the slab breaks up into a jigsaw of angular blocks many of which remain intact on the journey down the slope. It need hardly be said that a large hard slab avalanche possesses enormous destructive power.

Hard slab has a dull, chalky appearance and occasionally emits a booming noise when walked upon. A lack of adhesion to the underlayer is characteristic of all hard slabs and indeed in some cases it is not attached at all over a considerable area. Such circumstances give rise to sudden local subsidence which can be most alarming, even on the flat. In Alpine areas hard slabs are frequently associated with strong temperature gradients and a consequent build up of depth hoar. A dangerous slab exhibits an almost hair-trigger sensitivity and may be released by the passage of a climber or skier.

WET AVALANCHES

Common in spring and following thaw conditions at any time during the winter, wet avalanches result from water weakening the bonds between crystals or lubricating some potential sliding surface within the snowpack. Obviously, they can only occur when the snow temperature is close to the melting point. Depending on the degree of saturation they can start on shallow angled slopes (20° and occasionally less than that). The danger is especially great after a heavy snow storm which starts cold and finishes warm. The cold snow is light and dry forming a weak substratum for the warmer and more dense snow above and a poor anchorage to the old snow surface below.

Wet avalanches may be loose or slab in form. They travel at relatively low speeds and can sometimes be outrun by a competent skier or occasionally by making a fast exit on foot out of the avalanche path. Great turbulence is set up as the avalanche flows down the slope, producing snow boulders which gouge long grooves in the bed surface. A big wet slide acts like a giant bulldozer picking up a mass of debris on the way (trees, shrubs, rocks, etc), all of which add to the very considerable destructive force. In a channelled avalanche the debris sets like concrete immediately on stopping and this greatly reduces the chances of survival of anyone caught in it, as well as impeding the rescue effort. These avalanches can be very big with debris accumulating up to 30 m (100ft) deep.

This is possibly the easiest hazard to anticipate because of the conditions which initiate a wet avalanche cycle; namely a rapid temperature rise after snowfall, usually late in the winter and often in damp, overcast weather. Rain, wet snowfalls, warm winds and melting are all contributory factors. However, delayed-action avalanches of old, wet snow are amongst the most difficult to predict as regards time of release. A snowpit may reveal layers of wet snow on top of crust, or a layer of surface hoar which may be dangerously weakened by percolating water. There is likely to be little, if any, temperature gradient between the bottom and top of the snow cover. Local small scale avalanching, cracks in the snow, large snowballs rolling down the slope are some of the visible warning signs.

ICE AVALANCHES

Ice or glacier avalanches are the direct result of glacier movement. At the present state of knowledge they are quite unpredictable and can fall at any hour of the day or night. They vary from the fall of an individual serac to the collapse of a whole mountain side. In 1962 the collapse of a hanging glacier on Huascaran (6,768m) in Peru released 3 million tons of ice which travelled (10 miles) 16km in 15 minutes and wiped out five villages killing 4,000 people and 10,000 head of livestock.

Large blocks of ice and often masses of earth and rock are entrained within the slide. Additional debris may be brought down by avalanches triggered off by the first one. It may be accompanied initially by a cloud of pulverised ice but in its later stages becomes a flowing river of mud, rock and ice.

Overhanging ice, seracs, etc, are obvious danger spots. Large sections of ice above cliff tops or ridges. Heavy rain entering crevasses and lubricating the undersurface of the ice may accelerate ice movement and therefore increase the danger.

Cornices

Three conditions are required for cornice formation: a supply of snow, wind to transport it, and a steep lee slope (approximately 50°-60°). Under these conditions eddies form in the airstream at the top of the lee slope. The slowing of the airstream and its circular motion cause the broken snow particles to be deposited in the form of a cornice which gradually extends out to overhang the slope below. Much of the airborne snow which does not

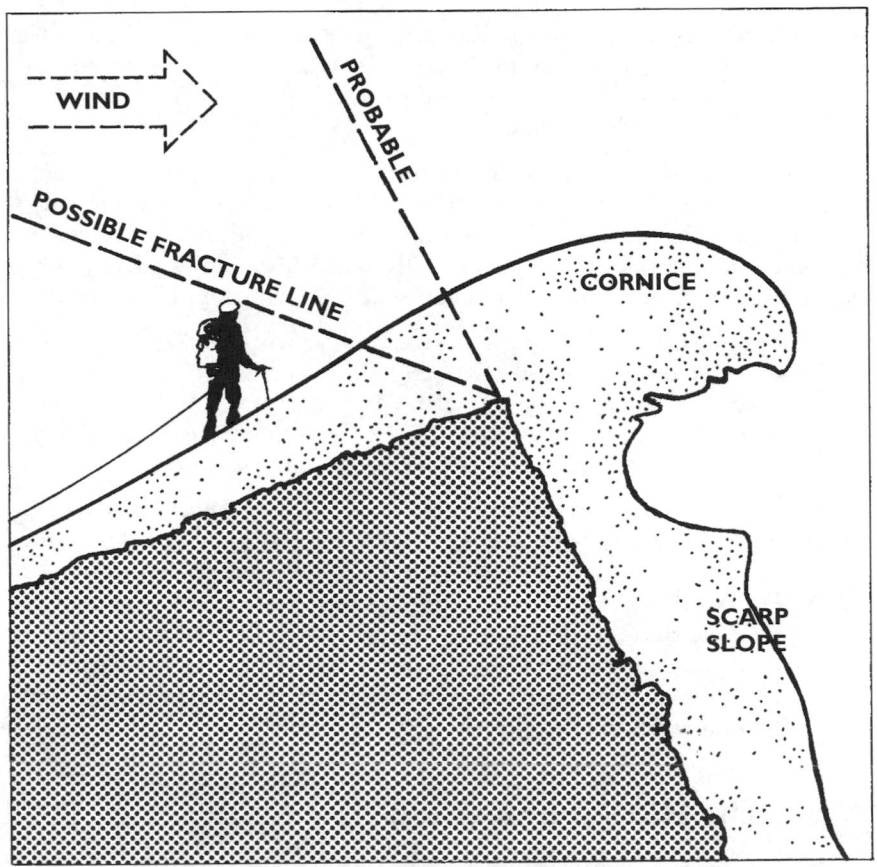

Fig. 208 *Cornice formation. Note the possible fracture line. Keep well back from the edge or the crest of the ridge.*

contribute to cornice formation accumulates on the slope below in the form of windslab. This slope is called the scarp slope and is often the focal point of avalanche activity.

Cornices are inherently dangerous and it is often difficult to judge their stability. The best advice is to give them a wide berth at all times. If you have to expose yourself to cornice danger then it should be for as short a time as possible. Sometimes a cornice will collapse simply as a consequence of its own weight. This frequently happens after a heavy snow storm. The falling cornice may trigger an avalanche of the scarp slope below. A common cause of cornice collapse is a sudden thaw and under these conditions it would be foolhardy to expose yourself unnecessarily to risk from this quarter. The more gradual spring thaw leads to the collapse of larger cornices as a result of the loss of cohesion due to warming during the day. Corniced slopes and gullies should be avoided at these times.

It is unwise to assume that there will be no build-up of cornices if there is no obvious snow fall in the valley. The wind may be active in sweeping snow from high catchment areas and depositing it on the upper slopes of crags and coire headwalls. This possibility should always be borne in mind and only a careful inspection on the spot will reveal whether or not this has happened.

Walkers are more likely to be at risk from cornices collapsing beneath them rather than on top of them. In negotiating a corniced ridge or cliff edge it is essential to take a line well to the windward of the possible cornice, remembering that overhangs in excess of 5m are common place and that the fracture line itself can be much further to windward than you expect.

This brief resume of the changes which take place in snow crystals and the processes which lead to the establishment of stable or unstable conditions is of general relevance. Conditions in the British Isles are different from those in the Alps or North America, so that although the basic processes are the same in all three areas the frequency and speed with which they occur can be very different. The scale too, is of a different order so that generally speaking avalanches in this country are smaller, less damaging to life and property, and confined to the higher mountain country.

Avalanche Hazard Evaluation

"*Whoever exposes himself to the danger of an avalanche without it being absolutely necessary is without doubt very stupid. However, in practice people expose themselves to this danger more often than they think; for snow can start to slide even on slopes with an incline of 30°. This means that virtually every mountain excursion presents a certain danger. Should one therefore give up wonderful trips into the mountains? Of course not, but one must try to act after consideration of all the factors in order to reduce the risk to a minimum. Nevertheless, even experts will be surprised again and again by avalanches.*"

André Roch

WINTER CLIMATE AND SNOW CONDITIONS

The maritime climate of the British Isles in winter gives rise to conditions in the mountains which are in some important respects quite different from those prevailing in the Alpine regions of mainland Europe. Precipitation levels, taken over all, are greater here than in the Alps, but of course a much smaller proportion of this falls as snow, even on our highest mountains. Higher average temperatures and dramatic variations in temperature within a very short space of time ensure a relatively rapid settling and stabilisation of the snow cover and, indeed thaws may be sufficiently protracted to remove the snow cover entirely from some mountain areas. If it were not for the wind which blows almost continuously above 600m (2,000 ft) in winter time, redistributing the snow and piling it into gullies and lee slopes, skiing and snow and ice climbing would be practically non-existent in this country. Thanks to the wind these thick localised deposits withstand the denuding effects of periodic thaws and provide high quality skiing and climbing well into the spring. By this time what remains of the winter's snow is coarsely crystalline and compact. Improved weather with clear night skies favours continuing melt/freeze metamorphism giving superb conditions for the late skier and climber - provided an early enough start is made!

Such unusual snow conditions suggest that there should be equally marked differences in the frequency of particular types of avalanches and this is indeed the case. The most important fact is that conditions do tend to stabilise quickly, the period of acute danger being during the snow storm itself and in the 24 hours immediately following. Rapid settling means that full depth avalanches are rare except in the Spring and during sudden heavy thaws when melting water destroys the attachment of the snow cover to the ground. It also means that the next snowfall frequently accumulates on a hard undersurface which may provide a poor anchorage, particularly if the snow is cold and dry at first, warming up later on. The freeze-thaw cycle together with the surface hardening effect of the wind gives rise to numerous icy crusts and these, too, provide potential sliding surfaces for subsequent snow layers. By far the most common type of avalanche is the surface slab, wet and dry, which is released from lee slopes during and after snowfall. Wind transported snow can give rise to substantial accumulations of wind slab in the complete absence of fresh snow. As previously stated the danger period is usually quite short, a matter of 24 to 48 hours, but this can be prolonged by cold weather.

The Scottish Avalanche Information Service (SAIS)

The basic purpose of this organisation is to address the problem of avalanche accidents in Scotland by providing the public with information on snow conditions and producing avalanche risk evaluations. Weather and forecast information supplied by the Met. Office is combined with local snowpack data gathered by SAIS own observers, in order to produce the daily Snow and Avalanche Report. This is made available to mountaineers in a variety of ways: local bulletin boards are placed at strategic locations in the three areas covered, namely Glencoe, Lochaber and the Northern Cairngorms: local radio stations in the Highlands as well as national newspapers also carry the Reports: a recorded message service giving all the Reports is operated by the police in Inverness, while commercial mountain weather lines also carry them. In these respects the service is not dissimilar to avalanche forecasting services in alpine countries.

The service is publicly funded and administered by the Scottish Sports Council and constituted the first initiative of the Scottish Mountain Safety Group (S.M.S.G.), which advises the Council. As well as providing the daily information, SAIS keeps a log of all avalanches recorded in Scotland and the rest of the UK. This work also includes retrospective material and details of avalanche occurrence provided by the general public. Such information is entered into a database also containing relevant weather and snowpack data.

A programme of educational work includes lectures to clubs and other organisations, as well as a series of publications, including input into the series of safety-related leaflets and posters produced by the SMSG.

SAIS has established links with avalanche forecasting agencies in other countries, principally Switzerland, France and the USA. A research grant from the British Council has facilitated the experimental deployment of the Swiss NXD Nearest Neighbours computer model to assist with avalanche prognosis in Scotland. This work continues.

Contact information:
SAIS Co-ordinator,
Scottish National Sports Centre,
Glenmore Lodge,
AVIEMORE PH22 1QU
Tel: 0479 810264 Fax: 0479 861212
Police Avalanche Information Line: 0463 713191

Assessing the Risk

It has already been stated that avalanche forecasting is about possibilities and occasionally probabilities, but rarely, if ever, about certainties   The mountaineer must make the best of it, selecting relevant information from a host of factors, weighing one against another, constantly updating information in an attempt to arrive at a realistic evaluation of snow stability and the likelihood of avalanches on one slope as against another. It is a daunting task and yet not an impossible one. A systematic approach to the subject is a great help and it should start before you even set foot on the hill.

Past Weather

Find out what the weather has been like, particularly in the previous week or so, noting any heavy snowfalls, strong winds and likely accumulation slopes for soft and hard slabs. Note also the temperature characteristics for the period and consider how this will have affected the settling process in the snow cover. From this historical information draw what inference you can about the present state of the snow in the general area of the proposed route. Your enquiries may reveal, for example, that there has been 15cm (6in) of fresh snow in the valley four days previously and that since then the weather had been cold, - 6°C, with clear night skies and 5-10 knot winds from the East. It would be reasonable to assume that the wind at 600m (2,000 ft) would be at least 10-20 knots and that it has redistributed the snow on to SW–NW facing slopes where soft to medium hard slabs may be expected. Cornice collapse may trigger slabs below. The cold weather will have delayed settling so that these slabs are likely to remain in an unstable condition. The hard surface of the old snow layer is unlikely to provide a secure anchorage. The snow profile may look something like this:

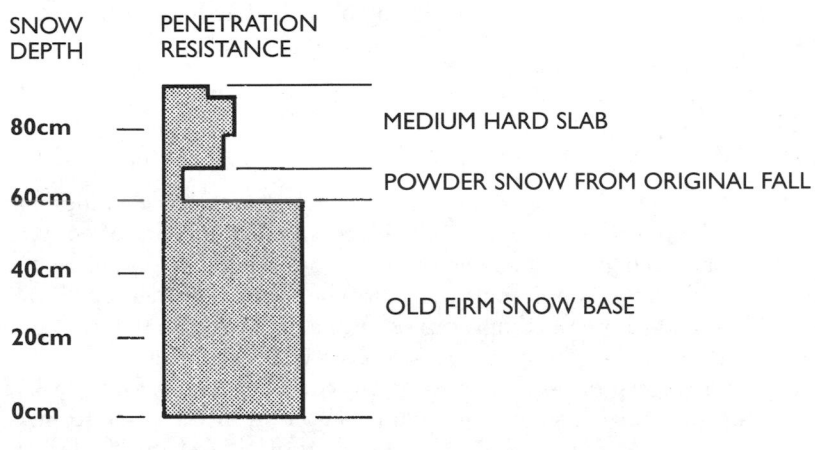

Fig. 209 *Resistance profile of a hard slab on top of a layer of powder snow with a thick base of consolidated old snow.*

Terrain

If you do not know the area it is common sense to talk to someone who does and discuss your plans and intended route. In particular find out if there are any peculiarities of terrain which might affect your choice of route, eg known avalanche paths, safe approach routes and so on.

ON THE MOUNTAIN

Once on the hill you should be subconsciously adjusting your assessment in the light of conditions as you actually find them. Clearly these will be changing as you gain altitude and you must make allowances for a fall in temperature of approximately 1.5° C for every 300 m, as well as for a likely increase in wind speed. Assess the prevailing weather conditions and how they are going to influence the situation. You have three main factors to consider: snowfall, wind and temperature and the effect that each of them may have on the old snow pack as well as on the accumulation of the new.

Snowfall

80-90% of avalanches are due to excessive loading caused by new snowfall. As a very rough guide, new snow depth in excess of 25cm (10 in) can create a serious avalanche risk in itself. The faster it accumulates the more serious the risk and rates of 2 cm (1 in) per hour or more should be considered potentially dangerous. The more dense and compact the snow, the greater the loading in relation to snow depth and the greater the hazard. The maximum loading of course comes from rain and wet avalanche cycles and extensive cornice collapse can be expected following a rain storm.

Wind

Wind has two important effects on snow. In the first place it erodes and transports it from exposed slopes and ridges and deposits it, often very unevenly, in sheltered gullies, hollows and lee slopes. In the second place, the snow crystals are broken up in transit so that when they are redeposited they accumulate in a much more compact mass with a distinctly layered structure. These accumulations are known as wind slabs and vary in hardness from almost the consistency of powder snow to rock hard deposits of marble-like quality. Huge amounts of snow may be transported in this way, the stronger the wind, the greater the volume of snow transported and the harder the resulting slabs. Slabs constitute the greatest avalanche hazard in mountains so it is of vital important to recognise both them and the conditions which give rise to them.

Temperature

It is difficult to estimate air temperature, partly because of the increased chill experienced when there is any wind at all and also because of the superficial warmth of direct sunlight. Nevertheless, indications can usually be found as

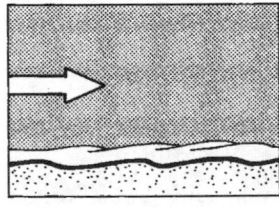
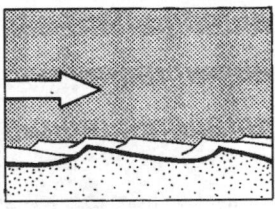

a Wind rippled surfaces — drifting snow

b Sastrugi — wind carved features

c Rime deposits

a   Ripples in the snow surface formed by drifting snow. The shallow slope of the ripples faces into the wind and the steep face away from it.

b   In harder, wind-packed snow, strong winds carve out sastrugi which present their steep faces to the wind.

c   Rime is deposited by moist winds on upstanding features such as cairns, fence posts, pylons, etc. The deposit grows into the wind so that it points in the direct from which the wind has come.

(Fig. 210)   *Indications of wind direction.*

to whether the air temperature is above or below 0°C. As we have seen, temperature plays a crucial role in the development of the snow cover. Sustained cold retards settling and prolongs the danger period. Cold new snow lacks cohesion and provides an unstable base for subsequent falls. By contrast, relatively warm air, above 0°C, accelerates the stabilisation of the snow cover and moist new snow tends to adhere to its underlayer.

On the other hand low temperatures can stabilise earlier surface layers of slush, at least till the next thaw. If the temperature is above freezing, wet sloughs of new snow can be expected immediately, but conditions quickly stabilise as the snow settles down. A continuing thaw will cause melting in older snow layers with the possibility of setting off a cycle of wet snow avalanches and cornice collapse. This is most common in the Spring, particularly after a succession of cloudy days which greatly restricts the amount of heat which can be lost by long wave radiation.

There are two types of surface deposit to look for. The first is surface hoar with its unmistakable flakey crystals which sparkle brilliantly in the sun. Once buried, however, they are more difficult to identify and provide a very unstable base for further snow falls.

The second type of deposit is caused by the freezing of water droplets carried by the wind on to solid objects in its path; rocks, fence posts, ski-lift pylons and so on. The deposit 'grows' into the wind and so is a useful indicator of earlier wind direction as well as signalling humid and relatively warm air. It is known as rime or fog crystal.

Be Observant

The most urgent warning of avalanche danger is an avalanche. Look around you. Are there any signs of avalanche activity? If so can you tell how recent? What type are they? Where are their starting zones and what is their general orientation? This information can provide invaluable guidance as to which slopes are vulnerable and which safe.

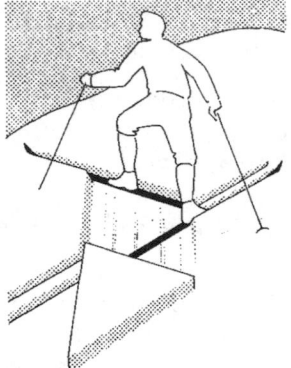

(Fig. 211) *A small slab breaking away as the skier makes a turn. This is a clear warning of serious avalanche risk, especially on lee slopes where the snow will have accumulated to greater depth.*

Practical Tests

DIGGING A SNOW PIT

Up till now your assessment of snow conditions has been almost entirely indirect, based on assumptions and deductions from historical information and from superficial observations of present weather and snow conditions. It makes very good sense before you venture on to a potentially hazardous slope to put your deduction to the test and to examine the profile of the snow in situ. This exercise need take no more than a matter of a few minutes since it is normally only necessary to excavate the surface layer with your ice axe to expose its junction with the layer below. Choose a spot which has a similar aspect to the suspect slope but is itself free from avalanche danger. The objective is to establish the depth of the surface layer and thus the seriousness of a possible surface slide and to identify any weaknesses, either within the layer itself, or in its attachment to the underlayer. In Scotland because of rapid settlement there is nearly always a distinct discontinuity between the new and recent snowfall(s) and the older snow underneath. An examination may then be made as follows:

The back wall is brushed smooth with a glove and investigated for different layers. A pencil or the edge of a compass is useful for this purpose. The magnifying lens found on most compasses may be used to examine snow grains. The physical properties of each layer are then assessed and graded.

(i) Hardness: penetration by objects.

1 Very low. Gloved fist.
2 Low. Gloved finger ends.
3 Medium. Single finger.
4 High. Pencil/axe spike.
5 Very high. Knife blade.
6 Ice.

(ii) Wetness: Try to form snowballs.

1 Dry. No snowball possible.
2 Moist. Dry snowball, no water visible.
3 Wet. Water visible but no drops can be squeezed out.
4 Very wet. Drops can be squeezed out.
5 Slush. Snow flooded with water.

Any abrupt change in these criteria, particularly in adjacent layers, would indicate a potential weak point in the snow pack.

Gross differences in the size of crystals in adjacent layers, as well as spaces between layers, icy crusts and layers of loose, unbonded crystals should also be regarded as possible sources of danger.

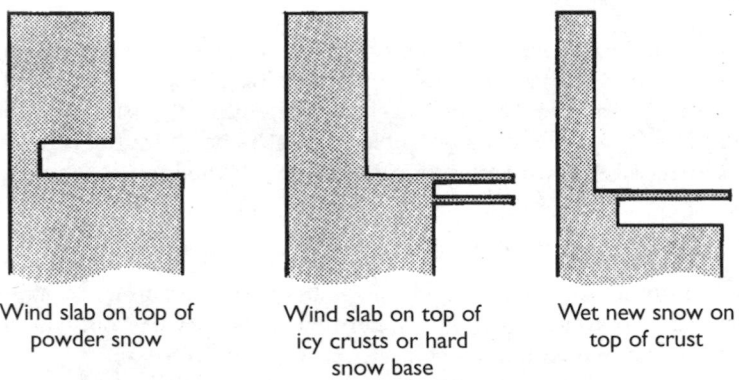

Wind slab on top of powder snow

Wind slab on top of icy crusts or hard snow base

Wet new snow on top of crust

Fig. 212 *What to look for. An inspection of the surface layer and its attachment to the underlying snow will provide vital information about the condition of the surface layer and its tendency to avalanche.*

WEDGE BLOCK TEST

After examination of the snowpit, further information as to the stability of surface layers may be gained by means of a shovel test. The simple Wedge Block test illustrated in Fig.213 is suggested as being the quickest and simplest.

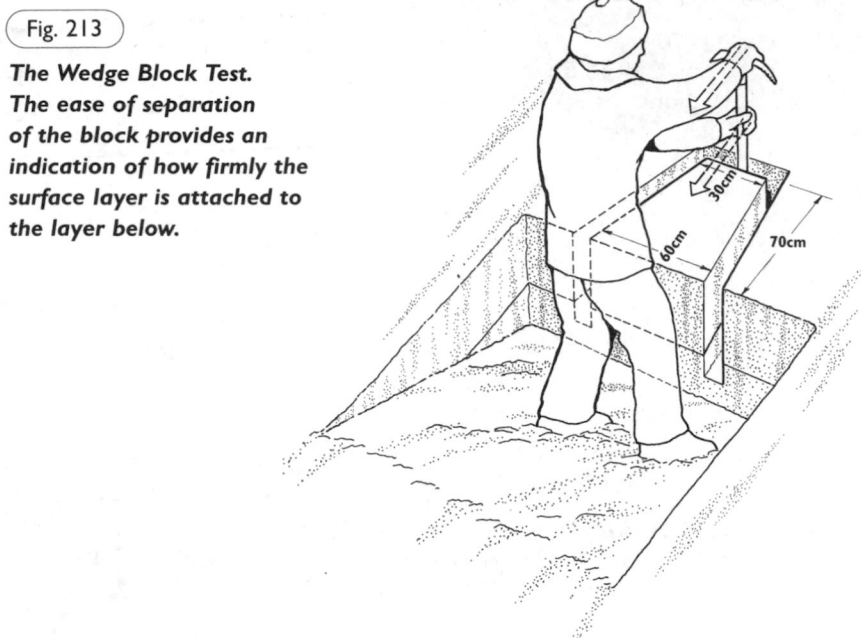

Fig. 213

The Wedge Block Test. The ease of separation of the block provides an indication of how firmly the surface layer is attached to the layer below.

The slots shown are cut to the depth of the first suspect layer. A shovel (or ice axe, or even gloved hands) may then be inserted at the back of the block, and a steady forward pull exerted. The ease of separation of layers is used as an index of the likelihood of a slab avalanche. This test is repeated for each suspect layer down either to ground level, or the highest substantial layer of nevé.

There are several disadvantages to this test:

1 It indicates stability at only one location, whereas snow layers may be relatively inhomogenous. Where possible, several tests in adjacent locations would provide a more reliable test.

2 The test does not take account of the loading effect of layers which have already been removed.

3 It still embodies a large degree of subjectivity.

4 It is not a good indicator of deep-seated instabilities within the snowpack. However, recent studies (PMB Fohn 1987) have shown that the effect of the passage of a climber or skier is unlikely to be significant in triggering avalanches when the weakness is situated at a depth greater than one metre. This objection is therefore relatively unimportant.

This test is recommended to climbers and skiers as being simpler and quicker than other available tests, while giving, with practice, useful results. It should be said that even the simple cutting of stances and dead-man placements during the course of a climb may provide valuable opportunities for observation of snow stability.

AXE TEST

An even quicker alternative to the Wedge Block Test, which can tell you a great deal about the surface layers, is to thrust your axe into the snow perpendicular to the surface. It is best to do this with a repetitive tamping action, applying the same amount of pressure on the spike of the axe each time. The axe will penetrate the snow a little further each time and any sudden variations in hardness will be apparent by an equally sudden difference in the extent of penetration. If this is the case, investigate by digging a surface pit. The safest profile would be indicated by a gradually increasing resistance with depth with no sudden variations. Obviously, this test is only valid in surface layers which are shallower than the length of the axe. A further limitation is that it may fail to show up very thin weak layers sandwiched between layers of similar hardness.

A number of other tests exist, including the RUTSCH BLOCK TEST and the LOADED COLUMN TEST but these take longer to perform.

Route Finding

It is unusual, though not unknown, for a party of mountaineers to be caught in an avalanche which they did not themselves trigger. Most avalanche accidents are caused by their victims. This is a thought to bear in mind when selecting a route through avalanche country. No matter how critical the risk of avalanche there is almost always a safe route to be found somewhere. Unfortunately, the decision to follow it is not always easy to make, partly because it is rarely possible to be absolutely sure of your evaluation of the degree of risk and partly because other factors tend to complicate matters. The safe route, for instance, might mean a substantial detour which you have neither the time nor the energy to accomplish. It is an inescapable fact that many avalanche accidents occur when circumstantial pressures have forced a party to ignore or minimise the obvious warning signs and take a chance.

Your choice of route will very much influenced by your assessment of snow conditions and how these might change in the course of the journey. The predominance of the lee slope slab in the Scottish mountains makes it essential to avoid these slopes during and immediately after heavy snowfall or drifting. Although avalanches have been known on slopes as shallow as 11°, the main danger lies within the range 30°-50°. Avoid bulging convex slopes where the snow cover is stretched under tension and favour concave shapes such as bowls and hollows where compressive forces tend to hold the snow in place. Given the choice, stick to ridges and the high ground above the avalanche paths and if you have to cross suspect slopes do so as high as possible so that, although you may be more likely to trigger a slide, you will be close to or right at the fracture line and therefore much more likely to remain on top of the debris or escape it altogether. Following a valley route may well be a safe option but bear in mind that an avalanche can flow out across a valley floor for a considerable distance. Small gullies and valleys with steep side walls

Fig. 214   *Danger in a narrow confined valley. Danger above! This party is walking into a potential death trap. Strong winds have deposited heavy masses of snow on the slopes above. There is no escape should an avalanche be released. Even quite small valleys can be extremely hazardous in these conditions.*

are particularly dangerous, even although the total amount of snow involved may be relatively small.

Snow can accumulate to considerable depths on the lee side, often topped by a cornice. If a slide is released, the debris can only pile up on top of the unfortunate party below. An open slope is much to be preferred to a confined one and, if there is a degree of risk, always work out what is likely to happen in the event of a slide.

A knowledge of the terrain is obviously a great advantage in working out a safe route since the places most exposed to avalanches can be avoided. Occasionally, the evidence of previous avalanche activity is clearly to be seen by its effect on the vegetation: a swathe cut through the forest, trees and bushes permanently bent downslope, and so on. It must be said though that few avalanches reach the timber line in this country. The presence of trees, particularly thick forest, do provide a measure of protection, but often a good deal less than many assume. An avalanche is unlikely to start on a forested slope but the presence of trees is no guarantee of protection from an avalanche released from the slopes above.

CROSSING A SUSPECT SLOPE

The first question to ask yourself when faced with the crossing of a suspect slope is, "do I have to?" A number of factors must be weighed in the balance and every possible alternative considered before making the decision to cross. Usually, it is not possible to choose the time of your crossing, but this is a factor which should be borne in mind when planning your route. A slope on which there is every likelihood of a wet avalanche may be frozen solid and perfectly safe in the early hours of the day before the sun has had a chance to do its work.

Having decided to cross, the next question to ask is, "where?" Where is the slope likely to fracture and where is the best crossing point? As we have seen, the fracture is likely to be across an area of tension in the slope and if at all possible you want to be above this area.

It is quite common for the upper fracture to follow a line connecting islands of stability on the slope, such as a group of rocks or trees. Such islands can provide useful anchor points if it becomes necessary to use the rope to safeguard a particularly exposed section. If you do elect to use the rope, the person providing the security should be belayed but should not be tied onto the same rope as the person crossing since a big avalanche would simply result in both being swept away. Try to visualise what will happen if the slope does go and work out what your escape options will be. Inform your party of your plan of action.

Before you embark on an avalanche prone slope there are certain basic precautions to take. Make sure that any encumbrances can be shed at a moment's notice. Undo your rucksack waist belt and at least one shoulder strap, take off the axe wrist loop, zip-up your clothing, put on gloves and pull on your anorak hood, securing it over your mouth and nose if possible. Skiers should ensure that safety straps are untied and wrist loops free. If you are carrying safety beacons make sure they are all switched to 'transmit' and carried inside the clothing (pages 417-419). A less effective alternative is to trail an avalanche cord. This is a 20-30m length of brightly coloured nylon tied to the waist at one end and left to trail behind you on the snow. Should you be taken by the avalanche it is possible that some part of this light cord will be thrown up on the surface, even if you are not. The cord has metal tags crimped on at 2m intervals with an arrow and the number of metres to the end of the cord (in the direction of the arrow) marked on. Just make sure you tie on to the right end of the cord!

The crossing should be made one at a time, if possible following a descending line which avoids too sudden an undercutting of the slope above. The others should keep a sharp look-out for anything higher up and be prepared to plot the progress of the victim should the worst happen. It has too often been a fatal mistake to assume that because one person, or even a whole party, has crossed a suspect slope in safety then it is safe for others to do so. Frequently, the earlier crossings simply bring the slope into a critical state of equilibrium ready to be released by the next person to cross.

Avalanche Search and Rescue

The rather depressing news conveyed by Fig 215 is that the chances of survival in an avalanche dwindle rapidly after $1\frac{1}{2}$ to 2 hours burial even when the victim is buried close to the surface. It also shows that the deeper the victim is buried the shorter the survival time.

Speed is therefore of paramount importance in any avalanche search operation. The chances of survival are greatly reduced as the burial time increases. Few victims are brought out alive after 2 hours or more in the snow. The operation may be considered in three phases.

1 A preliminary search by the survivors of the avalanche.

2 An advance party search carried out with people and equipment that can be got to the site without delay.

3 A systematic search using probes, dogs and other methods of detection.

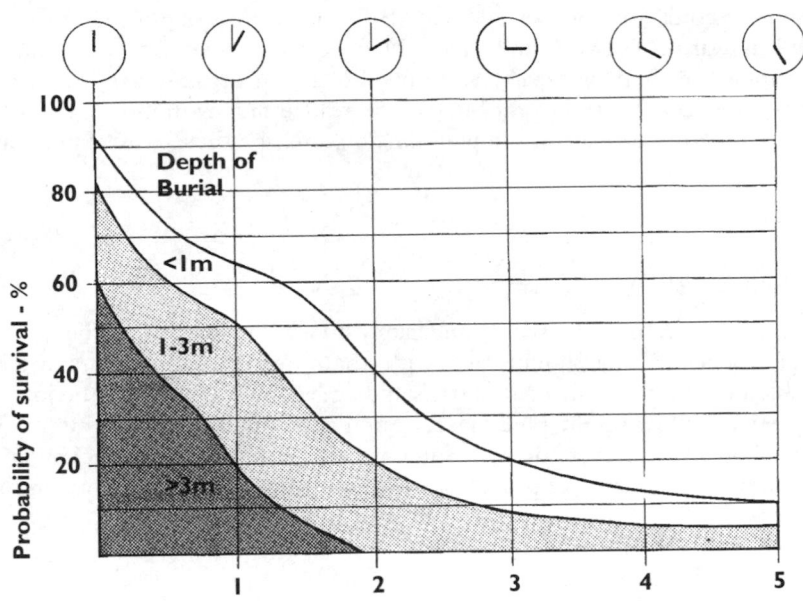

Probability of survival - %

Length of time victim buried ~ hours

Fig. 215   *Probability of survival of avalanche victims as a function of time, showing also the effect of depth of burial. In Switzerland, the survival rate for completely buried victims, is 19%. (From a study of avalanche accidents by de Quervain.)*

SEARCH BY SURVIVORS

It is remarkable how it is possible in many avalanche incidents for witnesses to follow the course of the victims during their descent, right up until their final burial. It is vitally important that the position of the victims when engulfed and when last seen be clearly marked with a stick, etc. The line connecting these two positions acts as a pointer to the likely burial area. This area and indeed the whole of the debris should be examined as closely as time permits for any sign of the victim, items of clothing or equipment. A reversed ski stick, an ice axe, or a stick with the basket removed makes a simple probe to test likely spots.

Obviously, the amount of time devoted to this preliminary search depends on the location of the accident and the number of survivors. However, this surface search is absolutely essential and half an hour is suggested as being of the right order.

Swiss records for the period 1960-1974 show that of the 777 people buried in avalanches and found alive, 371 freed themselves, 282 were found by members of their own party and only 124 by an organised rescue party. This is no reflection on the efficiency of the rescue organisation but serves to underline the importance of the preliminary search by those who witness an accident.

ADVANCE PARTY SEARCH

An advance party must be sent immediately and with all speed to the site of the avalanche. They should take with them only what is immediately available in the form of first aid, shovels and avalanche probes. It is the job of this party to follow up the preliminary search and concentrate their attention on the most likely areas of debris. Some rescue posts in the Cairngorms and elsewhere carry a supply of probes, shovels and other equipment required for avalanche work.

SYSTEMATIC SEARCH

A great many people may be involved in this phase and a high degree of accuracy and co-ordination is essential. For these reasons the search must be conducted with military precision and must be under the direct control of an experienced rescue co-ordinator.

In spite of all the scientific advances in this field, the two oldest methods of search remain the most effective for the moment namely, the use of avalanche probes and the use of dogs One of the most important reasons for this is the fact that neither method requires that the victim should be carrying some special device, such as a magnet or radio. They depend for their operation on natural and permanent properties of the human body and can therefore be employed with a good chance of success on all buried victims.

DANGER OF FURTHER AVALANCHES

There is more than a grain of truth in the statement that the safest place to be after an avalanche is in its track, but it is a statement which has to be qualified. Obviously, that particular avalanche will not fall again, at least not until after the next snowfall, but other avalanche paths may feed into this track and a sharp look-out must be kept against such a possibility.

USE OF AVALANCHE PROBES

These come in a variety of forms but are normally jointed metal rods up to 4m (13ft) in length. The rescuers are arranged in an extended line across the debris and advance up the slope probing at set intervals and to a predetermined depth. An area once searched in this way should be clearly marked with flags or sticks.

(Fig. 216) *Probing with an avalanche rod to detect a buried victim. Rocks or even lumps of snow may deflect the probe making it difficult to strike a deeply buried person.*

It is normal to probe to a depth of 2m (6ft) even although the depth of the debris may be considerably greater. The saving in time far outweighs the slim chance of finding a victim alive at a greater depth. Even with a team of 29-30 people the business of probing takes a very long time and here again a saving can be made by adopting a wide spacing between probes. Rescuers stand with their feet 0.5 m (20in) apart and separated from their neighbours' feet by a distance of 0.25 m (10in).

For coarse probing the rods are driven in between the feet. The whole line then advances by one 0.70m pace and the process is repeated. In this way each square metre of debris is probed twice. With this method 20 people can search an area of 1 hectare (100 x 100m) in 4 hours with a 76% chance of finding the victim.

For fine probing the rods are driven in at both toes and also centrally. The line then advances by 0.30m (1ft) and the process is repeated. Using this method each square metre is probed 13 times and it would take 20 people 20 hours to search 1 hectare with 100% chance of success.

The great disadvantage of sounding, effective though it is, is the length of time it takes to cover the ground, even with large numbers of rescuers. It is for this reason that a well trained dog is worth its weight in gold for it can search a given area in a tenth of the time that it would take a team of 20 people.

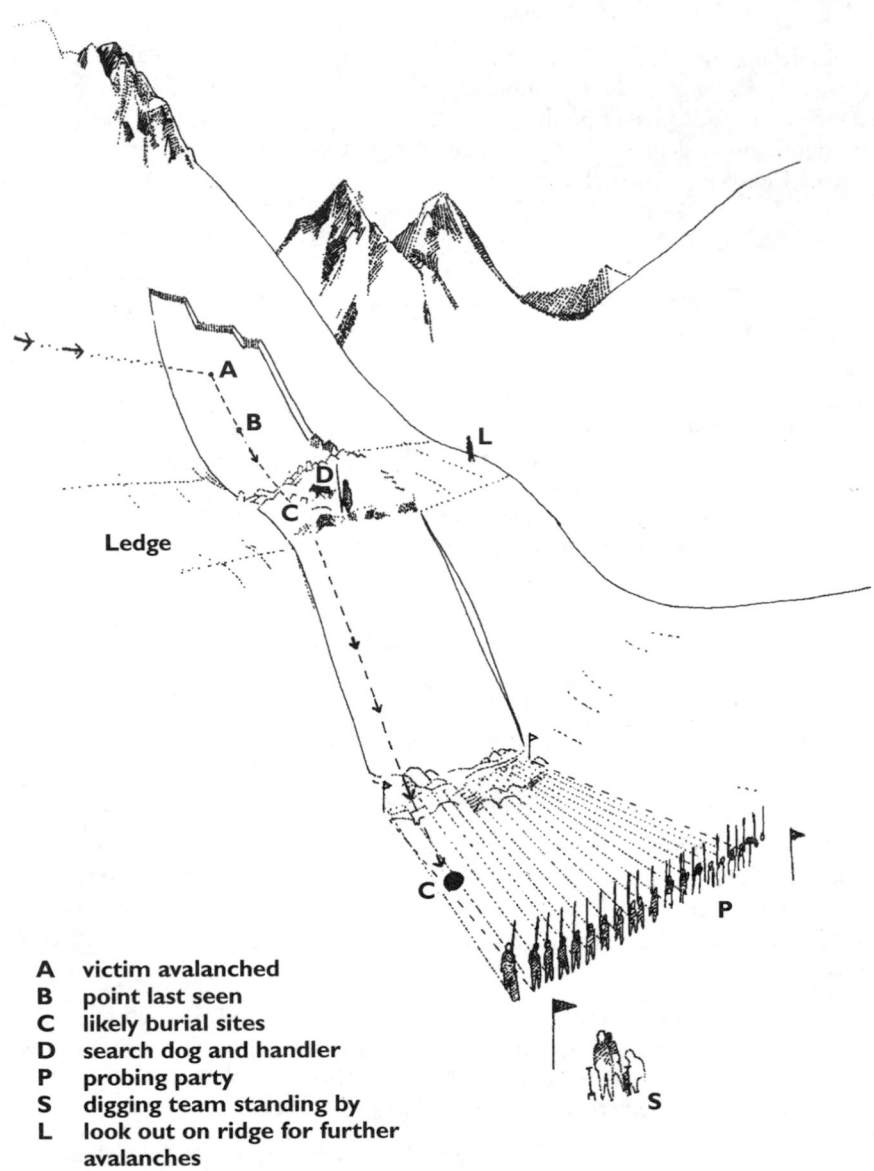

A   victim avalanched
B   point last seen
C   likely burial sites
D   search dog and handler
P   probing party
S   digging team standing by
L   look out on ridge for further
    avalanches

Fig. 217   *An avalanche search in progress.*

USE OF AVALANCHE TRAINED DOGS

Details of the Search and Rescue Dog Association have been given on page 311. The success of trained dogs in the search for buried victims is well documented. They will find all buried persons still alive or those who died shortly before, normally regardless of the burial depth and nature of the snow. The speed of search varies with the tenacity and stamina of the dog as well as with the prevailing conditions, but on average a trained dog will search an area of 1 hectare in about half an hour.

If dogs are to be used they should be brought to the site of the accident as soon as possible, preferably by helicopter. There is no reason why the search should be delayed till their arrival, but the site must not be contaminated by urine or discarded food.

TRENCHING

If these methods fail to locate the victim trenches must be dug into the debris. Theses trenches should be approximately 1m wide and spaced at intervals of 3m. The walls of the trenches should then be probed horizontally.

OTHER METHODS

Many other ingenious methods of detection have been devised. They can be divided roughly into those which require the victim to carry some device such as a VHF transmitter or a magnetic disc and those which depend on some natural function or property of the body. The latter offers the best hope for development since it is always difficult to persuade people to carry extra equipment, no matter how compact.

However, for organised groups and search parties avalanche transceivers or beacons are now routinely used. These greatly improve the chance of live rescue, but practice in their use is essential. Recent tests (1992) in Scotland have investigated the potential of ground radars for the location of buried victims carrying no transceiver or reflector. These tests, involving two separate systems, have been successful and the production of a portable unit is regarded as an imminent development. A separate research project using a microwave radiation detector is also well advanced.

Avalanche Beacons (Transceivers)

There is no doubt that the most effective insurance against being killed in an avalanche is to carry an avalanche beacon. This is a small portable transceiver which transmits a signal which can be picked up by other sets operating on the same frequency. Each member of the party should carry a beacon which is kept in the 'transmit' mode while in avalanche country. In the event of someone being buried in an avalanche the search is conducted by the remaining members of the party who switch their sets to the 'receive' mode. An increase in signal strength indicates an approach to the victim's position.

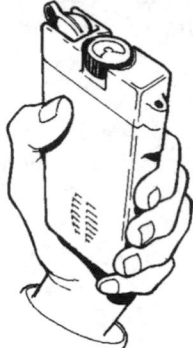

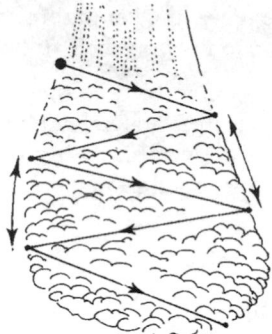

Fig. 218 — *An avalanche beacon or 'bleeper'.*

Fig. 219 — *Search technique using a single beacon. The distance apart of the turning points down each side should be just within the maximum range of the beacon.*

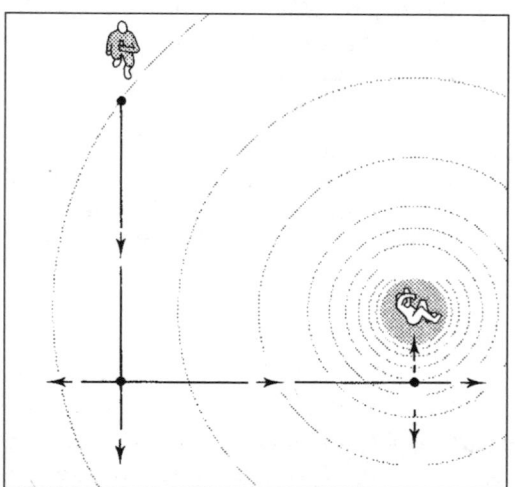

Fig. 220 — *Technique to be adopted after the first signal has been received from the buried beacon.*

It is very important to test all beacons in both modes before setting out. Replace used and partly used cells and carry a spare set in your pocket. Never carry beacons in your rucksack but attach them to your body in the recommended manner. All sets should be switched to 'transmit' at the start of the day and kept in that mode until your return.

Although the principle of operation and use is simple enough, the actual technique of searching requires a bit of practice. It is usually possible to pick up a signal at 50-100m range and to move fairly rapidly towards the victim. It is in the final 5m or so that some difficulty is normally experienced.

An internationally agreed frequency of 457 kHz will become universal on 1st December 1995. Transceivers using this frequency are in common use in Europe and dual frequency transceivers which are also compatible with the old 2275 Hz frequency, will continue to be sold until the agreed date. Groups should carefully check the compatibility of transceivers which they may be using.

FIRST AID

In about 80% of fatal avalanche accidents the cause of death is suffocation. If the victim is alive they may be suffering from shock, exposure, frostbite and other mechanical injuries to the body. If necessary, mouth-to-mouth resuscitation and/or external cardiac massage should be given immediately (remember that the mouth is likely to be full of snow.) Great care should be exercised in taking the victim out of the snow and into the casualty bag so as not to aggravate any injuries. The treatment should be continued as discussed in Chapter 11.

It should be remembered that a buried casualty is likely to be extremely cold and if unconscious may easily be mistaken for dead. Respiration and pulse may be undetectable. Always assume that the patient is alive until a doctor confirms otherwise.

What to do if Caught in an Avalanche

This is the sort of advice which is easy to give but which may be quite impossible to follow. Nevertheless, it is the distillation of the experience of many victims over a period of years. There are, of course, a number of physical variables, to say nothing of human ones, and the best course of action depends to a large extent on them. For instance, what may be a number one priority in a powder snow avalanche may be of little importance in a wet slab.

Remove rucksack and skis (these should already be in the quick release position if there is any risk of avalanche). A good skier, may of course, be able to traverse or schuss out of danger. Do not be too hasty in throwing away your ice axe until it is clear that it is likely to do more harm than good.

Make a quick assessment of the avalanche; whether you are at the top, bottom, middle, or to one side; what type it is (wet, dry, etc) and where your best line of escape lies. If you have already made a proper evaluation of the risk and considered the emergency options you will be much more likely to find the appropriate response when the need arises.

Delay your departure as long as possible by thrusting your ice axe into the stable underlayer and hanging on with all you have got. The more you let past you at the start the less is likely to bury you at the finish.

It may be advantageous to work out to the side of the avalanche and escape in that direction possibly by swimming or rolling.

If swimming movements are possible, then a sort of double-action back stroke seems to be the most effective, with the back to the force of the avalanche and the head up. Obviously, if you are in danger of being struck by blocks and slabs of snow then your arms will have to be used to protect your head and face. There is no cut and dried procedure here – ride it out as best you can and save your greatest effort for the last few seconds.

Keep your mouth shut! In a powder avalanche cover the mouth and nose with the top of your sweater or anorak or your rucksack if you have not already disposed of it.

A supreme effort should be made in the last few seconds as the avalanche loses its momentum and begins to settle. This may be the only time that you are able to obtain some purchase on the moving debris. Two things are paramount: an air space; and a position as near to the surface as possible. The chances of survival are greatly reduced if deeply buried.

Don't panic!

Avalanche Protection - A Summary

Precautions Before Leaving

Consult local expert advice and find out the recent weather history and snow conditions. Obey avalanche warning notices.

Carry first aid kit and basic rescue equipment, including shovels, in the party.

Carry avalanche beacons set to 'transmit' and be practised in their use.

Never expose more than one of the party to risk at any given moment.

Do not assume that the passage of another party is proof that slope is safe.

Never go alone.

Know how to improvise a rope or ski stretcher.

Weather Indications

Lee slopes are particularly prone to soft slab avalanches. Keep clear of accumulation areas during immediately after a snow storm. Know which way the wind has been drifting the snow.

Low temperatures prolong avalanche risk.

Any sudden increase in temperature after snowfall, especially with a dry wind, creates avalanche danger.

Rain on unconsolidated snow give rise to wet avalanches, especially where the underlayer offers poor attachment.

Powder avalanches are rare in Scotland, but occasionally occur after 30cm (1ft) or more of new snow in cold weather. Slopes take 2-3 days to settle and longer if cold and out of the sun.

Things to watch for in the Topography

Most avalanche accidents are caused by their victims. Keep high and on the ridges and avoid being the trigger which releases a slide.

Avoid cornices and the slopes below them after drifting or during a thaw.

Avalanche slopes which run out into gullies where the debris can pile up are especially dangerous.

The most dangerous slope angles are between 30° and 45°.

Fracture commonly takes place on the convex part of the slope.

Thin forest offers no protection.

Things to watch for in the Snow

The most reliable indication of unstable conditions are signs of recent avalanches in the neighbourhood.

Be on the look out for other warning signs: large snowballs (sunballs) rolling downslope, sudden collapse of snow cover under weight, hollow feeling and noise of slabs, cracks appearing in the snow, mini slabs released from boots or ski, signs of melting etc, etc.

The attachment of snow layers to each other is of fundamental importance. Assess this by carrying out a Wedge Block Test or by probing with an axe or ski stick. Adjoining layers which differ markedly in hardness are likely to be poorly attached to each other. Note particularly any weak layers and crusts.

The deeper the snow, the greater the danger. An accumulate rate in excess of 2cm (1in) per hour can lead to avalanche hazards.

17

Cold Injury

Frostbite

Frostbite is a condition which is fortunately relatively rare in this country. When it does occur, it is usually associated with emergency situations involving forced bivouacs or with fractures or other injuries. Nevertheless it is very important to be able to give the right treatment in the field to avoid permanent damage or loss of tissue. The condition is closely related to mountain hypothermia, previously described (Chapter 9), since one of the body's reactions to general cooling is to reduce the supply of blood going to the extremities in order to conserve heat in the core. This is done at the expense of a greatly increased risk of frostbite since a sluggish circulation is stage one of the frostbite process. It is unusual, therefore, to have simply a frostbite problem to deal with. It must be appreciated that frostbite normally reflects a more serious general condition of body cooling and that both must be dealt with simultaneously. If for any reason this is not possible, then treatment for hypothermia must take precedence. As in other things a knowledge of avoidance is paramount, coupled with early recognition and treatment before irrevocable damage is done.

Frostbite is the freezing or partial freezing of parts of the body, usually the face and extremities, the hands and feet. Provided blood circulation to these parts is adequate and tissue remains warm and nourished there is no danger of frostbite. Excessive surface cooling, almost invariably exacerbated by faulty clothing or a condition of exhaustion, shock or general cooling of the whole body, leads to a progressive reduction of circulation in the exposed part. Once circulation becomes negligible the tissue freezes. The initial stage of the process is known as 'frostnip'. This is speedily reversible provided action is taken in time. Keep a watch out for white nose, cheeks or ears on your companions and rewarm immediately. It is not possible to watch the hands and the feet as these are normally covered, but cessation of feeling or even a feeling of warmth following cold, are danger signs which must not be ignored. It should be noted that local cold injury is possible at temperatures above freezing, usually following a period of prolonged exposure to wet cold conditions.

While it is fairly easy to rewarm the hands it takes a great deal of will power in a difficult situation to go to all the trouble of removing gaiters and boots to warm up the feet. However, if these warning signs are ignored, true frostbite may be the result with a long and painful period of recovery and perhaps the risk of permanent tissue damage or even loss.

TREATMENT

'Frostnip' should be treated immediately by thawing the exposed part on some warm part of the anatomy. Fingers can be warmed under the armpit, ears by the hands, and feet on the belly of a companion. The important thing is to recognise this first stage of frostbite, especially in the feet, and rewarm immediately.

Frostbite may be superficial or deep. Superficial frostbite is confined to the skin and surface tissues which take on a greyish-white appearance, frozen hard on the surface, but resilient underneath. With proper treatment a full recovery with no loss of tissue is likely. Deep frostbite, on the other hand, affects not only the surface tissues but involves the deeper structures of muscle, tendon and bone. Recovery is a slow and painful process almost inevitably resulting in some permanent loss of tissue.

The preferred treatment is active rewarming, but once rewarming has taken place the greatest care is absolutely essential to protect the injury from further cooling or physical damage. For this reason it is best to head for home or for a base where adequate protection can be guaranteed. It is considerably less damaging to walk out on a frozen foot than a thawed one and in the likely circumstances a great deal safer for all concerned. In this country in almost every case the rule must be immediate evacuation to a place where professional medical help is available. In a situation where the victim is immobilised by other injuries and may have to wait some considerable time for rescue, treat for exposure by providing shelter, warmth and nourishment, but do not attempt to rewarm the frostbitten part by exercise or by any other means. In particular:

Do not rub with snow or, for that matter, anything else.
Do not give alcohol or cigarettes.
Do not apply direct heat to the injury from a hot water bottle or stone.
Do not apply traction to fractures.
Do not prick or burst blisters.

This treatment or, more accurately, non-treatment ensures the maximum chance of recovery later. Fractures should be treated with a well padded splint (not inflatable) and periodic checks made as to the state of the extremities. Footwear must be removed gently and the foot carefully padded with spare socks and sweaters and placed inside a rucksack.

It is highly unlikely that in this country it should ever be necessary to do more than is outlined above. The treatment at base would normally be supervised by a doctor or carried out in hospital. Experts on cold injury are agreed that immediate rapid rewarming for 20 minutes in a hot bath at 42°C - 44°C offers the best hope of recovery and minimal loss of tissue. In the field when speedy evacuation is not possible, as on a major expedition abroad, this treatment should be administered at base camp.

Whether rewarming is induced or spontaneous, as could happen if the victim was evacuated to a warm tent at a low level or indeed if any early diagnosis of the injury has not been made, it is important to realise that further exercise or use of the frostbitten part is out of the question. In the case of a frostbitten foot the victim must be regarded as a stretcher case and evacuated accordingly. Everything must be done to prevent further damage or cooling. A dry, loose cotton wool dressing is all that is required after the injury has been gently cleaned by dabbing with warm (not hot) soapy water. Pads of wool may be required to separate the fingers or toes. A cage of some sort must then be improvised to prevent accidental contact and the pressure and drag of sleeping bag or blankets. On no account touch or prick blisters or interfere in any other way with the injury.

PREVENTION

Frostbite is inextricably related to the general temperature balance of the whole body, and the preventative measures previously recommended (see Chapter 8) to combat hypothermia are equally valid to give protection from frostbite. Basically a party that is fit, well fed, clad and watered, and in good spirits has little to fear. This assumes that the equipment and clothing worn, particularly on the hands and feet, will give adequate insulation from the cold. Boots must be roomy and allow for the wearing of one or two pairs of warm socks or stockings (of wool and preferably loop stitched). A fitting which allows socks to wrinkle up under the heel or at the toes creates local pressure points which may become the focal point of frostbite injury. Do not wear wet socks or mitts (which, incidentally, are much superior to gloves as far as insulation is concerned), and carry spares of both. Change into dry socks at night and, if there is a risk that your boots might freeze up, put them into a polythene bag and keep them with you inside your sleeping bag.

The temperature of deep powder snow may be many degrees below the ambient temperature so that your feet may be much colder than the rest of your body. Gaiters not only provide additional insulation but they prevent snow from getting into your boots, a sure recipe for frostbite. In very cold weather avoid touching or handling metal with bare hands (you are liable to stick to it) and do not let your hands get wet with stove fuel or other liquids which freeze below 0°c.

In cold weather keep a watch on your companion's faces for any sign of frostnip (local pallor on nose, cheeks or ears). Stop and rewarm immediately. Rewarming the feet is a time consuming business, but impress on everyone the importance of taking action before it is too late. A feeling of numbness or even warmth following chill are warning signs which are ignored at your peril. Remember, too, that an exposed or injured person is much more liable to frostbite and, finally, that the 'freezing power' of the environment depends on wind as well as temperature (see Wind Chill Chart, Fig 116, page 234). The effect of a 40 m.p.h. wind at -7°C is exactly the same as that of a 2 m.p.h. breeze at -20°C.

Non-Freezing Cold Injury

Immersion Foot is due to prolonged exposure of the extremities to water and is characterised by painful, swollen feet or hands and, in more severe cases, by muscle damage, ulcers and gangrene. It is not known to what extent the condition occurs among mountaineers but there is no doubt that the early stages of the injury are occasionally encountered among inexperienced hillwalkers taking part in expeditions lasting two or more nights, where the feet may be wet or damp more or less continuously for the whole period. Two distinct types are recognised due to warm water (tropical) and cold water immersion. It is the latter which concerns us here.

While the main cause is exposure to water for a period in excess of 48 hours, contributory factors show a striking similarity to those which lead to mountain hypothermia: general chilling of the body, exhaustion, dehydration, lack of proper nutrition, etc. More specific factors include constricting clothing and footwear which tend to restrict the circulation in the extremities.

The condition may develop insidiously over a long period of time and early symptoms such as numbness or pins and needles and slight swelling may well be ignored. Removal of the boots results in increased swelling, tingling and sometimes severe pain. Later on the skin may turn yellow, blue or black and may remain in this condition for several hours or even days. This is followed by a stage which lasts 1 - 10 weeks, where the feet become red, hot and dry, and blisters may develop as in frostbite. The patient experiences burning and shooting pains accompanied by a bounding pulse. In the most severe cases there may be muscle wastage and the development of ulcers and superficial gangrene.

Rest in a horizontal position is the best treatment with the feet kept cool by exposing them to the air. Analgesics should be given to reduce pain. In most cases recovery is complete within 2 - 5 weeks, although severe cases may take considerably longer. The patient may be left with some after effects, such as increased sensitivity to cold.

Preventative measures are obvious. Keep your feet dry or if that is not possible, make sure that you change into a dry pair of socks as soon as practicable. The quality and fit of socks or stockings is of crucial importance in minimising the risk of cold injury. Well fitting loop- stitched or woollen stockings are effective in preventing the condition.

Snow Blindness

This has been referred to earlier when considering the effects of heat. Snow blindness is an extremely painful and debilitating condition brought about by exposure to intense ultra-violet radiation. Symptoms may not appear for 8-12 hours after exposure and by that time the damage has been done. This radiation increases with altitude. Snow reflects about 90% of ultra-violet light, so that it is not enough merely to shield the eyes from direct sunlight. Goggles, or glasses with light shading all round the lenses are required and, in addition, they must filter at least 90% of the ultra-violet radiation. In an emergency glasses can be improvised by cutting a horizontal slit in a piece of cardboard. It is a common error to believe that eye protection is not required on dull, overcast days, and this has resulted in a number of unnecessary cases of snow blindness. The situation is further aggravated by internal reflection from the cloud base, which has a multiplication effect on the ultra-violet radiation.

The eyes initially feel simply irritated or dry, but later they feel as though they are full of sand. Moving or blinking the eyes becomes extremely painful. Even exposure to light may cause pain. Swelling of the eyelids, redness of the eyes and excessive watering may occur. A severe case of snow blindness may be completely disabling for several days.

Snow blindness heals spontaneously in a few days; however, the pain may be quite severe if the condition is not treated. Cold compresses applied to the closed eyes, and a dark environment may give some relief. The patient must not rub his eyes. Local anaesthetic agents should not be used since they rapidly loose their effectiveness and may lead to damage of the delicate corneal surface.

Readers are reminded that over-exposure to ultra-violet radiation can also result in painful and, occasionally, serious sunburn. Reliable preparations which effectively filter this should be applied to all exposed areas, particularly the nose and cheeks, the lips and the underside of the chin and ears.

18

Snow Shelters

There are two quite distinct sets of circumstances under which snow shelters might be used. The first is in an emergency situation arising from an accident or from an error of judgement when a party is forced to spend a night in the open without the benefit of camping or bivouac equipment. In snow conditions it may be that the only possible form of shelter available would be a snow shelter of some kind. Obviously, every effort should be made to get off the exposed tops and down to a more sheltered location and it may be that the time and energy spent in constructing a shelter might be better spent in getting off the mountain. Nevertheless, there is no doubt that lives have been saved as a result of a prompt decision to dig in before darkness and storm dictated their own terms. In these circumstances time is likely to be short, with darkness already falling and the resources available to the party may be limited to that which would normally be carried on a winter walk: ice axes, rope, rucksack, emergency ration, spare clothing and so on. What can be achieved will depend very much on the physical condition and morale of the party, the nature of the terrain and snow cover and the weather conditions.

The second set of circumstances is quite different and arises from a deliberate decision taken in advance to spend the night in a snow shelter. Special equipment can be carried to aid the construction of a shelter, such as a snow saw and shovel and to make living conditions more comfortable eg. sleeping bag, insulation mat, stove, food, etc: in fact all the gear that would normally be carried for an overnight stop. In such a planned situation, sufficient time can be allowed to build a much more elaborate and spacious form of shelter. The value of such an exercise should not be underestimated. Snow shelters have been used to great advantage in polar regions and on expeditions to mountainous areas in all parts of the world.

A well designed snow shelter affords complete protection from the wind. It is well insulated by the snow, which is a poor conductor of heat and is, therefore, quickly heated by body warmth alone. It is quiet, easily lighted and adaptable. Unfortunately, it is time consuming work. It takes approximately one hour per person sheltered to build and for that reason it is wise to seek a suitable location well before dark.

A number of different types of shelter are discussed in this chapter each suited to particular snow and weather conditions. In Scotland the snow cave is the most reliable, since it is the only one with the structural strength to withstand sudden and devastating thaws. It is normally possible to construct some kind of snow shelter, provided there is sufficient snow. This is not likely to be found on exposed ridges or plateaus. Seek out the deeper drifts in more sheltered locations lower down. Some of these present a steep face on the lee side into which it is possible to tunnel and quickly gain a degree of protection from the elements.

It is quite common for large cornices to contain hollows where the snow has canopied over the top. In dire emergency they are certainly worth investigating for possible enlargement into a snow hole. Any investigation should be carried out on a rope secured from above and under no circumstances should a cornice or lee slope site be used if there is any likelihood of an avalanche, remembering that such sites are among the most sensitive trigger points.

The most useful tool for digging is a broad, short handled shovel which, together with a special saw for cutting blocks, can make relatively light work of moving quantities of snow. Anyone who has had to use an ice axe for making a snowhole will vouch for the fact that it is far from being the ideal tool for the job. However, in an emergency it may well be all that is available and for this reason it is sensible to get some practice in using it for this purpose. If possible, to save time and energy, blocks should be quarried above the site of the shelter using the snow layer which has the most suitable consistency. Wind blown snow usually provides excellent building material.

Precautions

Certain precautions need to be taken when using snow shelters to ensure maximum safety and comfort.

Only dry clothing and sleeping bags will keep you warm during the night. In addition, there is always the danger of wet clothing freezing during the night: therefore every care should be taken to see that they are kept dry and the following points need to be borne in mind:

Digging snow is warm work. Strip off to avoid making clothes damp with sweat which may freeze later.

Ensure adequate ventilation at all times.

All equipment must be brought inside.

Remove any wet clothes before settling in and place them in a rucksack.

If it is freezing hard, wrap your boots inside a polythene bag and take them into your sleeping bag.

Brush off all particles of snow clinging to clothing before entering the shelter. These may melt in the warm atmosphere, wetting clothing.

Water vapour given off during cooking may condense, wetting clothes also. If possible, avoid having liquids boiling or simmering. Increase ventilation.

Use a torch instead of candles, or if this is not possible, use only one candle.

Insulate the body from beneath as much as possible. Avoid sleeping on polythene or other slippery material, or you are liable to find yourself suddenly outside the cave.

Take a shovel or digging implement into the shelter with you in case you have to dig yourself out.

Leave a light on in the shelter if you have to leave it for any reason during the night. It may help you to find it when you come back.

If there are several snow shelters in use connect them up with a climbing rope firmly secured inside the entrance of each. This will ensure that communications can remain open even during the most severe drifting and that the shelters can be quickly located afterwards.

Ventilation

Nearly all the recorded accidents in snow shelters have been caused by carbon monoxide (CO) poisoning. It can not be stressed too strongly that ensuring adequate ventilation is the most important single precaution which must be taken. Normal stove burning produces little CO. However, if the flame touches a cool surface, such as a billy filled with melting snow, combustion is not completed and considerable unburnt CO will result. The danger can be reduced by avoiding direct flame contact with the billy, but increased ventilation, both at the door and above the stove, is the only safe procedure. If you get a headache after cooking it is a clear sign that the ventilation is inadequate.

In a freshly built shelter there will always be a certain amount of air movement through the walls. This will be reduced in time, as glazing takes place on the inside. In these circumstances it is quite possible for the supply of oxygen to become exhausted. This means that even if there is no burning stove or candles, additional ventilation must be provided. The door, or at least a section of it, should be left open at all times and if drifting occurs, it should be cleared out every 2 hours, or more often if drifting is fast.

Ventilation is also necessary to prevent over heating and melting. If the external temperature is below -10°C there should be no problem. At higher temperatures, which are common in this country, some dripping is inevitable and close to freezing the structure itself may be in danger of collapse. In this event the door should be kept fully open and if the shelter has been in use for some time, the roof can be skimmed to a thickness of a few inches to increase heat loss. A ventilation hole in the roof greatly improves the through draft.

SNOW CAVE

The best location for a snow cave is in a drift of snow with a fairly steep face. This will ensure that there is sufficient depth of snow and that it can be easily disposed of down the slope. It also means that shelter can be obtained reasonably quickly and that the snow is likely to be in good condition for cutting. It is relatively easy to make and, for Scottish conditions and emergencies, probably the most dependable type of shelter. There are many variations between the elaborate snow palace and the simple burrow which normally would have to suffice in an emergency. The classic snow cave is constructed as follows. (Fig. 221)

Mark the top of the projected cave with a ski stick, axe etc. Otherwise you may have unexpected company dropping in through the roof.

For the maximum insulation and structural stability the walls and ceiling should be at least 60cm thick.

Although the final entrance should be small, for ease of working it is best to make this larger to start off with and fill it in later. Dig a deep slot into the drift, high and wide enough to allow you to work upright. Blocks should be cut with a saw or shovel when possible and loose snow can be removed on a polythene bag or anorak.

Excavate the snow on either side of the slot to create an open living area. The roof should taper from head to feet so that you are sleeping in the warm air created by your own body and not underneath it.

Smooth off the roof to remove dripping points.

Reduce the entrance to a size which will allow access by crawling. A sack or polythene bag filled with snow makes an excellent door.

Make a ventilation hole in the roof. This is often in the thinnest part of the cave wall which is most likely to remain relatively unaffected by drifting. It may be the best escape route in the event of a complete drift-in.

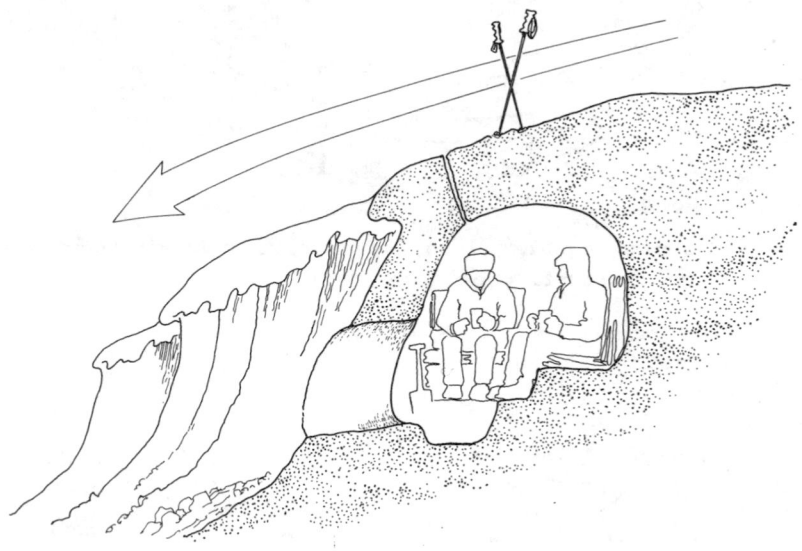

Fig. 221 *A snow cave in a drift. The entrance must be cleared of drifted snow at regular intervals throughout the night to allow adequate ventilation.*

IGLOO

There is a good deal of fun and interest in building an igloo but it is not a suitable type of shelter for conditions in the British Isles. The design has been developed by the Eskimo for use in the Arctic where sub-zero temperatures persist for months on end. Even in the Cairngorms the likelihood is that thawing or near-thawing conditions would cause an igloo to buckle and collapse. However, there are occasions when it is possible to build an igloo-like extension to a snow cave, using material cut from the cave, so that an understanding of the technique is not without relevance. Wind-packed snow provides the best building material because it can be conveniently cut into blocks of just the right size and shape. Although it is possible to do without, a snow saw greatly assists construction.

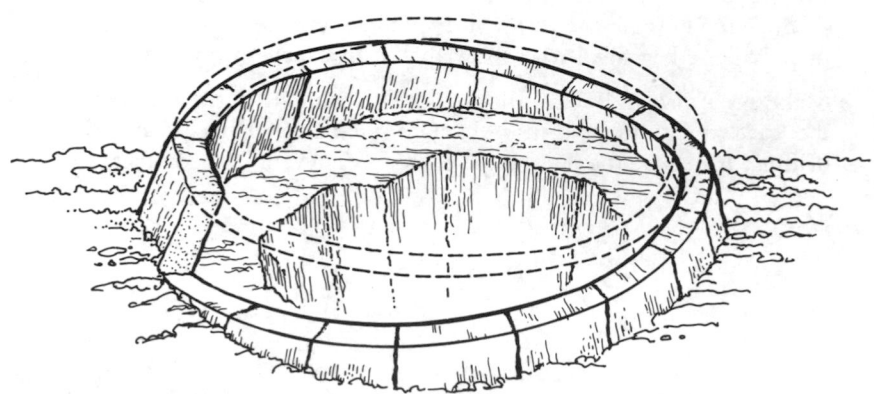

Starting to make an igloo. The first course of full-sized blocks is laid and then cut to form a ramp.

Fig. 223 *Igloos showing alternative entrances and wind break.*

To build an igloo, proceed as follows:

Select a safe site close to a source of good building snow. The way the blocks are mined is determined by the layering but, if possible, cut the blocks with their largest surface vertical.

Mark out a circle, the diameter of which will be dictated by the number of people to be accommodated. As a guide, a diameter of 2m (7ft) should be allowed for one person, plus 0.3m (1ft) for each additional person. Thus, a two person igloo will have a diameter of 2.30m (8ft). Since, for stability, the igloo must approximate to a hemisphere, anything with a diameter greater than 3m (10ft) would not be practicable.

The blocks should be as large as can be handled, the thickness being determined by the conditions. The bigger the blocks the quicker the igloo will be made. Do not spend too much time trimming the blocks to the exact shape. This can be done when they are in position by running the snow saw back and forth along the joints.

Fig.222 explains the method of construction. The builder stands inside, placing the blocks in an inward leaning spiral and making sure that each one has three points of contact with the previous one. To do this the bottom and the side face in contact may be made slightly concave. As the igloo rises and closes in, there comes a time when the blocks have to be passed in through a temporary opening cut in the side. The final opening in the roof is sealed by passing a block through, end on, and then lowering it into position. Before closing the roof, smooth off the inside of the igloo and throw out any loose snow.

All the small holes in the igloo can be filled in with pieces of broken blocks and the whole structure should be covered with loose snow.

The door should be placed at right angles to the prevailing wind and may be cut at floor level or as a trench. A straight forward opening with a short tunnel, somewhat larger than the door, would seem to be the best answer. An air vent should be opened in the roof.

If high winds are expected a low wall should be built to windward to protect the base of the igloo against erosion.

If the igloo is on a slope, a level floor should be excavated first and the wall built up until it is level. A ramp can be cut and the igloo continued as before.

Furnishings and fittings can now be added the last word in luxury being a slab of clear ice inserted as a window!

SNOW PIT

This is not a satisfactory shelter and should only be used when no other alternatives are possible. The actual construction is simple enough except that all the material has to be thrown out of the pit. It follows much the same pattern as the Snow Cave and indeed it can be regarded as a variant of it.

(Fig. 224) *A snow pit dug into a level snow field.*

Dig a pit big enough to work in comfortably, at least 1m (3'4") x 0.75m (2'6") by 1.5m (5') deep. Enlarge the bottom to provide an area wide enough to sit or lie in. Roof over the top of the pit with snow blocks.

SOFT SNOW MOUND

This unusual design of shelter originated in the U.S.A. where it has been successful in areas of shallow snow cover, below the timberline. When snow is disturbed it undergoes a process known as age hardening. It is this process which is used to consolidate shallow, loose masses of powder snow, which are later excavated to provide a shelter.

Snow is collected and shovelled into a mound, 3.5m (11½ft) in diameter and 2m (6½ft) high. Do not pack it down by patting or tramping since this causes uneven hardening. If necessary the snow can be reshovelled to accelerate the age hardening process. The mound should be as close to a hemisphere as is possible. A considerable saving in time and energy can be achieved by stacking up all the rucksacks to form the core of the mound before piling snow on top. They can be extracted later when the mound is excavated.

Fig. 225   *A soft snow mound excavated to provide a rudimentary shelter.*

When the mound has reached the required height it should be left for at least one hour, preferably longer, to consolidate. Considerable shrinkage will take place over-night, even in cold weather and due allowance must be made for this.

After consolidation, dig into the centre of the mound. The finished product looks very much like an igloo, complete with door and air vent.

SNOWBALL SHELTER

In heavy damp snow it is possible to make various types of shelters from giant snow balls. These can be rolled together, preferably to a gathering area at the foot of a slope and then used as they stand, or cut into blocks to make a crude form of igloo.

COMBINATION SHELTERS

All sorts of combinations between the various types of shelters mentioned in this chapter are possible. The choice will be determined by the terrain and the snow condition. There is considerable scope for the fertile imagination in the ultimate design. However speed is often a vital safety factor and that must always be considered. It is quite likely that in a real emergency some sort of combination shelter will be the most appropriate and some suggested designs are given in Figs. 226 and 227. The choice of site is all important and advantage should be taken of the natural configuration of the snow, using drifts, cornices, half-buried rocks, etc. to save time and energy. Blocks can be cut with the pick of the ice axe, snow can be shifted with a dinner plate,

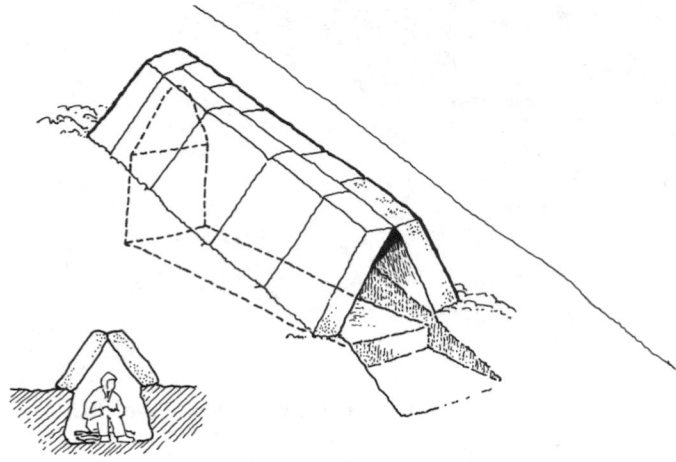

Fig. 226 *One person emergency snow shelter.*

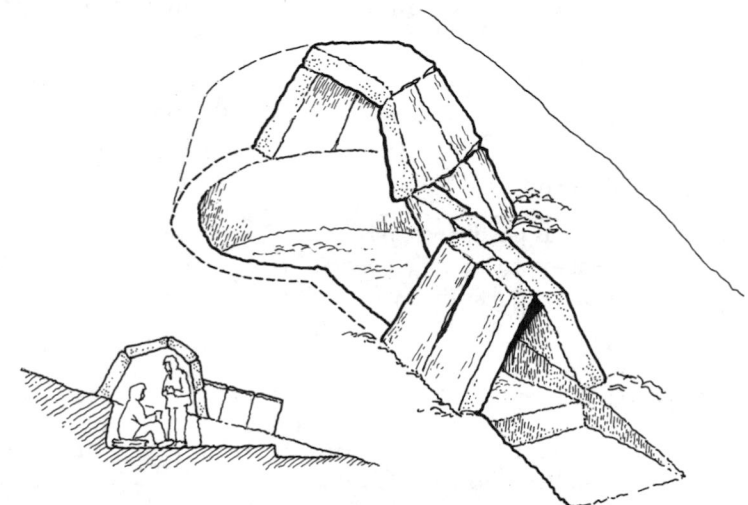

Fig. 227 *Two person emergency snow shelter.*

The one and two person shelters shown in Figs 226 and 227 can be built very quickly given reasonable snow and for this reason they are recommended as Emergency Shelters.

while a dead man can double up as a shovel. Even the wire can occasionally be put to good use, rather in the manner of a cheese-cutter.

A word of warning. It is very easy to lose small items of equipment in a snow shelter, so be careful and methodical in all that you do. It is also a temptation to leave behind waste food and unwanted packaging and other bits and pieces under the illusion that they will somehow remain out of sight. They will only remain out of sight until the spring thaw reveals the full extent of such thoughtlessness.

Appendix I

Bibliography

This bibliography is a selection from the vast literature on the subject of mountain craft.

Titles have been chosen to support and expand the text and have been listed according to the chapter(s) to which they refer. At the time of writing all are in print and most are available in bookshops or from the distributers. The principal U.K. distributer of outdoor literature is Cordee Books, 3a De Mountfort Street, Leicester LEI 7HD.

Mountaineering has a rich literature and candidates for leadership awards are encouraged to read as widely as possible. Books out of print may often be obtained second hand or from libraries.

GENERAL - ALL CHAPTERS

"Mountaincraft and Leadership", Langmuir. 1995 - Scottish Sports Council and Mountain Leader Training Board. ISBN: 0-903908-75-1.

"Mountaineering: The Freedom of the Hills". The Mountaineers. 1992 - Cordee. ISBN: 0-89886-309-0.

"Safety on Mountains", BMC booklet.

NAVIGATION - CHAPTER I

"Land Navigation: Route finding with maps and compass", Keay, 1989 - Duke of Edinburgh Award. ISBN: 0-905425-06-5.

"Mountain Navigation", Cliffe. 1991 - Cordee. ISBN: 1-871890-55-1.

"Orienteering, The Skills of the Game", McNeill (1989 - Crowood Press. ISBN: 1-85223-151-3.

HILLWALKING, CAMPCRAFT AND EXPEDITIONS, FOOD AND NUTRITION - CHAPTERS 2, 3, 4

"Expedition Planners' Handbook and Directory, 1993-94" (Royal Geographical Society). ISBN: 0-907649-54-8.

"The Backpackers Handbook", Townsend, 1991 - Cordee. ISBN: 0-87742-357-1.

"The Expedition Cook Book", Gunn. 1988 - Cordee. ISBN: 0-904405-69-9.

ACCESS AND CONSERVATION - CHAPTER 5

"Access for Mountaineers and Hillwalkers," Scottish Landowners Federation and Mountaineering Council of Scotland.

"Bird Life of Mountain and Upland," Ratcliffe. Cambridge University Press.

"Forbidden Land: Struggle for Access to Mountain and Moorland," Stephenson, 1989 - Manchester University Press. ISBN: 0-7190-2966 X.

The High Kingdom. The Living Countryside. Readers Digest.

Geological maps of the British Isles 1: 625000 :- North (solid geology). South (solid geology).

"Living Isles: A Natural History of Britain and Ireland", Crawford - BBC 1985. ISBN: 0563203692.

"Mountains and Moorlands", Pearsall. - New Naturalist Series, Collins.

"Rights of Way: A Guide to Law and Practice". Open Spaces. ISBN: 613734. Rambler's Association.

"Rights of Way. A Guide to Law in Scotland", Scottish Rights of Way Society, 1986.

"Tread Lightly", British Mountaineering Council booklet.

"Upland Britain, A Natural History", Atherden, 1992 - Manchester University Press. ISBN: 0-7190-3494-9.

SECURITY ON STEEP GROUND - CHAPTER 6

"Climbing Knots", British Mountaineering Council booklet.

"Rock Climb", Long, 1993 - Chockstone Press USA - (Cordee).
ISBN: 0-934641-64-1

"Rope", British Mountaineering Council booklet.

"The Handbook of Climbing", Fyffe and Peters. 1990 - Pelham.
ISBN: 0-7207-1805-8

MOUNTAIN WEATHER - CHAPTER 8

"Mountain Weather, Guide for hillwalkers and climbers in the British Isles".
Pedgley, 1980 - Cicerone. ISBN: 902-363-22-0.

"The Weather Handbook", Watts, 1994 -Waterline. ISBN: 1-85310-409-4.

FIRST AID AND MOUNTAIN RESCUE - CHAPTERS 11 AND 12

"Medical Handbook for Mountaineers", Steele, 1988 - Constable.
ISBN: 09-468570-3.

"International Mountain Rescue Handbook", McInnes, 1984 - Constable.
ISBN- 0-09-463449-8.

"Mountain and Cave Rescue Handbook". Mountain Rescue Committee.

"Wilderness Search and Rescue" Setnicka 1980 - Appalachian Mountain
Club USA - (Cordee). ISBN: 0-910146-21-7.

PARTY LEADERSHIP - CHAPTER 13

"Leading and managing groups in the Outdoors". Ken Ogilvie, 1993 -
National Association for Outdoor Education - ISBN: 1-89855-00-1.

"The Adventure Alternative", Mortlock, 1994 - Cicerone.
ISBN: 1-85284-012-9.

TECHNIQUE AND SECURITY ON SNOW AND ICE - CHAPTERS 14 AND 15

"Crampons", British Mountaineering Council booklet.

"Scotlands Winter Mountains". Moran – David and Charles.

"The Handbook of Climbing," Fyffe and Peter, 1990 – Pelham. ISBN: 0-7207-01805-8.

SNOW AND AVALANCHES - CHAPTER 16

"A Chance in a Million", Barton & Wright, 1985 – Scottish Mountaineering Trust. ISBN: 0-907521-11-8.

"Avalanche Safety for Skiers and Climbers", Daffern – Diadem. ISBN: 0-906371-26-0.

"The Avalanche Handbook", McClung and Schaerer, 1993, Cordee. ISBN: 0-898886-364-3.

Appendix II

Useful Addresses

NATIONAL PARKS OF ENGLAND AND WALES

Brecon Beacons National Park
Glamorgan Street
BRECON
Powys LD3 7DP
Tel: 01874 624437

Broads Authority
Thomas Harvey House
18 Colegate
NORWICH
Norfolk NB3 1BQ
Tel: 01603 610734

Dartmoor National Park
Parke
Haytor Road
Bovey Tracey
NEWTON ABBOT
Devon TQ13 9JQ
Tel: 01626 832093

Exmoor National Park
Exmoor House
DULVERTON
Somerset TA22 9HL
Tel: 01398 23665

Lake District National Park
Busher Walk
KENDAL
Cumbria LA9 4RH
Tel: 01539 724555

Northumberland National Park
Eastburn
South Park
HEXHAM
Northumberland NE46 1BS
Tel: 01434 605555

North York Moors National Park
The Old Vicarage
Bondgate
HELMSLEY
North Yorkshire YO6 5BP
Tel: 01439 70657

Peak National Park
Aldern House
Baslow Road
BAKEWELL
Derbyshire DE4 1AE
Tel: 01629 814321

Pembrokeshire Coast National Park
County Offices
HAVERFORDWEST
Dyfed SA61 1QZ
Tel: 01437 764591

Sowdonia National Park
PENRHYNDEUDRAETH
Gwynedd LL48 6LS
Tel: 01766 770274

Yorkshire Dales National Park
Yorebridge House
Bainbridge
LEYBURN
North Yorkshire DL8 2BP
Tel: 01969 50456

MOUNTAINEERING & RAMBLING ASSOCIATIONS/BODIES

British Mountaineering Council
177-179 Burton Road
West Didsbury
MANCHESTER
M20 2BB
Tel: 0161-445 4747
E-mail: register@thebmc.co.uk

Mountaineering Council of
Scotland
National Officer
4a St Catherines Road
PERTH
PH1 5SE
Tel: 01764 654962

Mountaineering Council of Ireland
c/o ASAS
House of Sport
Longmile Road
DUBLIN 12
Tel: 003531 509845

The Scottish Mountain Leader
Training Board
Caledonia House
South Gyle
EDINBURGH
EH12 9DQ
Tel: 0131-317 7200

Rambler's Association (Scotland)
Crusader House
Haig Business Park
MARKINCH
Fife
KY7 6AQ
Tel: 01592 611177

Open Spaces Society
25a Bell Street
HENLEY ON THAMES
Oxon RG2 2BA
Tel: 01491 573535

Rambler's Association
1/5 Wandsworth Road
LONDON
SW8 2LJ
Tel: 0171-582 6878

Mountain Leader Training Board and
United Kingdom Mountain Training
Board
Siabod Cottage, Capel Curig
Gwynedd
LL24 0ET
Tel: 01690 720314
E-mail: info@mltb.org
Website: http://www.mltb.org

Northern Ireland Mountain Leader
Training Board
Sports Council for Northern Ireland
House of Sport
Upper Malone Road
BELFAST
Tel: 01232-381222

Wales Mountain Leader Training
Board
Plas Menai
Llanfairisgaer
CAERNARVON
Gwynedd
LL55 1UE
Tel: 01248-670964

NATIONAL CONSERVATION BODIES

Countryside Commission
John Dower House
Crescent Place
CHELTENHAM
Gloucestershire GL50 3RA
Tel: 01242 521381

Association for the Protection of
Rural Scotland
483 Lawnmarket
EDINBURGH
EH1 2NT
Tel: 0131-225 7013

Countryside Council for Wales
Plas Penrhos
Ffordd Penrhos
BANGOR
Gwynedd LL57 2LQ
Tel: 01248 370444

Environment Service
Countryside and Wildlife Branch
Commonwealth House
35 Castle Street
BELFAST
BTI 1GU
Tel: 01232 314911

Council for the Protection of Rural
England
Warwick House
25 Buckingham Palace Road
LONDON
SW1W 0PP
Tel: 0171-976 6433

Campaign for the Protection of
Rural Wales
Ty Gwyn
31 High Street
WELSHPOOL
Powys SY21 7JP
Tel: 01938 552525/556212

Scottish Natural Heritage
12 Hope Terrace
EDINBURGH
EH9 2AS
Tel: 0131-447 4784

Ulster Society for the Preservation of
the Countryside
West Winds
Carney Hill
CRAIGAVAD
County Down
Tel: 01232 540540

English Nature
Northminster House
PETERBOROUGH
PE1 1UA
Tel: 01733 340345

Council for National Parks
246 Lavender Hill
LONDON
SW11 1LN
Tel: 0171 924 4077

Scottish Council for National Parks
15 Park Terrace
STIRLING
FK8 2JT
Tel: 01786 465714

The National Trust
PO Box 39
BROMLEY
Kent
BR1 3XL
Tel: 0181-464 1111

The National Trust for Scotland
5 Charlotte Square
EDINBURGH
EH2 4DU
Tel: 0131-226 5922

The John Muir Trust
13 Wellington Place
EDINBURGH
EH6 7JD
Tel: 0131-554 9101

NATIONAL RECREATION BODIES

The Sports Council
16 Upper Woburn Place
LONDON
WC1H 0QP
Tel: 0171-388 1277

The Scottish Sports Council
Caledonia House
South Gyle
EDINBURGH
EH12 9DQ
Tel: 0131-317 7200

The Sports Council for Wales
Sophia Gardens
CARDIFF
CF1 9SW
Tel: 01222 397571

The Sports Council for Northern
Ireland
House of Sport
2a Upper Malone Road
BELFAST
BT9 5LA
Tel: 01232 381222

Appendix III

Personal and Group Clothing and Equipment for Hillwalking and Camping Expeditions

Notes

It is the Leader's responsibility to see that the party is adequately clothed and equipped.

See that individual loads do not exceed one-third of the body weight of the individual and in no case more than 30lb.

The delineation between LOW and HIGH level is taken to be approximately 500m (1,640ft) above sea level. 'High level' assumes a greater degree of technical difficulty although this may not necessarily be the case.

Clothes not worn must be carried in the pack. A spare set of clothing must also be carried in a polythene bag and used only for night wear.

Ideally each member of a party should carry a personal map, compass, watch and whistle, plus a torch in winter.

It is not intended that these lists should be slavishly followed in every detail. They are offered as a guide or check list from which appropriate items may be chosen.

Individual Equipment

SUMMER

Low Level Walk	Low Level Camp	High Level Walk	High Level Camp
Day rations	Day rations	Day rations	Map
Whistle	Whistle	Compass	Day rations
Boots	Rucksack	Watch	Compass
Stockings	Boots	Whistle	Watch
Trousers	2 Stockings	Boots	Whistle
Shirt	2 Trousers	Stockings	Rucksack
Sweater	2 Shirts	Trousers	Boots
Anorak	2 Sweaters	Shirt	2 Stockings
First Aid	Anorak	2 Sweaters	2 Trousers
Overtrousers	First Aid	Anorak	2 Shirts

Toilet requisites	First Aid	2 Sweaters
Sleeping bag plus	Large polythene	Anorak
inner	survival bag	Gloves
K.F.S. mug	Overtrousers	First Aid
Polythene bag	Hat	Toilet requisites
Overtrousers		Sleeping bag plus
		inner
		K.F.S. mug
		Polythene bag
		Overtrousers
		Hat
		Karrimat
		Torch

WINTER

Low Level Walk	Low Level Camp	High Level Walk	High Level Camp
Day rations	Day rations	Map	Map
Whistle	Whistle	Compass	Compass
Boots	Boots	Watch	Watch
Stockings	Rucksack	Whistle	Whistle
Trousers	2 Stockings	Torch	Torch
Underclothes	2 Trousers	Day rations	Day rations
Shirt	2 Underclothes	Boots	Rucksack
2 Sweaters	2 Shirts	2 Stockings	Boots
Anorak	2 Sweaters	Trousers	2 Stockiings
* Balaclava	Anorak	Overtrousers	2 Trousers
Gloves	Balaclava	Underclothes	Overtrousers
* Overmitts	Gloves	Shirt	2 Underclothes
* Light scarf	* Overmitts	2 Sweaters	2 Shirts
Gaiters	Light Scarf	Anorak	2/3 Sweaters
First Aid	Gaiters	Balaclava	Anorak
	First Aid	Gloves	Balaclava
	Toilet requisites	Overmitts	Gloves
	Sleeping bag plus	Light scarf	Overmitts
	inner	Gaiters	Light scarf
	K.F.S. mug	Ice axe	Gaiters
	Polythene bag	Goggles or	Ice axe
	Karrimat	sunglasses	Goggles
		Crampons	* Crampons
		First Aid	First Aid
		Large polythene bag	Toilet requisites
			4 Season Sleeping
			bag
			K.F.S. mug
			Polythene bag
			Karrimat

* Optional equipment depending on conditions and aim of expedition.

Common Equipment: Shared

SUMMER

Low Level Walk	Low Level Camp	High Level Walk	High Level Camp
Map 1:2 Compass 1:2 Watch 1:2 Rucksack 1:4	* Torch 1:2 Map 1:2 Compass 1:2 Watch 1:2 Stove Fuel and bottles Billies Rations Water carrier Tin opener Matches Toilet paper Shovel Tent	Rucksack 1:3	Mountain tent Stove Fuel and bottles Billies Rations Water carrier Tin opener Matches Brillo pads Toilet paper Shovel

* Optional equipment depending on conditions and aim of expedition.

WINTER

Low Level Walk	Low Level Camp	High Level Walk	High Level Camp
Rucksack 1:4 Compass 1:2 Whistle 1:4 Torch 1:4	Torch 1:2 Compass 1:2 Whistle 1:4 Stove Fuel and bottles Billies Rations Water carrier Tin opener Brillo pads Toilet paper Shovel Tent	Rucksack 1:4 Thermos flask	Mountain tent Stove Fuel and bottles Billies Rations Water carrier Tin opener Matches Toilet paper Shovel

Additional Equipment for Leader

SUMMER

Low Level Walk	Low Level Camp	High Level Walk	High Level Camp
First Aid kit	First Aid kit	30m (9mm) nylon rope First Aid kit Bivi or survival bag Sleeping bag Emergency ration	30m (9mm) nylon rope First Aid kit Bivi or survival bag

WINTER

Low Level Walk	Low Level Camp	High Level Walk	High Level Camp
First Aid kit	First Aid kit	120ft (9mm) nylon rope First Aid kit Red flare Emergency ration Sleeping bag Torch, batteries (extra) Large bivouac tent	120ft (9mm) nylon rope First Aid kit Red flare Emergency ration Large polythene bag Torch, batteries (extra)

Appendix IV

First Aid Kit

It is emphasised that the list of items given below is a suggested First Aid kit to be carried by the leader of a party of up to 10 people walking or climbing on the mountains of the British Isles and absent from medical services for a period of less than three days. A First Aid kit is a very personal thing and it is quite impossible to produce a pack which will satisfy everybody. However, most people would agree with the general principles on which this list of items has been based. These are:

1 It should be simple and avoid offering alternative treatments.
2 It should contain readily available and reasonably cheap items.
3 It should be light in weight and small in bulk.
4 As far as possible single items should be able to be used for a number of functions.
5 It should be effective and comprehensive within the above limitations.

I am greatly indebted to Dr Peter Steele and Dr Neil Macdonald for their advice and comments on the contents of this kit.

Item	No.	Use	Carried by individual
Bandaid strip 6cm x 30cm.	1	Quick cover for cuts and grazes	
Dumbel sutures	4	Wound closure in place of stitches, finger dressings, awkward places	2
Zinc Oxide plaster 2.5cm x 5m	1	Holding gauze dressings in place to secure bandages	1
Bandages 10cm x 4.5m crepe	2	Elasticity for support/absorbent for bleeding	1
Triangular (compressed)		Arm sling/head bandage, etc.	
Dressing Melolin gauze squares 10cm x 10cm. 5cm x 5cm.	2	Non-stick absorbent cover	1
Plain gauze squares 10cm x 10cm	1		
Wound dressing (compressed gauze)	1	To stop bleeding in large wound	1
Antiseptic, sachet or cream	2	For dirty wounds	
Scissors, blunt/sharp	1		
Soap	1	Small bar	
Waterproof matches	1	Box	
Forceps, oblique end	1	For splinters	
Needle	1		
Scalpel blade	1		
Safety pin (nappy)	1		
Luggage label, pencil (wax and plain)	4	For written messages	1
Paracetamol, Codeine	24	For pain	
Antihistamine 'promethazine'	25	For hay fever, bites, allergies	
Tea bag	1	For sore eyes	
Amethocaine	drops	Eye anæsthetic	Op.
Calamine cream	1	For sunburn/itching	
Insect repellant	1	Mosquitos/midges, etc.	Op.
Sunscreen (factor 15) lip salve.	1	Optional - should filter U.V.	Op.
Wintergreen cream	1	Optional - aching muscles, sprains.	Op.
Steristrip plaster		In place of stitches	
Molesckin		For blisters	

Appendix V

Training of Mountain Leaders

PURPOSE

The purpose of the Mountain Leader Training Schemes is to promote the safe enjoyment and understanding of the hills by young people. The schemes provide training and assessment in the skills required by those who wish to lead groups of young people in the mountains and moorlands of the British Isles. There are schemes for Summer and for Winter Mountain Leader Awards.

Since their introduction in 1964, the Schemes have achieved widespread recognition by authorities responsible for the welfare of young people involved in hill and mountain based activities, including Education Authorities, youth organisations, parents and individuals.

OPERATION

The Schemes are operated by the Mountain Leader Training Boards within the UK which approve training and assessment courses and develop syllabus content. Arrangements exist for the co-ordination of the work of the four Home Country Boards through the UK Mountain Training Board.

SCOPE

The Mountain Leader Training Schemes provide the opportunity for experienced hillwalkers and mountaineers to gain the minimum technical competence for leading parties in the hills.

The Schemes provide training and assessment in technical and party management in the hills in a variety of testing conditions. They integrate training, experience, and assessment in a context relevant to the leadership of groups.

The Summer Mountain Leader Award specifically excludes training or assessment in the skills required to cope with the special hazards of winter conditions, particularly ice and snow. Specific training and assessment for winter conditions is covered within the scheme for the Winter Mountain Leader Award operated by the Scottish MLTB.

The completion of a training course alone is not a qualification in itself, and the Boards recommend that organisations do not use it as such.

QUALIFICATION OF ENTRY

Candidates are expected to be committed and experienced hillwalkers or mountaineers prior to registering for each Scheme. They should have a genuine practical interest in party leadership. They must hold the Summer Mountain Leader Award before registering for the Winter Scheme.

The Schemes are not intended as a first introduction to proficiency in mountaineering. There are other courses run by schools, colleges, outdoor centres, and voluntary organisations, which are suitable for beginners.

RESPONSIBILITY OF EMPLOYERS AND ORGANISERS

It is the responsibility of the employer or organiser to decide whether a leader possesses the personal attributes needed for leadership, for example, consideration, responsibility, empathy and understanding of young people.

It is the combination of technical skills, extensive experience and personal qualities which forms the foundation for effective leadership.

It is not intended that the adoption of the Mountain Leader Schemes by organising authorities or employers should exclude from party leadership those highly competent walkers and mountaineers who are known to possess the necessary qualities but do not hold a Mountain Leader Award.

While Mountain Leader training may well be of positive benefit to leaders of parties using lesser hills, which do not pose potential hazards arising from objective dangers or remoteness, it would be contrary to the purpose of the Schemes for employers to insist on the Mountain Leader Awards as necessary training for leaders in such familiar local terrain.

The employment of a holder of a Mountain Leader Award does not absolve an employer from their responsibility to ensure the suitability of staff for party leadership.

THE MOUNTAIN LEADER SCHEMES AND THE MOUNTAIN ENVIRONMENT

Mountains mean freedom, adventure, beauty and solitude, as well as the opportunity to earn a living from the land. Therefore, whilst pursuing their own ends and fostering a love of the hills, leaders of parties of young people have a responsibility to have due regard for other hill users and to encourage an understanding of the problems of mountain conservation, access and erosion. Consideration of these aspects is vital if the ethics and traditions of mountain life are to be preserved.

MORE ADVANCED AWARDS

Holders of the Summer and of the Winter Mountain Leader Awards are eligible to enter schemes of training and assessment for Mountain Instructors and European Mountain Leaders.

INFORMATION

Full information, syllabi, registration forms, etc. are available from the joint publishers of this book.

Index